Smoke & Mirrors

THE CANADIAN TOBACCO WAR

Smoke & Mirrors

THE CANADIAN TOBACCO WAR

ROB CUNNINGHAM

Foreword by JAKE EPP
Introduction by JUDITH MACKAY

INTERNATIONAL DEVELOPMENT RESEARCH CENTRE
Ottawa • Cairo • Dakar • Johannesburg • Montevideo • Nairobi • New Delhi • Singapore

Published by the International Development Research Centre
PO Box 8500, Ottawa, ON, Canada K1G 3H9

© International Development Research Centre 1996

Canadian Cataloguing in Publication Data

Cunningham, Rob

Smoke & mirrors : the Canadian tobacco war

Includes bibliographical references.
ISBN 0-88936-755-8

1. Smoking — Canada — Prevention.
2. Tobacco industry — Canada.
I. International Development Research Centre (Canada).
II. Title.
III. Title: The Canadian tobacco war.

HV5770.C3C86 1996   362.29'6'0971   C96-980380-X

IDRC BOOKS endeavours to produce environmentally friendly publications. All paper used is recycled as well as recyclable. All inks and coatings are vegetable-based products.

Contents

Part V. The War Goes Global

Part VI. Winning the War: An Agenda for Victory

Part VII. Final Thoughts

Foreword

It was not long after I was appointed Minister of National Health and Welfare in 1984 that I realized that the tobacco epidemic was a critical issue requiring a significant solution. Tobacco use was then — and, lamentably, remains today — public health enemy number one.

For many years, tobacco use has been the leading preventable cause of disease, disability, and death in Canada. It causes cancer, heart disease, and lung disease. Smoking during pregnancy harms the baby. Nonsmokers are at risk through exposure to secondhand smoke. Yet, despite this knowledge, cigarette sales remain unacceptably high, especially among teenagers.

Most of the responsibility for the tobacco epidemic lies at the door of the tobacco industry itself. Tobacco companies have publicly denied the truth. They have insisted on more research when scientific consensus had long been reached. They have aggressively contested virtually every meaningful regulatory initiative. They have advertised to those who are most vulnerable, including to teenagers and to those who are less educated. They have targeted women, as well as men. Through advertisements, they have portrayed smoking as glamorous, attractive, fun, and healthy; nothing could be further from reality.

The ability of the tobacco industry to stay healthy while its customers get sick is, according to an article in *Report on Business Magazine*, "One of the most amazing marketing feats of all times."

While Health Minister, I introduced Bill C-51, the *Tobacco Products Control Act*, in the House of Commons. This bill banned tobacco advertising, regulated other forms of tobacco marketing, and created authority to require health messages on packages. Even though the bill enjoyed all-party support in Parliament and strong public approval, it was 14 months before the bill received Royal Assent, surely convincing evidence of the industry's tactical abilities.

Canadians can be proud of what has been achieved after several decades of effort to reduce smoking. In 1964, when Health and Welfare Canada began its smoking and health program, just under 50% of adults were smokers. That has fallen to about 30%. Health professionals, scientists, nongovernmental organizations, private citizens, and governments have all played constructive roles. The multipronged strategy to reduce smoking — tax increases, advertising restrictions, prominent health warnings, smoking restrictions in workplaces and public places, educational campaigns, and transitional assistance to tobacco farmers — has delivered results.

At the same time, it is with extreme personal frustration that I witness continuing tobacco industry efforts to undermine health policies. Tobacco companies weakened the advertising ban by shifting money into sponsorship promotions, promotions that conveyed the same lifestyle images Parliament intended to eliminate through the *Tobacco Products Control Act*. The industry initiated legal proceedings that resulted in the invalidation of the advertising ban. The industry exported to the United States large quantities of cigarettes, products that returned to Canada as contraband. Widespread smuggling led to a rollback in tobacco taxes.

Despite these setbacks, we must press on to not only recapture lost ground but to advance our strategy into new areas. And we must be vigilant to protect each new health gain.

As we succeed in Canada and some other developed countries, tobacco companies increasingly shift their attention to the less developed world. We have an obligation not only to share our experience with other countries, but to actively assist in the implementation of successful tobacco-control policies and programs. The same issues that Canada has had to confront are now being addressed in many other places. Tobacco is a global issue: the industry, the health consequences, and the solutions to reduce consumption are similar around the planet. A smoke-free world is a monumental challenge, but one that we must relentlessly pursue.

The Honourable Jake Epp, P.C.
Minister of National Health and Welfare, 1984–1989

23 September 1996

Preface

Doctors and health organizations decry the harm caused by tobacco use and demand that the government impose tough regulations to control the tobacco industry. Tobacco manufacturers and farmers oppose regulation, arguing that there is no proof that smoking is harmful, that government intervention in the marketplace is unjustified, that regulation will cost jobs and hurt the economy, and that there is no proof that regulation will accomplish intended objectives. Does this sound familiar? These arguments were made in 1903, the year Canada considered banning cigarettes altogether.

Canada's tobacco war is nothing new. The battle to reduce smoking has been around for more than a century. At times the war has raged savagely, at times the war has waned, but always the stakes have been high.

In recent years, the tobacco war on Parliament Hill has been ferocious: the lives of tens of thousands of Canadians have been pitted against the enormous profits of the transnational tobacco industry. The lobbying from both sides is incessant. Other issues may only be around for a while, but tobacco never goes away.

The use of *war* to refer to the battles over tobacco is clearly appropriate. The tobacco industry, a foreign-controlled aggressor, knowingly kills tens of thousands of Canadian citizens each year. The industry knowingly addicts tens of thousands of children each year, thereby taking away their freedom, perhaps for a lifetime. To protect and expand its empire, the industry uses a finely tuned propaganda machine. Loss of life, loss of freedom, propaganda — these are the characteristics of war.

Successfully controlling the tobacco industry would produce major benefits for public health. But significant change does not come without significant resistance, as these major health reforms of the past show:

- ✦ When in 1854 England's Dr John Snow was faced with a cholera epidemic, he shut down the Broad Street water pump believed to be the source of the problem. In doing so, Snow encountered fierce opposition from the privately owned water companies. But Snow prevailed, and public health was the winner.

- ✦ In 1938, the Province of Ontario made the pasteurization of milk mandatory to prevent typhoid, undulant fever, and bovine tuberculosis. Premier Mitch Hepburn forced the reform through, despite a split in Cabinet and despite a massive storm of protest from dairy farmers not wanting to pay increased costs.

It has been more than 45 years since the publication of the first large-scale studies that found a statistical association between smoking and lung cancer[147,359,648] and some 35 years since the Canadian Medical Association declared that the relationship was one of cause and effect.[76] Yet despite the fact that more than 45 000 Canadians die every year from tobacco use, tobacco products in Canada have historically been virtually unregulated compared with narcotics, prescription drugs, or a whole range of products less hazardous than cigarettes. Why?

When an airplane crashes, killing passengers, the story makes front-page headlines around the world. Journalists go to great lengths to expose those at fault. Tobacco, in contrast, kills more people in North America every day than two jumbo jets colliding head on and killing everyone aboard. Yet for decades, tobacco executives have not been held accountable for their actions by the media, by Parliament, or by the courts. Why?

This book seeks to answer these questions by presenting a history of tobacco and tobacco control in Canada, by exposing the true nature of the tobacco industry, by placing the tobacco epidemic in a global context, and by presenting an action plan to minimize tobacco use.

Although the tobacco epidemic in this country is still horrific, Canada has been recognized as a world leader for its antitobacco strategy and its regulation of the industry. Canada's actions have dramatically succeeded in reducing smoking. Lower smoking rates have prevented many thousands of cases of disease and early death. That Canada is a world leader may be encouraging, but when one thinks about it, it is also discouraging. Imagine what the health situation is like — or will be like — in countries that have had little success in controlling the industry.

Canada's tobacco story is worth sharing, both with Canadians and with those outside the country. Antismoking and health groups (which in this book are often described together as health groups) have out-lobbied the industry in battles to obtain a ban on advertising, higher tobacco taxes, prominent health warnings, and restrictions on smoking in workplaces and public places. In many countries the tobacco industry emerges victorious time after time, but in Canada the health lobby has its share of victories too. On occasion, those victories have spread internationally as other countries emulate Canada's initiatives.

But the road ahead is a long one. The industry is successful at blocking reforms and at undermining or even reversing some of Canada's most significant accomplishments. For example, the tobacco industry is responsible for substantial reductions in tobacco taxes and for the Supreme Court of Canada striking down the ban on tobacco advertising.

The International Development Research Centre, which provided the financial assistance that made this book possible, wanted Canada's experience to be shared globally so that less-developed countries could learn from Canada's successes and failures.

People often ask me why I became so interested in tobacco control. In 1988, in my first year of law school at the University of Toronto, I and other students in my constitutional law class were given an assignment to write a paper on whether the proposed ban on tobacco advertising infringed the freedom of expression provision in the *Canadian Charter of Rights and Freedoms*. In the course of research, I discovered that persons under 18 in Ontario could not buy tobacco. Here I was at 23, having only recently been a teenager, and I thought the minimum age was 16. But the law went unenforced and was tantamount to a joke, so several students formed a group to do something about it. We called the group the Student Movement Aimed at Restricting Tobacco, or SMART for short.

Early in my second year, SMART sent teenagers into 30 Shoppers Drug Mart outlets in Ottawa and Toronto and found that 25 of these pharmacies illegally sold cigarettes to the underage purchasers. Shoppers was chosen because it is owned by Imperial Tobacco's parent company, Imasco Ltd. SMART then sent a minor into the Shoppers outlet in Toronto's Eaton Centre and had four law students witness a successful attempt to buy cigarettes. Several days later, we laid a private charge in court and announced our actions at a news conference. We told the media this law was not being enforced but should be because it is during the teen years that almost all smokers begin. The maximum fine of $50 had not been increased since Ontario first passed the law in 1892. The prosecution resulted in a $25 fine for the Shoppers Drug Mart outlet, generated considerable media coverage, and led to a statutory amendment increasing the fines for selling tobacco to minors.

In later years, I became a more active advocate for tobacco-control legislation, as a volunteer and employee with the Canadian Cancer Society and as a consultant to other organizations. The more I learned about tobacco issues and tobacco companies, the more convinced I became of the need for decisive action. Several times I moved on to other things, but each time I was drawn back to antitobacco work. Like many others involved in tobacco control, I found that the more you learned about the industry's behaviour, the more compelled you were to stay around and fight. Let there be no mistake: this book was written by a public critic of the industry who is still active within the tobacco-control movement.

Rob Cunningham
4 September 1996

Acknowledgments

This book would not have been possible without the support of many people and organizations. I am especially grateful to the International Development Research Centre (IDRC) for its financial support. This support allowed me to spend the time necessary to undertake this project.

I would like to thank IDRC's Don de Savigny, who endorsed the project and provided encouragement, and Anne Phillips, who directly oversaw the progress of the book and provided ongoing assistance and continual cheerfulness. Don and Anne both provided appreciated comments on my manuscript. Bill Carman, Managing Editor of IDRC Books, kindly demonstrated enormous patience and capably ensured that my manuscript became a book.

Neil Collishaw, of the Tobacco or Health Programme at the World Health Organization, provided a comprehensive critique of the book. His comments led to many improvements. Ken Kyle, Director of Public Issues for the Canadian Cancer Society, reviewed my manuscript and provided valuable advice.

Professor Prakit Vateesatokit of Thailand's Mahidol University gave me useful suggestions for portions of the manuscript, as did Kathleen Clancy of IDRC. Margaret Cunningham, my mom, provided helpful comments on my manuscript. Kelly McCann provided research assistance by locating pertinent historic debates from the House of Commons.

Each chapter begins with an editorial cartoon; Figure 13 contains a map of the Akwesasne reserve; page 235 contains a photo by James Lukoski. I thank the creators of these works for kindly granting permission to reproduce these items.

IDRC, the Canadian Cancer Society, the National Clearinghouse on Tobacco and Health, and the Non-Smokers' Rights Association made their files and resource collections available to me. These records were of tremendous value.

Several hundred people generously gave of their time by agreeing to interviews, answering questions, forwarding helpful documents, or helping in many other ways. It would be impossible to name all of these individuals, but I gratefully acknowledge their contribution and know that the book is far richer as a result.

The content of this book would have been substantially incomplete had it not been for the thousands of people who, since the 1950s and especially since the 1980s, have worked to reduce tobacco use. It is because of this legion of individuals that there have been victories in the war against the tobacco industry and that there is some good news in the tobacco story. Their contribution to public health has long been underrecognized.

It should be noted that I attempted to interview public relations representatives of each of the three major tobacco manufacturers in Canada, but in each case either I was refused or my telephone calls were not returned. I also attempted to interview a representative of the Canadian Tobacco Manufacturers' Council. When I reached the representative, I was told to call back, but when I called back and left messages, my calls were not returned.

And finally, notwithstanding the able assistance of others, I take full responsibility for any errors or shortcomings that remain.

Rob Cunningham
4 September 1996

Tobacco, Development, and the Canadian Experience

Judith Mackay
Director, Asian Consultancy on Tobacco Control

The global tobacco epidemic continues to rage. In many countries of the industrialized North, smoking rates are increasing, and the epidemic is rapidly spreading from the North to the developing countries of the Southern hemisphere. It is an epidemic for which the developing world is unprepared.

The transnational tobacco companies, reeling from hard-hitting tobacco-control successes in Canada and other Western countries, now appear even more determined to conquer developing-country markets. They confidently predict, for example, an increase in sales of 33% in Asia between 1991 and 2000. And, with developing-country governments only now grasping the political nettle of tobacco control, tobacco hangs like the sword of Damocles over the "Third World," threatening deterioration in health, the economy, and the environment.

Smoking and Development

Smoking kills one in two long-term, regular smokers, half of them in middle age. As a result, developing countries will lose many able leaders prematurely. Smokers who suffer tobacco-related illness have minimal access to health care, and 80% of rural dwellers in developing countries have no, or extremely limited, access. This may be critical for a pregnant mother with tobacco-related complications such as haemorrhaging or low birth weight.

Tobacco inflicts substantial economic costs upon governments, upon business and industry, upon individuals and their families, and upon the environment. This economic burden includes medical and health costs, lost productivity (as smokers are less productive workers than nonsmokers), loss of the use of land that could be used to grow nutritious food, and loss of foreign exchange if cigarettes are imported (and two thirds of developing countries spend more importing cigarettes than they gain from exporting cigarettes). On the environmental side, tobacco farms are notorious for their heavy-handed use of fertilizers and pesticides to maintain high production levels. Other environmental costs include fires caused by careless smoking, deforestation as wood is cut down to cure tobacco, and the cleaning up of smokers' litter.

Spending money to buy cigarettes can lock smokers and their families into poverty. In some countries, this cost exceeds 25% of an individual's income, taking away money that could otherwise be spent on food, clothing, and shelter. Studies from Asia show that smokers spend more money on cigarettes and alcohol than on either medical needs and the education of their children (in the Philippines) or on grains, pork, and fruits (in China).

Smokers who are paid daily or on a piecemeal rate lose income if they are off sick. Since smoking often kills smokers in their working years, smoking may deprive the smoker's family of many years of income. Following a smoker's premature death, a partner, children, or elderly parents may even be left destitute.

Even though domestic production and consumption of tobacco remain problems in developing countries, of particular concern is the penetration into domestic markets by the transnational tobacco companies. Their tactics include denial of the health evidence, aggressive promotional campaigns, obstruction of national tobacco-control action, and the use of political and commercial pressures to open up markets and to promote foreign cigarettes. Tobacco advertising revenue discourages the media from reporting on the hazards of tobacco, a particularly serious problem in developing countries where awareness of the harmfulness of tobacco is low or even nonexistent.

Tobacco and Development

In June 1995, Canada's International Development Research Centre (IDRC) organized a meeting of 22 international organizations and individuals at the Rockefeller Foundation's Bellagio Study and Conference Center. This meeting examined the implications of current global trends in tobacco production and consumption, especially in developing countries, for sustainable development. It concluded that in the developing world tobacco poses a major challenge, not just to health, but also to social and economic development and to environmental sustainability. In reaching this conclusion, the following key facts were noted:

+ World-wide, there are only two major underlying causes of premature death that are increasing substantially: HIV (the AIDS-causing virus) and tobacco.

+ Each year, 3 million of the 30 million adult deaths in the world are attributable to tobacco. Based on current smoking patterns, by about 2025 this annual number will rise to 10 million deaths, of which 7 million will then be in developing countries.

- The net economic costs of tobacco are profoundly negative: costs of treatment, mortality, and disability exceed estimates of the economic benefits to producers and consumers by at least US $200 billion annually, with one third of this loss being incurred by developing countries.

- There are today about 800 million smokers in developing countries, and the number is increasing. It is estimated that 50% men and almost 10% of women in developing countries smoke.

- Smoking during pregnancy substantially reduces birth weight, and low birth weight is strongly associated with infant mortality and illness.

- Parental smoking increases the incidence of acute respiratory infections and asthma in children.

- Women and youth in developing countries are being targeted as a growth market for tobacco.

Tobacco control needs to be more widely recognized as a development priority; however, it is not on the agenda of most development agencies. Resources available from the donor community to assist in studying and responding to this pandemic are inadequate in view of the growing global burden of tobacco-attributable disease.

There is no central, coordinated global funding for tobacco control. Most developing countries find it extremely difficult to find even small amounts of money to undertake a prevalence survey, organize a symposium on tobacco or health, or implement health-education activities. The rich countries of the West have only been able to reduce smoking slowly over long periods of time, so development aid to combat the epidemic in the poor countries is absolutely crucial.

The "Third World" War

The objectives of fighting the tobacco "war" are similar to those of most general wars: to protect countries from being invaded and overpowered, to save people from being disabled and killed, to return land to growing food, to improve the economy, and to protect the environment. Yet, governments in developing countries are often preoccupied in fighting wars over other health or general matters, such as high infant mortality and communicable diseases. Few have experience in combatting this new type of epidemic, and the number of smokers in developing countries is on the increase, for a number of reasons:

- By 2025 there will be about 3 billion more people, mostly in developing countries, so there will be more smokers, even if prevalence rates remains the same.

- More young people, especially girls, are taking up smoking.

- Increasing disposable income is making cigarettes more affordable.

- The transnational tobacco companies are a major obstacle to tobacco control.

- Funding for antismoking health education is minimal or entirely absent in developing countries.

- Many smokers in poor countries are illiterate, live in remote rural areas, and are therefore difficult to reach with health education.

- Despite this gloomy forecast, systems are slowly being put into place that will eventually reduce this epidemic. For example, 10 years ago in the Asia–Pacific region, virtually no developing country had implemented tobacco-control measures. Now, all countries have introduced health education, most have a national tobacco-control coordinating organization, and many have taken legislative measures.

Canada as an Example

Canada has a responsibility not only to its own citizens in reducing the tobacco epidemic but also to the rest of the world in the global field of tobacco control.

- **The exemplar role** — Canada has shown that "it can be done." Smoking rates can be reduced, tax increases and strong health warnings can be implemented, and campaigns such as the "Smoke-free Skies Campaign" can lead to airlines worldwide becoming totally or partially smoke free.

- **The political role** — Canada has shown the crucial importance of government commitment to reduce the tobacco epidemic.

- **The sharing role** — Canada has shared experience, expertise, and funds in countering the global tobacco epidemic.

- **The supportive role** — Canada has given myriad different types of support to groups committed to fighting the well-heeled, well-established tobacco lobby (for example, Canadian specialists have given extensive advice on advertising bans and tax increases to developing countries).

The Canadian tobacco war has been marked by some bitter battles. In 1995, for example, the Canadian Supreme Court ruled to overturn Canada's advertising ban on tobacco. This caused immense problems globally, and the transnational tobacco companies seized upon the ruling to pressure developing countries into abandoning proposed legislation on tobacco advertising. Despite this, the global plea is for Canada to continue fighting the tobacco war, for, if a country like Canada does not take firm action, countries like Malawi or Cambodia have little hope in doing so.

Smoke & Mirrors, therefore, is both timely and valuable. And, as the publisher, IDRC is again on the cutting edge of development thinking. In outlining the Canadian experience and the current global picture in the tobacco epidemic, this book will serve as a baseline study on the "vector" of the tobacco disease: the tobacco industry. It will provide valuable insight to policymakers, decision-makers, researchers, and activists, and it will assist in the design of strategies for controlling tobacco use and distribution in developing countries and throughout the world. For years to come, *Smoke & Mirrors* will be a valuable resource in the fight for a healthier and more sustainable society.

Professor Judith Mackay, in addition to serving as Director of the Asian Consultancy on Tobacco Control, sits on the WHO Expert Advisory Panel on Tobacco and Health and is Regional Chair on Tobacco and Cancer for the International Union Against Cancer (UICC), Senior Consultant of the Asia Pacific Association for the Control of Tobacco, Senior Advisor to the Chinese Association on Smoking and Health, and Visiting Professor at the Chinese Academy of Preventive Medicine.

PART I

Setting the Stage:
Wealth Versus Health

CHAPTER 1

Individuals and Their Stories

Anthony Jenkins, *Globe and Mail*, Toronto

When people talk about the health consequences of smoking, they often cite statistics. But these statistics represent real people, as the following personal stories help to show.

Roger Perron

Roger Perron, who now lives in Vancouver, recalls that he was 13 when he started smoking. "I was in a store and some fella, an older student, just gave me a cigarette. After that I became a regular smoker. Smoking was cool. It seemed like everyone was smoking. I smoked Export 'A', in the green pack. It was a man's brand."

When he was in his twenties, his legs began to feel numb. When he was 28, his left leg was amputated below the knee. The pathologist's report revealed that Roger had thromboangiitis obliterans, commonly known as Buerger's disease. This disease causes inflammation of the arteries that impairs blood circulation, especially in the limbs. Buerger's disease almost always occurs in a smoker. Some doctors colloquially refer to Buerger's disease as "smoker's leg."

Despite being told by his doctor about the disease and the impact of smoking on the disease, Roger continued to smoke. Problems with his remaining leg got worse, and he had to sleep with it elevated. "The pain was incredible. It felt like someone was hammering 100 000 nails into me." When he was 31, his right leg was amputated below the knee.

Then he stopped smoking. The numbness in his arms went away. He regained the enormous amount of weight that he had lost and started to feel much better. Now he gets around with two artificial limbs, but the story doesn't end there.

"One day I was going down the street and I saw these kids smoking. They must have been 12 or 13. I wanted to do something about it. So I spoke to my lawyer about what could be done to stop stores from breaking the law by selling to these kids. Russell [Stanton] looked into it, did some research, and then one thing led to another and he suggested I take a different approach and sue RJR–Macdonald."

Roger filed a lawsuit in 1988, becoming the first Canadian to do so, but 8 years later his case has not come anywhere close to going to trial. RJR–Macdonald hired one of the top lawyers in the city and tried unsuccessfully to have the claim dismissed outright because it was filed too late.

After all that he has been through, Roger was taken aback when his 13-year-old son was seen smoking at elementary school. "We got together and had a long talk and I think he understood. Since then, I haven't heard of him smoking. At least I hope he hasn't.

"Smoking is in the news all the time now, but I think a point is being missed in the papers. If a person is addicted and you need something to get off, that's negligence. That's somebody's fault, whether the government or tobacco companies.

"Often people fail to understand that when something takes over your mind and takes control of your body, then it has got to be wrong. Once you're hooked, ... they [the tobacco companies] have got you hook, line, and sinker. It's a crock that tobacco companies say tobacco is not harmful to the body."

Julie Laperle

Julie Laperle is 16 years old and a high school student in Sherbrooke, Quebec. She smokes two to three packs a week, although just recently she is smoking less because her mother no longer lets her smoke in the house. Before, she was able to smoke in her bedroom.

Julie was 12 and in her first year of high school when she had her first cigarette. She was at a school dance one night, and the students were allowed to smoke in the cafeteria. The first cigarette came from one of her girlfriends. "I was influenced by my friends. I wanted to feel big," she recalls. "I knew a little bit that it could be harmful to my health, but I didn't believe it. My father seemed in shape like everyone else and he smoked."

When asked today why young girls begin to smoke, she replied "I've asked myself that question a lot myself. They don't know. Its a trip between childhood and adolescence. It's to try. Some are able to quit, others not."

By age 14, Julie was smoking daily. She usually got her cigarettes from a corner store. Only rarely was she refused because of her age. One winter she had problems with her breathing. Her doctor advised her to stop smoking to help the situation, but she continued.

In biology class in her third year, she saw lungs of smokers and nonsmokers. "It looked really bad. Everyone said 'we are going to stop, we are going to stop'." But despite the good intentions, neither Julie nor her friends quit.

Julie thought about trying Nicorette chewing gum, but it cost $15 a box and she did not want to end up having wasted her money if the gum did not work and only part of the box was used up.

At 15, she wanted to quit "because it was expensive and because I wasn't in perfect health. I imagined all the advantages it could have." Julie and a friend started to cut down together. "We tried to keep ourselves busy without thinking about it," she remembers. That generally worked, except that sometimes they cheated. Then Julie and her mother went on a trip to the United States, and Julie quit altogether. But she couldn't hold out. She bought one pack, and by the time she got back to Sherbrooke, she was back to her regular number of cigarettes.

In Julie's group of friends, some have now quit smoking. "You get to an age where you know more what you've done and you want to do something about it," she says. "If prices went back up to $7 a pack, I think I would quit because that's really expensive. My allowance is $10 a week and $7 a pack is hard." Julie makes it quite clear. If she was able to quit immediately, she would.

George Knudson[168,338,383,396,531–533,593]

George Knudson grew up in Winnipeg, and from his early days he had a passionate interest in golf. As early as age 10 he was hanging around the St Charles Golf and Country Club. He started to work there, picking up balls on the driving range and later on working as a caddy. His own golf game improved quickly, and by the age of 14 he was winning junior tournaments and getting press coverage.

George went on to become Canada's greatest golfer ever. By the time Knudson had stopped playing full time on the PGA Tour in 1979, he had won more PGA events than any other Canadian (eight wins between 1961 and 1972). At the time he left the tour, he was ranked in the top 50 of all-time money winners. He was a five-time winner of the Canadian PGA championship and was part of Canada's first World Cup victory in 1968. Jack Nicklaus and many other top players felt that George had one of the most efficient swings in the game.

On and off the golf course, George and his cigarette seemed inseparable. He called smoking a stinking habit. He often tried to quit but without success. His kids even tried to get him to stop. He smoked for 30 years and thought that cancer wouldn't get him.

At age 50, professional golfers become eligible to play on the Senior PGA Tour, a tour George was planning to join. But just days before his 50th birthday, George felt chest pains on his way home from a fitness club in Toronto, where he was then living. He checked into a hospital. A few hours later, after a series of tests, he was told he had lung cancer and could expect to live 18 months. The next day he began chemotherapy. Soon he lost his bushy head of hair, along with his eyebrows, although some hair did come back later. During the treatment, George was violently sick to his stomach but would later tell a reporter that he was lucky because he didn't react as badly as some people do.

In fact, George's recovery went so well that he played in the Legends of Golf Tournament in Austin, Texas, part of the Senior PGA Tour. Newspaper articles noted the event with headlines such as "Knudson's sweet swing returns to the tour."[532] Unfortunately, this would be his last tournament. He flew to another tournament on Rhode Island, but he was too weak to play and had to return home.

The cancer had spread to his brain. Nine months later George was dead, leaving behind his wife, Shirley, and his sons, Kevin, Paul, and Dean. George had quit smoking after he was diagnosed with lung cancer, but it was too late. At 51, 19 months after the diagnosis, George died, tragically and unnecessarily. Canadian golf had lost its best.

Part of the irony is that the thing that killed George, the cigarette, was for years sponsor of the Canadian Open, Canada's premier golf event. The Royal Canadian Golf Association has even spoken publicly against legislation that would stop tobacco sponsorship of sporting events.

George's son Dean, now 25, spoke about his dad on what turned out to be the anniversary of his father's death. Dean commented on the lost potential, both personal and professional. "He won't see his grandchildren. He won't grow old with my Mom. And God only knows what he could have done on the Senior Tour." Dean now has strong anti-smoking views, and he is not shy about making his opinion known to friends who smoke.

Dean recalls that as his father's 50th birthday approached, the family was strongly encouraging a return to professional golf. His dad had become more enthusiastic about golf than he had been in years. Dean also remembers being with his father at the Rhode Island tournament. "On the first shot of the practice round, he hit the ball in a perpendicular direction. I had never seen him make a bad shot in my life. He had lost his sense of balance and right then he stopped. As we were walking off the course, I saw players like Palmer and Rodriguez. To me this showed how close my father was to returning to the game. Yet his passion was taken away from him."

Julieta Albuquerque de Oliverira[312]

Julieta Albuquerque de Oliverira lives in Arapiraca, Brazil's northeastern tobacco capital. When she was 13, she learned how to smoke from her cousins. At the time, her father gave her a warning: "Little one, if I ever see you smoking, I'll set fire to these lips of yours!"

But Julieta didn't take him seriously, because he and all her siblings smoked. "If you guys can smoke, I can smoke, too!" she replied.

Now 20 and pregnant, Julieta works in a big tobacco warehouse owned by her uncle. With about 500 other women, she sits on the floor stemming leaves. The warehouse is humid and smells terrible. Among the female workers, headaches, vomiting, nausea, shortness of breath, dizziness, and stomachaches are common. Julieta's hands are blackened from handling tobacco leaves.

She sometimes works at a day care. There she smokes in the bathroom so that she is not a bad role model for the children. Even though Julieta knows that smoking is dangerous for her health and for her baby, she smokes about 40 cigarettes a day. She doesn't quit because tobacco leaves are always right in front of her. If she is out of cigarettes, she will make them from the leaves with which she is working. Julieta has no intention of quitting, sometimes even preferring a cigarette to a snack.

CHAPTER 2

Tobacco *or* Health: The Consequences of Tobacco Use

Theo Moudakis, *[Halifax] Daily News*

An unparalleled epidemic

The tragedy of the stories about Roger, Julie, George, and Julieta is that their experiences are repeated thousands of times each year. Although many people believe that smoking is harmful, few appreciate just how much damage it really does. Annually, more than 45 000 Canadians suffer early deaths because of tobacco use.[161,467] This frighteningly large total exceeds the 42 000 Canadian deaths in all the years of World War II. The total also exceeds the number of annual deaths from car accidents, suicide, murder, AIDS, and illicit drug use **combined**.[380] For AIDS, the total number of deaths reported in 1993 was 998, lower than the 1992 record of 1 116. During the entire period 1979–93, the total number of reported deaths from AIDS in Canada was 6 439.[233] In 1993, the total number of fatalities from traffic accidents, including those caused by drinking, was 3 601.[595] It has been estimated that for the period 1955–2005, a total of 12.3 million Canadians will have died prematurely from tobacco use.[467]

The Canadian Medical Association (CMA) has strong words regarding tobacco and health. As long ago as 1969, the CMA said that

> the story of the health hazards created by cigarette smoking represents an unrivalled tale of illness, disability and death. The potential benefits to be derived from the cessation of smoking place it at a level of importance in preventive medicine with pasteurization of milk, the purification and chlorination of water, and immunization.[76, p. 689]

The total number of smoking-related deaths per year has increased in this century as smoking has increased. The total, when adjusted for an aging population, is now leveling off among men but continues to increase among women, because increases in smoking among women took place later than in men. It normally takes several decades before smoking results in death, so there is a delay before higher smoking rates translate into higher death rates. Similarly, it takes time before lower smoking rates translate into lower death rates.[369] Even with lower smoking rates, though, the total number of smoking-related deaths will increase in future years because of Canada's growing population and aging baby boomers. Of all smokers who die prematurely, half will die before age 70 and lose an average of 23 years of life.[467] The half who die after age 70 lose an average of 8 years of life.[467]

The rise in the health consequences due to tobacco is partially illustrated by Figure 1, which shows the rise in lung cancer since 1950. More than 80% of lung cancer deaths and about 30% of cancer deaths are caused by tobacco use. Unlike some other forms of cancer, lung cancer is usually lethal. Within 1 year of diagnosis, 66% of men and 62% of women are dead; within 5 years, 85% of men and 80% of women are dead.[427] Smoking also causes cancer of the throat, mouth, tongue, lip, larynx, pharynx, bladder, kidney, and pancreas. It has been associated with several other cancers, including cancer of the stomach and cervix.

As important as smoking is as a cause of cancer deaths, it is responsible for an even greater number of deaths due to heart attacks, stroke, and other forms of heart disease. American research indicates that of all tobacco-related deaths, 46% are due to cardiovascular disease, 26% to lung cancer, 14.3% to chronic bronchitis and emphysema, 7% to other cancers, and 6.7% to other causes.[602] Of all heart disease deaths, about 30% are

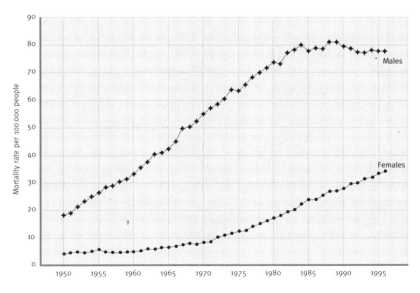

Figure 1. Age-standardized lung cancer death rate
for males and for females, 1950–96.[428,567]

attributable to smoking. Smoking also causes 80%–90% of chronic obstructive lung disease and is the major cause of emphysema and chronic bronchitis. Smoking can cause and aggravate asthma.

Employees exposed to chemicals in certain types of workplaces have an increased risk of certain diseases. If an employee smokes, the risk increases dramatically and is far greater than if just risks from smoking and from workplace chemicals were added together. For example, lung cancer death rates (per 100 000 people) for cigarette smokers exposed to asbestos dust has been reported at 602, compared with 123 for cigarette smokers not exposed to asbestos dust, 58 for nonsmokers exposed to asbestos dust, and 11 for nonsmokers not exposed to asbestos dust.[541]

Smoking during pregnancy increases the risk of complications, low birth weight, miscarriages, stillbirths, premature births, bleeding during pregnancy, and sudden infant death syndrome. Smoking has been linked to lowered immunity, early menopause, reduced fertility, and peptic ulcers. In men, smoking has been associated with a higher risk of impotence. Smoking can cause gum disease and tooth loss.

Quitting smoking can have a tremendous effect on reducing health risks and on improving life expectancy, especially if quitting occurs early in life. The benefits of quitting can be immediate, and within days or weeks some of the effects of smoking are reversible, including some respiratory problems. After 3 years, on average, the risk of sudden cardiac death approaches that of never smokers. However, increased risks still remain compared with the never smoker. For example, after 10 years of not smoking, the risk of lung cancer remains at 30%–50% of that for continuing smokers[236] and considerably higher than that for never smokers. And the greater the number of years a person smoked and the higher the number of cigarettes smoked daily, the greater the risks.

One of the most important studies ever done on the health consequences of smoking was carried out in the United Kingdom starting in 1951.[148] The study involved 40 000 doctors and followed them over the next 40 years, monitoring their smoking and, when applicable, their age at and cause of death. The study, released in 1994, concluded that "half of all regular cigarette smokers will eventually be killed by their habit."[148, p. 901] The study also concluded that earlier studies "substantially underestimated the hazards of long term use of tobacco."[148, p. 901] Smoking was significantly associated with 24 different causes of death. Interestingly, smokers were less likely to die from Parkinson's disease, although no explanation is offered. Partway through the study, in 1978, the alcohol consumption patterns of the doctors were monitored. In contrast with smoking, the study found that moderate consumption of alcohol actually increased life expectancy. However, heavier drinking (more than three units a day) led to increased death rates.[1]

Cigarette smoke contains more than 4 000 chemicals. At least 43 of these have been identified as carcinogenic in humans or animals, and others have been identified as toxic, so it is no surprise that smoking is so harmful. The substances in smoke include carbon

---

[1] One pint of beer = 2 units; one glass of wine = 1 unit; 25 mL of liquor = 1 unit.

monoxide (found in car exhaust), acetone (used in paint strippers), hydrogen cyanide (used in gas chambers), ammonia (used in fertilizers and bathroom cleaners), mercury, lead, benzene, cadmium (used in car batteries), formaldehyde, arsenic, and toluene (used in industrial solvents).[61,231] Unburnt tobacco has more than 2 500 chemical compounds, including pesticides applied during growing and sometimes substances added during the manufacturing process.[606] Nicotine itself is a potent toxin that has been used in insecticides and rat poison. Indeed, nicotine has been around as a poison since at least the 19th century. For humans, a lethal dose when swallowed has been estimated at only 40–60 milligrams (mg).[618] That's a mere drop, next to nothing. A smoker may consume more nicotine than that in two packages of cigarettes, but of course the dose is spread out.

There is no such thing as a safe cigarette, including so-called light cigarettes. Tobacco products are the only products legally available on the market that are harmful when used exactly as the manufacturer intends. The industry kills its best customers.

Apart from the health consequences, smoking can yellow fingers, yellow teeth, and speed the onset of facial wrinkles. It can cause clothes and hair to stink and as the saying goes, make kissing a smoker taste like kissing an ashtray.

For most new smokers, the taste of smoking a cigarette is awful. Smoking is an activity that has to be learned, but once learned, it may be extremely difficult to stop. Just ask an ex-smoker. Smokers often fail in attempts to quit because of intense cravings for nicotine and because of withdrawal symptoms. It is not unusual for smokers to need a cigarette in the morning, their body having gone without a fix for 8 hours. In the most extreme and unusual cases, smokers cannot even get through the night without a cigarette. In 1988, the US Surgeon General concluded that nicotine is the drug in tobacco that causes addiction and that the pharmacologic and behavioural processes that determine tobacco addiction are similar to those that determine addiction to drugs such as heroin and cocaine.[605] Data from Imperial Tobacco indicate that in 1989, 43% of smokers attempted to quit in the previous six months but only 1.8% of the total population did so,[290] strong evidence of the power of nicotine. Even after surgery for lung cancer, nearly half of smokers resume smoking. One study found that 40% of smokers who had their larynx removed tried smoking again.[248]

Tobacco is considered by many to be a gateway substance to illicit drug use. Research indicates that preventing tobacco use may help reduce the potential for use of illicit drugs.[605]

The harm caused by smoking is not limited to smokers. Nonsmokers are harmed by second-hand smoke, technically known as environmental tobacco smoke (ETS) but sometimes referred to as passive smoking or involuntary smoking. ETS includes both the smoke emitted from the lit end of the cigarette and the mainstream smoke exhaled by a smoker. ETS can cause fatal lung cancer in otherwise healthy nonsmokers and has a particularly harmful impact on children's respiratory systems.

Cigarettes are not the only harmful tobacco product. Cigars, pipes, and smokeless tobacco (chewing tobacco, snuff) are not safe alternatives to cigarettes. All of these products can cause cancer in the mouth area, including cancer of the lip and tongue.

No one should assume that he or she is immune to the risks of smoking. Those whose deaths are attributable to smoking include King George VI, musician Nat King Cole, actor Humphrey Bogart, actress Betty Grable, film maker Walt Disney, "Marlboro Man" Wayne McLaren, tobacco company head R.J. Reynolds, as well as descendants R.J. Reynolds, Jr and R.J. Reynolds III.

Economic and other nonhealth consequences

Nonsmokers as taxpayers have to pay for the medical costs resulting from smoking-related disease. Health Canada estimates that the direct health-care costs attributable to smoking in 1993 totaled $3 billion. If lost productivity, including foregone household income, is added, the total rises to $11 billion.[237] In the United States, researchers have estimated that smoking-related health-care costs in 1993 totaled US $52 billion. When lost productivity was taken into account, the total economic burden rose to more than US $100 billion.[643]

Cigarettes are the cause of preventable fires. These fires cause millions of dollars of property and environmental damage, result in the injury and death of innocent victims, risk the safety of fire fighters, and generally increase fire insurance premiums.

The economic consequences of tobacco use are staggering, but there are also significant intangible costs. Nothing can place a value on the pain and suffering caused by disease, the grief of losing a friend or loved one, or the financial crisis created by the death of a family's wage earner.

Tobacco is harmful to the environment. In addition to the damage from forest fires, the outdoors has to deal with about 2 billion empty cigarette packages annually, several billion plastic and metallic foil overwraps (used to keep the product fresh), and about 50 billion discarded cigarette butts. The butts are often made with cellulose acetate tow, a substance with poor biodegradability. A vast number of trees are cut down each year to produce cigarette paper, packages, cartons, shipping boxes, matches, and matchbooks.

The industry's position

In the face of the avalanche of knowledge about tobacco and health, the tobacco industry still denies that smoking is harmful to anyone. The industry denies that smoking has been proven to cause lung cancer or any other disease, that anyone has ever died from smoking, that nicotine is addictive, or that ETS is harmful. The transnational (multinational) industry maintains a united stand, regardless of the company or the country.

From the 1950s through the 1960s, and even later, the industry in Canada argued strenuously that smoking did not cause lung cancer. It offered alternative explanations for the rise in lung cancer, such as genetics, a virus, diet, or air pollution. Although the industry has long acknowledged a statistical association (sometimes referred to as risk) between smoking and lung cancer, it has argued that statistics do not prove causation. The industry's position is that although it is true that smokers are statistically more likely than non-smokers to get cancer and heart disease, the cause of the diseases might be explained by other factors. Today the position is unchanged, but now the industry does everything possible to avoid speaking about smoking and health questions. The industry knows that when it says "smoking is not a proven cause of lung cancer," all credibility is lost.

On the question of ETS, however, industry representatives put on their best face, go on the offensive, and deny the dangers of ETS just as vigorously as they once did with direct smoking, saying there is no "scientific consensus." They seek to create the impression that the debate remains open, a decade after the US Surgeon General concluded in his 1986 report that ETS could cause lung cancer.

Because many people find it difficult to believe that the industry still denies that smoking causes any harm to health, a few examples are worth citing. In 1987, Jean-Louis Mercier, then President of Imperial Tobacco, appeared before a House of Commons Committee and was asked whether he believed that any Canadians die of smoking-related diseases. He replied "No, I do not."[401, p. 13:29] He also stated that the "role, if any, that tobacco or smoking plays in the initiation and the development of these diseases is still very uncertain. The issue is still unresolved."[401, p. 13:22] Patrick Fennell, the President of Rothmans, Benson & Hedges Inc. (RBH), asserted that "science has not established that there is a causal relationship between smoking and illness."[171, p. 13:23]

The following is an exchange aired in 1994 on the Canadian Broadcasting Corporation (CBC) *Sunday Morning* radio program between journalist Lynn Glazier and Rob Parker, the industry's chief lobbyist, in his capacity as President of the Canadian Tobacco Manufacturers' Council (CTMC):

Q: Do cigarettes cause cancer?
A: It's an impossible question for me to answer. I'm not a scientist. I can certainly tell you that the industry's view is that there is a statistical link between tobacco consumption and a long list of health ill effects. Cause cancer? That's a scientific question. I'm not qualified to answer it. But I don't believe that there is an established scientific causal link. The risk is clear.
Q: Are cigarettes addictive?
A: What are you planning to do here?
Q: Is nicotine the substance that addicts people to cigarettes?
A: I can't answer the question. I'm not qualified to.[97]

On another occasion in 1994, Rob Parker stormed off a CBC *Midday* television set in midinterview when David Sweanor of the Non-Smokers' Rights Association (NSRA) asked him a smoking and health question. Parker said that this was violating an agreement made before coming on the show. Also in 1994, Imperial Tobacco spokesperson Michel

Descôteaux told *CTV National News* that "we don't say that smoking is good for you, we don't say that smoking is bad for you. All we are saying is that in the state of current knowledge we do not know."[129]

At the 1994 annual meeting of Imasco, the parent company of Imperial Tobacco, Chairman Purdy Crawford, was asked how many deaths were caused by tobacco use. "We have no view on that," he replied.[242, p. D2] When another questioner asked how the company would respond if it was ever proven that smoking caused lung cancer, Crawford avoided the question and stopped the person from asking further questions, all to a crescendo of applause from shareholders assembled in Montreal's plush Monument national.

In the November/December 1994 issue of *The Leaflet*, an Imperial Tobacco publication for employees and their families, an article entitled "Clearing the Air: Smoking and Health, The Scientific Controversy" contained this excerpt:

> The facts are that researchers have been studying the effects of tobacco on health for more than 40 years now, but are still unable to provide undisputed scientific proof that smoking causes lung cancer, lung disease and heart disease .... 'The fact is nobody knows yet how diseases such as cancer and heart disease start, or what factors affect the way they develop. We do not know whether or not smoking could cause these diseases because we do not understand the disease process'.[30, p. 2]

For decades, the industry has tried to muddy the waters. It has sought to create doubt about the health risks when no such doubt was justified. With a slick, sustained public relations (PR) campaign, the industry has used misinformation to help remove the stain from its products and to protect enormous corporate profits. If consumers do not believe smoking is harmful, their motivation to quit is reduced. If politicians underestimate or do not accept the health consequences of smoking, their motivation to pass tobacco control laws is decreased.

In 1994, Imperial Tobacco commissioned a study by economist Jean-Pierre Vidal in response to other studies showing tobacco to be a net loss to the economy. Vidal stated that tobacco-caused deaths are economically beneficial, in part because people are killed off before becoming a burden to society.[617] Naturally, this report touched off a storm of criticism. Should children's hospitals be closed because this would save money? Should all Canadians aged 55+ be denied medical care? Imperial Tobacco quickly responded that it did not agree with the study (of course not, because the company denies that cigarettes kill) and claimed that the study was not supposed to be made public.

Canadian trends in smoking

According to data from Imperial Tobacco, the proportion of Canadians aged 15 and over who smoke declined from 47% in 1971 to 29% in 1993.[290] Figure 2 shows the overall trend. Prevalence among men peaked at 62% in 1961. Among women, prevalence peaked at 40% in 1974. However, per capita consumption (age 15+) — the average number of

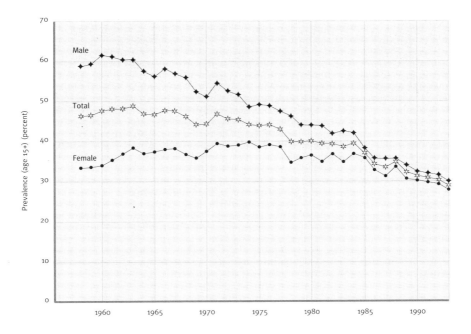

Figure 2. Prevalence of smokers among adults (age 15+) for men, for women, and for men and women, 1958–93. Source: 1958–70, derived from Rose (1981);[508] 1971–89, Imperial Tobacco (1989);[290] 1990–93, Imasco (1993, 1994),[278,279] and derivations from these.

cigarettes (including roll-your-own) smoked per person — may be a better measure of smoking because it takes into consideration both the number of smokers and the amount smoked. These rates peaked in 1966, declined slowly with some ups and downs until 1982, and then began a dramatic decline that lasted until 1993 before rising somewhat in 1994 as lower taxes made smoking more affordable. Figure 3 shows the historical trend.

Even though smoking rates were declining, a growing population meant that tobacco companies enjoyed increased overall sales until 1982. This was the peak year for total tobacco sales in Canada, with 73 billion cigarettes, including roll-your-own, sold. In 1995, the comparable figure, including contraband, was about 51 billion cigarettes, although exact figures are impossible to obtain because of smuggling.

Smoking patterns vary greatly. A Health Canada survey in 1994 found that although 31% of Canadians aged 15+ were smokers (6.6 million smokers), prevalence varied from a low of 25% in British Columbia to a very high 38% in Quebec. Thirty-two percent of men were smokers, compared with 29% of women. Men reported that they smoked an average of 21 cigarettes a day and women reported 17, although actual numbers are somewhat higher than obtained from self-reporting. Of the 31% of the population who were smokers, 25% were daily smokers and 6% were nondaily smokers. Prevalence generally decreased with age, reflecting both successful quitting and early death: 38% of those 20–24 years old smoked, compared with 34% of those 25–44 years old, 29% of those 45–64 years

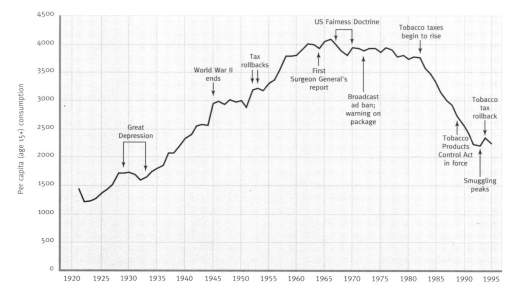

Figure 3. Canadian per capita (age 15+) cigarette consumption (including roll-your-own), 1921–95. Consumption during 1990s includes contraband estimates, and as a result there is some uncertainty. Imports, which are typcially very low, have not been included. Source: For legal sales, Goodyear (1994);[203] Statistics Canada (1995–96);[566] for contraband, Canadian Tobacco Manufacturers' Council (1993),[90] Lindquist Avey Macdonald Baskerville Inc. (1993, 1994),[364–366] Imasco Ltd (1996),[284] and personal calculations.

old, and 16% of those aged 65+. Among those 15 to 19 years old, 29% smoked.[235] A 1991 study found exceptionally high rates of smoking among indigenous people: 56% of Indians and 72% of Inuit were smokers,[241] rates among the highest anywhere in the world. Smoking decreases with education: 33% of people with less than high school education smoke, compared with 19% of people with university education. Among men, 4% smoke cigars, 2% smoke pipes, and 1% use chewing tobacco or other forms of smokeless tobacco.[235]

Trends in youth smoking are shown in Figure 4. There was a particularly large decline in smoking among teenagers during the 1980s.

A total of 5.9 million Canadians are former smokers (27% of the population aged 15+). Of the 6.6 million current smokers, 4.9 million (74%) have made a serious attempt to quit by giving up smoking for at least 1 week.[234] Among current smokers, younger people are more likely to have attempted to quit in the previous 3 months than older people: 29% for those aged 15–19, 22% for those aged 20–24, and about 10% for those aged 25+. Older smokers may be less likely to try quitting because of previous failed attempts; if they had been able to quit, they would no longer be smokers. Thirty percent of smokers smoking 1–10 cigarettes per day attempted to quit in the previous 3 months, compared with 5% smoking 11–25 cigarettes.[235]

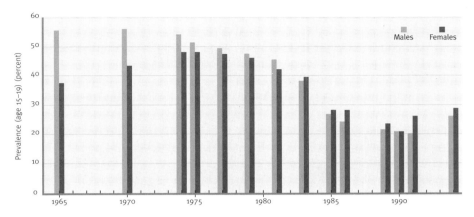

Figure 4. Smoking prevalence reported by 15–19 year old Canadians, 1965–1994, according to government surveys. Source: National Clearinghouse on Tobacco and Health.[429]
Note that the *1994 Youth Smoking Survey* found a smoking prevalence among 15–19 year olds of 23% for males and 24% for females,[240] lower than the results from the
Survey on Smoking in Canada illustrated in the graph.

Overall, the good news is that the number of smokers has been going down. The bad news is that some 6.6 million Canadians still continue to smoke. The bad news is made worse by the fact that tens of thousands of teenagers start smoking each year. Apart from the addictiveness of nicotine, why do so many people continue to smoke and so many teens begin smoking? The answer lies largely with the wealth, power, and skill of the tobacco companies — the merchants of death.

CHAPTER 3

Industry Wealth:
"More Money Than God"

Tribune Media Services, by Mike Peters

From a profit perspective, the cigarette business is an exceptionally lucrative business. A cigarette can cost about a penny or two to make, it can be sold at a high profit margin, and most of all, because of addiction, customers will remain loyal whether they want to or not. The business is recession proof, and it is huge. The total retail value of Canadian tobacco sales in 1992 was $9.8 billion.[89]

In Canada, despite declining sales, tobacco industry profits in 1995 again set an all-time record high. Profit levels surpassed records set in each of the previous 8 years. As Figure 5 illustrates, lower smoking rates clearly have not hurt the industry's bottom line. High profitability is not new. Imperial Tobacco has shown a profit every year since 1928 (its financial data are not available for earlier years). Imperial was even profitable during the Great Depression.

Here is what one American company executive said about the tobacco industry and its profitability:

> I'll tell you what I like about the business. First, there are no surprises. There is nothing more to be said or discovered about the cigarette business or the industry. And there's no way to write an article that could do us any more harm than what has already been written. Second, no new company wants to get into the tobacco business. That's great. Third, we have the best partners in the world: the governments. In a lot of countries, it's incredibly important to the whole welfare state that we sell our products to

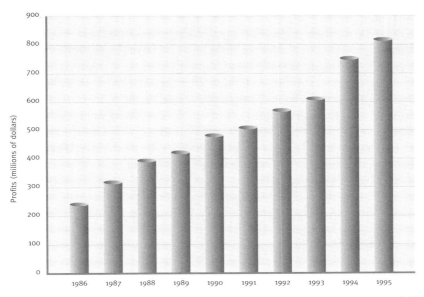

Figure 5. Combined pretax profits of Imperial Tobacco Ltd and Rothmans Inc., 1986–95.[276,512] Profits for RJR–Macdonald Inc. are not available for all years in this period and thus are not included.

collect taxes. ... So no matter how you look at the cigarette business, it's incredibly predictable, it's extremely secure as an investment vehicle and, therefore, it's a great business to be in — if you can deal with the fact that some people are not going to like you.[509, p. 41]

The tobacco manufacturing industry in Canada is 99% dominated by an oligopoly of three foreign-controlled, transnational tobacco companies (TTCs). Each is discussed in turn below.

Imperial Tobacco Ltd

Montreal-based Imperial Tobacco Ltd is the dominant player in Canada, with a 67% share of the domestic cigarette market. The company's performance has consistently improved since 1975, when its market share was 36.7%.[290] Imperial is 100% owned by Montreal-based Imasco Ltd, which in turn is controlled by British-based tobacco conglomerate B.A.T Industries plc (BAT). BAT owns about 41% of the Imasco shares. Imperial Tobacco's leading brand families are Player's and du Maurier, which together account for 59% of Canadian cigarette sales. Imperial also sells Matinée, the company's third most important brand family, as well as Cameo, Peter Jackson, Avanti, and Medallion cigarettes. In the United States, Imperial's sister company is Brown and Williamson, a company also controlled by BAT.

Imperial Tobacco's roots go back to 1895, when the American Cigarette Company moved into Canada and started to manufacture cigarettes in Montreal. Soon afterward, the American Tobacco Company of Canada Ltd was created by a merger of the American Cigarette Company and D. Ritchie & Company, a Montreal firm dating from 1885. Over time, American obtained controlling interest in the Empire Tobacco Company, the B. Houde Company, and the Joliette Tobacco Company. In 1907, the American Tobacco Company obtained a 50% interest in a company later known as the National Tobacco Company, a firm now best known for marketing smokeless tobacco. Imperial Tobacco sold this 50% interest in 1986.[289] In 1908, Imperial Tobacco was created by a formal merger of the American Tobacco Company of Canada and Empire Tobacco Company. In 1912, the present Imperial Tobacco Ltd was incorporated as a successor to the Imperial Tobacco formed in 1908. At this point, controlling interest in Imperial Tobacco was no longer with the American Tobacco Company but with British–American Tobacco Co.

In subsequent years, Imperial acquired other tobacco companies: in 1921, General Cigar Co., a firm that included another company, S. Davis & Son; in 1930, Tuckett Tobacco Company, which controlled Tobacco Products Company of Canada and Philip Morris Co. Ltd, both Canadian firms; in 1936, Landau & Cormack Ltd; in 1942, L.O. Grothé; and in 1949, Imperial Tobacco Company (Newfoundland) Ltd, just as Newfoundland was entering Confederation. Imperial purchased Canadian rights to certain brands and trademarks from British–American Tobacco (now known as BAT) in 1921 and from US-based Brown and Williamson in 1950.

In 1964, when the smoking and health issue was really heating up, Imperial started to diversify, fearing that tobacco was on the road to disappearance. Imperial obtained interests in Canada Foils Ltd, Growers' Wine Company Ltd, and Welland Winery Ltd. In 1968, it acquired Simtel Incorporated and Editel Productions, both of Montreal, and in 1969, it acquired S & W Foods Inc. of San Francisco and Uddo & Taormina Corp. of New Jersey. Imperial also purchased Pasquale Bros Limited (later called Unico Foods), a food distributor based in Toronto. Imperial does not own any of these subsidiaries today.

In 1970, the company's name was changed to Imasco (IMperial and ASsociated COmpanies). Imasco Ltd was the holding company for the various corporate interests. Other companies that Imasco has owned or in which Imasco once had a significant interest include Amco Services (Canada) Ltd (a vending machine company, which subsequently purchased other vending machine companies), Chalet Wines, Grissol Foods, Marché aux Escomptes S & M Ltée (Quebec discount health and beauty aid stores), Collegiate Sports (later Arlington Sports), Red Carpet Coffee Service Ltd, Ski Oberson Boutique Inc., Rancho Francisco, Toltec Foods (tortilla producer), Topmost Foods, Biscuits Montmagny Inc., Henri & Fils, PoP Shoppes of America, Inc., The Outdoor Stores, Lido Biscuit Cie Ltée, Canadian operations of Anco International (a cheese company), La Fromagerie de Comeville Inc., Cavalier China & Gift Shops, Burger Chef Systems, Inc., Flame Oil & Gas Ltd, Ingersoll Cheese, Embassy Cleaners, Tinder Box International (tobacco and gift shops), Peoples Drug Stores (based in the United States), and Canadian Northwest Energy Ltd.[173,285] In 1995, Imasco sold off its long-standing ownership of United Cigar Stores.

A lot of these investments turned out to be big mistakes. It was the huge cash flow generated by tobacco that made the acquisitions possible in the first place, and it was the cash flow that allowed the company to get away with errant acquisitions. Many of the now discarded Imasco subsidiaries lost money or were simply not generating profits the way Imperial Tobacco was.

Today, in 1996, Imasco has interests in several large companies. Imasco owns Shoppers Drug Mart/Pharmaprix (Canada's leading pharmacy chain), 98% of Canada Trust (Canada's biggest financial institution after the big five banks), Hardee's (the fourth largest hamburger fast-food chain in the United States), and Genstar Development (a land development company). Imasco's ownership of Shoppers Drug Mart dates to 1978. Since then Shoppers Drug Mart has gobbled up other pharmacies.

In 1993, the conglomerate Imasco was the sixth largest publicly traded company in Canada when ranked by profits. Only Bell Canada, Seagram, and three banks enjoyed greater profitability.[485] This ranking dropped to 12th in 1994 as other companies with more variable profit than Imasco's moved ahead.[486]

Imperial Tobacco is the driving factor behind Imasco's financial success. Although Imperial's net revenues only accounted for 16% of Imasco's system-wide total in 1994, tobacco profits represented 51% of Imasco's total pretax earnings from operations. This does not include the tobacco profits arising from retail tobacco sales by Shoppers Drug Mart. A study by University of Quebec accounting professor Léo-Paul Lauzon estimated that for the period 1987–93, the total amount of money provided by Imperial Tobacco to Imasco was greater than the total dividends paid out by Imasco.[355] Not only was Imperial the source of all Imasco dividends, but also it provided money to reinvest in other Imasco ventures.

Imasco has had many influential individuals on its Board of Directors. In 1996, the directors include Bernard Roy, former Principal Secretary to Prime Minister Brian Mulroney and partner at the Montreal law firm of Ogilvy Renault, the same firm at which Mulroney is now a partner. Rob Pritchard, President of Canada's largest university, the University of Toronto, is a director. Russell Palmer, former Dean of the Wharton Business School at the University of Pennsylvania, is a director. Former directors include Paul Martin, now Minister of Finance; Bill Bennett, one-time premier of British Columbia; and Torrance Wylie, previously a senior official with the Liberal Party of Canada. Claude Castonguay, a former Quebec Minister of Social Affairs and later a Progressive Conservative Senator, was a director in the 1970s. Pauline McGibbon was on the board briefly before she became Lieutenant-Governor of Ontario. McGibbon has also had a long association with the du Maurier Council for the Performing Arts, now known as du Maurier Arts Ltd, a sponsorship-granting body connected with Imperial Tobacco.

Some directors have had simultaneous appointments seemingly at odds with their directorship of a tobacco giant. For example, Nan-Bowles de Gaspé Beaubien, a director since 1987, is also a director of the Terry Fox Humanitarian Award Committee, an award in memory of Canada's most famous cancer victim and in whose name millions of dollars for cancer research are raised annually. Murray Koffler, the founder of Shoppers Drug Mart, was a director of the Canadian Council on Drug Abuse and a director of Imasco at the same time.

Rothmans, Benson & Hedges Inc.

RBH is Canada's second largest tobacco company. The company's brand families include Rothmans, Craven "A", Benson & Hedges, Number 7, Belvedere, Mark Ten, Viscount, Dunhill, Black Cat, Sportsman, Peter Stuyvesant, Belmont and Canadian Classics.

RBH's stock is 83% foreign controlled. Forty percent is owned by a subsidiary of Philip Morris, the largest tobacco company in the United States. Philip Morris is the world's largest consumer products company through sales of not only cigarettes, but also Kraft products, Miller beer, Toblerone chocolate, Post cereals, Maxwell House coffee, Jell-O desserts, Kool-Aid drinks, and Oscar Mayer meats. Philip Morris also owns 20% of Canada's Molson Breweries. The remaining 60% of RBH stock is owned by Rothmans Inc., a Canadian holding company, which through a series of other holding companies is 71.2% owned by Rothmans International B.V., now based in the Netherlands. Rothmans International is ultimately controlled by the Rupert Family Trusts in South Africa. In 1994, there were 11 corporate levels between RBH and the ultimate South African interest.[565]

RBH was formed in 1986 with the merger of Rothmans of Pall Mall Limited and Benson and Hedges (Canada) Inc. The former was controlled by Rothmans International, and the latter was a subsidiary of Philip Morris.

RBH's market-share performance has been steadily eroding. In 1975, the combined cigarette market share of Rothmans and of Benson & Hedges was 43%. That has fallen to 20% and may continue to fall, in part because smokers of its brands are older than smokers of competitors' brands.

Benson & Hedges started in Britain in 1873, expanded to New York around 1895, and from there expanded to Canada, opening a store in Montreal in 1906. The company was not a major player until Benson & Hedges (Canada) Ltd, along with its New York counterpart, merged with Philip Morris in 1954. In 1961, Benson & Hedges (Canada) Ltd opened a new cigarette factory near Brampton and started to market aggressively. In 1962, Benson & Hedges (Canada) purchased Tabacofina of Canada, the makers of Belvedere.

Rothmans of Pall Mall started operations in Canada in 1957 at a time when its British parent company was expanding throughout the Commonwealth. In 1958, Rothmans' parent company acquired a controlling interest in Carreras Limited of London, United Kingdom. Carreras had a controlling interest in Canada's Rock City Tobacco Company, a firm based in Quebec City since being founded in 1899 and best known for its

Craven "A", Black Cat, and Sportsman brands. In 1963, all outstanding stock of Rock City Tobacco was acquired by Rothmans of Pall Mall Canada Ltd.

In the late 1960s, Rothmans started to diversify. At one time Rothmans has owned Alfred Dunhill of London Ltd (luxury goods and accessories) and Carling O'Keefe Breweries, which in turn has owned Jordan Valley Wines, Star Oil and Gas, the Canadian Football League's Toronto Argonauts and the National Hockey League's Quebec Nordiques. Carling O'Keefe was sold in 1987, and the Dunhill subsidiary was sold in 1990. RBH now focuses exclusively on tobacco.

Like Imperial Tobacco, Rothmans has had its share of prominent directors. The Chairman of the Board is Progressive Conservative Senator William Kelly. Kelly was appointed as a director shortly after the Conservatives won the 1984 election. Also on the Board of Directors is Roch Bolduc, a fellow Conservative Senator. Pierre des Marais II is President and Chief Executive Officer (CEO) of Unimédia Inc., a firm that owns several French language newspapers including *Le Soleil* in Quebec City and *Le Droit* in Ottawa.

Louis St Laurent, Liberal Prime Minister from 1948 to 1957, was Chairman of the Board of Rothmans during most of the 1960s. For part of the period that St Laurent was Chairman of Rothmans in the early 1960s, he was also President of the Canadian Heart Foundation. Other directors have included John Wettlaufer, former Dean of the business school at the University of Western Ontario; Alistair Gillespie, former Liberal cabinet minister; and Robert Winters, a former Liberal cabinet minister under St Laurent. After being on the Rothmans Board of Directors, Winters returned to politics and became Minister of Trade and Commerce. Winters later ran for the leadership of the Liberal Party but lost to Pierre Trudeau.

Joel Aldred, a high-profile radio and television announcer who recorded hundreds of cigarette commercials during the 1960s and early 1970s, sat on the Board of Directors.[525] Maurice Sauvé, a former Liberal cabinet minister and husband of Jeanne Sauvé (who became Canada's first female Governor-General), sat on the Benson & Hedges (Canada) Board of Directors before the company merged with Rothmans. Murray Koffler sat on the Rothmans Board of Directors before he sold the Shoppers Drug Mart chain to Imasco, after which he sat on the Imasco Board of Directors.

RJR–Macdonald Inc.

Canada's third largest company is RJR–Macdonald Inc., with a 12% market share. A government publication shows the company is 100% owned by its immediate parent firm, RJR Tobacco Consolidated IHC, Inc. of the Bahamas, a Caribbean tax haven.[565] This Bahamas company is related to US-based RJR–Nabisco Inc. and R.J. Reynolds Tobacco Company. Like Philip Morris, RJR–Nabisco is a huge global conglomerate that sells not only cigarettes but also such brand-name products as Planters peanuts, Life Savers candies, Oreo cookies, Ritz crackers, and Fleischmann's margarine.

The overwhelming majority of the Canadian subsidiary's cigarette sales come from the Export "A" brand family. RJR–Macdonald also manufactures Vantage, Macdonald, and Contessa Slims cigarettes and imports small quantities of Camel, Winston, Salem, and More cigarettes made by its US parent.

The company was established as Macdonald Tobacco in Montreal in 1858 by W.C. Macdonald, for decades the dominant man in Canada's tobacco industry. The company was a family-owned business until it was sold to R.J. Reynolds in 1974 and renamed. There were some moves toward diversification, such as owning the X-Y Textile Company, but today RJR–Macdonald's business is exclusively tobacco. In the 1990s the company began exporting cigarettes made under contract for its parent company.

Liberal Senator Michael Kirby, a prominent strategist and spokesperson for his party, has been a director of the company for many years. Another past Liberal connection has come through Jeffrey Goodman, who went from Prime Minister Pierre Trudeau's press office to PR for RJR–Macdonald.

Other companies

All cigarette sales other than by the big three companies constitute less than 1% of the Canadian market. This includes all cigarette imports, as well as a small volume of products made by Bastos du Canada Ltée, based in Louisville, Quebec. Bastos makes house brands and generic products for grocery store chains and other retailers. There are a number of other very small manufacturers.

There is no smokeless tobacco made in Canada. All such products sold in Canada are imported. Cigar sales, which declined substantially during the 1980s and early 1990s, are made up of both domestic and foreign brands.

Corporate wealth

The worldwide revenues of the tobacco transnationals operating in Canada total CA $168 billion:[2] Philip Morris has global annual revenues of US $65 billion;[470] BAT, GB £21 billion;[32] R.J. Reynolds, US $15 billion;[491] and Rothmans, GB £7 billion.[519] This mammoth sum provides enormous economic power. The total is greater than the revenues of any single government in Canada, whether federal or provincial. Moreover, unlike many governments, tobacco companies are not laden with horrific debts and deficits. Most significantly, the $168 billion (US $123 billion) in annual revenues is more than the individual gross domestic products of 180 of the world's 205 countries.[599]

The profits allow the industry to pay its Canadian executives handsomely, as indicated by reports filed under securities laws. In 1994, Donald Brown, President of

---

[2]Foreign exchange rates used were US $1 = CA $1.37 and GB £1 = CA $2.08.

Imperial Tobacco, earned $758 846 in salary, bonus, and other compensation. As well, he was given options to purchase 10 000 shares at $36.00 any time before 2 May 2004. Because the market price of the shares was $36.00 at the time the options were awarded, Brown gets a risk-free opportunity to take advantage of any increase in share price over a 10-year period. Purdy Crawford, Chairman of Imasco, did even better, earning $2 030 576 in total compensation plus the option to purchase 24 000 shares.[283] For fiscal year 1995, Joe Heffernan, President and CEO of Rothmans, Benson & Hedges Inc., earned $466 000 in total compensation. As well, he can benefit further under long-term incentive plans.[517]

Professor Lauzon's study[355] of the industry's financial statements is revealing. He found that over the period 1987–93, the companies earned almost $2 billion in profits, which in his view ridiculed government antitobacco policies. Dividends equivalent to more than 99% of these profits were declared, 58% of which (more than $1 billion) was sent out of the country, thereby substantially reducing the real value of the tobacco industry to the Canadian economy. The 58% does not include a further special dividend of $99 million declared by RBH in early 1994. Each of the companies is generating plenty of cash. In RBH's case, dividends were actually greater than profits. Lauzon also found that the companies were reinvesting very little of their profits in Canada: 17% for the industry as a whole and as low as 5% for RBH. As a proportion of net sales, only 2.4% was reinvested in Canada.

Annual after-tax return on shareholders' investment for the industry as a whole over this period was a very high 33.3%.[355] In 1993, pretax return on capital used was 84% for Imperial, 69% for RBH, 38% for RJR–Macdonald, and 69% for the industry as a whole[60] — not bad in a year when individuals owning Canada Savings Bonds were earning interest at the pretax rate of 6%.

Why is the tobacco business so profitable in Canada? According to the Five Forces model of Harvard Business School professor Michael Porter,[479] tobacco can be considered a five-star industry:

1. Buyers have little power relative to that of the industry, including when it comes to manufacturer price increases. The 6.6 million consumers are spread out across the country, and a great many of them are addicted. Consumers thus do not have the clout to prevent price increases. Intermediate buyers, the wholesalers and retailers, are numerous and normally competitive.

2. The industry's suppliers have little bargaining power because what they supply (tobacco, paper products) are mostly commodities that could be obtained from other suppliers.

3. Few products can directly substitute for cigarettes in the same way that margarine can substitute for butter. Although nicotine gum and the nicotine patch do exist, their sales are small by comparison.

4. Large barriers prevent new competitors from entering the market. Normally, massive returns on investment would entice new entrants, but there have been no new players in Canadian tobacco in almost 40 years. In a business in which trademarks are everything, the biggest barrier is established brand names. With advertising restrictions making it much more difficult to establish new brand names, it becomes almost impossible to break into the Canadian market. As well, there are economies of scale in manufacturing and distribution. Manufacturing is technologically advanced and highly automated, and the equipment is expensive. Distribution requires a trained sales force that must span the country. Instead of there being any new companies in the market, the industry has consolidated from four main companies to three, with more rationalization forecast for the future. In 1989, Patrick Fennell, President of RBH, predicted that Canada's three manufacturers would eventually shrink to two through the amalgamation of RBH and RJR–Macdonald.[573,587]

5. Rivalry within the industry is relatively tame. Imperial Tobacco is the leader of the oligopoly. When Imperial raises its prices, the other two companies happily follow suit. There has not been a price war since 1986. Advertising restrictions — when in place — have helped reduce the rivalry, although companies still compete by paying retailers for stocking and prominently displaying various brands.

The high profitability of tobacco companies gives them the cash to pay for high-priced lobbyists, lawyers, PR specialists, advertising agencies, and junk-science researchers. One representative of an advertising agency working for a tobacco company said that the client had "more money than God." Tobacco's enormous profit potential provides a tremendous incentive for keeping the industry sales high. When it comes to efforts to combat tobacco control measures, the industry can write a blank cheque at any time. As the next chapter indicates, attempts to control tobacco use are hardly a recent phenomenon.

PART II

Early Battles

CHAPTER 4

An Historical Look

Toronto Saturday Night

MAKING A CLEAN SWEEP.
What we may expect the ladies of the W.C.T.U. to accomplish,
now that our law-makers have foresworn the cigarette.

Tobacco spreads to Europe

Tobacco use in the Americas dates back thousands of years.[608] By the 1st century BC, the Mayas of Central America were known to have smoked tobacco in religious ceremonies.[289] Centuries later, the smoking of tobacco spread to parts of North and South America. When Europeans arrived in the 15th century, tobacco was being grown by indigenous people in many parts of the Americas, including along Lake Erie and Georgian Bay in what is now southern Ontario. The indigenous nations in this area — including the Petuns, the Tobacco Nation — traded some of their tobacco commercially with other indigenous people in exchange for furs and other items.[577]

When Christopher Columbus arrived in the Western Hemisphere in 1492, some of his crew saw indigenous people smoking and became the first Europeans to encounter tobacco. On returning to Spain, one of Columbus' crew members, Rodrigo de Jerez, was seen smoking and was imprisoned by the Inquisitors for it. Townspeople had seen smoke coming from his nose and believed he had been possessed by the devil.

On Jacques Cartier's second voyage to North America in 1535, he was offered tobacco by the indigenous people he met when he arrived at the island of Montreal. Cartier described this in his diary:

> In Hochelaga, at the head of the river in Canada, grows a certain herb which is stocked in large quantities by the natives during the summer season, and on which they set great value. Men alone use it, and after drying it in the sun they carry it around their neck wrapped up in the skin of a small animal, like a sac, with a hollow piece of stone or wood. When the spirit moves them, they pulverize this herb and place it at one end, lighting it with a fire brand, and draw on the other end so long that they fill their bodies with smoke until it comes out of their mouth and nostrils as from a chimney. They claim it keeps them warm and in good health. They never travel without this herb.[289, pp. 8–9]

"We tried to imitate them," Cartier wrote, "but the smoke burnt our mouths as if it had been pepper."[58, p. 90] Smoking was a part of indigenous ceremony, religion, and medicine, and smoking a peace pipe marked the resolution of conflicts with enemies.

In 1560, France's ambassador to Portugal, Jean Nicot, shipped tobacco seeds to the Queen Mother of France in the belief that tobacco would cure many diseases. In Nicot's honour the botanical name *Nicotiana* was given to the tobacco plant, and centuries later the word *nicotine* would also be derived from his name. By the late 1500s, Sir Walter Raleigh was actively promoting tobacco in England. In time, smoking became popular throughout Europe.

As tobacco use increased, some countries moved to curb the practice:

> In 1606, Philip III of Spain issued a decree restricting the cultivation of tobacco. In 1610 Japan issued orders against both smokers and planters. Things really got tough in Russia where the patriarch placed smoking and snuffing in the category of deadly sins! The Czar, in 1634, issued a ukase against the use of tobacco, stating that first offenders — smokers or vendors — would have their noses slit. In a number of cases, repeat offenders were sentenced to death. In Berne, smoking was considered as sinful as adultery and was punished accordingly. The Pope ordered that persons taking tobacco or snuff into a Roman Catholic Church be excommunicated — cigar and pipe smoke were competing with the aroma of incense, and some monks were coughing during the solemn chants. ...
>
> Murad IV of Turkey is said to have gone to extremes in his antismoking crusade. He reportedly roamed the streets of 17th century Istanbul in disguise trying to get vendors to sell him tobacco. If they did — an act against his official policy — he would behead them on the spot, leaving the body in the street as a grisly warning to other would-be lawbreakers.[628, p. 33]

In 1604, England's King James I anonymously wrote *A Counterblaste to Tobacco*, in which he thoroughly and colourfully condemned the emerging product. He concluded by describing the use of tobacco as

> a custome lothsome to the eye, hatefull to the Nose, harmefull to the braine, dangerous to the Lungs, and the blacke stinking fume thereof, neerest resembling the horrible Stigian smoke of the pit that is bottomelesse.[314, p. 36]

In 1670, the Sovereign Council in New France imposed duties on tobacco and liquor. From 1676 to 1759, citizens were prohibited from smoking on the street or carrying tobacco.[419] Because the retail sale was also prohibited for a period, the French colonists tended to grow tobacco for their own use, typically for smoking in pipes. That Canada's tobacco industry is today based in Quebec is an outgrowth of the early start in this region. As well, for a long time much of the country's population was centred around Montreal.

In 1739, Canadian tobacco was exported to France for the first time.[419] However, these exports were tiny compared with those from some British colonies in America. Starting in the early 1600s, tobacco was an important cash crop for the Jamestown (Virginia) colony and helped the colony survive.

The spreading popularity of tobacco occurred partly because many perceived tobacco as having positive medicinal qualities. However, there were occasional reports of tobacco being harmful, and in 1761 Dr John Hill, an Englishman, made what is believed to be the first clinical report of tobacco as a cause of cancer in his *Cautions Against the Immoderate Use of Snuff.*[628]

The popularity of the cigarette in Western Europe has its origins in the Crimean War (1854–56). English and French officers returned home with hand-rolled cigarettes obtained from the Turks. Smoking of tobacco products generally, not just cigarettes, became more popular, despite Queen Victoria's personal disapproval. A 1906 article made the following comment:

> Before the Crimean war, no well bred man would think of being seen in the daytime in a fashionably frequented part of London with a cigar in his mouth. Nowadays a fragrant Havana, if not an emblem of aristocracy, is regarded anyhow as a proof of means.[69]

Development of the modern industry

Tobacco consumption received an enormous boost with the 1881 patenting of the cigarette-rolling machine by American James Bonsack. The machine, which after improvements became operational in 1884, replaced the inefficient hand-rolling method, thereby dramatically decreasing the costs of production. The machine could produce 120 000 cigarettes a day, equivalent to the production of 48 workers.[581] Another critical breakthrough occurred around the turn of the century with the development of the safe, portable match. Cigarettes could then easily be smoked at any moment of the day; there was no need to be near a fire or an oil or gas lamp. The new match eliminated the risks of the early, dangerous versions of the match.[628] Before the emergence of cigarettes, including hand-rolled cigarettes, tobacco consumption was dominated by cigars, pipe smoking, snuff, and chewing tobacco.

Development of an antismoking lobby

As cigarettes grew in popularity in the United States, a strong anticigarette lobby developed. The lobby focused on cigarettes because cigarettes were seen to cause harm that other tobacco products did not. By 1890, 26 states and territories had prohibited the sale of cigarettes to minors (with ages set somewhere from 14 to 24). Many states soon went further: starting with Washington in 1893, at least 14 states prohibited all or some of the following: the sale, manufacture, possession, advertising, and use of cigarettes. Some 21 other states and territories considered prohibition.[581] The campaign got a boost from prominent businessmen who believed cigarettes contributed to both criminality and inefficient workers. Henry Ford spoke out against cigarettes, writing *The Case Against the Little White Slaver*.[180] Thomas Edison was another prominent anticigarette business leader. In Canada, Timothy Eaton never allowed tobacco to be sold in his stores.

In 1878, Reverend Albert Sims of Ontario published *The Sin of Tobacco Smoking and Chewing Together With an Effective Cure for These Habits*.[547] A later edition in 1894 was retitled *The Common Use of Tobacco Condemned by Physicians, Experience, Common Sense and the Bible*.[548] This 173-page book discussed health and spiritual consequences of tobacco use and described the progress of the antitobacco movement. It also contained charts showing how much money would be wasted yearly on smoking, with amounts compounded over time by forgone interest.

In 1889, the Anti-Tobacco Association of Saint John, New Brunswick, published *Prize Essays on Tobacco*.[16] One essay, by R.A.H. Morrow, said that the carbon in tobacco smoke causes "'the smoker's sore throat', which sometimes ends in cancer."[410, p. 30] Morrow approved of those who said that doctors "have failed to do their duty, in not warning against the baneful nature of tobacco."[410, p. 32] Miss Laura Bigney of Lunenberg, Nova Scotia, said that a great man had once remarked that tobacco "was leading thousands of young men and boys away from the Promised Land instead of into it."[43, p. 58] She supported total prohibition and cited cases of insanity caused by smoking, testimony of doctors on the health effects, and cases in which smoking by men had harmed wives and children (that is, ETS). Reverend Robert Wilson cited seven reasons why he did not smoke: it is expensive; it is filthy and offensive; it is injurious to health; it impairs the mental powers; the practice tends to immorality; it would be inconsistent with his speaking out against tobacco; and he had religious grounds for not doing so.[633]

Despite what may be indicated from these publications, cigarettes were slow to catch on in Canada. In 1895, only 66 million cigarettes were sold:[289] that's an average of only 13 per person per year. But there was a persistent, well-coordinated antismoking lobby, the Women's Christian Temperance Union (WCTU), which was also lobbying for the prohibition of alcohol. Other organizations and individuals were calling for control over cigarettes, but none was as large or effective as the WCTU.

Early on, several jurisdictions passed laws preventing the sale of tobacco to minors. British Columbia passed legislation in 1891 (age 15); Ontario, in 1892 (age 18); Nova

Scotia, in 1892 (age 16); New Brunswick, in 1893 (age 18); and the Northwest Territories, in 1896 (age 16) (parts of the Territories became the provinces of Alberta and Saskatchewan in 1905 and carried on the same laws). Several of these laws made it an offence for minors to smoke or purchase tobacco, punishable by a fine (such as a maximum of $2) or even imprisonment. Also the vendor who supplied the tobacco could be fined or imprisoned, with or without hard labour, as was the custom of the day. However, these laws were not enforced and did not curb the growth of smoking. As popularity grew, more grocers and drug stores joined traditional tobacconists in selling tobacco and cigarettes.

Some Ontario municipalities tried to control the sale of cigarettes by imposing extremely high licence fees. However, this movement was dealt a heavy blow in 1906 when a court struck down a $200 cigarette licence fee in the City of Peterborough as being prohibitive, not merely regulative.[578]

The threat of alcohol prohibition was of concern to tobacco companies in Canada. They believed that if the government banned alcohol, men could not go into a saloon and enjoy a cigar with a drink. Decreased cigar sales were feared. Further, an alcohol ban would make it easier to argue that cigarettes should also be banned. Tobacco companies gave money to the campaign funds of the liquor interests to help slow the prohibition movement. However, when some provinces adopted prohibition, the fears of the tobacco men proved groundless. Tobacco sales were barely affected.

Notwithstanding these concerns, the tobacco industry was on a massive upswing at the turn of the century. Commented the *Canadian Cigar and Tobacco Journal* in 1902, "Never in the history of our industry have times been so prosperous, nor the opportunity so good for the aggressive development of individual trade."[67, p. 477] The industry had not seen anything yet — a far larger prosperity lay ahead.

This journal, a detailed information source on Canada's early tobacco industry, reported on testimonials of people refuting health claims against smoking or, alternatively, extolling certain health benefits. The journal disseminated this information to help counter the opposition to smoking. For example, one item in 1899 referred to smoking as "preventive of pulmonary diseases."[66]

Dominance by the American Tobacco Company

Around the turn of the century, the American Tobacco Company of Canada dominated cigarette sales in Canada, just as its parent company, the American Tobacco Company, was doing in the United States. In Canada, the firm had 80% of cigarette sales.[529, p. 7] This dominance was maintained by a contract system that effectively prevented wholesalers or retailers from carrying brands of any other cigarette company. Further, the manufacturers set the prices at which products could be resold. Protests from smaller Canadian-owned companies and from tobacco growers led to a Royal Commission. The Commission's report in 1903 concluded that although the contract system was not illegal, it was in general use and it did prejudicially affect other tobacco manufacturers.[529]

The subject of the American Tobacco Company's effective monopoly and its use of anticompetitive measures was raised in Parliament. There was much concern about preventing the tobacco monopoly from maintaining its strong foothold in Canada. In the end, Parliament adopted legislation to prevent the exclusive contract system of the sort then in use by the American Tobacco Company.

Parliament considers tobacco issues

The lobbying by the WCTU, with support from many church organizations and some doctors, led to much debate in Parliament. Cigarettes were attacked on moral and health grounds. The precise impact of cigarettes on health was not well understood and sometimes it was misunderstood, but even at that time medical experts believed there was sufficient evidence to support restricting the product.

In 1903, the House of Commons approved — by 103 to 48 on a free vote — a remarkable resolution supporting an outright ban on cigarettes. The resolution, introduced by Montreal Member of Parliament (MP) Robert Bickerdike, read as follows:

> That the object of good government is to promote the general welfare of the people by a careful encouragement and protection of whatever makes for the public good; and by equally careful discouragement and suppression of whatever tends to the public disadvantage.
>
> That the smoking of cigarettes has been proved by overwhelming testimony to be productive of serious physical and moral injury to young people; impairing health, arresting development, weakening intellectual power, and thus constituting a social and national evil.
>
> That legislation licensing and restricting the sale of cigarettes has not proven sufficient to prevent these evils, which will continue while the public sale of the course of the mischief is permitted to go on.
>
> That this House is of the opinion, for the reasons hereinbefore set forth, that the right and most effectual legislative remedy for these evils is to be found in the enactment and enforcement of a law prohibiting the importation, manufacture and sale of cigarettes.[40]

Prime Minister Sir Wilfrid Laurier voted against the resolution, although he would have supported legislation prohibiting the sale of tobacco to minors. Laurier was of the view that smoking was injurious to boys but not to adults.[353] Within 3 weeks of this expression of opinion by the House of Commons, Bickerdike introduced a private-member's bill to prohibit cigarettes. The Bill later had to be withdrawn after it was ruled out of order on a technicality.

Shortly afterward, still in 1903, the Minister of Justice, Charles Fitzpatrick, introduced a bill to amend the Criminal Code to include a provision to prohibit the sale of tobacco to persons under 18. This led, however, to dissatisfaction from both sides of the debate. Those in the tobacco business felt the proposal went too far and would be a "gross injustice" to honest traders because the law would create a "gang of informers who will seek, by tempting children, to create trouble for those who would not otherwise be interfered with in carrying on their business."[178] Furthermore, the bill provided no penalty for the youth purchaser and placed the legal responsibility only on the vendor. The tobacco trade sent a deputation to meet the Minister, as well as many MPs, to express their opposition. The WCTU, in contrast, felt the measure did not go far enough because it did not completely prohibit the sale of cigarettes. Women from across Canada sent letters and telegrams expressing their opposition. The provision dealing with tobacco was deleted from the bill at the Committee stage.

In 1904, the House of Commons again agreed to a resolution supporting the prohibition of cigarettes,[257–259] although some in the tobacco industry felt that many MPs treated the vote as a joke and voted yes just to appease the women. The day after the resolution, Huntingdon (Quebec) MP William Maclaren introduced Bill 128 to enact the resolution. The Bill was approved at second reading on a vote of 52 to 28 and sent to the Committee of the Whole House. The sections of the bill were narrowly approved during clause by clause consideration. Although it was reported back from Committee, the Bill never received final approval before the end of the parliamentary session.[260–262]

Had the law been adopted, at a time when cigarette consumption was not yet widespread, Canada's tobacco history might have been different. However, public pressure would have eventually forced a repeal as cigarette consumption rose in the United Kingdom, the United States, and other countries. All of the US states that outlawed cigarettes eventually repealed their bans, with Kansas' law the last to go, in 1927.[122]

In 1907 and 1908, the House of Commons again debated (without voting on) resolutions supporting the prohibition of cigarettes. The resolutions were introduced by Peel MP Richard Blain, who was persistent in his efforts to get Parliament to take action on tobacco.[263–265]

Finally, later in 1908, the Minister of Justice, Allen Aylesworth, introduced Bill 173, the *Tobacco Restraint Act*. The bill, adopted without dissenting votes, prohibited the sale of tobacco to persons under 16 years of age. The House of Commons had approved a minimum age of 18, but Senate amendments reduced the age to 16. Maximum fines were set at $10 for a first offence, $25 for a second offence, and $100 for third and subsequent offences. A provision prohibited persons under 16 from smoking or chewing tobacco in a public place or from purchasing or possessing cigarettes or cigarette papers. A minor's first offence brought a reprimand; a second offence, a maximum fine of $1; and a third offence, a maximum fine of $4. A justice had the authority to order the removal of a vending machine if persons under 16 were using it. The *Tobacco Restraint Act* was a compromise: it addressed tobacco, but it did not go so far as to prohibit cigarettes altogether. The Act would remain on the books unamended until it was replaced in 1994 — 86 years later.

Much of the debate in the House of Commons would foreshadow future debates. Those in support of a ban cited the health effects and other evils of smoking. Bickerdike, the MP who introduced the first resolution, had nearly 100

certificates from most eminent physicians, throughout the country, from the Atlantic to the Pacific, and all these documents go to prove that the cigarette habit, with the boys at least, is very, very injurious."[41]

The late Dr Christie, who had been an MP, was quoted by Robert Holmes, another MP:

I believe that it is the almost universal opinion of medical men that the cigarette habit is most deleterious to the young, producing physical degradation, and the habit should be denounced in trumpet tones by all who have the welfare of humanity at heart.[250]

Other medical opinions were cited:

W.O. Lambly, M.D., Cookshire, Province of Quebec. — The effect of cigarette smoking on the young undeveloped system is certainly most injurious, not only affecting the mucous membranes of the nose, throat and lungs, but also having its most injurious effect on the nerve centres.

James Stuart, M.D., Prescott, Ontario. — There are not two sides to this subject. Cigarette smoking is a pernicious habit, injurious to body, mind and soul. ...

Sir William Hingston, M.D., of Montreal, on being asked his opinion, said: 'To youth generally, hurtful, sometimes disastrous, never beneficial'. When asked in what way or on what organs, replied, 'The digestive, nervous and circulatory chiefly'.[404]

The House of Commons debate included reference to "coffin nails" and to the view that cigarettes led to the consumption of narcotics. *Addicted* was sometimes used, directly or indirectly. Said one MP, "When boys acquire the habit in their youth, it gets fixed and they are not able to give it up afterwards."[555]

In 1907, a letter from the superintendent of Montreal's Old Brewery Mission was quoted in the House:

Men who have been saved from drink tell me that they find the desire for cigarettes stronger than that for liquor. ... I have had many others cry out to me about their slavery and curse the day they began to smoke the cursed things.[45]

Although the overwhelming consensus in Parliament was that smoking was harmful to youth, the view was not unanimous. One MP stated that

it has not been proved that tobacco is a poison. It is no worse to smoke tobacco than it is to use hundreds or thousands of other articles that are in common use in this country.[193]

One MP, who had been smoking since the age of 10, felt it was good for his health.[356] Another MP, addressing his remarks to the women supporting a ban on cigarettes, said that there was more indigestion from bad cooking than from smoking.[458]

Many American businesses refused to hire boys who smoked, and this was cited as further evidence of public recognition of the evils of the cigarette. Also cited were the views of educators that smoking had a bad effect on academic results and led to increased juvenile criminality. It was mentioned that smokers were increasingly likely to be rejected by the armed forces.[257]

Much of the concern in Parliament was due to the rapid rise in cigarette consumption. Total consumption increased from 89 million in 1898, to 184 million in 1903, to 277 million in 1906.[44] In 8 years, sales had tripled (but averaged just 45 per person per year). Cigarettes, according to Laurier, were particularly obnoxious because of their cheapness: a boy would get 5 cents and spend it on a pack of cigarettes instead of on candy: "Nothing can be more offensive to me than to meet on the street a young boy of ten or twelve with a cigarette in his mouth."[354] A few MPs lamented that even some girls were smoking.

Some MPs were opposed to a total ban on cigarettes, rather than a ban on their sale to minors. Some felt that an outright ban on cigarettes would not work because it would be "entirely inoperative, because you cannot prevent the smoking of cigarettes by adults."[162] One MP cited the "flourishing establishments that manufacture [cigarettes], and which thereby carry on a legitimate trade."[135] He objected that their investments would be wiped out without compensation. He said that a total ban on cigarettes was an unacceptable intrusion on liberty and wondered what would be next:

> We might just as well prescribe the diet that each one should follow at his evening meal, in the pretext that there are people who eat too much, and who thereby injure their health.[136]

Others felt that education in the home and in the schools was preferable to legislation.

Some felt that if cigarettes were banned, it would still be possible to use papers to roll cigarettes. Others felt that banning cigarettes did not go far enough: all forms of tobacco should be prohibited.

It was the WCTU that kept the issue alive in Parliament. WCTU members wrote letters, sent telegrams, prepared publications, gathered medical opinions, met with MPs, organized petitions, and even met with the Prime Minister. The WCTU did not stop its efforts with the passage of the *Tobacco Restraint Act* but continued to call for a complete ban on cigarettes.

Select Committee on Cigarette Evils

In 1914, the House of Commons set up the Select Committee on Cigarette Evils. The Committee was asked to consider whether cigarettes should be banned or whether any alterative measures could be adopted for "the purpose of remedying or preventing any evils arising from the use of cigarettes." Public hearings were held, and judges, probation officers, and representatives of insane asylums and children's welfare organizations all gave testimony.

One witness, Dr L.J. Lemieux, administrator of the Montreal juvenile court, proposed a list of measures far ahead of its time:

✦ Placing nicotine levels on cigarette packages;

✦ Prohibiting anyone but tobacconists from selling tobacco;

✦ Enforcing laws against selling tobacco to minors, setting higher fines, and revoking licences of those stores that do sell to minors;

✦ Increasing the national minimum age to 18;

✦ Establishing a Central Bureau in Ottawa, with branches in several cities, to collect data and circulate literature on the evils of excessive smoking; and

✦ Ending incentives, such as getting a free umbrella if you returned enough empty packs.[357]

Another witness, J.J. Kelso, Ontario Superintendent of Neglected and Dependent Children, had his own set of policy recommendations:

✦ Raising the minimum national age to 18 and appointing special officers to enforce the law, instead of regular police officers;

✦ Raising tobacco taxes to discourage smoking and increase government revenue;

✦ Restricting advertising — "In Toronto, Montreal and all our large cities the most costly, the most conspicuous signs are usually erected by the cigarette people";[329, p. 51]

✦ Prohibiting free samples and prohibiting pictures or prize coupons in cigarette packages;

✦ Imposing high licence fees and prohibiting tobacco sales at retail by anyone not a tobacconist;

✦ Restricting the depiction of women smoking in moving pictures and in theatre productions, as this "has a bad effect on young people because it suggests that it is a correct thing to do";[329, p. 52] and

✦ Prohibiting women from smoking in public places.

Kelso also expressed concern that some vendors were selling single cigarettes to boys who could not afford a whole package.[329]

Most other witnesses focused on the effects of smoking, including juvenile delinquency, and on the lack of enforcement of laws prohibiting the sale of tobacco to minors. It was said that juvenile delinquents were almost always "cigarette fiends." Substantial testimony addressed smoking as a cause of insanity.[320]

The Committee wanted to hear from cigarette manufacturers and the WCTU but ran out of time. Because the parliamentary session was nearing an end and because "the greater part of the evidence adduced to date [was] based more or less on theory," the Committee made no policy recommendations.[266]

Cigarette popularity continues to rise

The advent of World War I later in 1914 dealt a devastating blow to the WCTU campaign. It became patriotic to send tobacco overseas to soldiers. Here is the view in 1915 of the *Canadian Cigar and Tobacco Journal*:

> The greatest compliment the weed ever received is through the present national crisis. True, there has been a general setback to the trade. That was expected because of the tightening up of money, the fear of hard times. But the war has proved beyond doubt the value of tobacco to the human race. There is no greater boost for cigarettes than the soldiers' appeal for them and the manner in which the people at home are responding to that appeal.[70]

After the war, the WCTU still campaigned for a number of years to drive out the cigarette, but to no avail. Many soldiers, who returned as heroes, were smokers who provided smoking with an excellent endorsement. The cigarette continued to rise in popularity, including, slowly, among women. In 1921, as perhaps a sign of the times, the Canadian Pacific Railway said it would add railway sleepers with smoking rooms for female passengers.[71] The total number of cigarettes consumed per year in Canada rose from 87 million in 1896 to 2.4 billion in the 1920s, a 28-fold increase.[112]

Early marketing techniques

During the early years, cigarette advertising was more sophisticated than many imagine. The American Tobacco Company advertised aggressively and contributed to the rapid rise in cigarette smoking. Advertising was commonly in print or at point of sale, especially with sophisticated window displays made up of empty packages. Barns visible from rail lines had advertising painted on them; fences were plastered with large posters; and billboards and streetcars were used to advertise products. Associating a brand with special events was another technique. For example, Pall Mall, a cigarette for the elite, was promoted in concert and gala programs. Another promotional technique was the use of stunts, such as the Red Cross tobacco brand — yes, Red Cross — in 1903 sponsoring a person dressed up as a Red Cross package crossing Quebec's Montmorency waterfalls on a high wire, an event witnessed by a reported 30 000 people. The package featured the international Red Cross symbol: a red cross on a white background. Red Cross was one of the most heavily advertised brands in Canada. Other promotional activities included parades on city streets, balloon ascents, and parachute drops.

Manufacturers included cigarette cards with many brands as a way to help maintain brand loyalty. These collectible sets of cards featured politicians, British soldiers, animals, and all sorts of images. The origins of cigarette cards go back to the 1800s, when cigarettes first appeared. Plain cardboard stiffeners were used to protect cigarettes when they were overwrapped with paper. Eventually, someone got the idea that these otherwise useless stiffeners could be used in marketing.

Many early advertising themes and brand images reflected Canada's close connection to the British Empire. Early brands included Hyde Park, Empire, and High Admiral. One important brand at the turn of the century was Athlete. Of the 50 brands made by Imperial Tobacco from 1908 to 1919, only three are still sold today: Player's, Sweet Caporal, and Pall Mall, the latter two of which are only marginal. For years, a quotation that had somehow appeared in the British medical journal *The Lancet* — "The purest form in which tobacco can be smoked" — appeared on advertisements for Sweet Caporal, accompanied by a depiction of Miss Sweet Caporal. Cigars were often named after famous people such as Byron (a poet), Lord Roberts (a famous field marshall from the Boer War), and Baden-Powell (a Boer War hero and later founder of the Boy Scout movement). Laurier cigars were on the market while Sir Wilfrid Laurier was Prime Minister.

A historical look by Imperial Tobacco at some of its brands shows that from early on, advertising portrayed certain images. Player's was often associated with famous naval stations such as Malta and Gibraltar, especially with the advent of World War II. Turret was "oriented towards the blue collar class."[297, p. 4] To boost sales, Turret offered cash prizes in 1932 for estimating the number of goals scored by National Hockey League teams (prizes doubled when the estimate was attached to Turret package front panels). Another incentive was a weekly prize of a brand-new Chevrolet Standard Coach for the person with the most interesting handwriting features submitted on four front panels of Turret cigarettes.

Sweet Caporal pioneered sponsorship of the first Canadian football radio broadcasts, including the Grey Cup in the 1930s. The 1930s also saw some product innovations, such as cellophane wrapping and the "easy opening" tear strip. Macdonald's Menthol was launched in 1934, and Cameo mentholated was launched by Imperial Tobacco the following year. During the 1930s, Imperial Tobacco continued to dominate, but its market share of 91% in 1930 fell to 83% by 1939.[297]

Cigarettes and other tobacco products were popular Christmas gifts. Manufacturers sometimes placed regular products in specially decorated Christmas packages, and retailers had displays for special occasions. Father's Day was another big promotional occasion, so much so that International Pipe Week was held in June each year.

Some people had been smoking for several decades, and as cigarette smoking increased, more smokers were feeling effects such as a sore throat or shortness of breath. Advertising seems to reflect this. In 1929, Buckingham cigarettes sponsored the Buckingham Booster [radio] Orchestra. Here is the copy from one advertisement:

> 'Every member of the Buckingham Booster Orchestra is a Buckingham smoker', says Geoff Waddinton, leader. 'They smoke Buckinghams because they prefer them for their "throat-easy" qualities. The "Buckingham Baritone" and "Marguerite" whose wonderful voices have made them so popular with listeners-in to the Buckingham hour say that singers who wish to guard their throats should smoke only the "throat-easy" Buckinghams'.[468]

The throat-easy slogan would still be used in the 1940s. A 1951 advertisement for Craven "A" extolled that "Craven 'A' will not affect the throat."[504]

Smoking restrictions

As cigarette sales increased, so did the number of areas in which smoking was permitted. In 1903, the *Canadian Cigar and Tobacco Journal* urged that smoking sections be established in streetcars. Existing prohibitions in various cities harmed sales and were "distasteful alike to the trade and the smoking public."[68] In 1933, an editorial in the journal called for smoking to be permitted in theatre balconies.[73]

Anticompetitive activities by the tobacco industry

In 1938, a Commission was instituted to investigate anticompetitive practices of various sectors of the tobacco industry in Alberta. The Commission found a system of price fixing, boycotts, and trade-related restrictions detrimental to the public. A massive prosecution was eventually initiated. Charges were laid against 36 companies and individuals involved in the tobacco business, including seven manufacturers and numerous wholesalers. In 1941, an Edmonton jury found the accused guilty of price fixing and participating in a monopoly that substantially controlled tobacco distribution. Fines totalling $221 500 were levied, but all the accused except one appealed the conviction. On appeal, the trial decision was set aside on a technicality. A new trial was never held.[571]

Cigarettes sent overseas during World War II

During World War II, efforts were again organized to send massive quantities of cigarettes overseas to soldiers, in addition to the individual gifts sent by friends and relatives. Many groups pitched in to supply soldiers with cigarettes, including the Canadian Red Cross, the Overseas Tobacco League, the Canadian Legion, the Young Men's Christian Association (YMCA), and the Knights of Columbus.[298] Tobacco advertising continued during the war, though ad budgets were restricted. Some Sweet Caporal ads also promoted Victory bonds, Red Cross blood clinics, and a "nearly-new shop in aid of war charities." Sweet Caps sponsored entertainment for Canadian soldiers during World War II and again during the Korean War (1950–53).

Sales growth continues

As Figure 3 (Chapter 2) illustrates, tobacco sales grew enormously in the 1920s, 1930s, and 1940s. During this period, relatively negligible health concerns over smoking and a lack of organized antismoking groups facilitated this growth. However, health issues would soon reappear at the forefront of the smoking debate.

CHAPTER 5

The Evidence Builds

Don Wright, *Miami News*

Differing views on the health question

During the 1920s, 1930s, and 1940s, more scientific evidence linking smoking and ill health was unearthed, but little reached the mainstream. What did reach the public was typically countered by views dismissing the health effects of smoking.

In 1924, *Reader's Digest* published an article entitled "Does Tobacco Injure the Human Body?" The author, Irving Fisher, concluded that "from every indication, it behooves the man who wishes to remain fit to omit tobacco from his daily schedule."[177]

In 1938, *Science* published the results of a study by Johns Hopkins University biostatistician Raymond Pearl. After looking at the longevity of 6 813 men, Pearl concluded that 45% of smokers lived until age 60, compared with 65% of nonsmokers, and that a reduction in longevity was found at every age until age 60.[462]

In 1940, the federal Department of Pensions and National Health produced "Smoking," a booklet in a series of publications on health matters.[142] The booklet was "not intended as a forthright condemnation, on all and every count, of a custom which is the solace of millions" but to give the "considered opinion of modern medical science on the effects of smoking" and to contribute to "public information on a matter of vital public health concern."[142, p. 2] Inhaling tobacco smoke was said to give rise to "stomach, teeth and eye trouble," "smoker's breath," and loss of "wind" for an athlete.[142, pp. 5, 14] The booklet said that excessive smoking was blamed "for promoting nervous symptoms and circulatory disturbances."[142, p. 5]

> Any research chemist knows that pure nicotine is twice as deadly as strychnine. ... Practically every confirmed smoker is a walking, coughing example of the effect of tobacco on throat and voice.[142, p. 5]

The booklet cited a study showing that smoking was associated with reduced life expectancy. Smoking by mothers was of concern because smoking damaged the blood supply, and babies depended on mother's blood supply for nourishment. The booklet said smoke from filtered cigarettes was no more beneficial than smoke from standard cigarettes. As for cancer, there was "no proof that smokers are more susceptible ... than non-smokers."[142, p. 10] The booklet offered tips for giving up smoking and noted that "it is not undignified to decline gift cigarettes with the simple explanation that you no longer smoke."[142, p. 13]

In 1941, retired world heavyweight boxing champion Gene Tunney, then head of the US Navy's physical fitness program, wrote an article in *Reader's Digest* entitled "Nicotine Knockout, or the Slow Count."[598] Tunney strongly criticized smoking, writing that "I can bluntly say that few things could be worse for physical fitness than promoting the cigarette habit."[598, p. 23] Tunney described tobacco advertising as a "national menace," recalling that when he was a boxer, he declined an offer of US $15 000 to endorse a brand of cigarettes, politely saying that he did not smoke. He was then offered US $12 000 if he would agree to have his picture used with the statement that the brand "must be good, because all my friends smoke them."[598, p. 23] He declined this offer as well. The article prompted a report in the *Globe and Mail*, entitled "Tobacco deadly foe, says Gene Tunney."[74] Alfred H. Dunhill of London, UK, wrote a letter in reply to the *Globe and Mail*, stating that "the fact, of course, is that with smoking and drinking and many other pleasant habits, vice lies in excess. Nobody, for instance, defends the chain cigarette smoker.[74] These events were reported in the *Canadian Cigar and Tobacco Journal* in an article entitled "Eminent American Physician Blasts Tunney for His Tirade on Tobacco."[74]

In 1943, *Maclean's* magazine carried an article entitled "This is the Truth About Tobacco."[170] Estimating that 60%–80% of adults smoked, clearly an overestimate if women were counted, the article dismissed almost all the health effects once said to be caused by tobacco. The only exceptions were said to be Buerger's disease (with 99% of the victims of this rare disease said to be smokers) and dimness of vision. The fact that life insurance companies no longer asked about smoking was cited as evidence that smoking did not lead to higher death rates. In 1948, an article in *Saturday Night* magazine appeared with the title "You May Puff Peacefully While Doctors Disagree."[105]

Uncovering the link between smoking and lung cancer

As early as 1912,[5] scientific reports suggested that the rise in lung cancer might be attributable to cigarette smoking, but few offered hard evidence. A small-scale, seminal study published in Germany in 1939 found that patients with lung cancer were much more likely to smoke and to be heavy smokers than were healthy men of the same age.[415]

The first large-scale study traces its origins to 1947, when Canadian physician Dr Norman Delarue was working in St Louis, Missouri, with Dr Evarts Graham. At that time Graham was depressed by his unsuccessful attempts to treat lung cancer with female hormones, on the premise that lung cancer was sex-linked. Few women at this time were getting lung cancer. A disgusted Graham asked that "someone please find out what is causing this epidemic."[134, p. 431]

In response, Delarue compared 50 patients with lung cancer and 50 patients hospitalized with some other disease. He found that more than 90% of the lung cancer patients had smoked, but only 50% of the other patients had any smoking history. Graham, a chain smoker, was unimpressed. He initially thought that the suggestion that smoking caused lung cancer was nonsense. Nonetheless, Delarue boldly proclaimed that by 1950 no one would be smoking.[134]

Graham eventually changed his views. In 1950, Ernest Wynder (a medical student) and Graham co-authored the first large-scale smoking study providing scientific evidence of the relationship between smoking and lung cancer. The study, published in the *Journal of the American Medical Association* (JAMA),[648] found that of 605 men hospitalized with lung cancer, only 1.3% had been nonsmokers throughout the preceding 20 years, whereas 51.2% had smoked more than 20 cigarettes a day over this period. In a control group of general hospital patients without cancer, 14.6% were nonsmokers and only 19.1% had been smoking more than 20 cigarettes a day. After this study, Graham successfully quit smoking in 1953, but it was too late. He died of lung cancer in 1957.

A second study published in the same issue of JAMA, this one by Morton Levin and others, found a statistical association between cigarette smoking and lung cancer.[359] A study published in September 1950 in the *British Medical Journal* by Dr Richard Doll and Dr Bradford Hill examined the smoking patterns of lung cancer patients in 20 London hospitals and also found that lung cancer was associated with higher rates of cigarette smoking.[147]

Resolution debated in Parliament

The evidence was mounting and in 1951 the House of Commons debated a resolution introduced by Liberal MP Daniel McIvor from Fort William, Ontario. The resolution read

> That, in the opinion of this house, early consideration should be given to the advisability of appointing a special committee of the House to consider the entire cigarette problem; its effect on moral, mental and physical health, especially teenagers and unborn children; fire hazard and other related details.[394]

Although the debate was short, references during the debate provided an interesting exposé of the state of affairs at that time. One reference was to the fact that there did not seem to be any effective organizations presenting information that smoking was bad for health. As well, some commercials were said to be coming over the air "almost as though cigarettes are a good thing for health," sometimes with testimonials from a voice "you can imagine being the family physician."[221] Another MP referred to a cigarette advertisement in a magazine published by the Health League of Canada. The ad included the words "Awarded the certificate of the institute of hygiene for quality and purity" without saying exactly what the institute was.[222] One MP commented on the exceptionally high percentage of boys who smoked appearing before the courts.

The Health Minister, Paul Martin, Sr, voted against the resolution. Martin had suggested that the motion not be pressed "on the understanding that for the time being the matter could be given consideration at the departmental level." However, the Cooperative Commonwealth Federation, forerunner to the New Democratic Party (NDP), forced a vote. The resolution was defeated.

The increase in smoking naturally increased the number of smoking-related fires. There was criticism in the House of Commons, including an accusation in 1950 that manufacturers saturated cigarette paper with chemicals to keep the cigarette burning.[337] The matter of fires caused by cigarettes would be raised several times in subsequent years. In the 1950s, the industry initiated public education campaigns on fire safety but blamed smoking-related fires on negligent individuals instead of on cigarettes.

Industry offers reassurance

In November 1951, in a Canadian Cancer Society (CCS) newsletter, the Executive Director of the National Cancer Institute of Canada (NCIC) drew attention to the possible existence of a link between cigarette smoking and lung cancer.[65] As time elapsed, more studies provided more evidence of the health consequences of smoking, and many studies made headlines. In 1954, the CMA issued its first public warning on the hazards of smoking. The same year, industry representatives met with NCIC and the CMA to discuss research. In 1954, the industry gave NCIC the first of three scheduled $100 000 grants to do research on lung cancer.

In 1954, the *Canadian Medical Association Journal* published a report showing that the age-standardized lung cancer death rate in Canada had skyrocketed over the period 1932–54 from 3.0 to 17.0 deaths per 100 000 in males and from 1.6 to 3.7 in females.[472] By 1958, the rate had further increased to 26.3 in males and to 3.8 in females. Thus in just 26 years, lung cancer mortality had jumped by a multiple of 8.8 in males and 2.4 in females.[473]

In the 1950s, the sale of filtered cigarettes soared in response to all the media coverage of lung cancer. One well-known item was the 1952 *Reader's Digest* article "Cancer by the Carton."[452] Filters gave smokers the impression of health protection, and advertising enhanced this perception. Filters had another benefit for manufacturers: filter material cost less than tobacco as a cigarette component.

However, filters were sometimes too strong. In the United States, large sales of Kent filtered cigarettes followed the product's introduction in 1952. Advertising focused on the filter. However, after a while, smokers were finding that their nicotine craving was not satisfied. So in 1956, Lorillard, the manufacturer of Kent, changed the filter to allow more smoke, tar, and nicotine through. By 1958, Kent was satisfying consumers and was the fifth leading brand in the United States.[629]

During the 1950s, much advertising addressed health issues. In 1958, Rothmans took out a series of full-page newspaper ads that discussed lung cancer and then pointed out that Rothmans King Size filtered cigarettes had lower tar intakes (at 18–20 mg) than other cigarettes. Figure 6 reproduces one of the ads in the series. This advertisement noted that

> as a precautionary measure in the interest of smokers, ... Rothmans Research Division accepts the *statistical* evidence linking lung cancer with heavy smoking [but that] the exact *biological* relationship between smoking and cancer in mankind is still not known and a direct link has not been proved.[518]

The ad described the company's techniques to reduce tars in its cigarettes. Near the end of the text, Rothmans reiterated its pledge "to continue its policy of all-out research" and "to impart vital information as soon as available." Rothmans concluded that "as with all the good things of modern living, Rothmans believes that with moderation smoking can remain one of life's simple and safe pleasures."[521] A different ad stated that the company had developed a filter that could filter "virtually 100% of the total solids in tobacco smoke" but that "such extreme filtration is unnecessary."[520]

In the United States, advertisements also reassured smokers with slogans such as "More doctors smoke Camels than any other cigarette!" and "Play safe — smoke Chesterfield." A Philip Morris advertisement advised smokers to "Stop worrying about cigarette irritation" and proclaimed "The cigarette that takes the fear out of smoking!"[339,628] During the 1950s, Ronald Reagan, Bob Hope, Bing Crosby, and other celebrities appeared in ads endorsing cigarettes.

In 1954, Canada's Department of National Health and Welfare decided to conduct its own study of smoking. Beginning in 1956, the Veterans Study followed the smoking behaviour and causes of death of Canadian veterans of the two world wars and the Korean War. Preliminary results released in 1960 showed that the group of cigarette smokers had 60% more deaths than the group of nonsmokers, that smokers who smoked more cigarettes had higher mortality rates, that smokers who quit reduced their risk of premature death, and that cigarette smoking was associated with an increase in lung cancer and heart disease.[38] Further data released in 1963 essentially confirmed the preliminary evidence: the group of cigarette smokers had 52% more deaths than the group of nonsmokers. Of the excess deaths, 62% were attributed to heart and circulatory diseases and 33% to lung cancer and other forms of cancer.[39]

The International Cancer Congress and Cigarette Smoking

On July 6-12th. in London, England, 2,000 scientists from 63 countries attending the 7th. International Cancer Congress — an event held every four years — were given the latest data on cancer and smoking by the world's foremost cancer experts. Rothmans Research scientists were also there and have examined the papers submitted along with their own findings.

SINCE THE publication on June 23rd. of the first in this series of research announcements, there has been widespread interest shown in the Canadian press and smokers have asked for more information. Here is a brief summary of the facts as they stand today:-

1. Rothmans Research Division accepts the *statistical* evidence linking lung cancer with heavy smoking. This is done as a precautionary measure in the interest of smokers.

2. The exact *biological* relationship between smoking and cancer in mankind is still not known and a direct link has not been proved.

3. In research laboratory work, inhalation studies on animals have been largely negative. However, the application of tobacco tar on the skin of certain animals has produced cancer and therefore indicates that tobacco smoke condensate contains carcinogenic substances which are at least active to those animals.

4. The suspected chemicals in tobacco smoke that have produced cancer in animals have been identified. In fractionation studies, the majority of the active carcinogenic agents were located in the fraction which is eluted with carbon tetrachloride from the neutral tar. This fraction represents only 1.7% of total tobacco tar and, when applied in the heavy concentration of 10%, produced 100% cancer on animal skin.

5. Further studies were then conducted to determine whether there was a threshold level at which total tobacco tar would *not* produce cancer on animal skin. It was discovered that there was a dose level at which the development of animal cancer was so small, and the latent period before the formation of tumours so long, that for all material purposes it represented a *threshold* level. This minimum level is about one-third the optimum level.

6. Transposing this data to cigarette smoking, an increasing section of scientific opinion believes that if the tar intake from a single cigarette were reduced to the range of 18 to 20 milligrams (mgs.), there would be a significant reduction in the *possible* risk of lung cancer. Most of the world's cigarettes today yield in the vicinity of 30 mgs. and there are many which exceed 40 mgs.

N.B. *The control at 18-20 mgs. of the tar intake from a single Rothmans King Size cigarette is achieved as follows:-*

(i) *the use of tobaccos of lower tar content,*

(ii) *the fitting of an effective filter which reduces further, and in correct proportion, the amount of tar entering the mouth and lungs, and*

(iii) *the stubbing out of the butt of a cigarette equivalent to about one-third of its total length (for which purpose the extra length of Rothmans King Size is provided).*

The balance between satisfaction, filtration and ease of draw is constantly checked by scientific instruments.

7. There are no scientific grounds to justify the reduction of tar in a single cigarette to less than 18-20 mgs., except in the case of very heavy smokers of more than 2 packs (40 cigarettes) a day.

N.B. *To such smokers Rothmans advocates moderation.*

Reducing the tars in cigarettes to the level of 18-20 mgs. does not affect the pleasure of smoking. Indeed, once people have smoked such cigarettes, they find satisfaction and enjoyment in the cleaner smoke. Below 18-20 mgs., tobacco begins markedly to lose its taste and aroma, and there would be less and less satisfaction as the readings drop.

8. Unburned tobacco contains no cancer forming agents. They are formed only during combustion. Any plant material sets free cancer forming agents when burned at a high temperature. (If lettuce were smoked, the result would be the same.)

From about the middle of a cigarette length to the butt, the temperature reaches 880°C. (± 30°C.). When this temperature is reduced below 700°C., the biological activity on the skin of animals is reduced to almost nil.

As a further precautionary measure, research projects on this problem include the search for a chemical to make tobacco burn at a lower temperature.

N.B. *The present straight virginia manufacturing process as used by Rothmans employs no chemicals whatsoever. Nor would any chemicals be used unless a direct biological link (as distinct from a statistical link) makes it necessary to treat tobacco with such a catalyst.*

9. Some statistical studies indicate a higher mortality rate from lung cancer among cigarette smokers than among smokers of cigars and pipes. However, in laboratory experiments, the carcinogenic activity from cigar and pipe smoke was found to be greater than in cigarette smoke, because, burning at a high temperature for a longer time, combustion is more complete in cigars and in pipes.

10. The tobacco-cancer problem is difficult and nebulous. It has brought forth many conflicting theories and evidences. But great knowledge and a better understanding have been gained through research. The controversy is a matter of public interest. The tar contents of the world's leading brands of cigarettes are today under the scrutiny of medical and independent research.

A list of cigarettes, some of which have achieved significant tar reductions of up to 40% in the past year, was tabled at the International Cancer Congress by an eminent cancer expert.

N.B. *The performance of Canadian made Rothmans King-Size cigarettes (as previously certified by independent research) showed that:-*

Rothmans King Size Filter yields from 14.4% to 38.7% less tars than the four other best selling Filter brands in Canada.

Rothmans King Size Untipped yields from 26.5% to 34.0% less tars than the three best known plain end brands in Canada.

ROTHMANS Research Division welcomes this opportunity to reiterate its pledge:-

(1) to continue its policy of all-out research,

(2) to impart vital information as soon as available, and

(3) to give smokers of Rothmans cigarettes improvements as soon as they are developed.

In conclusion, as with all the good things of modern living, Rothmans believes that with moderation smoking can remain one of life's simple and safe pleasures.

This announcement has been issued by

ROTHMANS INTERNATIONAL RESEARCH DIVISION

Figure 6. A 1958 full-page Rothmans advertisement in the *Toronto Daily Star*.[521]

In 1958, a special committee of NCIC concluded that

> while it has not been established that cigarette smoking is a cause of lung cancer, sta-
> tistical studies show that cigarette smokers have a greater risk of dying of lung cancer
> than have non-smokers and the risk increases with the amount smoked.[425, p. 568]

In 1962, a second report was far stronger:

> the available statistical and epidemiological evidence of the association between smok-
> ing and lung cancer favours the conclusion that cigarette smoking is an important fac-
> tor in the causation of lung cancer and is largely responsible for the dramatic and
> continuing increase in the recorded lung cancer death rates.[426]

In 1960, the CMA voiced concern about a possible relationship between tobacco
smoking and bronchitis, bronchiectasis, emphysema, and coronary heart disease. In 1961,
the CMA accepted the "weight of evidence [implicating] cigarette smoking as the principal
causal factor in the increased incidence of lung cancer in Canada."[76, p. 690]

In July 1961, the Canadian edition of *Reader's Digest* reported that Craven "A" had
the lowest tar and nicotine of any Canadian cigarette. Afterward, Craven "A" sales "soared
spectacularly," according to Rothmans, the brand's manufacturer.[525, p. 11]

In 1962, the Royal College of Physicians of London released a report on smoking
and health. The report concluded that

> cigarette smoking is a cause of lung cancer and bronchitis, and probably contributes to
> the development of coronary heart disease and various other less common diseases. ...
> The number of deaths caused by diseases associated with smoking is large.[528, p. S7]

As well, the report stated that "decisive steps should be taken by the Government to curb
the present rising consumption of tobacco, and especially of cigarettes."[528, p. S8] The report
listed seven possible measures:

- ✦ More education;
- ✦ More effective restrictions on sales to minors;
- ✦ Restrictions on advertising;
- ✦ Restrictions on smoking in public places;
- ✦ Tax increases;
- ✦ Information on tar and nicotine content for consumers; and
- ✦ A look at the value of antismoking clinics.

The report was followed by a decline in cigarette sales in Britain, a decline that lasted only
1 year.

In 1963, the CMA president urged doctors to stop cigarette smoking, at least during
professional duties.[76] Subsequently during the 1960s, the CMA publicly advocated measures, including legislation, to control smoking and was far more active than its American
counterpart.

Canada's smoking and health program begins

On 17 June 1963, Canada's Minister of National Health and Welfare, Judy LaMarsh, made a landmark statement in the House of Commons acknowledging the harmfulness of smoking. "There is scientific evidence that cigarette smoking is a contributory cause of lung cancer, and that it may also be associated with chronic bronchitis and coronary heart disease," she declared.[350, p. 1214] A national conference would be held, and representatives of the provinces, health agencies, tobacco companies, and tobacco growers would be invited to attend. LaMarsh herself quit smoking.

Cabinet records now show that LaMarsh had planned a stronger statement but that her ministerial colleagues succeeded in getting her to tone down the words. The draft statement originally said that smoking was an "important contributory" cause of lung cancer, but this was changed to *contributory*. For chronic bronchitis and coronary heart disease, it was suggested that the words *may also be* replace the words *is probably also* to describe the association with smoking. Ministers urged her to be as "neutral and dispassionate" as possible "so as not to frighten people unnecessarily." Interestingly, just 2 months before the statement, Cabinet had decided to permit smoking at its meetings.[217]

Held in the Parliament buildings, the 1963 national conference was chaired by Minister LaMarsh. Ashtrays were scattered throughout the room, and the amount of smoking increased as the meeting went on. The conference was one of the few occasions when health organizations and the tobacco interests were brought together under one roof. Naturally, the perspectives were wildly different. Tobacco growers objected to some of the antismoking publicity of health charities, arguing that donations would be better spent on research. They objected to the "cancer stick" type of campaign, calling it "macabre."

Tobacco manufacturers had a detailed written brief criticizing existing health studies and calling for more research. "The fact is," asserted the industry,

> that the 'mounting evidence' consists of repetition of the same charges restated by different people. This 'evidence' was and remains inconclusive no matter how often it is repeated and restated.[3, p. iv]

The industry recommended that the difference in lung cancer rates between provinces be studied and explanations sought in terms of air pollutants, industry, population density, ethnic composition, climate, and smoking habits.

The briefs of health organizations tended to emphasize evidence supporting the scientific link between smoking and health. The Minister's June statement on the health consequences of smoking was affirmed by most health participants. Although some people at the conference supported a legislative approach, the consensus favoured health education and research.

The federal government announced a 5-year, $600 000 antismoking budget starting in 1964: $200 000 for scientific and behaviourial research ($40 000 a year) and $400 000 for health education ($80 000 a year). This was the real beginning of Canada's smoking and health program. Before this, the federal government had an explicit policy of not being involved in any smoking-related education.[407]

On 11 January 1964, the landmark report of the US Surgeon General's Advisory Committee on Smoking and Health was released.[612] The Committee comprised 11 scientists, 5 of them smokers. Their report was much anticipated. January 11 was a Saturday, chosen because stock markets were closed. An auditorium in the State Department provided a location with excellent security. The report's contents had been a closely guarded secret. Even the White House did not get copies before 7:30 AM on the day of release. Media were allowed into the auditorium at 9:00 AM and "locked in," unable to phone out until the media session was over.

The Committee's report concluded that cigarette smoking was a cause of lung cancer and laryngeal cancer in men, a probable cause of lung cancer in women, and the most important cause of chronic bronchitis. As well, the report stated that "cigarette smoking is a health hazard of sufficient importance in the United States to warrant remedial action." The Committee based its conclusions on several thousand articles on smoking and health. The Canadian Veterans Study was one of seven prospective studies cited in the report.

The Committee's report received enormous press coverage. The credibility of the report was enhanced because the tobacco industry had been given the opportunity to vet all the Committee members before the work had begun. Thus, it was much more difficult for the industry to attack the report. Cigarette sales in both the United States and Canada dropped following release of the report but recovered after the initial impact wore off.[523,628]

In Canada, the Rothmans 1964 annual report tried to downplay the Committee report:

> This report has created a further storm of controversy, since many eminent doctors, scientists and statisticians have questioned the conclusions reached in this report on the basis of the available scientific evidence. ... The problems confronting the industry cannot be solved by charges and counter-charges in the press, but only by a continuing co-operative program between Government, the tobacco industry, and medical and scientific research.[523, p. 18]

At the same time as the federal government was launching Canada's antismoking program, it was giving large amounts of assistance to tobacco interests: $120 000 for antismoking initiatives versus $575 414 for research on tobacco growing in fiscal 1964/65. Between 1954 and 1966, a total of $4.9 million was spent on tobacco-growing research.[216] In 1965, the Department of Trade and Commerce appointed a commodity officer, who would be "exclusively responsible for serving the needs of the tobacco industry in relation to export market research and trade promotion."[215] Nonetheless, tobacco farmers were still upset at the mere existence of an antismoking program. To assuage the farmers the government asked the House of Commons Agricultural and Colonization Committee to initiate hearings on help for tobacco growers.

Clearly, the political environment in which the tobacco industry operated had changed, and the industry responded. In 1963, the four major companies formed the Canadian Tobacco Manufacturers' Council. The industry retained clout in high places, with former Liberal Prime Minister St Laurent as Chairman of Rothmans. For the new Liberal government considering measures for its antismoking program, St Laurent's position was powerful evidence of the industry's connections.

The goals of Canada's new antismoking campaign were threefold: to inform the public of the health risks, to encourage smokers to quit, and to dissuade nonsmokers from smoking. By today's standards, the efforts were relatively modest. The Department of National Health and Welfare prepared and distributed *Smoking and Health Reference Book,*[139] which was sent to every doctor in the country, the Teacher's Information Kit, educational materials (primarily aimed at youth), and public service announcements for radio and television. *The Drag*, an educational film commissioned by the Department and produced by the National Film Board in 1967, was nominated for an Academy Award in the animated cartoon category. In 1965, the government conducted a national survey on smoking. To the surprise of many, the survey found that a bare majority of adults were nonsmokers (a majority of men, however, were smokers).[141] In 1968, the Post Office introduced a cancellation mark with the slogan "The safe cigarette is the one you don't light."

In 1965, a Canadian Youth Conference on Smoking attracted 70 teenage participants from the 10 provinces. The Department of National Health and Welfare organized the conference to learn first hand from youth about smoking issues. Many ideas for action were generated, including a suggestion to restrict tobacco advertising.[140]

Support for Canadian legislation grows slowly

In 1964, the Canadian tobacco industry announced a voluntary code to restrict advertising, several months before the American industry announced its own code. Advertising was to be directed to adults, models were to be at least 25 years old, health claims in ads were restricted, athletes and celebrities were not to be used, and poster or bulletin-board advertising was not to be "immediately adjacent" to schools. No advertising was to "state or imply that cigarette smoking is essential to romance, prominence, success, or personal advancement." Not surprisingly, the use of the word *essential* meant that this provision would be completely ineffective at curbing lifestyle advertising. The existing practice of not placing television commercials until after 9:00 PM was included in the code.[286]

In the United Kingdom and the United States, there were some early legislative controls. The United Kingdom banned tobacco advertising on television in 1965. The same year, the US Congress adopted a law requiring a mild warning on packages: "Caution — Cigarette Smoking May Be Hazardous to Your Health."

Through most of the 1960s, Canada was slow to consider legislative action against tobacco. The Department of National Health and Welfare emphasized an explicitly cooperative rather than confrontational attitude with the tobacco industry. Why? Tobacco growers and manufacturers represented a major industry. Memories of the failed attempt at alcohol prohibition lingered and discouraged the government from taking action. There was also a view that research and technology could find ways to make smoking safe, such as identifying the harmful substances in smoke and filtering them away. Another factor was that federal tobacco taxes made up fully 7% of all federal budgetary tax revenues.[526] A 1970 National Health and Welfare publication recalled that "the Department of Finance was sharply conscious of the $400 million annual tax revenue which the tobacco industry provided."[141, p. 2]

In the 1960s, more than 20 private-member's bills were introduced in the House of Commons. More than half were authored by Vancouver area MP Barry Mather (NDP), a tireless and visionary supporter of tobacco-control legislation. Mather persistently pressured the government to take action, and he dismissed arguments about the insufficiency of medical evidence:

> Then it is sometimes said that they do not really know the cause of lung cancer. The same was once said of cholera and typhoid, which were brought under control long before the germs causing them were discovered. This was based on observation that drinking polluted water was associated with disease. If the provision of clean water had had to wait until the discovery of bacteria, thousands of preventable deaths would have occurred.[388]

Mather's first bill, Bill C-75, was introduced immediately after LaMarsh made her 1963 statement. This bill would have given the government the authority to regulate the labeling, packaging, and advertising of cigarettes.[387] Mather and other MPs presented proposals to place tobacco under the *Food and Drugs Act*, to restrict advertising, to require a warning on packages, and to limit tar and nicotine content. Other issues came up in Question Period, for example, tobacco sponsorship of skiing; and tobacco advertising on programs broadcast by the government-owned CBC.

Tobacco-belt MPs from southwestern Ontario led the parliamentary opposition to antitobacco legislation. In criticizing one of Mather's bills, tobacco-belt MP Jack Roxburgh proclaimed that "if this bill is passed it will be the first step toward doing away with everything for which democracy stands, from freedom of speech to the freedom of free enterprise."[527]

In the second half of the 1960s, health and medical organizations increased their support for a legislative approach. Inside the Department of National Health and Welfare, proposals to restrict advertising and require health warnings, with the support of officials like Harold Colburn, were actively considered.

Cabinet documents obtained under the *Access to Information Act* reveal that in May 1967 Cabinet approved a recommendation by National Health and Welfare Minister Allan MacEachen to have legislation prepared to require tar and nicotine levels on packages and in advertising and to prohibit advertisements "likely to create an erroneous impression regarding character, merit or safety of cigarettes or cigarette tobacco."[204, p. 7] Despite initial Cabinet approval, this legislation was never introduced.

The first World Conference on Smoking and Health was held in New York in September 1967, giving a boost to the movement. Also in 1967, the NDP and Conservatives were pressuring the government to restrict tobacco advertising. They were also calling on MacEachen to refer all existing private-member's bills on tobacco to the House of Commons Standing Committee on Health, Welfare and Social Affairs. Eventually, on 29 November 1968, the government agreed with this second alternative and referred the bills to Committee. This decision set in motion an unprecedented, comprehensive examination of tobacco issues in Canada.

CHAPTER 6

The Second Attempt at Regulation

James Reidford, *Globe and Mail*, Toronto

Cigaret?

The Isabelle Committee

The all-party House of Commons Standing Committee on Health, Welfare and Social Affairs was chaired by Dr Gaston Isabelle, a Liberal MP from Hull, Quebec. Some Committee members, such as Barry Mather, were well known for their antismoking views. On the other hand, the Committee had tobacco-belt representatives who were sympathetic to the industry. This ensured that the proceedings investigating smoking were lively.

The industry viewed the hearings with some significance. A week before the hearings began, the President of Brown and Williamson, Imperial Tobacco's American sister company, wrote to a senior official at parent company BAT that

> Paul Paré and Leo Laporte have kept me advised of the latest developments on the health situation in Canada. We are very disturbed at the situation and feel that whatever happens in Canada will have a direct bearing on what may happen in this country.[174]

On 19 December 1968, Health Minister John Munro opened the hearings with a statement calling for advertising restrictions, a warning on packages, legislated maximum tar and nicotine levels, and some voluntary research by the industry on ways to make smoking less dangerous. Munro strongly condemned cigarette advertising, saying that

> almost every minute of every day, we are urged, coaxed, and cajoled to buy a variety of different brands of a potentially dangerous product — namely cigarettes. ... On the ads we are told that cigarettes increase pleasure, attractiveness, sophistication, and sexual potency.[417, p. 130]

The Health Minister was committed to action, but the government as a whole was not. In 1968/69 and 1969/70, it spent about $500 000 each year on tobacco development research, more than double the amount it spent on antismoking research and programs. Further, the Department of Industry, Trade and Commerce spent $15 000 on a trade mission promoting Canadian tobacco exports, and the Department of Regional Economic Expansion granted $909 000 to the tobacco growing and manufacturing sectors.[319]

The Committee hearings received substantial publicity. On the one side were health and medical organizations that all confirmed the harmful consequences of smoking and recommended remedial action, including legislation. The CMA noted that over the preceding 15 years, the proportion of doctors who smoked had dropped from 65% to 35%.[76] On the other side were those with an economic interest in opposing controls, such as tobacco manufacturers and growers, the National Association of Tobacco and Confectionery Distributors, and the union representing workers in tobacco factories. The manufacturers brought to the Committee scientists and doctors who denied that smoking was harmful and who delivered testimony consistent with industry views. Some of the industry witnesses had previously given similar testimony before US congressional committees. By using this tactic, the industry sought, at a minimum, to demonstrate that medical opinion was divided on health issues, despite the fact that no credible scientific body anywhere was known to agree with the industry position. The industry sought to put forward more witnesses than the Committee was willing to hear.

Partway through the hearings, on 7 May 1969, the CBC announced that it would voluntarily stop tobacco advertising. "We took action on our own initiative rather than have government action push us as reluctant dragons into it," said the CBC President.[558] This decision and similar decisions by some private radio and television broadcasters added support to the call to ban advertising.

The tobacco industry's oral and written presentations to the Committee, delivered on 5 June 1969, were a classic example of industry deception and misinformation. The heads of the four companies appeared under the banner "Ad Hoc Committee of the Canadian Tobacco Industry," with Imperial Tobacco President Paul Paré designated as the principal spokesperson. He claimed that

> the tobacco industry — in Canada as elsewhere — has been and continues to be deeply concerned over the question of tobacco's possible effect on some people and has been doing something about this through scientific research and investigation.[461, p. 1539]

Here are some other excerpts from his testimony:

> ... efforts are made to blame cigarettes for every ailment with which they may be statistically associated.[461, p. 1541]
>
> It is actually a disservice to those millions who enjoy smoking to be constantly assaulted with some of the extreme and unsubstantiated propaganda that is spread about the so-called evils of smoking.[461, p. 1542]
>
> With respect to people who should not have carrots but eat them, carrots could then be described as being harmful to health.[461, pp. 1554–1555]

When asked whether there should be controls on heroin, Paré replied,

> Of course, I do not think the positions can be equated in terms of the dangers of the use of the products you are speaking of. Heroin is not only addictive, it is destructive of human life. This has been demonstrated. There is no question of statistical association. There is proof.[461, p. 1570]

A written brief detailed the industry's position on the "health controversy," gave the industry's views on legislative issues, described the industry's support of health research, and provided information about the industry's economic importance.[4] The brief said the "riddle of lung cancer remains basically unsolved."[4, p. 1615] The industry went on to describe what it saw as the benefits of smoking: in small quantities, smoking improved concentration and had a stimulative effect; in larger amounts, smoking was relaxing; and smoking helped with weight control.

The industry opposed advertising restrictions, arguing that manufacturers only competed for market share and did not seek to increase overall sales like the coffee, tea, and milk sectors did. An advertising ban would penalize the media and all sectors of the tobacco industry and would "largely eliminate" competition among tobacco companies. "Restrictions could tend to freeze the present marketing pattern among companies and would make the successful launching of new competitive brands almost impossible," said the brief.[4, p. 1657] New companies might be effectively excluded. The industry disputed that an advertising ban would work and asked what other suspects might be next. Automobiles? Eggs? Beefsteak? The industry recommended voluntary self-regulation as an alternative.

The industry suggested that health warnings might be counterproductive and encourage rebellious youth to smoke. Further, the industry saw as unjustified this requirement to advertise against its own product at its own expense. It opposed maximum tar and nicotine limits because there was no proof lower levels were safer. It even opposed printing tar and nicotine levels on packages because this would imply that brands with lower levels were safer and therefore to be preferred.

In the end, the Committee thoroughly rejected the industry's position. On 18 December 1969, a year after the study on tobacco began, the Committee presented a well-written and far-reaching report:

> We believe it sufficient to point out that there is no longer any scientific controversy regarding the risk created by cigarette smoking. The original statistical observations

have been validated by clinical observation and the evidence is now accepted as fact by Canadian medicine.[269, p. 2:12]

The production, distribution and sale of cigarettes should no longer be considered in the same light as the production, distribution and sale of other products. ... The cigarette stands unique among health and social problems. Therefore, society is justified in seeking unique solutions and in rejecting arguments based on technicalities. It is clearly contrary to the public interest for the use of a harmful product to be actively promoted even though a ban on production and sales would be unacceptable.[269, p. 2:52]

Young people can hardly be expected to believe that governments really consider cigarette smoking to be hazardous if they allow unlimited cigarette promotion. Further, large numbers of smokers wish to stop smoking or stay stopped and anything that could be done to support their resolve and reduce the pressures to smoke, which are part of our society, would be desirable.[269, p. 2:54]

The report recommended that

- ✦ A complete ban on advertising be phased in;
- ✦ Warnings be placed on packages, on vending machines, and, during the advertising phase-out period, on ads as well;
- ✦ Tar and nicotine levels be listed on packages and in warnings;
- ✦ Maximum levels for tar and nicotine be set;
- ✦ Placement of vending machines be restricted;
- ✦ Prominent displays of cigarettes be discouraged;
- ✦ Standards be set to make cigarettes less of a fire hazard;
- ✦ The sale of tobacco in hospitals and health facilities be discontinued;
- ✦ Coupon-premium schemes and free distribution be banned;
- ✦ Public education be increased;
- ✦ More surveys be undertaken; and
- ✦ Coordinating committees be established at national, provincial, and local levels.

All in all, the report represented an unprecedented Canadian call for legislative action to control tobacco.

Incentive promotions spread like wildfire

In 1970, Imperial Tobacco got into trouble with a brand of cigarettes called Casino. This brand contained potential instant winnings of $5 to $100. A printing error on game cards resulted in consumers winning prizes repeatedly. Some people were claiming winnings of $20 000 and $30 000, but Imperial Tobacco, at least at one point, refused to honour many claims. Once the error was discovered, the company quickly removed the brand from the market. Imperial eventually paid out vast sums of money. Further, the company was convicted of misleading advertising because it promoted the cigarettes as "$5 in every pack of new Casino," when in fact there was only a chance to win $5.[483]

The Casino controversy came at a time when incentive promotions for cigarettes had spread like wildfire, rising to a point in 1970 when 63% of the cigarette market carried some type of incentive.[524] Apart from being costly to the industry, the incentives also brought much public criticism. MP Mather complained in Parliament about a Mark Ten promotion inviting smokers to save coupons found in cigarette packs and turn them in for a television. He calculated that at one pack a day, it would take 243 years for a smoker to earn enough coupons to earn a colour television.[389] During 1970, tobacco companies got together and voluntarily agreed to stop incentive promotions.

Committee recommendations move to Cabinet

During 1970 and 1971, Cabinet actively debated the extent of legislative restrictions that should be imposed on tobacco. Although the Cabinet Ministers generally agreed with the recommendations of the Standing Committee, a few ministers were still opposed. As described in Cabinet documents obtained under the *Access to Information Act*, reasons for opposition included the following:

 ◆ There would not be that much of a reduction in consumption.

 ◆ New forms of advertising would be created to get around the law.

 ◆ Individuals should be left to make their own choices.

 ◆ It would be inconsistent to restrict tobacco advertising and to continue to allow liquor advertising.

Some ministers felt that it was inconsistent of the government to discourage smoking at the same time as it encouraged the export of tobacco and the Department of Regional Economic Expansion and the Department of Agriculture were encouraging tobacco growing in Canada.[205–208] The Liberal caucus, however, strongly held the view that tobacco advertising should be banned in newspapers in addition to broadcast media.[205]

Bud Drury, President of the Treasury Board, suggested that tobacco companies be encouraged to do more research into the effects of smoking.[206]

On 18 June 1970, Cabinet agreed that it would enact legislation "at the earliest convenient time" to prescribe maximum levels for tar, nicotine, and other constituents, to prohibit incentive promotions and the free distribution of cigarettes, and to prohibit advertising in electronic media and in newspapers. Health Minister Munro was asked to report back on the feasibility of eliminating the tax deduction for tobacco advertising. Cabinet also decided to require, through regulations under the *Hazardous Products Act*, the disclosure of levels of tar, nicotine, and other constituents on packages and in remaining advertising.[206] These regulations, however, were never adopted. It would be another year before new legislation was introduced in Parliament.

Cabinet minutes from 6 May 1971 state that "all tobacco companies recognize a world-wide ban on advertising is inevitable and there may be little advantage in Canada going faster than the United States in this regard."[208, p. 5] The minutes reveal that the government had held ongoing discussions with the tobacco industry about voluntary restrictions. Because one of the companies changed its mind after initial agreement, legislation became necessary. Given that a by-election for a riding in the Ontario tobacco belt was scheduled for 30 May 1971, it was decided to not introduce a bill until after the by-election. On 7 June 1971, before the summer recess, the Cabinet agreed to introduce a bill "for first reading only at this time."[209] There was no commitment to ensure the bill went beyond initial introduction.

Bill C-248 introduced

Finally, on 10 June 1971, Health Minister Munro introduced Bill C-248, the *Cigarette Products Act*. This bill would have eliminated cigarette advertising effective 1 January 1972, would have required a warning on packages and on vending machines, would have created authority to set maximum limits for nicotine and other constituents, and would have required disclosure of tar and nicotine yields on cigarette packages. In announcing the Bill, the Minister told reporters that he had reduced his own smoking from three packs a day to a pack and a half. Health groups roundly applauded the Bill's introduction.

The tobacco industry wasted no time in opposing the legislation. Imperial President, Paré, held a news conference in Ottawa on the same day the Bill was introduced. Paré said that the advertising restrictions would not affect the industry but that reducing tar and nicotine levels could have a devastating impact. He pointed out that a new Imperial Tobacco brand with a too-effective filter was a failure in the market because smokers were unsatisfied.[196]

Despite support from opposition parties, Bill C-248 was never even debated. On 21 September 1971 the industry announced a package of new voluntary measures:

- ✦ It would stop advertising cigarettes on radio and television. [This measure was less significant than it appeared because the CBC and some private stations had already stopped accepting cigarette advertising.]

- ✦ Packages would bear the warning "The Department of National Health and Welfare advises that danger to health increases with amount smoked."

- ✦ There would be a maximum tar yield of 22 mg per cigarette and a maximum nicotine yield of 1.6 mg per cigarette. [This measure affected only four brands then on the market.]

- ✦ Advertising expenditures would be restricted to 1971 levels.

✦ Free distribution would be restricted to new brands, to employees, and to consumers sending in complaints.

✦ The ban on poster and bulletin-board advertising would be extended from "immediately adjacent to schools" to "in the immediate vicinity of schools."[36]

The same day, Munro said that he still planned to press ahead with legislation. He also announced that spending for antismoking research and publicity would be doubled. This was a clear sign that the government and the industry had been actively communicating, perhaps negotiating, before the simultaneous announcements. The industry's initiative was a shrewd public relations move that not only deflated the government's sails but tamed the calls for action by the opposition and by the health community. Bill C-248 died when the parliamentary session ended.

When the new parliamentary session opened in 1972, the government included cigarette legislation on a list of 29 bills it intended to introduce. However, no bill was ever introduced, and Cabinet documents reveal that cigarette legislation was not on the list of bills really intended for passage. The second round of trying to legislate the industry, and the first since the turn of the century, had ended unsuccessfully. There were five important reasons for this:

1. The antismoking lobby was not as big or effective as it would later become. Although health and medical groups did call on government to take action, they did not have the lobbying experience or did not commit the staff resources to ensure the government carried through on legislative proposals.

2. A relatively high proportion of Canadians still smoked, especially among men, who dominated policy-making. Smoking was not as socially unacceptable as it would later become.

3. The historic uncertainty of the medical evidence on the health consequences of smoking was still within memory.

4. Industry self-regulation proved to be a strong counter to the legislative approach.

5. The tobacco industry was seen to be economically important, and parts of the federal government were taking measures to foster further growth.[230]

In 1972, Industry Minister Jean-Luc Pepin boasted in the House of Commons about the government's efforts to support the tobacco sector:

> I do not think you will find many people in the tobacco industry in Canada who will say that they have not been fully supported by the Department of Industry, Trade and Commerce. The recent sale to China which I announced was a direct result of the efforts of the department. If my friend knows of other ways in which we can support the tobacco industry, I will be glad to look into them.[463]

In 1971/72, aid to improve tobacco crops had risen to $965 000, still far outpacing the amount spent on nonsmoking projects, now up to $381 000 a year.[484]

Initiatives in the 1970s

In late 1972, Marc Lalonde became Minister of National Health and Welfare, replacing Munro. During Lalonde's 5-year tenure as Health Minister, the government had no anti-tobacco legislative initiatives. However, the Health Department released the landmark report *A New Perspective on the Health of Canadians*.[348] Following the release of this report, influencing people to make lifestyle changes (exercise, nutrition, smoking, drinking) became a more widely accepted principle of national health promotion.

During the 1970s, the government's antismoking program produced television spot announcements, films, posters, leaflets, and teachers' guides to educate the public. The amount spent by the government, however, was a pittance compared with the millions in advertising dollars spent by the industry. Health and Welfare Canada cooperated with the Department of Agriculture in research on less hazardous tobaccos and tobacco products. A new research laboratory at the Delhi Research Station was jointly opened in 1973 by Lalonde and Agriculture Minister Eugene Whelan.[118] Health and Welfare Canada continued a practice started in 1968 of publishing a list of the tar and nicotine yields of the most widely available cigarette brands.

In the mid-1970s, Health and Welfare officials "negotiated" with the industry, urging it to further reduce tar and nicotine yields in the belief that this would have notable public health benefits. Although some officials were dissatisfied that terms like *light* and *mild*, once used to describe low-tar and low-nicotine products, now appeared on cigarettes having relatively high tar levels, there was no tobacco legislation to permit the officials to take remedial action.

In 1975, the industry amended its voluntary code:

◆ Roll-your-own tobacco was now covered by the code.

◆ Advertising of sponsored events in broadcast media was prohibited, as was the use of direct mail.

◆ The rule limiting expenditures to 1971 levels was altered to allow for inflationary increases. [This was a very significant weakening of the code.]

◆ Average tar and nicotine yields would be placed on packages and print advertisements.

◆ *Avoid inhaling* was added to the end of the package warning. [This measure was meaningless and comparable to advising a person consuming a soft drink to avoid swallowing.]

◆ The warning would also be displayed in print advertising and "prominently displayed" on all transit and point-of-sale advertising greater than a certain size. [Once in place, however, the warnings on advertisements were often illegible, let alone prominent. The warnings on packages appeared on the side in colours that often blended in with the package design.]

The tobacco companies continued to use the code as a shield to deflect arguments that legislation was necessary. Health ministers used voluntary restrictions as an excuse for not introducing legislation. All in all, the code continued to be an extremely weak restraint on industry marketing.

As the 1970s progressed, the nonsmokers' rights movement grew, and municipalities began to pass bylaws restricting smoking in public places. NSRA was founded in 1974. The same year, acting on a formal recommendation of the 1973 national conference on smoking, health organizations created an umbrella group known as the Canadian Council on Smoking and Health (CCSH). However, it would be another decade, well into the 1980s, before proposals for meaningful national tobacco legislation were again firmly on the parliamentary agenda.

PART III

Key Issues:
The Major Battlegrounds

CHAPTER 7

The Battle to Ban Advertising

Alan King, *The Ottawa Citizen*

The impact of tobacco advertising

When tobacco companies sell cigarettes, they are selling two main things. First, there is the physical product itself, the most important component of which is nicotine. Second, there is "imagery," the intangible life-style characteristics created by marketing.

Few teenagers begin smoking for a cigarette's inherent physical qualities. Instead, teens are attracted to smoking for its imagery attributes, such as the five S's: sophistication, slimness, social acceptability, sexual attractiveness, and status. Marketing gives a cigarette a false "personality." Imperial Tobacco explains that imagery attributes are "derived from product and package design or the association of a brand with certain advertising campaigns or sport or cultural activities."[289, p. 28] According to Imperial, the image of a cigarette brand "may be as important as the physical characteristics of the cigarette in satisfying consumer needs."[289, p. 28]

Different brands of cigarettes may be virtually the same physically, but it is marketing that gives them life and makes them attractive to different consumer target markets. Here is an excerpt from a report by Brazil's Souza Cruz, a sister company to Imperial Tobacco:

> The inspired person who designed the cigarette made it masculine in men's hands; feminine in women's hands. Sophisticated among the sophisticated; rough among the rough. To the young, a token of rebellion; to the elderly, a tool of quietness ... a warm ally in the moments of action and a solitary companion during reflection.[247]

It is easy to understand why health organizations strongly oppose tobacco advertising. The portrayal of an addictive, carcinogenic, and lethal product as innocuous and even desirable is simply incompatible with responsible public health. There is as much justification for promoting tobacco as there would have been for promoting rats during the Plague. It is not possible to prohibit cigarettes altogether, because of addiction, but it is possible to prevent the use of imagery to make cigarettes more attractive.

Tobacco advertising can increase consumption in a number of possible ways. Advertising can encourage nonsmokers to start, perhaps earlier than would otherwise be the case. Advertising can induce ex-smokers to start again or to remain smoke free for shorter periods. Advertising can persuade consumers to get their nicotine from a tobacco product instead of from a nicotine alternative such as nicotine gum or a nicotine patch. Advertising can increase the amount smoked daily and can discourage or delay quitting. As part of this, advertising can enhance the social acceptability of smoking. Advertising can stimulate price competition, leading to lower prices and consequently higher sales volumes. Advertising can induce consumers to switch to a lower priced product instead of quitting or cutting down.

Advertising can buy silence by influencing news content in the media. On numerous occasions smoking and health articles have been suppressed or edited to avoid offending tobacco advertisers.[628] The result is a public without the full knowledge necessary to make informed decisions about smoking. An American study covering the periods 1959–69 and 1973–86 found that magazines without tobacco ads were 43% more likely to cover smoking and health than those that did not. Among women's magazines, the likelihood was 234%.[623] The following 1979 excerpt from *The Ottawa Citizen* illustrates how the industry can inflict financial punishment on those media who discourage smoking:

> Imperial Tobacco Ltd. has pulled the balance of its June and July advertising from *The [Ottawa] Citizen* in the wake of an intensive stop-smoking campaign launched by the newspaper June 9. ...
>
> Imperial marketing vice-president Anthony Kalhok, in a telephone interview Tuesday from Montreal, said he was 'surprised' *The [Ottawa] Citizen*'s sales department hadn't called his department to 'let us know you were running this type of campaign and ask us in advance if we wanted to run our ads during that time. Some papers do that and I'm just surprised that someone didn't tell us in advance that you were planning to run a series of articles'.
>
> Kalhok refused to explain the reasoning behind the company's decision. 'We don't ask you to explain or justify your editorial content, so I don't see why we have to

answer any questions. We don't have a contract that says we have to run an ad simultaneously in all newspapers in one city, or in all cities across Canada at the same time'.[411]

The October 1984 issue of *Chatelaine* had a feature on cancer, a further article on smoking, and no tobacco ads. The magazine had informed advertisers in advance, and no tobacco advertising was placed, even though tobacco ads had regularly appeared in the magazine.[132]

Concern about the influence of advertisers is not new. During the 1903 House of Commons debate about banning cigarettes, MP Bickerdike made these observations:

> Heretofore many of the papers have been very generous in commenting editorially in favour of the movement against cigarettes. But now I notice that in some of them are appearing long articles stating that cigarettes are quite harmless, and really nourishing and beneficial. Of course there is no hint that these articles are advertisements, and that the space is paid for, probably by some one interested in the tobacco trust. One of the editors being asked about it, answered: Well, we get higher rates than we do for ordinary advertising matter.[42]

Cigarette advertising can neutralize health concerns or can at least affect perceptions of the severity of the risks. Advertisements portray energetic and happy young people, often engaging in athletic, healthy activities. Teenagers want to be like the people in tobacco ads, and they want to participate in the activities shown in the ads. It is no accident that many ads feature backdrops of the pristine outdoors. These positive images counter negative images such as lung disease and cancer.

The industry's position is that advertising only affects a company's market share by influencing smokers to select a particular brand and that there is no proof that advertising increases overall consumption. This position is nonsense. If advertising did not affect overall consumption, the industry would not oppose a ban on advertising. Companies could save tens of millions of dollars annually without fear of a new or existing competitor using advertising to take away market share. In the United States, more than US $6 billion is spent annually on tobacco advertising and promotion.[169] Yet despite this potential opportunity for dramatically increased profits through cost savings, the industry is fervently opposed to a ban on tobacco advertising.

The US Surgeon General[608] and the US Food and Drug Administration[611] are among those who have examined the evidence and concluded that tobacco advertising does increase overall consumption. The World Health Organization (WHO) is a strong supporter of a total ban on advertising.[639] In countries like Japan, Austria, and Cameroon, where in the past there has been only one tobacco company (a monopoly), tobacco advertising has continued.[99] This is irrefutable evidence that advertising is used to affect more than market share.

Campaign to ban advertising regains momentum

In Canada, after the failed 1971 attempt to ban advertising, health groups were not actively pressing for a ban. A small breakthrough occurred in 1979, when NSRA, led by Executive Director Gar Mahood, mounted a successful campaign (opposed by the industry) that resulted in the Toronto Transit Commission voting to refuse tobacco ads. In 1980, the Hamilton–Wentworth Transit Commission made a similar decision.

In 1983, the Fifth World Conference on Smoking and Health was held in Winnipeg. David Nostbakken, Chair of the Conference, recalls that "the conference really helped to send a message to the federal government just how important tobacco issues were." Although the conference nearly left CCSH (the organizer) bankrupt, it did raise the profile in Canada of smoking issues.

Later in 1983, NSRA, CCS, CCSH, and the Canadian Heart Foundation formed the Coalition of Health Interests to oppose RJR–Macdonald's Export "A" sponsorship of amateur skiing. The Canadian Ski Association's Medical Committee opposed the tobacco sponsorship, and the issue developed into a media controversy. Dr Andrew Pipe sat on this committee, and it was through his involvement on this issue that Physicians for a Smoke-Free Canada was later formed. The antisponsorship effort was given a boost when Olympic skiers Ken Read and Steve Podborski each refused to accept awards for their performance in the Export "A" Cup, the name given to the national championships.

Although the campaign failed to block the sponsorship immediately, in 1984 Health Minister Monique Bégin joined with the Sports Minister to announce that the government planned to end tobacco sponsorship of amateur skiing eventually.[132] The following year, Sports Minister Otto Jelinek announced that amateur sports organizations that wished to receive federal funding would not be able to accept any new tobacco sponsorships.[408] The best outcome of the ski sponsorship campaign was that health groups gained experience working together as a coalition. Other collaborative efforts followed, including a news conference in 1984 to urge newspapers to refuse tobacco ads. Health groups said such advertising violated a rule of the *Canadian Code of Advertising Standards*, which stipulated that no advertisements should encourage unsafe or dangerous practices. In reply, the advertising industry, which is responsible for the Code, revised the rule to make it clear that tobacco advertising could continue. Although this was not a surprise, it made it clear that the advertising industry was not willing to eliminate tobacco advertising through self-regulation.

In 1984, the tobacco industry strengthened its voluntary code by requiring the health warning to appear on cartons in addition to packages, on packages of imported cigarettes, and on billboard advertising. The text of the warning was unchanged, and the size of the warning on billboards often made the message unreadable except at close range.

In 1985, the federal Department of Agriculture wanted to establish a Canadian Flue-Cured Tobacco Marketing Agency that would subsidize farmers and promote leaf-tobacco sales. Health groups banded together to fight the plan. The proposal was eventually dropped, and health groups gained more lobbying experience.

Throughout this period, NSRA was leading a campaign to persuade newspapers to voluntarily refuse tobacco advertising. The *Kingston Whig-Standard*, a small but award-winning Ontario newspaper, set a precedent when it decided in October 1984 to do just that. A couple of small publications followed. In August 1986, the country's most important English-language newspaper, the *Globe and Mail*, followed suit. The Globe's announcement forced policymakers and other media to sit up and take notice. These decisions gave a major boost to efforts to ban tobacco advertising.

When Jake Epp became Health Minister in 1984, he took a more determined position against tobacco advertising than his predecessor. In 1985, Epp wrote to Imperial Tobacco asking that ads be removed from the premises of Canada's Wonderland and from the theme park's official guidebook. Stated Epp, "Many citizens, including myself, have concluded that these cigarette advertisements are being addressed to persons under eighteen, in contravention of [the code]."[164]

Early in 1986, RJR–Macdonald launched a new cigarette brand called "Tempo." Tempo advertising featured youthful-looking models wearing "cool" clothes. Although the company denied the brand was targeted at youth, health groups quickly condemned the company for attempting to do just that. Health Minister Epp publicly criticized Tempo advertising several times and called on the company to stop the campaign. Eventually, Tempo was taken off the market, although it is unclear whether poor sales or public pressure was the main reason for the decision. A marketing study done for the company later revealed that the reasons for poor sales included the fact that Tempo advertising was perceived as too explicitly youth-oriented to be successful in the 18–24 age group.[495]

The controversy over Tempo advertising highlighted the inadequacy of the industry's voluntary code. Over the years, the industry simply rejected requests by the Department of Health and Welfare to strengthen the code if it did not like the proposed changes. For example, in 1980 an attempt to have carbon monoxide levels listed on the package ended up with the manufacturers merely undertaking to lower the levels without printing anything on the package. In 1982 an attempt by Health Minister Bégin to ensure that there was 500 metres between ads and school property was never implemented. When further restrictions to the code were accepted by the industry, the changes were typically minor and had been years in the works.

Violations of the code usually went unaddressed. When Bégin wrote to CTMC requesting that ads appearing on closed-circuit television be removed, CTMC replied with an alternative interpretation of the code: the ban on television advertising did not apply to closed-circuit TV. When the public and Bégin complained about ads placed within 200 metres of schools, as the existing code prohibited, the industry placed the blame on advertising agencies and billboard companies.

Meanwhile, the industry maintained that the code was working well. Indeed, from its perspective, the code clearly was effective. The industry had ample opportunity to promote its products as it saw fit while pointing to self-regulation to indicate that heavy-handed legislation was unnecessary.

The increasing public support for a ban on tobacco advertising, coupled with a health minister who had taken a hard line on advertising, prompted the industry to propose further self-regulation in an effort to pre-empt discussion of legislative action. CTMC wrote to Epp in early 1986 regarding the code:

> From time to time, the four member companies of the Canadian Tobacco Manufacturers' Council review the industry's Advertising and Promotion Code. ... We believe that this is an appropriate time to examine the present Code and determine what, if any, changes should be considered.[393]

Over the next 6 months, Epp and the industry met a number of times and exchanged letters. Epp expressed his displeasure with violations of the code and indicated he was seeking major improvements to code provisions. The industry rejected many of his proposals, including the premise that all advertising would be prohibited except what was explicitly permitted. Eventually, Epp decided that the voluntary approach would not work and that legislation was necessary.

Epp was helped by the increasing number of representations made to government by health groups and the public. In January 1986, NSRA released "A Catalogue of Deception,"[442] a report that outlined violations of virtually every major rule in the code. This comprehensive brief documented how self-regulation by the industry was completely ineffective. The brief also noted that a manufacturer could simply opt out of the code, just as Rothmans of Pall Mall did in 1985. As well, because only manufacturers, not members of the public, could file complaints, obtaining effective enforcement was illusory indeed. The brief proved to be a particularly valuable reference. It rebutted industry arguments that legislation was unnecessary because, according to the industry, the Code had "operated responsibly and in the public interest" for 22 years.[255, p. 2]

Additional initiatives increased the pressure to take action on tobacco. In 1986, Air Canada announced that it would have some smoke-free flights in the Ottawa–Toronto–Montreal triangle. NSRA and the Society of Obstetricians and Gynaecologists filed an unfair business-practice complaint with the Ontario government, alleging that tobacco manufacturers were "withholding material facts" about the dangers of smoking during pregnancy.[132] No action was taken on the complaint. Physicians for a Smoke-Free Canada filed an application in Federal Court to force the federal Minister of Consumer and Corporate Affairs to add tobacco to the *Hazardous Products Act*, an application that was unsuccessful. NSRA placed full-page ads in 23 newspapers, calling on the government to treat tobacco as it would any other addictive, lethal product. Maureen Law, then Deputy Health Minister, later recalled "that non-government organizations created a climate where it would be difficult for the government to not ban tobacco advertising."

What really made the difference, though, was Bill C-204, the *Non-smokers' Health Act*. This private-member's bill, introduced in the House of Commons by MP Lynn McDonald (NDP) in October 1986, proposed to restrict smoking in federally regulated workplaces, as well as on planes, trains, and boats. The bill placed tobacco under the *Hazardous Products Act*, thereby prohibiting all advertising and sales except what was permitted by regulation.

Normally, private-member's bills have almost no chance of being passed by the House of Commons, but parliamentary reform improved the odds. Bill C-204 was drawn as one of 20 items in a lottery of about 150 private-member's bills and motions. A committee then selected 6 of the 20 items to be votable. Bill C-204 was one of the six. The Bill received five separate hours of debate over the next 5 months. Health groups lobbied MPs to support it. As support grew, Epp used Bill C-204 behind the scenes to gain support in Cabinet and caucus for the government's introducing its own bill to prohibit tobacco advertising.

On 22 April 1987, just 10 days before Bill C-204 was scheduled for a second-reading vote, Epp announced that he would soon be introducing a bill to ban tobacco advertising and sponsorships and to require rotated health warnings. The government also announced that smoking would be prohibited in the federal public service and that the Labour Minister would restrict smoking in other federally regulated workplaces. Health groups were jubilant. The industry denounced the government. It was quite a fight to introduce Epp's legislation, Bill C-51, the *Tobacco Products Control Act* (TPCA), but that was nothing compared with the battle to come.

The Parliamentary campaign over Bill C-51 and Bill C-204

Although Bill C-204 obtained second reading shortly after Bill C-51 was introduced, Bill C-51 quickly got a much higher profile. The tobacco industry initiated a massive, multifaceted $2.5 million campaign to oppose Bill C-51. The industry retained The Houston Group, a PR firm, which put together an information kit to help generate a letter-writing campaign against Bill C-51. A major ad campaign was launched to create public opposition to the Bill (Figure 7). Imperial Tobacco held news conferences in various parts of Canada threatening to withdraw its sponsorship of locally held sporting events. As a test case, 15 000 letters were sent to homes in the riding of Toronto-area MP John Bosley.

In opposing a ban on tobacco advertising, the industry argued that the ban was an unconstitutional infringement of freedom of expression, that the ban would not reduce smoking, that arts and sports groups would lose funding, and that thousands of jobs in the advertising industry would be lost. As well, because advertising for brands in American magazines would be exempt from the ad ban, the Canadian industry argued that American cigarettes would gain market share in Canada, especially with the pending implementation of the Canada–USA Free Trade Agreement. Jobs in the Canadian tobacco industry would be lost, it was claimed. In response to this point, health groups noted that American cigarette imports represented just 1% of the Canadian market. Health groups also pointed out that American cigarettes used a different type of tobacco and did not taste the same as Canadian cigarettes.

Why the proposed Government legislation banning tobacco advertising deserves a sensible second look.

Even by people who don't smoke.

The Federal Government has proposed legislation banning all Canadian tobacco advertising, promotion and brand sponsorship.

Whether or not you smoke, if you're a Canadian who cares about civil liberties, you owe it to yourself to examine this issue and come to your own conclusions.

A VIOLATION OF THE CHARTER OF RIGHTS AND FREEDOMS?

Never in the history of Canada has a legal product been totally denied the right to advertise. Bill C-51 denies tobacco manufacturers the right to provide information through advertising and the consumer the right to receive it. So the proposed legislation may well be a direct violation of the Charter of Rights.

Many Canadians believe banning advertising for a legal product is in violation of Canada's Charter of Rights and Freedoms.

REASONABLE CONSTRAINTS YES. OUTRIGHT CENSORSHIP NO.

Nobody questions the need for reasonable constraints on tobacco advertising. Tobacco advertising has been controlled through a voluntary industry code for more than 20 years.

Under the voluntary code, tobacco manufacturers withdrew from television and radio advertising. They limited expenditures, included government health warnings and ensured that outdoor advertising would not appear adjacent to primary and secondary school areas. Within the last year, the industry has further offered to eliminate people from all advertising and enlarge and modify Health and Welfare messages in advertising and on packages. With this record of co-operation and control, is outright censorship really necessary?

WHAT ADVERTISING DOES AND DOESN'T DO.

Today's tobacco advertising is designed to encourage current smokers to try one brand over another. That's all advertising does. It doesn't get people to start smoking and it doesn't get them to smoke more. In countries where tobacco advertising has been banned, such as Norway, Sweden, Finland and Singapore, consumption has not declined, and in some cases, has actually increased.

Advertising also doesn't encourage young people to start smoking. A recent study of Canadian children undertaken by the respected Children's Research Unit of the United Kingdom shows clearly that advertising has little, if any, influence.

JOBS LOST FOR NOTHING.

There is ample evidence to suggest that Bill C-51 will not achieve its aims. What it will achieve is massive economic dislocation. Up to 2,500 people in Canada's advertising and media industries stand to lose their jobs and many other industries will feel the economic impact.

With tobacco brand sponsorship outlawed, organizations such as the Royal Canadian Golf Association, Tennis Canada, the Canadian Equestrian Federation and many major opera companies, dance companies, theatre companies and symphony orchestras could lose up to $10 million a year in sponsorship grants. All in all, a heavy price to pay for ineffective legislation.

TOBACCO ADVERTISING TODAY. WHO'S NEXT?

If the rights inherent in the Charter of Rights and Freedoms can be conveniently trampled upon in the tobacco advertising issue, whose rights will be denied next?

Will alcoholic beverage advertising be made illegal? Will advertising for certain food products be outlawed? Will trade unions be told that they can't plead their case through advertising because the Government doesn't want Canadians exposed to their ideas? Once we start down the road of banning information, where do we stop?

In a study conducted among Canadian children by the highly respected Children's Research Unit of the United Kingdom, the myth that tobacco advertising encourages young people to smoke was shattered. Among the major findings:

- Peer pressure, parental role models and socio-economic status are the primary influences leading to smoking among young people.
- Advertising was cited as an influence by less than 2% of the young people surveyed.
- Cigarette consumption among young people is substantially higher in Norway than in Canada. Tobacco advertising has been banned in Norway since 1975.

If you're concerned about this basic point of principle, or if you'd like more information on the proposed tobacco advertising ban, we urge you to write to P.O. Box 80, Station "H", Montreal, Quebec H3G 2K8.

Canadian Tobacco Manufacturers' Council ● Committee of Concerned Tobacco Area Municipalities
Ontario Flue-Cured Tobacco Growers' Marketing Board ● National Association of Tobacco and Confectionery Distributors
Bakery, Confectionery and Tobacco Workers International Union ● I.T.W.A.L. ● Nova Scotia Flue-Cured Tobacco Growers' Marketing Board
New Brunswick Flue-Cured Tobacco Growers' Association ● Association of Canadian Advertisers ● Smokers' Freedom Society
P.E.I. Tobacco Commodity Marketing Board ● Office des producteurs de tabac jaune du Québec

Figure 7. Sample advertisement placed by the industry to oppose Bill C-51.

To help oppose the Bill, RBH retained the PR firm Burson-Marsteller. This firm put together Coalition 51, a group of academics, artists, and sports figures opposing the Bill. The group was launched with slick same-day, satellite-linked news conferences in Toronto and Montreal. Health advocates attending the Toronto conference informed the media of the presence of Cynthia von Maerestetten, RBH Corporate Affairs Vice-President. Exposing the fact that the tobacco industry was behind Coalition 51 dramatically decreased the impact of this initiative opposing the Bill.

As part of the industry's campaign, retailers and others were sent letters and pre-stamped envelopes that they could simply sign and mail to their MP. The letters were designed to appear as if the retailer was the author: for example, the retailer's return address was included. Letters were made to look different in form, text, colour, and paper, all varied by automated equipment. Retailers received up to three follow-up calls to ensure that the letters got sent in. Many letters were sent in, and the industry's attempt to create an impression among MPs of grass-roots opposition to the Bill was succeeding.

By the end of the summer of 1987, support for Bill C-51 was slipping. The Bill had been publicly criticized by the Agriculture Minister and the Sports Minister.[132,551] Liberal health critic Sheila Copps said the letters she received were 9 to 1 against Bill C-51. Epp's initial plan to have the Bill passed within 2 months proved to be wishful thinking. He informed health groups that unless their campaign was stepped up, the Bill would not pass, despite the large majority the government had in the Commons and despite support from opposition parties.

The health lobby had been planning a campaign and went into high gear. Health groups emphasized that a ban on advertising would reduce smoking, especially among youth; they rejected industry forecasts about the economic harm the Bill would cause; and they said that in any event public health must come first. The CMA announced that it would ask its 48 000 member physicians to vote against any MP opposing the Bill.[77] Doctors were asked to call their MPs.[78] NSRA published full-page ads outlining support for the Bill within the cultural community. NSRA also prepared a pamphlet, "Give Kids a Chance."[424] Physicians for a Smoke-Free Canada launched a small-scale radio campaign in Toronto. CCS and the Canadian Public Health Association initiated meetings with more than 25 MPs. CCS announced that it would ask its volunteers to send MPs 35 000 black-bordered cards asking for speedy passage, one card for each person who died from tobacco-related causes each year. *The Ottawa Citizen*[24] and the *Montreal Gazette*[409] announced that they would no longer accept tobacco ads. Fifteen health groups blitzed the office of the Government House Leader with phone calls asking when Bill C-51 would be brought forward. CCS released a Gallup poll showing that 62% of Canadians supported an ad ban and only 30% were opposed.[189]

An important part of the campaign occurred when NSRA exposed the phony letter-writing campaign involving retailers. After obtaining copies of the letters and documenting accounts of how people were being urged to send the letters in, NSRA informed the media and MPs of how the flood of letters opposing the campaign was in fact orchestrated by the tobacco industry.[443,444] NSRA's initiative undermined the effectiveness and credibility of the letters opposing Bill C-51.

Neil Collishaw, who at the time was the key official on tobacco issues inside Health and Welfare Canada, later recalled that the preparation of "A Catalogue of Deception," the unmasking of Coalition 51, and the unmasking of the phony letter campaign were "three examples of outstanding lobbying efforts."

As health groups stepped up their campaign, government ministers were feeling the heat. In particular, the full-page ads and the phone calls from doctors had an impact. The total number of letters on tobacco or smoking received by the Health Minister in the first 10 months of 1987, regardless of viewpoint, was 5 499, up from 1306 in 1986 and 92 in 1982.[112] Finally, Bill C-51 received second reading on 23 November 1987 and was sent to the committee studying Bill C-204.

Committee hearings on Bill C-204 had been ongoing for several months. One of the Conservatives on the Committee was Ron Stewart, a tobacco wholesaler and former Chairman of the National Association of Tobacco and Confectionery Distributors. He had opposed his own party's Bill C-51 at second reading.[132] NSRA and CCS held a news conference in Stewart's constituency, arguing that he had a conflict of interest.[144] A circular was sent to homes in his riding with the message that he was not properly representing his constituents because of the conflict of interest. Shortly thereafter, Stewart stopped serving on the Committee.

The lobbying battle continued before the Committee. Health groups wanted Bill C-51 strengthened, and the industry wanted the opposite. The hearings were often testy, with MP Chris Speyer (Conservative) opposing the thrust of the Bill, and MPs Copps (Liberal) and McDonald (NDP) strongly supporting it. Conservatives Arnold Malone and Paul McCrossan were also strong supporters. Much of the debate centred on whether an ad ban would reduce consumption. The industry and health groups both brought in experts to help make their respective cases. Sports groups receiving sponsorship testified that they would be unable to replace industry support. The advertising industry protested the loss of revenue and jobs. Throughout the hearings and the debate generally, the industry tried to position the issue as one of freedom, whereas supporters tried to position the issue as one of health.

To strengthen the industry's hand, Bill Neville was brought in as the new President of CTMC. Neville was the consummate well-connected political insider. He had been Chief of Staff to former Conservative Prime Minister Joe Clark, a Conservative strategist in the 1984 election campaign, and then part of the transition team for the newly elected government of Prime Minister Mulroney. Neville was personally close to the Prime Minister.

Health groups were worried about how this development might affect passage of the ad ban. Part of the response was a full-page ad published in the *Globe and Mail*. This controversial ad, drafted by NSRA, revealed the "Neville Factor" (Figure 8) and came at a time when the Prime Minister had been under significant criticism for giving special treatment to his friends. Failing to pass the Bill would open the government to more criticism.

HOW MANY THOUSANDS OF CANADIANS WILL DIE FROM TOBACCO INDUSTRY PRODUCTS MAY LARGELY BE IN THE HANDS OF THESE TWO MEN

Prime Minister
Brian Mulroney

Lobbyist
William H. Neville

In a few hours, a small group of Members of Parliament will begin the clause-by-clause review of two proposed bills. They could become the most important federal laws in disease prevention and health promotion in over a decade. In fact, the health community believes that the Committee's decisions will greatly influence illness and death rates from cancer and other diseases for decades to come.

The House of Commons Committee, dominated by Conservative MPs, will review two critical bills: the **Tobacco Products Control Act** (Bill C-51) and the **Non-smokers' Health Act** (Bill C-204). We believe the wishes of two powerful Canadians, Prime Minister Brian Mulroney and tobacco lobbyist William Henry Neville, will have a major influence on the final outcome. ·

At 35,000 deaths each year, tobacco industry products kill more Canadians annually than would be killed by the collision of two fully-loaded jumbo jets every week for a year. These bills are moderate, reasoned responses to a health problem of this magnitude.

Bill C-51 would ban tobacco advertising and prevent the industry from using arts activities and sports/fitness events for the purpose of promoting tobacco sales. Bill C-204, MP Lynn McDonald's private member's bill, would bring tobacco under the **Hazardous Products Act**. It would also regulate involuntary smoking in inter-provincial transportation and workplaces under federal jurisdiction.

Bills C-51 and C-204 are supported by hundreds of organizations representing millions of Canadians. These bills constitute world precedent-setting legislation. Passage of this legislation would represent the first time a government, in a tobacco growing country, had sufficient integrity to withstand the muscle of the tobacco lobby.

Let us be clear. To date, the Prime Minister's government has acted with courage and integrity to bring the government bill this far. As it stands, Bill C-51 represents policy for a government with a huge majority. To their credit, the Liberal and New Democratic parties have set aside partisan politics to give Bill C-51 all-party approval. **In other words, if the Prime Minister wants Bill C-51 to pass without being weakened, we think the House of Commons Committee will support him.**

If these bills pass, the Prime Minister and Health Minister Jake Epp will be the recipients of praise from coast-to-coast. And the government will attract international acclaim.

THE NEVILLE FACTOR

One thing could stand in the way. Bill Neville, perhaps the most powerful lobbyist in Canada and a friend of the Prime Minister. Neville is also the newly-appointed President of the Canadian Tobacco Manufacturers' Council.

The industry knew what it was doing when it hired Bill Neville. He was Chief of Staff for one conservative Prime Minister and was responsible for setting up the Prime Minister's Office for the current government. Neville's credentials as a professional lobbyist are impeccable.

Bill Neville's assignment has been to derail these Bills or, at the very least, to extract compromises from the government which will minimize the reduction in tobacco sales. Unfortunately, his task flies in the face of the health objectives of the government and the entire Canadian health community.

Given the enormous death rates caused by the tobacco products Bill Neville is defending, there is a danger that every point he wins and every compromise he extracts could have the potential to translate into tens of thousands of deaths over time.

On the other hand, the Prime Minister has renewed a commitment to progressive social policy. Given the enormity of the death rates, every pro-health amendment the government-dominated Committee approves, every time the Committee votes to maintain the integrity of these bills, there is a potential for the savings of tens of thousands of lives.

NO COMPROMISES WITH EPIDEMICS

The pro-tobacco influences are seeking one amendment which has the potential to "gut" Bill C-51. They can live with a ban on conventional advertising as long as arts and sports sponsorships are protected. The industry knows that the money spent on conventional advertising can simply be shifted to sponsorships. And, frequently, sponsorships can more effectively promote tobacco products than conventional ads. The protection of sports sponsorship would provide the industry with the perfect escape route.

Our position has to be **"no compromises on epidemics. No compromises with death rates of this magnitude. And no compromises on sponsorship!"**

THE ISSUE IS INTEGRITY

The issue in the eleventh hour is simply this. Will the influence of a powerful industry and a skilled lobbyist override 50,000 scientific studies demonstrating the association of tobacco industry products with death and disease? Will the millions of dollars spent by this industry to defeat this bill run roughshod over the courageous leadership of the Minister of Health and his entire department, over Canadian health and human service organizations united as they have never been before, over the leadership of the Liberal and New Democratic parties, and over the substantial majority of Canadians which polls demonstrate consistently support these legislative initiatives?

We appeal to the Prime Minister and the Committee on Bills C-51 and C-204 to back integrity. Young Canadians will be in their debt for generations to come. And, we think that William Henry Neville, deep down, will understand.

**ASSOCIATION DES CONSEILS DES MÉDECINS,
DENTISTES ET PHARMACIENS DU QUÉBEC**

CANADIAN CANCER SOCIETY

CANADIAN COUNCIL ON SMOKING AND HEALTH

CANADIAN TEACHERS' FEDERATION

NATIONAL ACTION COMMITTEE ON THE STATUS OF WOMEN

NON-SMOKERS' RIGHTS ASSOCIATION

PHYSICIANS FOR A SMOKE-FREE CANADA

Figure 8. The Neville ad.[22]

Bill C-51 made it through Committee substantially intact, and no amendments were made that would gut the Bill. Some amendments strengthened it, such as creating authority to require package inserts of detailed health information. Bill C-204 was also approved and sent back to the House of Commons, with the added proviso that if Bill C-51 passed, the part of Bill C-204 that would ban tobacco advertising would be of no effect. However, the battle was still not over. Epp remained firmly in support, but most of the Cabinet remained opposed. Even though both opposition House Leaders had promised to permit the Bill to pass with little debate, and even though there were days when the Commons ended early because there was no business before it, the government did not bring Bill C-51 up for third reading.

Eventually, health groups stepped up their lobbying in support of final passage. Time was running out. The government was expected to call an election in the fall, and if Bill C-51 was not passed before the summer recess, the Bill might die.

Meanwhile, over a number of months, third-reading debate over Bill C-204 was proceeding. The Bill was scheduled for a vote of final approval on 30 May 1988. The government rescheduled the vote to the next day so that its own Bill C-51 could be brought forward and passed and McDonald's Bill C-204 could be defeated.

May 31 proved to be a critical lobbying day. Several health lobbyists (including NSRA's Mahood, David Sweanor, and Gabriel Durocher; CCSH's Victor Lachance; and CCS's Ken Kyle and David Hill) waited outside the Commons and urged arriving MPs to support both bills. Malone and McCrossan lobbied fellow MPs to either support Bill C-204 or stay away. When a rumour spread that the two bills were incompatible and could not both be passed, health representatives worked with Malone to prepare a short statement that the bills were indeed fully compatible.[378] The statement was signed by Malone, copied in McDonald's office, and distributed to MPs.

The lobbying worked. Malone said that at the start of the day more than enough MPs to approve or reject the Bill were undecided. In the end, Bill C-204 passed by a vote of 77 to 58, with all Cabinet ministers in the House voting against it; Epp was absent. Just nine MPs voting differently would have changed the outcome. Many government backbenchers, who felt the government was not paying enough attention to them, asserted their independence by supporting the opposition bill. Bill C-51 was also approved with all-party support, thus giving health groups a double reason to celebrate. Epp was present for the passage of Bill C-51.

However, the battle was not yet over. Press reports indicated that the industry would turn its attention to the Senate, of which Rothmans Chairman, William Kelly, was a member. Health groups launched a letter-writing campaign. The fight would not be long, though: both Bill C-51 and Bill C-204 were passed within 4 weeks. Victory was at hand (see Figure 9). The *Globe and Mail* reported that Epp praised health groups:

> 'That was based on one of the best lobbying efforts ever seen on Parliament Hill', Mr. Epp said, adding that the lobby that fought on behalf of the two bills was remarkable for its cohesiveness, its broad base of support and its effectiveness.

Figure 9. Gathering in the Parliament buildings 28 June 1988 following Royal Assent of Bills C-51 and C-204. Left to right: Ken Kyle and David Hill, Canadian Cancer Society; Senator Stanley Haidasz; Neil Collishaw, Health and Welfare Canada; Lynn McDonald, MP; Byron Rogers, Health and Welfare Canada; Jake Epp, Minister of National Health and Welfare; Gar Mahood, Non-Smokers' Rights Association; Victor Lachance, Canadian Council on Smoking and Health; David Sweanor and Gabriel Durocher, Non-Smokers' Rights Association. Present but not in picture: Gweneth Gowanlock, Legislative Assistant to Jake Epp; Cynthia Callard, Legislative Assistant to Lynn McDonald; Rob Cunningham, Canadian Cancer Society.

'If you're looking at a strategy, I think what happened was a strategy whereby the traditional manner the tobacco lobby entered this fray didn't work', he said. 'They were outgunned, they were outmuscled, and quite frankly they were outfinessed'.[183]

The critical role of Lynn McDonald's Bill C-204 should not be underestimated. At every step in the legislative process, Bill C-204 preceded Bill C-51 and placed significant pressure on the government to move the government's Bill forward.

Some time in the months after the TPCA was passed, the Privy Council Office tried to get the Department of Health and Welfare to hire von Maerestetten, who had been RBH's spokesperson, as the Department's head of communications. Health and Welfare steadfastly refused. At a minimum, the recommendation to place a former tobacco-industry apologist in the Health Department showed the government's lack of sensitivity to the tobacco issue.

Illegal advertising

When the tobacco industry's voluntary code was in place, violations by tobacco companies were commonplace. Even after restrictions on tobacco advertising became law, the industry's behaviour was hardly exemplary. Tobacco manufacturers were responsible for numerous violations of the Act, but only a few charges were laid, and none of these charges had made it to trial by the end of 1995. Examples of violations included placing large displays of packages at retail when the packages were not intended for sale; placing tobacco ads at retail, when such ads were not allowed; placing promotional inserts in packages for a new brand; using cigarette brand names on nontobacco goods such as lighters and cigarette papers; including free calendars with cigarettes; and placing price-discount information on packages when such extraneous information was not permitted.[131] Notwithstanding this list, the companies maintain that they have always been in full compliance with the TPCA, sometimes (but not always) providing alternative interpretations of the Act.

Economic consequences of the advertising ban

The TPCA made significant progress toward reducing tobacco promotions, despite problems with illegal advertising and the far bigger problems with sponsorship promotions (see Chapter 8). Despite dire forecasts of the devastating economic impact that would be caused by Bill C-51, no such adverse impact ever materialized. Seven years after the Act was passed, industry profits stood at record levels. Despite American cigarette ads continuing to appear in American magazines, imports from the United States actually went down, with sales at less than 1% of the overall market.[560] Though CTMC had told a parliamentary committee in 1987 that Bill C-51 threatened up to 25 000 Canadian jobs,[86] there is no credible evidence that the TPCA has been responsible for any job losses.

Advertising firms did not suffer the disaster that had been predicted. In 1995, the President of the Outdoor Advertising Association of Canada, Bob Reaume, wrote a letter to the editor of *Marketing* magazine, stating that

> the *Tobacco Products Control Act* was arguably one of the best things to ever happen to our industry. It so drove our members to develop other advertising categories that, today, packaged goods clients, not tobacco, are our largest spending group, and the loss of tobacco revenues has been completely recouped and then some.[482]

Canadian Advertising Foundation Vice-president Suzanne Keeler told Kentucky's [Louisville] *Courier-Journal* that ad agencies had not suffered either. "There was concern ... that if ads for this product are banned it would lead to other bans," she said, adding that so far that had not happened.[635, p. 4] The Chairman of Magazines Canada, which represents the magazines with the largest circulation, said the ad ban "wasn't calamitous."[635, p. 4]

Industry begins legal challenge

Having been defeated in Parliament, the industry quickly shifted its attack to the courts. Within 10 weeks of parliamentary passage of the TPCA in 1988, all three companies had filed separate challenges to the Act. RBH launched a claim in the Federal Court, claiming that the Act was an unconstitutional infringement of freedom of expression as protected by the *Canadian Charter of Rights and Freedoms* and that the Act infringed on the author-ity of the provincial governments. CCS applied for and was given status as an intervenor, a role opposed by RBH.

This case never got off the ground, however. Instead, the legal dispute focused on the cases filed in the Quebec Superior Court by RJR–Macdonald and Imperial Tobacco. The position of these companies was similar to that of RBH, except that RJR–Macdonald also asserted that the health warnings were unconstitutional. RJR–Macdonald argued that it was being forced to say something with which it disagreed and that the warnings should be attributed to the government. The tobacco companies and their platoon of high-priced lawyers had been preparing for months. In contrast, the government was initially poorly prepared to defend the law, having been preoccupied with both the passage of the Act and the drafting of regulations under it. Tobacco companies tried a procedure to get a quick judgment, but that failed. The government now had more time to prepare its case.

An attempt by CCS to obtain intervenor status in the Quebec cases was rejected by Jean-Jude Chabot, the judge assigned to hear the case. Chabot had described parts of the CCS declaration in support of its position as smacking of a "puritanism and intolerance that is relentlessly irritating."[308, p. 560]

The Imperial Tobacco and RJR–Macdonald cases were heard together. The trial took 13 months. There were 28 witnesses (mostly experts) and more than 10 000 pages of tes-timony. The 560 exhibits were lengthy enough to fill a floor-to-ceiling bookshelf.[505] Walking into the courtroom, one would see filing cabinets lining both sides. Six lawyers were visibly working for the industry at one time, some with laptops; other lawyers came in on other days, depending on who the witnesses were. Some lawyers, including Ameri-cans, were in the back of the room, and other lawyers had a role to play elsewhere. The government responded with its own team of lawyers from both the Department of Justice and the private sector.

As part of the trial process, the government had access to tobacco-company market-ing documents. The small fraction of these that made it onto the trial record, and thus into the public realm, provided unprecedented insight into tobacco company strategies. Gov-ernment lawyers used these documents to contradict industry claims that they do not direct advertising to young people and that advertising does not seek to increase smoking.

Project Viking, a 1986 report prepared for Imperial Tobacco, talks explicitly in the foreword about expanding the market:

Background and Objectives

It is no exaggeration to suggest that the tobacco industry is under siege. The smoker base is declining, primarily as a function of successful quitting. And the char-acteristics of new smokers are changing such that the future starting level may be in question. ...

Within this somewhat alarming view of the mid-term program, Imperial Tobacco is embarking on a proactive program. Perhaps for the first time, the mandate under consideration is not limited simply to maximizing ITL franchises; it is now to include as well serious attempts to combat those forces aligned in an attempt to significantly diminish the size of the tobacco market in Canada.

This is the underpinning of Project Viking. There are, in fact, two components of the program, each having its own purposes, but also overlapping with the other in informational areas:

- ✦ Project Pearl is directed at expanding the market, or at very least forestalling its decline. It examines attitudes and issues with the potential to be addressed via advocacy. It also looks at the needs of smokers specifically.
- ✦ Project Day represents the tactical end by which ITL may achieve competitive gains within the market of today and in the future. Unmet needs of smokers that could be satisfied by new or modified products, products which could delay the quitting process, are pursued.[124, pp. 1–2]

One section of volume II of *Project Viking* begins "The ability to reassure smokers, to keep them in the franchise for as long as possible, is the focal point here."[125, p. 31] Smokers are classified in five groups: "Smokers with a Disease Concern," "Leave Me Alone," "Pressured," "Seriously Like to Quit," and "Not Enjoying Smoking/Smoking Less Now." Under "Pressured," the following appears:

> The final group of smokers does deserve particular attention as it is most vulnerable to quitting and is in urgent need of reassurance and stroking. It involves a similar proportion to the previous group [Leave Me Alone], one-quarter of smokers and 10 percent of the adult population.[125, pp. 33–34]

In volume I, the following appears under "Unsuccessful Quitters":

> Probably this is the most important group to examine. It is comprised of people in turmoil in the final stages of smoking. The extent to which they can be reassured and satisfied has a major impact on the extension of a viable tobacco industry.[124, p. 60]

In the mid-1980s, RJR-Macdonald also decided to fight back against declining tobacco industry sales:

> Key Issue #1 — Decline in Industry Volume ...
> Objectives
> a) Achieve stability of industry volume by directing all business efforts, including both our marketing and sales programs as well as our external corporate relations, towards this end.[494, p. 25]

Excerpts from other documents of both companies indicate how important advertising is to maintaining the social acceptability of smoking:

> Without price differentials and without easily perceptible product differentiation (except for extremes, e.g. Matinée versus Player's) consumer choice is influenced almost entirely by imagery factors.
> — Imperial Tobacco Ltd, confidential "1971 Matinée Marketing Plans"[292, p. 7]

> When image advertising [for Player's Filter] is used in response to specific regional strategies, creative will continue to reflect a lifestyle realization of youthful self-expression, independence and freedom with subject matter that is particularly relevant to **young males** [emphasis in original].
> — Imperial Tobacco Ltd, "Creative Guidelines," circa 1979[294, p. 5]

All lifestyle images in Player's ads will promote the social acceptability of smoking where appropriate. Scenarios and settings for the lifestyle imagery will be selected to invite the reader to associate a Player's brand with a pleasant peer group situation where product usage can be seen to be appropriate, acceptable and enjoyable.

— Imperial Tobacco Ltd, "Creative Guidelines," circa 1979[294, p. 3]

Role of lifestyle is to
... Promote and reinforce the social acceptability among the peer group to smoking as a relaxing, enjoyable self-indulgence [emphasis as in original].

— Imperial Tobacco Ltd, "Creative Guidelines," circa 1979[294, p. 13]

The Export smoker must also be constantly reassured that it is alright to smoke. **Especially** Export [emphasis as in original].

— RJR–Macdonald Inc., "Export Family Draft
Brand Positioning Statement," 1986[496, p. 2]

du Maurier (red)
F '81 Advertising Strategies
1. To continue to develop advertising that reflects a contemporary quality image, by ensuring that all advertising reflects a contemporary, perhaps even avant-garde, lifestyle and materialism to which the target market would aspire to.

— Imperial Tobacco Ltd, "du Maurier Trademark
[Fiscal] '81 Advertising"[307, p. 14]

Advertising Objectives [Player's Filter]
1. To communicate that the brand is for those who make their own choice about what they do, for people who want to assert their own individuality, and who are seeking a more independent lifestyle.

— Spitzer, Mills & Bates, "The Player's Family: A Working Paper
Prepared for Imperial Tobacco," 1977[554, p. 13]

When Justice Chabot rendered his judgment on 26 July 1991, these excerpts were not discussed anywhere in his reasons.[500] To the shock of health groups, Chabot declared the TPCA unconstitutional and accepted each of the industry's arguments. Chabot ruled that the ban on tobacco advertising infringed constitutional protection of freedom of expression and that the infringement could not be justified as a reasonable limit. He also decided that a tobacco advertising ban was a provincial responsibility and could not be implemented by the federal government. He further ruled that the health warnings were unconstitutional because they unjustifiably violated tobacco manufacturers' right to silence.

Health groups immediately called on the government to appeal, and many health organizations from outside Canada wrote to the Prime Minister with the same request. Within a few weeks, the government filed an appeal. Nevertheless, an elated industry was claiming victory on all fronts. The industry wasted no time in publicizing the court's ruling around the world, including in the European Union, where a tobacco advertising ban was being considered. When boasting about the decision, the industry failed to mention that the judgment was under appeal or that the advertising ban remained in force pending the appeal.

On 15 January 1993, the Quebec Court of Appeal reversed the trial court decision.[501] By a majority of 2 to 1, the court decided that the ad ban was a reasonable limit on freedom of expression because the government had provided sufficient evidence that a ban on advertising would reduce smoking. Unanimously, the court ruled that the health warnings were constitutional and the ad ban was within federal authority. This time, it was health groups that were overjoyed.

The Supreme Court of Canada

The industry appealed to the Supreme Court of Canada, and the case was heard in November 1994 before a full court of nine judges. Over the objections of the industry, five health groups were collectively given intervenor status in the case.

When the case was argued in the Supreme Court, the tobacco industry had seven lawyers in gowns. On top of this, another 15 or so industry lawyers and PR representatives from Canada and the United States kept an eagle eye on the proceedings from the back of the room. The industry was present with a small portion of its usual "wall of flesh." On the other side of the courtroom, the government had five lawyers of its own. Health groups had three. Seated behind them were a dozen representatives of health organizations. Clearly, both sides recognized that a lot was at stake.

The Supreme Court released its judgment on 21 September 1995.[503] The court unanimously ruled that a ban on tobacco advertising was within federal responsibility and was not exclusively a provincial responsibility. However, and more important, the Court ruled by a narrow 5 to 4 decision that the ban on tobacco advertising was an unjustified infringement of the *Canadian Charter of Rights and Freedoms.*

The majority held that the objective of reducing smoking was a valid objective and that because advertising could increase consumption, a ban on tobacco advertising advanced the government's objective. However, the majority held that the government had failed to demonstrate why a total ban, rather than a partial ban, was necessary. The majority indicated that it would have upheld partial restrictions consisting of a ban on lifestyle advertising and a ban on advertising directed at minors.

In contrast, the minority held that the government had introduced ample evidence to demonstrate that a total ban was necessary, noting that "in countries where governments have instituted partial prohibitions upon tobacco advertising, ... the tobacco companies have developed ingenious tactics to circumvent the restrictions."[503, p. 311]

The majority ruled that the government had failed to introduce evidence to demonstrate that attributed health warnings would be any less effective than unattributed warnings. The minority disagreed, holding that unattributed warnings were constitutionally valid, citing in support common sense and expert opinion.

One excerpt from the Court's judgment, endorsed by a majority of six justices, is worth repeating:

> Perhaps the most compelling evidence concerning the connection between advertising and consumption can be found in the internal marketing documents prepared by the tobacco manufacturers themselves. Although the appellants [the tobacco manufacturers] steadfastly argue that their marketing efforts are directly solely at maintaining and expanding brand loyalty among adult smokers, these documents show otherwise. In particular, the following general conclusions can be drawn from these documents: the tobacco companies are concerned about a shrinking tobacco market and recognize that an 'advocacy thrust' is necessary to maintain the size of the overall market; the companies understand that, in order to maintain the overall numbers of smokers, they must reassure current smokers and make their product attractive to the young and to non-smokers; they also recognize that advertising is critical to maintaining the size of the market because it serves to reinforce the social acceptability of smoking by identifying it with glamour, affluence, youthfulness and vitality.[503, p. 295]

Nonetheless, the final result was that the Court declared unconstitutional the sections of the TPCA concerning advertising, warnings, and the use of tobacco trademarks on non-tobacco goods. The few remaining parts of the TPCA — the provisions dealing with the ban on free distribution of tobacco products, the ban on incentive promotions, and reporting requirements for manufacturers — remained intact.

The Court's judgment proved to be very controversial. Although there were those who supported the judgment, significant criticism came from the health community, many members of the public, and numerous newspaper editorials. Said Janice Forsythe, Executive Director of CCSH, "The big losers as a result of the Supreme Court decision are Canada's children. ... The only winner is an industry which already reaps record profits from addicting its consumers." The judgment was a major setback for antismoking forces.

Naturally, the industry was exuberant with its victory. Regardless of how much the industry spent on legal fees to defeat the law — and the amount was in the millions — the industry received far greater value in return. Apart from striking down the key parts of the law, the court case delayed implementation of many additional reforms for tobacco control. Delayed reforms included requiring plain packaging, closing down the sponsorship loophole, and revising the initial round of health warnings under the TPCA. Once the Supreme Court decision was released, it was quickly cited by the tobacco industry when lobbying to prevent advertising restrictions in other parts of the world, including Hong Kong and the Unites States.

The federal government strikes back

On 11 December 1995, less than 3 months after the Supreme Court's decision, Health Minister Diane Marleau responded forcefully. She released a tobacco-control blueprint containing a comprehensive set of legislative measures.[239] Notwithstanding the Supreme Court's judgment, the blueprint proposed a total ban on tobacco advertising. Marleau said that the government would present the evidence that the majority said was missing to justify a total ban. The blueprint also proposed to do the following:

✦ Establish a legislative framework that would give the government authority over tobacco similar to what is found under the *Hazardous Products Act* and the *Food and Drugs Act*;

✦ Place significant new restrictions on sponsorship promotions, but stop short of a complete ban;

✦ Ban the use of tobacco trademarks on nontobacco goods;

✦ Ban mail-order sales and counter-top displays;

✦ Limit point-of-sale product displays to one sample package per product;

✦ Expand toxic-constituent information on packaging and increase manufacturer reporting requirements; and

✦ Create authority to implement plain packaging and regulate product design [but no specific measures were proposed].

As can be expected, health groups heaped praise on the Minister. Implementing the blueprint's measures would restore Canada's international leadership role in terms of tobacco-control legislation. Tobacco manufacturers criticized the plan, saying that the measures may not be possible in light of the Supreme Court's decision. Many arts organizations came out strongly against the restrictions on sponsorship advertising.

On 19 December 1995, shortly after the release of the blueprint, CTMC announced a new voluntary code restricting advertising. Once again, the industry was attempting to use self-regulation as a means to stave off government legislation. This new code prohibited tobacco advertising on radio and television, prohibited people in ads (but permitted other forms of lifestyle advertising), required advertising to be directed to adults, required advertising only to be for the purpose of increasing or maintaining market share, prohibited advertising within 200 metres of school entrances, and required a warning attributed to Health Canada at the bottom 15%–20% of ads. Many of the provisions were similar to those contained in the previous code. However, in contrast with the old code, sponsorship promotions were permitted on television.

Following release of the blueprint, the government opened a public consultation period. Written submissions could be submitted until 31 January 1996, with legislation to be introduced at some point after that. Opposing sides of the debate geared themselves for a major battle. The progress of the fight, to the extent known when this book went to press, is included in the Postscript.

Examples of tobacco ads

Men who fight for Canada on sea or land or air, lead a hard life . . . harder than most civilians can imagine. The little luxuries mean a lot to these men and the little luxuries are not easily come by in war-time Europe. That's why we appeal again for your support of:

THE OVERSEAS LEAGUE TOBACCO FUND
51 King St. East, Toronto

$1 to them means 400 cigarettes delivered to a sailor, soldier or airman who really needs them. So won't you send a subscription — as large as you can make it, today!

1943

Sometimes, you want now to last forever.
That's why Benson & Hedges 100's gives you more
to enjoy. More smoking mildness than you can
get from an ordinary king size cigarette.
And they're still the same price as ordinary kings.

**The longer the cigarette,
the smoother the smoke.
Benson & Hedges 100's.**

CONTEMPORARY TASTE — Precision. Flair. Intrigue. Presented for contemporary tastes. Vantage has the right combination of taste and enjoyment in a range of mild cigarettes. Now you don't have to compromise when it comes to smoking. Because Vantage has the taste for today. Vantage. Vantage Lights. Vantage Menthol Lights.

● VANTAGE. THE CONTEMPORARY CHOICE.

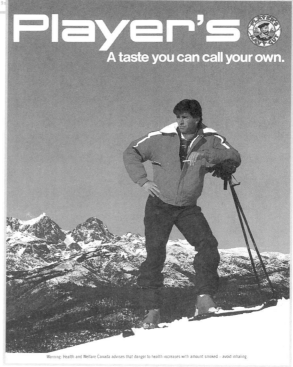

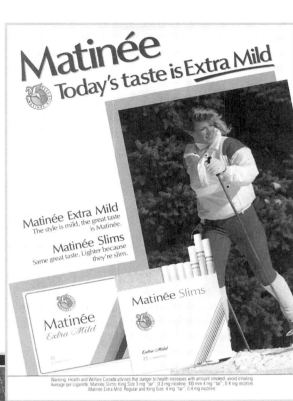

CHAPTER 8

Sponsorships: Buying Credibility

Alan King, *The Ottawa Citizen*

The impact of sponsorships

Tobacco sponsorship of sporting and cultural events — event marketing — is an extremely sophisticated and effective form of tobacco promotion. The following excerpt from a *Maclean's* report describes just how valuable sponsorships can be:

> [Imperial Tobacco] company officials said that they value the golf connection — including sponsorship of the $600,000 du Maurier Classic on the pro women's circuit — because that helps to instil confidence in a brand and spurs positive associations in smokers' minds with a so-called upscale event. Said Imperial president Wilmat Tennyson: 'If you stay with it long enough, the benefits are enormous because you are conveying a message to people that is much more memorable'. Donald Brown, Imperial's vice-president of marketing, said that even less affluent smokers may favor the brand because of its link with a comfortable lifestyle and because that 'says something about you'.[373]

In 1977, an executive with The Houston Group expressed a similar view: "Advertising is what you say about yourself. Sponsorship is what other people say about you."[92, p. 14] RBH spokesperson von Maerestetten stated that "basically it [sponsorship] is part and parcel with the marketing of your product. It is one of a range of tools. No one hands over big cheques just to give themselves a warm fuzzy feeling."[450]

Sponsoring an event can give a brand tremendous exposure. A study for CCSH found that sponsorship ads in Ottawa–Hull stores selling tobacco resulted in 280 million exposures (people seeing the ads) a year.[634] In a different study, Physicians for a Smoke-Free Canada taped a televised broadcast of a car race held in the streets of Halifax, Nova Scotia. During the 58.5-minute broadcast, the Player's Ltd name and logo were seen 580 times. The name was easily visible for 9 minutes and 4 seconds of the broadcast. The Sports Network covered the event on a tape-delayed basis, broadcasting the race on Saturday morning (when many children watch television) and rebroadcasting the race on three other occasions.[475] Clearly, sponsorship advertising is a way to get massive television exposure for a brand despite purported bans on tobacco advertising on TV.

In 1994 a national Youth Smoking Survey commissioned by Health Canada asked those 10–19 years old about the purpose of billboards and signs for sporting and cultural events sponsored by tobacco corporations. Fully 85% of smokers and 83% of nonsmokers agreed that these "billboards and signs are a way of advertising particular brands of cigarettes." Some 43% of smokers and 58% of nonsmokers agreed that these "billboards and signs are a way of encouraging people to smoke."[240]

Sponsorship lends social acceptability to smoking and neutralizes health concerns held by consumers. Tobacco companies associate their products with healthy and desirable activities, instead of with disease and death. Furthermore, no warnings have appeared on these promotions, as is required by law in the United States.

The industry openly acknowledges that sponsorship promotions are a form of brand advertising, but it denies that overall smoking increases as a result.[97] However, if sponsorships did not increase overall smoking, tobacco companies would not oppose a legislated ban on sponsorship. That way each company could save millions of dollars without worrying that other companies would be trying to take away its market share. Sponsorship advertising is the purest form of lifestyle advertising.

Sponsored events give tobacco executives a forum in which to win new friends, exert influence, and improve a tarnished image. Politicians and other elites are frequently invited as guests. For example, all Ottawa municipal councillors were given free passes to a 1994 du Maurier Ltd Classic golf tournament.

Tobacco companies defend their sponsorships on the basis of freedom, yet they do not always practice what they preach. In 1994, Cathy Rudick, Executive Director of Physicians for a Smoke-Free Canada, submitted an advertisement for the program of the du Maurier Ltd Classic golf tournament, the Canadian Open for women. The advertisement presented a factual message: "Last year cigarettes killed twice as many women as breast cancer. Physicians for a Smoke-Free Canada." The ad was rejected because du Maurier officials concluded the ad was "inappropriate for the sponsor and the event itself."[175] The advertising director at *Score* magazine, responsible for putting the program together, said the ad was

clearly detrimental to what the sponsor is trying to achieve. Look, there's no doubt about why companies like du Maurier get involved in sponsorships like this — they do it to get exposure for their brands. It simply doesn't make sense for them to carry an ad that contradicts those objectives.[175]

Streetlight poles along the Ottawa roads leading to the tournament site bore red banners promoting the du Maurier Ltd Classic. When Physicians for a Smoke-Free Canada put up their own "Cigarettes kill women" posters on poles, tournament personnel took the posters down, even though the poles were on municipal property.

In 1995, Cynthia Callard, the new Executive Director of Physicians for a Smoke-Free Canada, entered a team in a white-water rafting race sponsored by Canadian Classics Adventures Inc. Canadian Classics was a new cigarette brand with packages featuring a nature scene of forest and mountains. Callard and her five teammates wore T-shirts saying "Smoke Screen Team" with a picture of a broken cigarette and the message "Promote Health Not Tobacco." Even though the T-shirts would have been covered by life jackets, event organizers disqualified the team to ensure the race was "safe, professional and fun."[374]

Sponsorship advertising explodes

During the parliamentary debate over Bill C-51, one of the most troublesome issues for the government was tobacco-company sponsorship of arts and sports events. Arts and sports organizations spoke out against the Bill, thus giving opposition to the Bill a degree of credibility that the tobacco lobby alone could never provide. The possibility that these events would be adversely affected was something that manufacturers exploited, generating some public and political sympathy.

The final version of the TPCA banned tobacco advertising, but exceptions permitted certain forms of sponsorship promotion, in essence a form of tobacco advertising. The TPCA permitted promotion of sponsorships using a corporate name, provided this was not done "in association with a tobacco product," with the onus on the advertiser to show no such association.

Tobacco companies moved rapidly to take advantage of this exception, something they saw as a major loophole. Even before the Act came into force, Imperial Tobacco incorporated new shell companies, naming them Player's Ltd, du Maurier Ltd, and Matinée Ltd. RJR–Macdonald soon established Export "A" Inc.; RBH created Rothmans Ltd, Craven "A" Ltd, and Benson & Hedges Inc.[63] These new companies would do nothing except lend their names to sponsored events.

While Bill C-51 was being debated, Wilmat Tennyson, President of Imperial Tobacco, said on TVOntario that his company would not create companies named after brands because this would be "sleazy" and "I don't want to do that."[133] Given the speedy creation of shell companies, it is evident Tennyson's promise was not kept.

Because of the shell companies, tobacco sponsorships existing before the TPCA was enacted continued uninterrupted. Over time, sponsorship promotions became so widespread that the advertising ban in the TPCA was significantly undermined.

Whether or not the letter of the law was infringed, the array of sponsorship advertising infringed the spirit of the Act. Tobacco companies spent about $10 million on sponsorship in 1987.[86] In 1991, according to the industry, that amount had risen to more than $40 million.[88] By 1995, Imperial Tobacco said it alone was spending $35–40 million on sponsorships.[109] Just as in 1972 the industry shifted its advertising expenses from radio and television to other media, after the 1989 ban on advertising, the industry shifted its advertising expenses to sponsorship promotions.

The events sponsored have fit nicely with a brand's image. Export "A" Inc. and Player's Ltd, both of which have targeted young males, have sponsored car racing and other sports. Matinée, a predominantly women's brand, has sponsored fashion shows. The Matinée Ltd Fashion Foundation donated $500 000 to fashion designers but seemed to be spending more than this publicizing its donations. Other sponsorships have included auto racing by Rothmans Ltd, fireworks by Benson & Hedges Inc., and country music by Craven "A" Ltd. Some ads promoting Craven "A" Ltd country music have pictured a carefree, energetic young couple, just as lifestyle cigarette ads did before the TPCA was enacted.

du Maurier, which has an upscale status image, has sponsored professional golf and tennis tournaments, jazz festivals, and various arts events through du Maurier Ltd. Historically, du Maurier cigarettes have always been associated with the performing arts. The brand gets its name from Sir Gerald du Maurier, "a leading personality in theatre and a society trend-setter in the early nineteen hundreds," according to Imperial Tobacco.[299, p. 9] In the 1960s, some du Maurier advertising featured stars such as Robert Goulet (TV, movies, records) and Fred Davis (host of *Front Page Challenge*).[379] In 1970, Imperial created the du Maurier Council for the Arts and decided to use arts sponsorship in an effort to revitalize the brand.

Sponsorship promotions use colour combinations similar to those on cigarette packages: blue for Player's, red for du Maurier, yellow for Matinée, and so on. Logos for sponsored events are typically a variation of brand logos. The largest word in the promotion is typically the cigarette brand name or the name of the shell company, for example, Player's Ltd. Some promotions have not even had details of the sponsored event, simply stating "Player's Ltd" in brand colours. Sponsorship promotions have been regularly placed in stores alongside cigarettes and signs indicating the price of cigarettes. So much for not being "in association with a tobacco product."

Sponsorship promotions have appeared everywhere, including on transit vehicles that transport thousands of children to school daily. Some promotions are strategically placed to gain substantial TV exposure, such as on National Hockey League scoreboards overhanging centre ice or in the outfield at Olympic Stadium, where the Montreal Expos play baseball. Sponsorship promotions have even appeared directly as television commercials, despite the fact that they had been previously prohibited under the voluntary code between 1975 and 1988.

A way to eliminate sponsorships

Some groups on the receiving end of tobacco sponsorships have said that they would be unable to do without tobacco money. These fears may be unjustified. For example, during parliamentary hearings on Bill C-51, the Royal Canadian Golf Association stated that it would not be able to replace Imperial Tobacco as sponsor of its Canadian Open men's golf tournament.[218] Yet today the event continues successfully with Bell Canada as the title sponsor instead of du Maurier.

A Tennis Canada spokesperson stated in 1988, just after Bill C-51 was passed by the House of Commons, that replacing Imperial Tobacco as sponsor for the Canadian Open would not compromise the survival of the tournament. "We know other companies want to organize the event," he said.[46] Given the history, success, and prestige of the tournament, this is hardly surprising. Notwithstanding this one-time statement from its spokesperson, Tennis Canada normally maintains that Imperial Tobacco cannot be replaced. A new nontobacco sponsor for tennis is highly desirable, especially because the women's half of the tournament typically has several star teenagers competing. Young sports idols widely admired by teenage girls are being used to promote cigarettes, despite the fact that those players are too young to be sold cigarettes.

Health groups do not object to purely philanthropic donations by tobacco companies, but they do not want these contributions to promote a lethal product. Recognizing that a ban on tobacco sponsorships may affect some groups, the government has some options. Government funding could replace tobacco funding, possibly requiring the events to be named after a "Quit" (antismoking) theme as in Australia. Money for the government contributions could come from a special tax on tobacco-company profits. A variation of this would be to levy a one-time lump-sum tax on tobacco companies of $300–$500 million to create a permanent endowment to fund arts and sports. Canada's tobacco industry is clearly capable of paying this tax, especially when the companies would be permanently relieved of future sponsorship spending. One way or another, sponsorship promotions must come to an end.

CHAPTER 9

Warnings:
Getting the Health Message Across

Brian Gable, *Globe and Mail*, Toronto

New health warnings: round one

Once the TPCA had been passed on 28 June 1988, regulations requiring new health warnings were needed before the Act came into force on 1 January 1989. Warnings had the potential to add teeth to the legislation. On 29 July 1988, just weeks after the Act was passed, Health and Welfare Canada sent the tobacco companies a memorandum concerning the proposed warnings and requesting "comments and suggestions."[367] The memorandum was not distributed to health groups, thus giving the industry an unimpeded lobbying opportunity.

The government's initial proposals were significant. They included four warnings for cigarettes, one of which was a warning about addiction. Warnings were to be in place by 1 July 1989, were to be displayed in a striking circle and arrow format, and were to cover 30% of the front and back of the package. Billboards permitted during the phase-out period would also have to carry a warning in the circle and arrow format covering 30% of the sign. For smokeless tobacco, three rotated warnings would be required.

Tobacco lobbyist Neville went to work. On 17 August 1988, he wrote to the Chief of Legislative and Regulatory Processes at Health and Welfare Canada. In his letter, Neville asked 19 questions seeking details on the government's proposals and suggested a meeting on 23 August.[432] On 24 August, a day after this meeting date, J.R. Hickman, Acting Director General of the Environmental Health Directorate, sent a memo to Bert Liston, Assistant Deputy Minister of the Health Protection Branch. The memo proposed the content of the new warnings, but the addiction warning and the circle and arrow format had been dropped.[272]

On 31 August, Neville, on behalf of CTMC, submitted a detailed written response to the government's proposals of 29 July. In his covering letter, he requested that the document be kept confidential, stating that "it would be highly detrimental to our discussions at this stage if correspondence and related memoranda were to be made public before the consultative process is complete and the final regulations proclaimed."[433, pp. 1–2] In the submission, CTMC objected to the addiction warning, saying that it "trivializes the serious drug problems faced by our society."[87, p. 7] CTMC objected to the size of the proposed warnings because it showed "no respect for the integrity of our packaging."[87, p. 2] CTMC also objected to the warnings because they didn't indicate that the government was the author, as in "Health and Welfare Canada advises that … ."[87] A federal election was called on 1 October 1988. Neville then took up his duties as election strategist for the Progressive Conservatives.

As the election campaign progressed, the bureaucracy still did not disclose to health groups what had been disclosed to the tobacco industry. The groups could not meet with the Minister because of the election campaign.

On 7 November 1988 the government released draft regulations, and for the first time health groups were informed of the proposals.[368] However, the key decisions to weaken the regulations had already been made. The final version of the warnings, which was released in January 1989 and was in some respects further weakened, contained these provisions:

- ✦ On cigarettes and roll-your-own tobacco, there would be four rotated messages: "Smoking reduces life expectancy," "Smoking is the major cause of lung cancer," "Smoking is a major cause of heart disease," and "Smoking during pregnancy can harm the baby."

- ✦ The warnings would appear at the bottom 20% [down from the 30% proposed earlier] of the front and back of the package — English on one side, French on the other.

- ✦ The message was to be "legible and prominently displayed in contrasting colours."

- ✦ Packages of smokeless tobacco required only one warning, "This product can cause mouth cancer" [three rotating warnings had been proposed earlier].

◆ Packages of cigars and pipe tobacco required one of two messages: "This product
   can cause mouth cancer" and "This product is not a safe alternative to cigarettes."

When the final regulations were released, health groups slammed the government for not
including an addiction warning and for a general weakness in the regulations. Tobacco-
industry lobbying had won a victory at the expense of more health information for consumers. Clearly, though, the situation could have been worse. The new warnings were still
the largest and most prominent in the world. Further, the warnings were not attributed to
Health and Welfare Canada, something the industry had fought to have included.

It was not until June 1989 that health groups discovered how much industry lobbying had occurred in the early stages of regulatory development. NSRA obtained the relevant
documents under the *Access to Information Act* and released them to the media. The new
Health Minister, Perrin Beatty, came under heavy criticism, even though he had not been
Health Minister at the time regulations were being prepared. Beatty announced that the
government had commissioned a study to determine whether smoking was addictive and
that the results would influence the second round of regulations. This prompted media
criticism that the government was wasting money trying to ascertain something so
obvious.

During the summer of 1989, the first packages with new warnings arrived on the
market. Tobacco companies chose colour combinations for the warnings that minimized
their prominence and blended in with existing package design. On Medallion cigarettes,
for example, gold lettering appeared on a yellow background. On other packages, warnings were simply not discernible from some angles. Beatty, a former Minister of Defence,
quipped, "if our experts [at National Defence] knew as much about camouflage as the
tobacco company did, nobody'd ever find our fellows."[80] The industry abbreviated the
carbon monoxide listing to CO, a meaningless term to many Canadians.

On many packages, the industry used a white background for the scannable bar code
but not for the health warning. The industry was thus prepared to use stark colour con-
trasts for electronic eyes but not for messages intended for less-sophisticated human eyes.

Before the passage of the TPCA, the industry had said that it would take at least
2 years to complete the repackaging of all existing brands.[86] Once the text of the new
warnings was announced, though, the redesign of the packages was completed within
10 months and could have been done in even less time.

New warnings: round two

In response to the way industry printed the new warnings, health groups seized the initiative and started to lobby for stronger warnings in the second round of regulations. The
health lobby was aided by a Royal Society of Canada report supporting the use of *addictive*
when describing nicotine.[530] Neville had been threatening legal action if the government
decided to require an addiction warning, but the report undermined this threat.

In January 1990, Beatty announced that the government would put revised regulations into effect in July 1991. There would be eight rotated warnings, including one on addiction and one on ETS. The proposals would set a number of world precedents:

◆ Warnings would cover the top 25% of the front and back of the package.

◆ Warnings would be in black and white, not in the package colours.

◆ The colour combinations for each warning would alternate between black on white and white on black.

◆ Warnings would cover 25% of all six sides of a carton.

◆ The addiction warning would be included [for the first time in a major tobacco market].

◆ Inserts providing more detailed health information would be required in packages.

Beatty could be proud of his announcement. As usual, though, implementation of the new regulations was easier said than done. The industry argued that the new measures represented "economic and administrative harassment" because new warnings had just been put in place.[318] CTMC said that because there was no proof that the proposed revisions would be any more effective, there was no justification for tobacco companies incurring further expense. In addition, the industry decried the cost of including inserts.[435] CTMC asserted that "any attempt to brand six million Canadians who choose to smoke as 'addicts' is insulting and irresponsible."[435, p. 6] CTMC stated that "we do not accept that there is any credible or reliable scientific evidence to establish that environmental tobacco smoke (ETS) constitutes a genuine health hazard to non-smokers."[435, p. 6] The use of black and white was said to be "a direct infringement" of trademarks.[435, p. 11]

The industry also argued that smokers were already well aware of the risks of smoking and that revised warnings were unnecessary. Although tobacco companies for decades had denied the evidence against smoking, they still said that everyone (or at least everyone but themselves) knew the health consequences of smoking.

However, there was ample evidence that the public was unaware of or underestimated the health risks. Imperial Tobacco regularly surveyed smokers on their beliefs about the health consequences of smoking. One study done for Imperial Tobacco in 1986 showed that smokers and former smokers had a particular lack of knowledge. When asked to volunteer what they knew about the smoking and health relationship, only 13% mentioned cancer, 14% mentioned a respiratory-related item, and 5% mentioned the dangers of second-hand smoke. Although most people mentioned one health effect or another, 23% said there was no relationship between smoking and health. When prompted with statements, only 55% of smokers agreed that "life expectancy of a smoker is less." Similarly, only 55% were "concerned about effects of smoking on me." Only 66% thought that emphysema was associated with smoking, and only 50% thought stroke was associated with smoking. However, 96% agreed that lung cancer was associated with smoking.[124]

The argument the industry emphasized most was that it was in the middle of its legal challenge to the constitutionality of the TPCA: the industry objected to the amending of regulations while the matter was before the courts. The Department of Justice was of the view that there were no legal impediments to amending the regulations; nevertheless, it recommended against amendments until the Quebec Superior Court released a favourable judgment. Health Canada accepted this advice. However, in July 1991, the Court declared the legislation and the existing warnings unconstitutional. This dealt a devastating blow to plans to strengthen warnings. The government indicated that new warnings were "dead in the water."

The health groups would not take no for an answer. NSRA and the Heart and Stroke Foundation led a major campaign to have the revisions implemented. They noted that the TPCA remained in full force and effect pending the appeal. Opinions were sought from major law firms, and the conclusion was that there was no legal barrier to amending the regulations while the Court decision was being appealed. The groups met with departmental officials and had several meetings with Health Minister Benoît Bouchard. Bouchard was a strong supporter of improved warnings.

To gain more support at the Cabinet table, health groups wrote to every household in the ridings of each member of the Cabinet committee that would consider the new regulations. This initiative, designed to reach 1 million people, was announced at a news conference, which in turn drew further attention to the campaign. The groups met with as many of the ministers on the Cabinet committee, or their staff, as possible. A poll by health groups found that 89% of Canadians supported an addiction warning and 83% supported package inserts. Of 12 possible warnings, respondents ranked the addiction warning as the most effective.[310] The federal government commissioned its own study and found that the proposed new warning format at the package top was overwhelmingly preferred by smokers when compared with the existing format.[579]

Eventually, in January 1993, the Quebec Court of Appeal released its judgment that the TPCA was constitutional, reversing the lower court decision.[501] Because the government had for so long used the legal uncertainty as the reason for not proceeding with the new warnings, the favourable ruling forced the government to go forward. Bouchard immediately announced that he would move ahead with new regulations. Within 2 months, draft revisions to the regulations were announced. The revisions were along the lines of what Beatty had proposed in 1990, except that the requirement for package inserts was dropped.

Health groups wanted the final regulations in place before the June 1993 Conservative leadership convention because Bouchard would be stepping down at that time. There was fear that with Bouchard's presence at the Cabinet table gone, the warnings would never receive final approval. As it turned out, Bouchard did depart before the regulations were finally approved, but so did some of the other ministers who were very opposed to the revisions.

The date proposed for implementation of the new warnings was September 1993, just 6 months away. When this was announced, manufacturers stopped orders for packages, prompting packaging companies to immediately lay off workers. Manufacturers used the usual "jobs argument" to argue against, or at least delay, new warnings.

After further lobbying from both sides, the final text of revised regulations was announced in July by Mary Collins, the new Health Minister. The final version gave Canada the strongest health warnings in the world, although warnings that were better in some respects would subsequently be introduced in Australia. Canadian warnings were required to appear at the top of the cigarette package, covering 25% of the front and back (Figure 10). A border was to surround the warning, making the effective size of the warning 33%–39%, depending on package size. Messages included one on addiction and two dealing with ETS. Packages of cigarettes and roll-your-own tobacco were required to bear these warnings:

- ✦ "Cigarettes are addictive."
- ✦ "Tobacco smoke can harm your children."
- ✦ "Cigarettes cause fatal lung disease."
- ✦ "Cigarettes cause cancer."
- ✦ "Cigarettes cause strokes and heart disease."
- ✦ "Smoking during pregnancy can harm your baby."
- ✦ "Smoking can kill you."
- ✦ "Tobacco smoke causes fatal lung disease in non-smokers."

The messages had to appear alternately in black on white and white on black, giving a total of 16 message presentations in each official language seen by the consumer. On cigarette cartons, the message "Cigarettes are addictive and cause lung cancer, emphysema and heart disease" had to appear, surrounded by a border, on the top 25% of all six sides. Black lettering on a white background was required. On the side of packages and cartons, *Tar, Nicotine*, and *Carbon Monoxide* had to be spelled out in full and appear in black lettering on a white background under the heading "Toxic Constituents." The original implementation date of 1 September 1993 was extended to 12 September 1994 in response to industry representations.

Having lost the battle over new regulations in Cabinet, the industry again turned to the courts. Imperial and RJR–Macdonald filed motions in the Supreme Court of Canada seeking to block the warnings until 12 months after the Supreme Court ruled on the constitutionality of the TPCA. Four health groups, led by the Heart and Stroke Foundation, appeared before the Court as intervenors to support the government's position.

In a unanimous decision released in March 1994, the nine judges rejected the industry's argument for a delay.[502] The Court said that any cost of implementing new warnings

Figure 10. The evolution of package health warnings. Sample packages illustrating health warnings over time: voluntary warning on the side, 1972–1989 (the words *avoid inhaling* were not included until 1976); warnings on the front/back of package, 1989–1994; warnings at the top of the front/back in black and white, starting in 1994.

could be passed on to consumers:

> Any public interest in maintaining the current price of tobacco products cannot carry much weight. This is particularly so when it is balanced against the undeniable importance of the public interest in health and in the prevention of the widespread and serious medical problems directly attributable to smoking.[502, pp. 353–354]

The prominent Canadian warnings have sparked international interest, and other countries have considered copying what Canada has done. Already, Canada's lead has helped the case for new regulations on warnings in Australia and South Africa. At the Ninth World Conference on Tobacco and Health held in Paris in 1994, many delegates eagerly asked Canadians for sample packages featuring the new warnings.

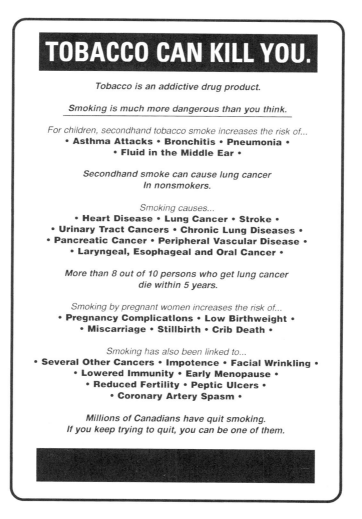

Figure 11. Sign required in New Brunswick stores.

Warnings at point of sale

In 1994, a new trend developed as Canadian provinces started to require health messages in retail stores selling tobacco. This is a very cost-effective way to get a health message out to the public. New Brunswick was first, setting a world precedent by requiring a message with 31 negative points about tobacco (Figure 11). Some other provinces followed New Brunswick's lead and now require their own health-based signs at retail, although the signs are far less comprehensive than the ones in New Brunswick.

CHAPTER 10

Clearing the Air

Historical evolution of smoking restrictions

It is amazing how times have changed. Smoking used to be everywhere. People smoked in the office, on elevators, on city buses, in restrooms, at staff meetings, in university class-rooms. Everywhere. Doctors smoked in front of patients and permitted smoking in waiting rooms. A person recuperating from surgery in a hospital might find that the patient in the next bed was a heavy smoker. The stereotypical journalist chain smoked while pounding away on the typewriter. Television anchors on the evening news might be seen with a stream of cigarette smoke rising by their side. Dr Mary Jane Ashley of the University of Toronto recalls giving an after-dinner talk in a smoke-filled room at the 1968 annual meeting of the North Bay Tuberculosis and Respiratory Disease Association. Smoking occurred at CCS meetings and fund-raising events, even into the late 1980s.

That has changed substantially. By 1994, 39% of Canadians had a completely smoke-free workplace; a further 41% had some smoking restrictions in their working environment. However, the degree of protection varied by province: in Quebec only 25% of people had a completely smoke-free workplace.[235]

Despite the improvement, a lot more progress needs to be made. It is one thing for an adult to choose to smoke, but it is another to force nonsmokers to smoke against their will. Unless indoor ETS is properly restricted, nonsmokers involuntarily inhale toxins and carcinogens. In this context, smoking is not strictly a matter of personal choice.

In Canada, some of the earliest smoking restrictions were a means of preventing fires or explosions. These restrictions were sometimes by order of the fire commissioner, sometimes by municipal bylaw. For example, in 1950 Ottawa prohibited smoking in retail shops with 10 or more employees. Some companies, such as those in the chemicals and food sectors, restricted smoking so that their product remained pure throughout the manufacturing process. The real drive for smoking restrictions started in the first half of the 1970s, when nonsmokers became more assertive about asking smokers not to smoke.

Interestingly, before — and after — smoking restrictions became popular, many restaurants and transit companies posted signs saying "cigarette smoking only" because customers were bothered by the smell of cigar and pipe smoke. Customers bothered by cigarette smoke were not treated so considerately.

In 1971, Air Canada divided seats on some flights into smoking and nonsmoking sections, putting nonsmoking at the front. This led to complaints from some smokers that they were being treated as second-class citizens because they had to sit "at the back of the bus." In 1974, Air Canada changed its policy so that smoking seats were on one side of the aisle and nonsmoking seats were on the other. Not surprisingly, this revised policy was a massive failure and produced a litany of complaints from nonsmokers. The smoking section was moved back to the rear of the plane.

The ordeals of nonsmokers were making headlines. A taxi driver who banned smoking in his taxi was told by a Metro Toronto licencing commission official to permit smoking by passengers or he would lose his taxi licence.[631] A student had to quit university because of smoking in the lecture hall.[326] The Unemployment Insurance Commission docked 3 weeks of benefits from a man who stopped attending a retraining course because he could not tolerate the smoke. The Commission denied his right to appeal because there was "no principle of importance" at stake.[123]

In 1973, North York, Ontario, prohibited smoking in supermarkets, and the Ontario municipalities of Pickering and Scarborough passed similar bylaws the following year. Soon, sprouting up across the country were dozens of local antismoking groups with names like Group Against Smokers' Pollution (GASP) and Society to Overcome Pollution (STOP). GASP organizations were typically affiliated with the Tuberculosis and Respiratory Disease Association, now known as The Lung Association.

In 1973, the Canadian National Railway set aside nonsmoking areas on Rapido trains between Montreal and Toronto. In 1974, the Canadian Motor Coach Association made a voluntary recommendation that the first five rows of buses be nonsmoking.

Also in 1974, private-member's Bill C-242 was introduced in the House of Commons by Liberal Ken Robinson, a Toronto MP, to provide nonsmoking sections in planes, trains, and intercity buses. The Bill, which was similar to one previously introduced by MP Mather, was approved at second reading, was applauded by Health Minister Marc Lalonde, and was the subject of hearings by the Health Committee, but as is the normal fate for a private-member's bill, never received final approval or came to a third-reading vote. Before the Committee, CTMC took the unusual position of not opposing the bill. Perhaps it was too early for the industry to fully realize the implications of smoking restrictions.

One of the most successful antismoking groups at that time was the Ottawa–Hull Nonsmokers' Association, an organization founded in 1973. Association members campaigned at a time when antismoking activity was hardly the norm. Edna Eisenberg, the Association's first President, recalls that some people ridiculed her, saying she needed "psychological help." In 1976, the Association mounted a strong campaign that led to the City of Ottawa passing Canada's first real antismoking bylaw. Many members of City Council had been extremely reluctant, but a newspaper ad placed by the City to obtain public views prompted 306 letters, with 574 signatures in support and just 11 opposed.

The Ottawa bylaw prohibited smoking in the following places: patient-care areas; service counters in financial institutions and municipal offices; reception areas; elevators, escalators, and stairways; service lines; school buses; taxis if driver or passenger requests; retail shops except in restrooms, office areas, or lunch counters; indoor places of public assembly except in designated smoking areas; and nonsmoking sections of restaurants. Restaurants had to post a sign visible from the outside indicating whether they provided a nonsmoking area.

In 1977, the City of Toronto followed suit with a bylaw restricting smoking in several public places, including parts of hospitals. This was done despite the opposition of the Ontario Hospital Association. Perhaps a sign that antismoking was still in its infancy, the bylaw followed Ottawa's example and specifically did not restrict smoking in restrooms.[197] The victory followed 3 years of lobbying and was important because of the city's large population and prominence and because of the media located there. Council approved the bylaw 21 to 0, in large part because of NSRA efforts. Mayor David Crombie, later federal Health Minister, described NSRA as

> the most impressive and intelligent lobby I have ever known. The information they supplied was reliable and complete; they answered our objections even before we raised them; they showed a talent for reasonable compromise; they didn't waste my time.[327]

Among the critics of the new bylaw was former Health Minister LaMarsh, who wrote in her *Toronto Star* column that it was a "dumb law" because it would be unenforceable.[351] LaMarsh's predictions proved wrong. The bylaw was mostly self-enforcing.

By the 1980s, many more municipalities had passed public-place bylaws. Some bylaws started to include partial restrictions on smoking in restaurants, although many restaurants had already voluntarily created nonsmoking sections. Early bylaw requirements were modest, such as a minimum nonsmoking area of only 10% or 20%.

Perhaps prompted by the advent of public-place bylaws, more employers voluntarily restricted smoking in their workplaces. In 1986, Vancouver passed a bylaw covering smoking in workplaces. Later, some other municipalities would also adopt their own bylaws covering all parts of workplaces, not just the public portion.

A major factor driving the movement to restrict smoking was increasing knowledge of the harmful impact of ETS on the nonsmoker. In 1969, the Isabelle Committee had noted an increasing recognition of the rights of nonsmokers and recommended that "out of consideration for the majority of Canadians who do not smoke, a gradually increasing number of no smoking areas or sections be provided in places or facilities used by the general public."[268, p. 2:88]

In 1972, the US Surgeon General raised the issue of second-hand smoke in his annual report. He concluded that

> an atmosphere contaminated with tobacco smoke can contribute to the discomfort of many individuals. ... The level of carbon monoxide attained in experiments using rooms filled with tobacco smoke has been shown to equal, and at times to exceed, the legal limits for maximum air pollution permitted for ambient air quality.[613, p. 7]

In 1975, the Surgeon General concluded that

> children of parents who smoke are more likely to have bronchitis and pneumonia during the first year of life, and this is probably at least partly due to their being exposed to cigarette smoke in the atmosphere.[614, p. 108]

Also in 1975, during the House of Commons debate on Bill C-242, Health Minister Lalonde stated that

> evidence indicates that individuals with asthma, allergies, advanced emphysema, or advanced coronary arterial disease can be seriously troubled by inhaling cigarette smoke, especially in closed environments over a period of time.[349]

Apart from this evidence, reasons put forward for early antismoking bylaws included protecting nonsmokers from smoke-caused discomfort and irritations, such as headaches, coughing, watery eyes, smelly hair and clothes, and contact-lens problems. ETS was recognized as harmful to children with asthma. There was also an awareness that second-hand smoke has greater concentrations of toxic substances than mainstream smoke.

In the early 1980s, new studies substantially increased the knowledge of the health consequences of ETS. Some of the early studies found that nonsmoking wives with smoking husbands were at greater risk of lung cancer. In 1986, the US Surgeon General dedicated an entire report to ETS, concluding that "involuntary smoking is a cause of disease, including lung cancer, in healthy nonsmokers."[604, p. 7] In 1992, the US Environmental Protection Agency (EPA) completed an extensive examination of ETS. The EPA classified ETS as a group A (known human) carcinogen, thus placing ETS in a category with only a small number of other substances, such as radon and asbestos. The EPA concluded that ETS was responsible for lung cancer deaths in adults. In children, ETS caused bronchitis and pneumonia, worsened the condition of those with asthma, and was a risk factor in new cases of asthma.[605] Although the EPA did not look at ETS as a cause of heart disease, there is evidence that ETS causes far more deaths from heart disease than from lung cancer.[194]

New Canadian health warnings on ETS to be put on packages were adopted in 1993 in recognition of ETS hazards. In Canada, it has been estimated that more than 330 Canadians die annually from lung cancer caused by exposure to ETS.[630] A 1994 survey found that 56% of Canadians are physically irritated in some way by ETS.[238] ETS has also been linked to sudden infant death syndrome.[609] Babies whose mothers are exposed to ETS during pregnancy tend to have reduced birth weights. Children exposed to ETS are at greater risk of impaired lung function; eye, nose, and throat irritation; and chronic middle-ear infections.[232]

In adopting ETS restrictions, Canada has generally lagged behind the United States. By 1976, more than 30 states had some form of nonsmoking law,[376] although many laws covered very little. In 1987, Beverley Hills became one of the first municipalities to completely ban smoking in restaurants. The ban was reversed 4 months later after a campaign engineered by the tobacco lobby. Industry front groups claimed that restaurant sales fell by 30% after the ban went into effect, but in fact a later study of sales-tax receipts showed that restaurant sales actually increased.[195,535]

Later, many other California municipalities, including Los Angeles and San Francisco in 1993, banned smoking in restaurants. By the end of 1995, California, Vermont, and Utah had statewide laws completely prohibiting smoking in restaurants.

In 1994, the US Occupational Health and Safety Administration held hearings on a proposed rule that would prohibit smoking in virtually all workplaces, whether open to the public or not. This would include restaurants and bars. The only exceptions would be separately enclosed, independently ventilated rooms used for no purpose other than smoking. Needless to say, the tobacco industry campaigned hard to prevent adoption of such a rule.[6] Even if the rule is adopted, the industry can be expected to launch a court challenge.

In Canada, it was not until 1987 that the first provincial law restricting ETS was in force. Surprisingly, the law was in Quebec, the province with the highest smoking rates in Canada.[227] By the end of 1995, only 4 of the 10 provinces had provincial laws restricting smoking in public places, and only Ontario and Newfoundland had legislation applicable to smoking in workplaces, albeit with only partial restrictions. Most of the action has been at the municipal level: by 1991, at least 280 Canadian municipalities with a population greater than 10 000 had a bylaw restricting smoking.[228] At the federal level, restrictions have been much stronger because of the *Non-smokers' Health Act.* The Act severely restricts smoking, but only in the approximately 10% of workplaces regulated by the federal government. Such workplaces include banks, transport and telecommunications companies, and federal Crown corporations.

The campaign for smoke-free skies

Despite historic lagging behind the United States when it comes to ETS restrictions, Canada is a world leader when it comes to controlling smoking aboard airlines. In 1986, Air Canada introduced completely smoke-free flights on some of the routes in the Toronto–Ottawa–Montreal triangle. A 3-month experiment proved so successful that Air Canada increased the number of smoke-free flights. In 1987, Air Canada, with smoke-free flights to New York, became the first major airline to have smoke-free flights in the United States. Canadian Airlines International followed suit in the same year with some smoke-free flights to the United States. Also in 1987, the federal government prohibited smoking on all domestic flights under 2 hours, a move later followed by the US Congress. In 1988, Air Canada prohibited smoking on all its charter and scheduled flights in North America.[10]

When the *Non-smokers' Health Act* came into force on 29 December 1989, it prohibited smoking on all flights of Canadian air carriers except flights specifically exempted by regulation. The major airlines lobbied strenuously against a complete ban on smoking on all international flights, arguing that they would lose up to $90 million in revenue and that a ban would be unenforceable.[152,191,202,459] Health groups joined with representatives of flight-attendant unions (led by tireless campaigner Carmen Paquin, an Air Canada attendant) to counter this lobby. This led to apparent victory when Labour Minister Jean Corbeil and Transport Minister Benoît Bouchard announced on 18 December 1989 that all domestic and international flights would be smoke free. Of course, when it comes to smoking, it is never over until it is over.

The airlines intensively lobbied the government. On 23 December, just days before the ban was to come into force, the government caved in and deferred the smoking ban on international flights to 1 July 1990. The complete ban on smoking on domestic flights, though, went into force as scheduled.

In June 1990, the government announced that smoking would be banned on international flights of 6 hours or less. On longer flights, the seating allocated to smoking would be phased out over 3 years. In 1993, the complete ban was deferred for another year. In 1994, implementation of the ban was again delayed, this time for 2 months, but only on flights to Japan.

Finally, in September 1994, Canada became the first country in the world to require that all domestic and international flights of its airlines be smoke free. Ken Kyle, Director of Public Issues for CCS, recalls that "it was only through persistent lobbying that the victory was achieved. Part of the argument we used was that a smoke-free flight would be a marketing advantage, not a disadvantage." After the total ban was implemented, Canadian Airlines International actually increased the number of seats on its Japan–Canada routes. An Air Canada spokesperson said that revenues "had not been negatively affected" by smoking restrictions. Air Canada was saving about $900 000 a year on all its routes by not having to clean ashtrays, not to mention the further benefits of being able to extend the interval between deep cleanings of its airplanes to 9 months from 6.[641]

In 1992, Canada sponsored a resolution that was adopted by the assembly of the International Civil Aviation Organization, a United Nations agency. The resolution urged countries "to take necessary measures as soon as possible to restrict smoking progressively on all international passenger flights with the objective of implementing complete smoking bans by 1 July 1996."[311] Although the resolution was not legally binding on countries, it set the desired international standard.

Adoption of the resolution did not happen by accident. It was preceded by a Campaign for Smoke-Free Skies Worldwide spearheaded by CCS and the American Lung Association. WHO also worked hard to gain support for adoption of the resolution.[346,640]

In another move that may be copied elsewhere, Canada, the United States, and Australia entered a trilateral treaty in 1994 in which they agreed that flights between their countries would be smoke free. The treaty provides for the inclusion of other countries willing to sign the agreement.

Restaurants and bars

Although smoking restrictions are becoming more extensive, smoking is still permitted in many restaurants and bars. Smoke-free restaurants and bars are not yet as common in Canada as in the United States, but the number is increasing. In 1994 McDonald's and other fast-food chains like Taco Bell and Subway made landmark decisions to go completely smoke free in corporate-owned outlets. A 1994 guide by the Airspace Nonsmokers' Rights Society lists 550 completely smoke-free places to eat in British Columbia alone.[11]

The need to ban smoking in bars and restaurants is all the more important because these places have high ETS concentrations, thus increasing the hazard. A study published in JAMA found a 50% increase in the risk of lung cancer among restaurant and bar employees.[544]

Restaurateurs often oppose any smoking restrictions because they fear a loss of business; they argue that smoking restrictions should be determined by the marketplace. At one time, restaurants even opposed the early bylaws that created a 20% nonsmoking section in restaurants. After the nonsmoking sections were in place, though, it was business as usual, without the terrible sales consequences the restaurants had forecast.

A survey in California found that adult nonsmokers eat out as often as smokers, that more than two thirds of smokers do not feel the need to smoke when they eat out, and that a smoke-free restaurant ordinance would likely lead to an overall increase in restaurant business because nonsmokers would eat out more.[476] Similarly, an Angus Reid poll in the Vancouver and Victoria areas in British Columbia found that restaurants would likely increase their business if there was a complete ban on smoking.[15]

Restaurants are not justified in placing profit ahead of the health of their employees and customers. Would it be acceptable for a restaurant to refuse to serve a particular ethnic group because sales would be harmed? Is a restaurant justified in not complying with sanitary standards because of the extra cost? Of course not.

The impact of smoking restrictions

Smoking restrictions protect the health of nonsmokers (and smokers, who also breathe ETS). Smoking restrictions also decrease the social acceptability of smoking. This contributes to the desire to quit. As well, restrictions, especially in the workplace, decrease a smoker's daily consumption, thus reducing the risk to health and increasing the likelihood an attempt to quit will be successful. Here is what a confidential Imperial Tobacco document (circa 1987) stated (emphasis in the original):

> The shift to **social pressure** has also moved to high gear. Passive smoking has moved from a fringe issue, to by-laws, to the implementation of smoking restrictions in the work-place. **Smoking restrictions have moved from abstract discussion to practice.** This increasing social isolation of the smoker will not only increase his ill-ease with smoking, but will also have **a measurable effect on daily usage rates** resulting in overall industry losses [emphasis as in original].[304, p. 9]

California researchers found that the implementation and continuation of a smoke-free work area was associated with a 26% reduction in per capita consumption among workers. Over time, a smoke-free policy led to quitting, especially among light smokers. When employees moved from a smoke-free work area to an area with fewer restrictions, their smoking increased.[476] Several other studies have found that the introduction of workplace smoking restrictions is followed by lower smoking rates among workers.[49,316,403]

A smoke-free workplace provides employers with a number of benefits, notably reduced costs from cleaning, maintenance, fire insurance, absenteeism, and sick pay. It has been estimated that among Canadian employees, absenteeism is 33%–45% higher for smokers than for nonsmokers.[641] Eliminating ETS means that repainting is less frequently needed. Productivity will increase as smokers take fewer breaks, and nonsmokers will have a better working environment. A ban also decreases the risk of legal action against the employer by an employee or customer harmed by ETS.

Actions nonsmokers can take

Nonsmokers have a number of possible remedies to reduce involuntary exposure to ETS. In the workplace, perhaps with the assistance of their union representatives, nonsmokers can persuade management to voluntarily implement a nonsmoking policy. Nonsmokers can verify whether federal, provincial, and municipal laws are being enforced. Under provincial occupational health and safety legislation, workers usually have the "right to refuse" to work in unsafe circumstances. Some nonsmoking workers have invoked this provision to force their employers to ban smoking. In some circumstances, workers could file a grievance against the employer in accordance with a collective agreement.

In Ontario, a Medical Officer of Health has the authority to declare something a health hazard and to order removal of the hazard. Up to the end of 1995, this measure had not been used to control smoking.

The courts have sometimes provided a remedy. In cases dating back to 1984, a couple of judicial orders prevented some husbands from smoking in homes shared with their wives. In British Columbia, a tenant obtained an injunction to prevent a neighbour from smoking because the smoke was travelling between apartments. In 1988, an Ontario court terminated the visitation rights of a father who would not stop smoking in the presence of his 6-year-old asthmatic daughter.

The failure to ban smoking discriminates against several groups and thus may violate provincial human rights codes. Permitting smoking in the workplace discriminates against pregnant women. Persons with asthma and other disabilities face discrimination because, through no fault of their own, they are unable to remain in a smoky environment. In certain circumstances, legislative exemptions permitting smoking could be challenged under the *Canadian Charter of Rights and Freedoms* on the grounds of discrimination on the basis of sex or disability.

The tobacco industry responds

What has been the tobacco industry's response to ETS? Tobacco companies deny the health consequences of ETS and work to oppose legislation, although in Canada the industry has not been as aggressive as in the United States. In 1978, a confidential research report prepared for the US tobacco industry warned that the ETS issue was "the most dangerous development to the viability of the tobacco industry that has yet occurred."[507, p. 5] The report recommended "developing and widely publicizing clear-cut, credible, medical evidence that passive smoking is not harmful."[507, p. 6]

A 1986 report prepared for Imperial Tobacco presented a strategy for dealing with second-hand smoke:

> Should a decision be made to enter public debate, two assumptions lead to a recommendation that the **passive smoking issue** is used as the focal point. The first is that, of all the health issues surrounding smoking, it is the one which the tobacco industry has most chance of winning; that the evidence proclaimed by the anti-group is flawed. Secondly, and related to the first, is that it is highly desirable to control the focus of debate. A broad discussion of smoking and health can only lead to a series of barrages in areas which the tobacco industry would have extreme difficulty in defending. And **offense** should be the watchword.
>
> Passive smoking has high relevance to the socially-concerned. An attack on the credibility of evidence presented to date may well provide the rational argument to soften their attitudes. At the same time, a halo would be created, bringing other undebated issues into question by inference, providing reassurance and reinforcement for the more emotionally-dependent health-concerned group [emphasis as in original].[125, p. 60]

In seeking an advocate to make the case for the industry's position, the report said "the challenge will be to find a sympathetic doctor who can be demonstrated to take a largely independent stance."[125, p. 60]

In 1987, during parliamentary hearings on the proposed *Non-smokers' Health Act*, the industry brought up its normal troop of experts to deny that ETS was a demonstrated health problem. When the Ontario legislature was considering the *Smoking in the Workplace Act*, CTMC submitted a detailed brief refuting the alleged dangers of ETS. When the new law came into effect — prohibiting smoking in workplaces except in designated areas — CTMC wrote to employers suggesting that each desk be designated a smoking section. This was a deliberate attempt to undermine the effectiveness of the law.

To prevent the adoption of bylaws restricting smoking, the tobacco industry has funded local opposition. For example, in British Columbia in 1995, the industry funded the Lower Mainland Hospitality Industry Group to oppose proposed bylaws that would ban smoking in all restaurants and bars. A tobacco industry organizer traveled to the province to help establish the group, and CTMC provided the group with ongoing strategic advice.

The next chapter, on taxation and smuggling, describes far more serious industry efforts to undermine the effectiveness of an antitobacco strategy.

CHAPTER 11

Taxation and Smuggling

Brian Gable, *Globe and Mail*, Toronto

Higher tobacco taxes play critical role

When the price of something goes up, people buy less of it. That's basic logic and basic economics. That's also the principle behind the most important factor in Canada's tobacco-control strategy: higher tobacco taxes.

Research shows that as the real (after-inflation) price of cigarettes rises, tobacco consumption decreases. Although the magnitude of the decrease varies and may differ by country and circumstance, one oft-cited American study found that a 10% increase in real price led to a 4% decrease in consumption.[360] Other studies have found decreases of 3%–9%.[608] Among teenagers, who have less money and are more price sensitive, the decrease has been measured at about 14%.[361] Were it not for nicotine's addictiveness, decreases would be larger.

Higher prices can work in a number of ways. Smokers may feel that the price is too high and decide to quit or smoke less. Higher prices might combine with other factors and finally push a smoker into quitting. Even if a smoker only decides to cut down, this produces health benefits. Fewer cigarettes a day may reduce the risk that a smoker will contract a tobacco-caused disease. As previously noted, people who smoke fewer cigarettes a day are more likely to attempt to quit and to quit successfully than people who smoke more cigarettes per day. For teenagers, higher prices may push cigarettes beyond the level of affordability or may delay the age when smoking begins, thus decreasing the long-term risk to health. Decreasing the amount smoked may reduce the risk that addiction will set in.

Tobacco-tax increases serve a dual purpose: they improve public health, and they increase government revenue. Tobacco taxes also partially allocate health-care costs to smokers, who as a class receive billions of dollars in extra health-care benefits.

Tobacco taxes in Canada have a history that predates Confederation. For just as long, there have been attempts to get the government to reduce those taxes. In 1869, the question of abolishing tobacco taxes was raised in the House of Commons and dismissed by the Minister of Finance.[181] In 1878, a resolution to eliminate tobacco taxes was debated and defeated. The mover of the resolution had argued that heavy excise taxes were suppressing the growth of domestically cultivated tobacco.[256] In response, Wilfrid Laurier, then Minister of Inland Revenue, questioned whether Canadian conditions were suitable for the growth of tobacco anyhow.[352] The Minister of Justice defended the tax in part, saying "this weed was injurious to the health of those who indulged in it,"[347] but for this he was promptly criticized by some Quebec MPs. Other MPs opposed the measure, saying that if the tobacco tax was abolished, other taxes would have to be raised to replace lost revenue.

For more than 100 years, motivated to protect its profits, the tobacco industry has led the fight against high tobacco taxes. For example, in 1876, in a brief entitled "Serious Loss of Revenue to the Country," the Tobacco Association of Canada complained that higher taxes had led to a large illicit tobacco trade. The Association called for strict enforcement of tax laws or, alternatively, abolition of the tobacco tax.[589]

At the turn of the century, representatives of the tobacco industry traveled to Ottawa each year to lobby the Finance Minister. However, the lobbying did not always work. After tobacco taxes were increased in the 1897 federal budget, an outraged industry formed the Dominion Cigar Manufacturers Association to improve lobbying effectiveness. In the early years of the tobacco lobby, trade associations seemed to have a short life, and this one seemed to disappear after a few years. Other short-lived associations included the Tobacco Trade Association of Canada, created in 1917, and the Dominion Cigar and Tobacco Association, created in 1919.

For most if not all of the last century, cigarette taxes have constituted a significant proportion of the retail price, usually more than 50%. Also throughout Canadian history, cigarettes have been smuggled from the United States into Canadian border cities, although the level of smuggling has varied. The tobacco lobby, in its representations to the government, has often cited the threat of more smuggling being brought about by higher tobacco taxes.

In 1951, during the Korean War, the federal government increased the taxes on a pack of 20 cigarettes by 3 cents. Although the Minister of Finance would later say that the increase was not intended to discourage smoking, the increase seems to have had this effect. The increase was followed by substantial protests from the tobacco industry. To bolster their position, manufacturers increased their prices by 2 cents a pack (nearly as much as the tax increase), a move that further decreased smoking and consequently government revenue. These increases raised the retail price to 42 cents a pack, 46 cents in Quebec (where there was also a provincial tobacco tax). The differential between prices in Canada and the United States (where prices were already much lower) widened. Cigarette smuggling increased substantially, especially in Ontario and Quebec near the US border. *Weekend Picture Magazine* reported that a carton of 200 black-market American cigarettes could be purchased for $3.00 to $3.50 when the legal price of a carton was about $4.20 in most parts of Canada and $4.60 in Quebec.[330] A strike at Imperial Tobacco resulted in a shortage of some popular brands, perhaps making contraband appear more attractive. Despite calls in Parliament for the Finance Minister not to be intimidated by the industry, tobacco taxes were reduced in 1952 by 3 cents a pack (thereby eliminating the 1951 increase) and in 1953, the last year of the Korean War, by another 4 cents. Though the Finance Minister felt that the extent of smuggling had been exaggerated, the contraband situation was the prime factor in his decision to roll back tobacco taxes.[1,2] After the rollback, manufacturers rescinded their own 2-cent increase. The industry's tactics had been enormously successful: taxes in 1953 were lower than they had been before the 1951 increase.

In the 1980s, tobacco companies used an array of arguments to oppose higher tobacco taxes. They argued that increases are inflationary, that increases jeopardize tobacco-related jobs in manufacturing and farming, and that tobacco products are being unfairly singled out for high tax rates.[172,434,436,513]

Tobacco companies also argued that high taxes are regressive and have a greater negative impact on the poor.[434,513] This argument, however, is countered by the fact that it is the health effects of smoking that are regressive. People from lower socioeconomic groups are more likely to smoke and thus die from tobacco-caused disease. Higher tobacco taxes benefit the health of the poor far more than they benefit the health of any other group because smokers with low incomes may be most likely to quit following an increase. Also, those low-income smokers who quit or cut back significantly will have more disposable income than before the increase.

In the 1950s, 1960s, and 1970s, the real disposable income of Canadians grew substantially, but the price of tobacco did not keep pace. In terms of disposable income, even with the price increases of the 1980s and 1990s, cigarettes were still cheaper in 1993 than they had been in 1949.[448] Tobacco prices did not even keep up with inflation. This was a major factor in the increase of per capita cigarette consumption to such high levels during this period.

It took some time before higher taxes were seen as a desirable part of Canada's tobacco-control strategy. The 1969 report of the Isabelle Committee contained no recommendation to increase taxes. By the late 1970s, officials at Health and Welfare Canada recognized the potential health benefits of a taxation strategy and regularly — and unsuccessfully — urged the Department of Finance to increase tobacco taxes. During the 1970s and early 1980s, there was little call outside government for higher taxes. Though some tobacco-control supporters thought increases were desirable,[580] others were opposed to increases because they perceived that governments would become more dependent on tobacco revenue and less likely to regulate the industry.

The 1981 federal budget introduced the *ad valorem* tobacco tax (*ad valorem* means a percentage of the value of the goods being taxed). Taxes went up any time the price of tobacco went up, whether because of inflation, manufacturer increases, or provincial taxes. A tax spiral started. When the price increased, taxes went up, meaning that the price was yet higher, so taxes would go up again. Because many provinces also had *ad valorem* tax structures, federal tax increases pushed up provincial taxes, which in turn pushed up federal taxes. The spiral was slow at first, but by 1982 and especially 1983 the real price of tobacco had noticeably increased. Consumption started to fall, and manufacturers were lobbying for changes.

At the 1983 World Conference on Smoking and Health, held in Winnipeg, Canada's Health Minister, Monique Bégin, urged that cigarette taxes be increased by 30% to reduce smoking.[249] The Conference agreed with this view, also urging that taxes be increased. However, Bégin had made her comments without first consulting Marc Lalonde, who was Finance Minister, and she was forced to retreat. Officials explained that her views did not represent government policy but instead were part of a "personal lobby."[79]

When the Progressive Conservatives were elected federally in 1984, the new government was much more concerned with deficit reduction than the previous Liberal government had been. With a need to find more revenue, the government turned to higher tobacco taxes as one possible avenue. Although the government responded to industry representations and eliminated the *ad valorem* system in 1985, the tobacco tax on cigarettes was increased by $2.00 a carton in 1985, a further $4.00 a carton in 1989, and a further $6.00 a carton in 1991. Michael Wilson was Finance Minister for each of these increases. Arguably, Wilson can be credited with doing more to reduce smoking than any other Canadian ever. Budget papers accompanying the 1989 increase stated that "these measures, besides increasing revenues, complement the government's comprehensive strategy of reducing tobacco smoking in Canada."[137, p. 56] In his 1991 budget speech, Wilson stated the following:

> Studies show that tobacco taxes are particularly important in discouraging younger Canadians from smoking. ... As a result [of the tax increase], it is estimated there will be about 100,000 fewer teenage smokers.[632, p. 22]

Provincial governments, also financially strapped, increased their own tobacco taxes considerably in the 1980s and early 1990s, contributing to much higher retail prices.

The results were dramatic. As Figure 3 (Chapter 2) indicates, tobacco consumption declined during this period at rates unprecedented in Canadian history. Prevalence surveys found the impact particularly strong among teenagers aged 15–19. Between 1979 and 1991, among Canadians aged 15–19, the proportion who reported they were occasional or daily smokers declined from 47% to 22%, and the proportion who reported they were daily smokers declined from 42% to 16%.[445,447] A 1993 Department of Finance study of the impact of higher taxes concluded that "federal tax increases since 1985 have resulted in a net decline in overall tobacco consumption in Canada"[138, p. vi] and that "younger Canadians are, indeed, more sensitive to price changes than adults."[138, p. iv]

Higher tobacco taxes resulted in tremendous increases in government revenue. Total federal and provincial revenue received from tobacco increased from $2 billion in 1981 to $7.2 billion in 1992, before declining in 1993 (a result of increased smuggling).[85,89] Although cigarette sales were falling, throughout the decade governments were collecting much more money.

Inside government, lobbying by federal Health ministers and Health Department officials helped convince Finance Minister Wilson and the Department to increase taxes. Outside government, the lead individual contributing to the tobacco-tax strategy was NSRA lawyer Sweanor, who provided expertise and pushed tobacco-control advocates so that taxation became a priority of the antitobacco lobby. In time, an effective lobby, led by NSRA, helped persuade federal and provincial governments to increase tobacco taxes. Well-researched prebudget submissions and compelling logic helped make the case to government.

Among other points, the submissions referred to public support for tobacco-tax increases. A 1987 Gallup poll done for CCS found that 44.1% of Canadians supported a tax increase of 40 cents a pack; 43.6% were opposed. However, when tax increases were pursued as part of a comprehensive strategy for tobacco control, support increased to 77.5%; only 17.3% were opposed. Even among smokers there was 2 to 1 support.[189] A 1989 Environics poll done for CCS, NSRA, and the Heart and Stroke Foundation found that 80% of all respondents and 68% of smokers either "strongly" or "somewhat" supported a tax increase of 50 cents a pack "if this were shown to greatly reduce smoking among young people."[64, pp. 17–22] The message is that if governments must raise taxes, they will receive more support by choosing tobacco as their revenue source. Increases during the 1980s received little opposition other than from manufacturers and their allies, thus making it easier for governments to further raise taxes.

It is unusual to have public support for higher taxes of any kind. Nigel Lawson, a former British Chancellor of the Exchequer, said,

> Such is the success of the anti-smoking lobby that the tobacco duty is the one tax where an increase commands more friends than enemies in the House of Commons. ... The tobacco duty is the one tax a Chancellor can increase and receive at least as much praise as execration for so doing.[643, p. 23]

The tobacco industry's response

Not surprisingly, the tobacco industry was furious with the massive increases in tobacco tax. Year after year, their annual reports blamed increases in tobacco taxes for decreases in industry sales volumes. In its 1984 annual report, Imasco Ltd stated that a reduction in tobacco taxes would "allow the industry to return to a pattern of modest but stable growth."[274, p. 6] In its 1986 annual report, the company said, "Excessive cigarette taxation continued to be the industry's major problem in fiscal 1986. Substantial increases in taxes at both the federal and provincial levels resulted in a further slowing of unit sales."[275, p. 2] Similarly, Rothmans complained in its annual reports and at annual meetings about "discriminatory" and "punitive" tax policies.[514, p. 6]

In 1989, the presidents of the three major companies wrote to tobacco-related businesses to urge them to send a letter to Ontario Treasurer Robert Nixon asking him to prevent further provincial tax increases. The presidents emphasized that "As the price of tobacco products is pushed ever higher by taxes, **sales go down** [emphasis as in original]."[172, p. 1]

In its 1990 prebudget submission to the federal Minister of Finance, CTMC decried the decrease in industry sales between 1981 and 1989, stating that "although lifestyles are changing and the debate on tobacco use and health explains part of this decrease, there is no doubt that taxation of tobacco products is principally responsible."[434, p. 2]

A 1990 Informetrica study commissioned by CTMC examined the impact of higher taxes. For the period 1973–88, Informetrica found that a 10% increase in the price of tobacco resulted in a 6%–8% long-term decrease in smoking, depending on the measurement of consumption used.[309] The industry used this in an attempt to show that higher taxes reduced smoking and in turn meant fewer jobs.

In the face of decreasing cigarette sales, companies developed and promoted lower priced tobacco products as alternatives to cigarettes. For example, the industry promoted the lower retail price of roll-your-own tobacco, a product taxed at a substantially lower rate than cigarettes. As cigarette taxes increased and taxes on roll-your-own tobacco failed to keep pace, sales of roll-your-own tobacco increased as a proportion of total tobacco sales. This shift in purchasing patterns reduced the health and revenue benefits of high tobacco taxes.

In 1988, RBH introduced a Custom Cut product consisting of tobacco sticks, paper tubes with filters, and a device to insert the tobacco stick into the tube. Because tobacco sticks were taxed at a rate lower than the cigarette rate, they provided a lower priced option for consumers. Imperial responded by introducing its own Insta-kit. RBH took Imperial to Federal Court for patent infringement and won an injunction preventing Imperial from marketing its product until 2005.

In 1991, RBH introduced its Maverick brand of cheroots. Cheroots resemble cigarettes except that they are wrapped in process tobacco leaf instead of paper. Because cheroots were not considered cigarettes, taxes and thus prices were lower. This new product, however, failed in the marketplace.

When the 1991 federal tax increase came, the industry accelerated its antitax campaign. Within months of the budget speech, the industry generated a tax protest. Imperial and RJR–Macdonald printed protest cards on the inside sliding portion of the package. The card, which could be mailed to the Prime Minister free of charge, read "I am of voting age. I want you to stop the unfair taxation of tobacco products in Canada. What are you going to do about it? I expect a reply."[186] Advertisements also urged smokers to fill out and send in these cards.

Up to and including 1991, the industry had emphasized the argument that tobacco-tax increases were bad for the economy and led to job losses in the tobacco industry. By 1992, however, the tobacco industry realized that governments were not listening to these arguments, so it reversed its strategy. Despite previous assertions to the contrary,[437,451] the industry now argued that the tax increases had had no impact on smoking by Canadians.[278] Said CTMC President Rob Parker, "It is not the case that increasing price leads to a decrease in consumption."[84, p. 25] Because the objective of a reduction in smoking was a key pillar of the support for tax increases, the industry decided it needed to knock down the pillar.

The rise of smuggling

As Canadian taxes increased, the differential between Canadian and US cigarette prices widened and thus increased the incentive to smuggle cigarettes in from the United States. The contraband issue became critical to the industry's antitax campaign. Tobacco companies publicized the growing problem of smuggling as part of their effort to pressure governments to lower taxes. For several years the industry hired a forensic accounting firm to calculate the size of the contraband market.[341,342,362,364] The resulting reports were released with great fanfare (at least once in conjunction with a cross-Canada media roadshow).

One of the reports, "1992 Contraband Tobacco Estimate,"[363] released to the media in April 1993, included errors that overestimated the size of the contraband market by 20%, or 1.6 billion cigarettes.[576] NSRA detected the errors, but no revised report[364] was released by the industry for 5 months, despite persistent dogging by NSRA (and without the media coverage accompanying the original report).

Although it is not suggested that the tobacco companies did anything illegal, the effect of certain industry actions, including the massive exporting of cigarettes, was to foster the contraband situation.

The major factor contributing to the rise of smuggling was a dramatic increase in manufacturer exports of Canadian cigarettes to the United States. Most of the exports went just over the border to upstate New York and returned to Canada as contraband, a fact openly acknowledged by the industry. As illustrated in Figure 12, total cigarette exports to the United States exploded from 1.2 billion cigarettes in 1989 to 18.6 billion in 1993, despite the absence of any added American demand for Canadian brands. Smuggling had a high profit potential, and tobacco companies happily supplied the cigarettes that became contraband. Said lobbyist Neville, "If there's smuggling, we're unapologetic that it should be Canadian cigarettes."[270, p. A6] The industry told the government it needed to defend its market share.[270] More than 90% of the contraband consisted of products originally manufactured in Canada.[279]

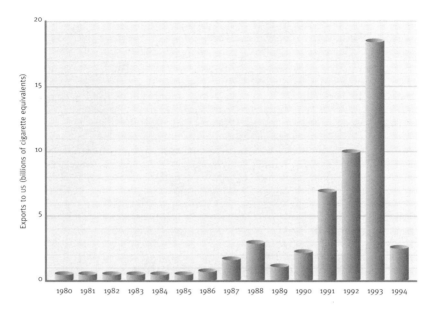

Figure 12. Exports of cigarettes and roll-your-own equivalents to
the United States, 1980–94.[559]

Not only was the industry not paying Canadian taxes on the exported product, often it was not even paying the lower US taxes. The industry shipped billions of cigarettes to US duty-free warehouses — despite the absence of corresponding large-scale increased demand from legitimate duty-free stores — before the cigarettes made it back into Canada. Payment of US federal and New York state taxes, amounting to about US $9.00 (CA $11.85) a carton, was avoided, thereby enhancing the price advantage of illegal products and further boosting the smuggling.[423]

Much of the contraband — estimated to be up to 80%[438] — entered Canada through the Akwesasne Indian reserve straddling the Ontario, Quebec, and New York borders (Figure 13). Once on the reserve, and despite strong opposition to the contraband trade by a large segment of the reserve population, massive volumes of illegal cigarettes then found their way to other parts of Canada. Enforcement on the Canadian side of the reserve was affected by the tense relationship between police and Mohawk Warriors, especially after the armed standoff during the Oka crisis just a few years earlier. Though contraband was openly stored and sold on the Quebec portion of the reserve, police avoided going on this portion to enforce the law.[160,596,94] Smugglers were well armed and well financed, and they threatened to resist a raid with force. Police officers feared for their personal safety. Furthermore, the reserve was in three different political jurisdictions, which complicated enforcement.

Some other Indian reserves, especially the Kahnawake reserve just outside Montreal and the Six Nations reserve near Brantford, Ontario, were important selling and distribution points for contraband. On Kahnawake, a carton could be easily had from any

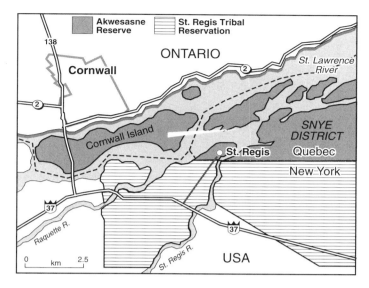

Figure 13. Map of Akwesasne reserve.
Source: Bernard Bennell, *Globe and Mail,* Toronto.

one of dozens of outlets for as little as $17 to $21, compared with the fully taxed price of $47.[62]

Another smuggling route was from the French islands of St Pierre and Miquelon to nearby Newfoundland. Canadian tobacco exports to the islands during the early 1990s far exceeded what was necessary for the few thousand residents of the fishing outport.[62]

In 1991, there was a surge of Canadian cross-border shopping in the United States. This was attributed to several factors: Canada's new Goods and Services Tax, the relatively high value of the Canadian dollar, and the lower American prices for many products, especially tobacco, alcohol, and gasoline. Because a large majority of the Canadian population lives within 150 kilometres of the US border, cross-border shopping was having a severe impact on Canadian businesses in border communities.

The cross-border shopping issue and a major increase in cigarette smuggling prompted the federal government to take action. On 12 February 1992, effective at midnight, the federal government imposed an export tax of $8.00 per carton of cigarettes. The objective was to push up the price of contraband returning to Canada and to narrow the Canadian–US price differential. On the day of the announcement, Imperial Tobacco rented every truck it could and had 50 vehicles headed to the United States to get as much tax-free tobacco as possible across the border before the midnight deadline.[270]

Exports plummeted from 760 million cigarettes in February to 233 million in March, as illustrated in Figure 14. The industry did not like it and began a major campaign to have the tax repealed. Soon 16 lobbyists were on board to get the industry's message across to the government.[270] Tobacco companies argued that if they were unable to

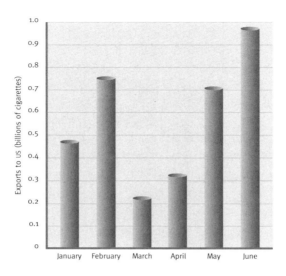

Figure 14. Monthly cigarette exports to the United States,
January to June 1992.[562]

export, then smugglers would simply obtain their contraband from US sources. The industry played hardball and threatened to get around the tax by shifting some production to the United States.[270,277,437]

As offensive as the industry's threats were, they worked. The industry orchestrated a large, well-publicized protest on Parliament Hill that involved hundreds, if not thousands, of bused-in demonstrators. The prime message was jobs. Unless the export tax was repealed, the industry argued, Canadian jobs would be lost. At the same time, RJR–Macdonald broke off negotiations with tobacco farmers for the next year's crop. Although this announcement was more symbolic than anything, it garnered a lot of publicity about possible economic harm to farmers. Naturally, this resulted in tobacco farmers being up in arms.

The overall campaign succeeded in placing tremendous pressure on the government and its Minister of Finance, Don Mazankowski. Mazankowski had been Agriculture Minister in his previous portfolio and was sensitive to farmer concerns. On 8 April, less than 2 months after the export tax was imposed, the government yielded to the pressure and repealed the tax. When the announcement came, leading tobacco-control advocates were out of the country at the Eighth World Conference on Tobacco or Health, in Buenos Aires, Argentina. Revenue Minister Otto Jelinek had to put the best face on the government's retreat:

> The tax was suspended, not as an act of Government capitulation, but rather as a result of an agreement between the Government and industry to work together in battling the trade in illegal tobacco products. My officials have negotiated with industry representatives and have arranged for much improved markings and identification codes on packages of tobacco products.[317, p. 1]

The codes were to identify the US wholesale purchaser, with the intention that this would facilitate the tracking down of the source of contraband once it was seized in Canada. The industry also agreed "to make every effort to ensure that exported tobacco products are delivered to bona fide wholesalers and retailers in the United States and other countries."[210, p. 2] The industry made its commitments during the negotiations, which were conducted behind closed doors without the participation of health groups.

Time would prove the commitments to be worthless. The coding system was never implemented. The industry strongly resisted the efforts by the government to have "Not for Sale in Canada" prominently displayed on the packaging. In the end, manufacturers placed the markings on the side of the package, often in colour combinations that blended in with existing package design. As soon as the tax was repealed, exports set new records, although one company (Imperial Tobacco) did show some restraint for about a year.

Further actions by tobacco companies contributed to the continued growth of the contraband market. Some Export "A" packages officially made for sale outside Canada were designed in a way that made it harder to distinguish what was legal in Canada from what was illegal. Some Player's and Export "A" cigarettes legally sold in Canada were marketed in tin containers. Some smokers would use these containers to hold their contraband cigarettes so that no one would detect what they were doing. The containers did not have the marking "Not for Sale in Canada." Even after the export tax was gone, RJR–Macdonald produced some Export "A" cigarettes in Puerto Rico, an indication that keeping production in Canada was not the company's priority.

While the industry was loudly decrying the high tobacco taxes, it was implementing huge price increases of its own. Manufacturer prices to wholesalers on cartons of 200 cigarettes increased from $4.86 in 1988 to about $8.50 in 1993, a 74% increase.[279,355] The industry was contributing to the Canadian–US price differential. Wholesale and retail margins also increased, from $2.86 in 1988 to $4.94 in 1992.[355]

The industry profited from the contraband situation itself. In part, this was because manufacturers were paying Canadian farmers substantially less for tobacco used in exported products.

Although Imperial Tobacco manufactured Player's, the trademark was owned by Philip Morris in the United States, a problem that prevented Imperial from exporting Player's cigarettes. To remedy the situation, Imperial Tobacco and Philip Morris made a deal so that these exports would be possible.[187,198] RBH made a similar deal with Philip Morris to increase exports of some of its brands.[515]

According to estimates by forensic accounting firm Lindquist Avey Macdonald Baskerville (Lindquist Avey), the proportion of the Canadian market made up of contraband increased from 1.8% in 1989 to 2.4% in 1990, to 12% in 1991, and then to 16% in 1992.[90,278,364] For 1993, estimates from a number of sources (Imasco Ltd[279] and Lindquist Avey,[366] for example) placed the illegal market at 25–31%. The problem was particularly serious in Quebec, where the contraband market was considerably more widespread.

As exports and contraband increased following the repeal of the export tax, so did all sorts of related problems. Criminality was widespread, with some smugglers becoming millionaires.[438] Disrespect for the law was encouraged. Ordinary Canadians possessed illegal products. Teenagers were being offered contraband cigarettes on school grounds. Lower prices undermined health objectives. Governments suffered decreased revenue. Tobacco farmers were receiving less money from manufacturers. Retailers and wholesalers, especially in Quebec, saw a tremendous reduction in tobacco sales. Tensions between the indigenous and nonindigenous communities escalated.

Anatomy of a tax rollback

Given the political sensitivity of the contraband issue, the government took little action in the run-up to the 25 October 1993 federal election. In Quebec, many candidates knocking on doors found that tobacco smuggling was the major issue. Shortly after the Liberals were elected, there were hints that a tax reduction was in the works. MP Don Boudria, whose riding of Glengarry–Prescott–Russell bordered the St Lawrence River where most of the contraband entered, started to publicly build the case for a tax reduction. In mid-December, Boudria invited Liberal caucus members to a meeting to discuss tobacco smuggling.

The subject of a tax rollback was raised in December at a federal–provincial conference of Finance Ministers. Quebec had long been publicly calling for a joint federal–provincial reduction in tobacco taxes, and now the federal government was willing to discuss the idea. At the conference, the Quebec Finance Minister tried to persuade others of the need for reduced tobacco taxes. Also in December, Quebec raised the stakes by threatening a unilateral reduction if Ottawa failed to act.

Meanwhile, health groups started to sense the urgency of the situation and increased the pace of their activity. On 10 January 1994, in Montreal, CCS released a detailed report containing 44 recommendations for controlling contraband and tax-exempt tobacco.[62] Montreal was chosen because it was in the heart of support for a tax reduction. The date was chosen because it was the day before the new Quebec government of Premier Daniel Johnson was to be sworn in. The report targeted the industry as being principally responsible for the extent of the smuggling. The main recommendation was a reimposition of the export tax, combined with measures to prevent tobacco companies from shifting production outside the country. If the export tax was reinstated, the industry would suddenly have a massive financial incentive to reduce smuggling. The report generated substantial media coverage and marked the beginning of the most intensive, exhausting lobbying period in Canadian tobacco-control history.

In Quebec, the new Revenue Minister, just after being sworn in, said that his number-one priority was a tobacco-tax reduction. In Ottawa, when an assistant to Revenue Minister David Anderson was asked about a tax rollback, she responded that "it is only one of the options the government is considering." When asked what the other options were, she was uncomfortably silent and unable to provide any. An export tax was not on the table. A tax reduction was being planned.

When Parliament resumed on 19 January 1994, the separatist Bloc Québécois (MPs exclusively from Quebec) pressed the government daily for action on smuggling. The party's demands received news coverage and increased support for a rollback. On 24 January, some Quebec retailers operating under the banner of the Mouvement pour l'abolition des taxes sur le tabac (MATRAC, movement to abolish tobacco taxes) started to openly sell contraband to the public as a means of increasing the pressure on government to reduce taxes. This received enormous publicity across Canada and even more in Quebec. Jubilant purchasers were pictured obtaining their low-priced cartons. Stocks sold out in a matter of hours. MATRAC took its protest and illegal sales to various municipalities around the province. The media, again especially in Quebec, continued to give ample coverage to this traveling circus. A 27 January MATRAC news release said, "To you, representatives of the media, THANK YOU!"[441, p. 7] The illegal sales had raised the contraband issue to crisis proportions.

MATRAC's illegal sales appeared to be a spontaneous tax revolt. However, André Noël, an investigative reporter with Montreal's *La Presse*, discovered that MATRAC had links with the tobacco industry. Jacques Larivière, Vice-President of CTMC, met with MATRAC leaders after a meeting on 11 January at which plans for the illegal sales were finalized.[372,440]

MATRAC received assistance from the Association des détaillants en alimentation du Québec (ADA, Quebec association of food retailers). Not only did ADA host the 11 January meeting in its offices, but it participated in the coordination of the sales campaign. For example, the local director of MATRAC in Sherbrooke, André Marcotte, was the regional director of ADA. Said Marcotte, "Behind MATRAC, one finds the ADA."[441, p. 9] ADA provided logistical help and PR expertise and prepared news releases. ADA even ensured that messages sent out by MATRAC members were consistent.

Tobacco companies were members of ADA and helped fund the organization. ADA's Director General, Michel Gadbois, formerly worked in PR for both Imasco and Benson & Hedges.[441] The open sale of contraband was not a new idea. In April 1993, Gadbois had raised the possibility at a news conference.[441] He later would say that they were waiting for a change in government in Ottawa and Quebec before their campaign went into full force.

While the antitax campaign was gaining steam, so was the campaign to maintain taxes. As part of the health lobby's efforts, representatives went on a tour of Western Canada to outline the industry's role in contraband, to build support for an export tax, and to oppose a tax reduction.

The tobacco-tax issue was in the news daily, and opposition to a rollback was becoming extremely vocal. MPs were receiving many letters and phone calls on the issue, mostly from people opposed to the decrease. Letters to the editor were pouring in. Some Liberal MPs made public statements opposing a tax decrease. Clearly, the health message was getting across. At the same time, government leaks reported in the media indicated that a tax reduction was closer to being announced and that federal and provincial governments were looking at a joint reduction.

Key tobacco-control advocates decided to heat up the campaign even further and concluded that a full-page, hard-hitting advocacy ad was urgently needed. NSRA drafted the text over the weekend. Major health groups held a conference call on Sunday night (30 January) to modify and approve the text. On Monday, in a matter of hours, CCSH succeeded in getting more than 30 organizations to endorse the ad. The ad ran the next day, Tuesday 1 February, in the *Globe and Mail*. Leading off with a picture of Prime Minister Chrétien, the ad read "Are 250,000 tobacco deaths and a federal tax giveaway of $1 billion your government's idea of bringing 'integrity' to Ottawa?" Readers were invited to write or call their MP to oppose a tax cut. The toll-free 1-800 number for Elections Canada was published for those who didn't know the name of their MP. Elections Canada was inundated with so many calls that its staff couldn't handle them. Health Minister Marleau apparently showed the ad to Chrétien, and Chrétien was not happy about it. The ad was effective and definitely enhanced the health lobby's campaign.

As the crisis escalated, the federal government knew it would have to act quickly. Chrétien personally lobbied provincial premiers to participate in a joint tax reduction. For reasons of national unity, it was highly undesirable that Quebec be the only province to reduce taxes. Ontario was key, given its large population and proximity to Quebec. However, the Premier of Ontario, NDP Bob Rae, was publicly opposing a tax decrease, calling instead for an export tax.[402] In Ottawa on Sunday 6 February, the federal government's top bureaucrat, Glen Shortliffe, met with Rae's top official, David Agnew. Attempts to bring Ontario on board were unsuccessful.

On Tuesday 8 February, the Liberals held a special caucus meeting to quell dissension within the party. Just afterwards, in the House of Commons, Chrétien announced the government's antismuggling action plan. The key component of the plan was a reduction in taxes. The federal tobacco tax on a carton of 200 cigarettes was reduced by $5.00 nationwide; in addition, on a province-by-province basis, the federal government would match provincial-tax decreases up to a maximum of $5.00, for a total possible federal reduction of $10.00 per carton. Taxes on other tobacco products, notably roll-your-own tobacco, would also be reduced. Enforcement by customs personnel and the RCMP would be increased.

In part to lessen the political fallout, the government announced that further measures would accompany the decrease. A 3-year health-promotion surtax, expected to raise $180 million, was imposed on manufacturers' profits. The money would be used to fund the "largest antismoking campaign this country has ever seen."[107] "Kiddie packs" (packs with fewer than 20 cigarettes) would be banned. The House of Commons Standing Committee on Health would be asked to consider plain packaging. The government reimposed the export tax of $8.00 a carton. And Chrétien had strong words for the industry:

> We do not want tobacco manufacturers to receive any benefit from the difficult decision we have made today. The fact is that the Canadian manufacturers have benefited

directly from this illegal trade. They have known perfectly well that their tobacco exports to the United States have been re-entering Canada illegally. I believe they have not acted responsibly.[107]

Premier Johnson of Quebec held a news conference immediately after Chrétien's statement. Quebec reduced its taxes by $11 a carton, bringing the total federal–provincial tobacco-tax reduction in the province to $21. Johnson also criticized tobacco companies and imposed a provincial corporate income surtax on cigarette manufacturers. New Brunswick was the only other province that day to announce that its provincial tobacco taxes would go down.

Overall, the decision was a major tobacco-control setback. Retail prices, including sales taxes, were cut by more than half in Ontario and Quebec, from about $47 a carton to about $23. The lower prices were almost inviting people, especially teenagers, to smoke more. It could have been worse, as little consolation as this may be. Had health groups not been so vocal and public opposition not been so strong, the health component of the government's announcement would probably not have been nearly as extensive. The federal tax-reduction formula permitted a smaller reduction in parts of Canada where contraband was less serious. In these provinces, the benefits of high taxes could be partially maintained.

The tobacco lobby had achieved an enormous victory, but the cigarette manufacturers received many black eyes in the process. In the month preceding the tax reduction, much of their contribution to the smuggling problem was exposed. Numerous news reports, editorials, editorial cartoons, letters to the editor, and comments on open-line shows painted them in a highly unfavourable light. Here is an excerpt from a *Globe and Mail* editorial published after the decrease:

> Any settling of moral accounts must begin with the cigarette manufacturers. It is not enough that, as a matter of ordinary routine, they knowingly make and market a substance that kills people — a substance that, uniquely among legal products, kills when used exactly as intended. By continuing to ship cigarettes to the U.S. in massive amounts, knowing that almost every last one would be smuggled back into Canada, they have actively colluded in the systematic evasion of the law. Among the guilty, they are scarcely better than the organized crime rings they [indirectly] supply.[199]

When CTMC President Rob Parker was asked on CBC radio's *Cross Country Checkup* what the tobacco industry was doing to fight contraband, he could only muster three things: placing markings on packages for export, measuring the size of the contraband problem through Lindquist Avey reports, and recommending a decrease in taxes to the government.[128] This was hardly a comprehensive or acceptable level of industry action, especially in view of the fact that the first item mentioned was required by law.

The strength of the public opposition to the tax rollback showed how far the public's sentiments toward smoking had evolved. Rothmans called the decision "politically courageous."[516, p. 3]

No one suffered more political fallout from the tax decrease than Health Minister Marleau. In the wrong place at the wrong time, she was placed in the exceptionally difficult position of trying to defend the government's decision. She was extensively criticized by health groups, including local groups in her Sudbury, Ontario, riding. She was roundly criticized at a federal–provincial meeting of Health Ministers that started, coincidentally, the same day as the tax reduction.

After Quebec and New Brunswick reduced their tobacco taxes, interprovincial smuggling became a problem. Low-priced cigarettes were being smuggled into the provinces that had not lowered their taxes. The situation in border areas was particularly serious. Retailers in Ontario and Nova Scotia pressured their provincial governments to lower their taxes to stem a decrease in retail tobacco sales. A domino effect ensued: Ontario reduced taxes within a few weeks, and a while later Prince Edward Island and Nova Scotia did the same.

Newfoundland, the Western provinces, and the territories were able to hold the line on taxes, in part because of their distance from the big markets of central Canada. Interprovincial smuggling did not affect these jurisdictions enough to force them to back down. Even after the federal tax decrease, British Columbia and Newfoundland still had nearly the highest levels of tobacco taxation in the world.

As anticipated, the industry used Canada's rollback to argue against tax increases elsewhere, especially in the United States. The Canadian experience was publicized in the United States by the National Coalition Against Crime and Tobacco Contraband. This organization was a front group funded by R.J. Reynolds.[156]

The tax decreases quickly and dramatically reduced smuggling into Canada,[282] which is not surprising. The tax reduction was so big in Quebec and Ontario that the legal price of cigarettes was in some cases lower than in the neighbouring US states of New York and Michigan. Also not surprisingly, exports plummeted, as illustrated in Figure 12.

There is no doubt that the tax rollback had an adverse impact on smoking rates after more than a decade of steady decline (see Figures 2 and 3, Chapter 2) — the prevalence of smoking increased according to several surveys.[57,273,569] In Ontario, the proportion of male students who smoked increased from 23% in 1993 to 28% in 1995; among female students the increase was from 25% to 28% over the same period.[457] In one Ontario study of smokers in grades 7 and 9, 34% said they smoked more as a result of the lower cost; only 3% said they smoked less.[506] In numerous media interviews, teenagers and adults said that they had increased the number of cigarettes they smoked a day; this is some anecdotal evidence of increased smoking.

In terms of per capita consumption, the overall increase two and a half years after the rollback was much smaller than expected. At a minimum, however, the long decline in consumption and industry sales had come to an end. The potential impact of other anti-smoking interventions may have been neutralized.

The magnitude of the health impact will depend on how quickly taxes return to their former levels. In February 1995, the federal and Quebec governments announced a total tax increase in Quebec of $1.20 a carton. The health lobby applauded the move as a small but desirable step. Small indeed — if increases continue at that pace, taxes will not return to their former levels until 2011.

The 1994 tax rollback was an unprecedented blow to antismoking efforts, and attention turned to another major tobacco-control issue, plain packaging.

CHAPTER 12

Plain Packaging

Alan King, *The Ottawa Citizen*

The importance of packaging

Packaging is an integral part of a tobacco product. As a form of advertising, it is essential to a brand's image. When Donald Brown was Vice-President of Marketing at Imperial Tobacco, he was asked in court whether as much time, energy, and expense went into designing a package as went into creating advertisements. He replied that packaging is "as important, more and more so."[56] RJR–Macdonald's Peter Hoult maintained that some young adults smoke a particular brand to influence what their friends think of them. "They buy it with their friends in mind," he said.[252] "Clearly, the package does communicate the cigarette they're smoking and we believe that people choose their cigarettes according to what those cigarettes are, and that includes imagery."[251]

In a 1982 publication celebrating the 25th anniversary of Rothmans, the company commented on the importance of packaging:

> The Company is very aware that every customer carries the Rothmans logo, on the package, with him or her all the time. That package comes out many times a day, and every time it is seen makes a personal comment about the person who carries and shows it. Trust in its quality must never be compromised through any lapse of attention to the smallest detail.[525, p. 7]

Similarly, Christian Hemain, President of Crealise Packaging Inc., which produced a special container for roll-your-own tobacco for RJR–Macdonald, said, "The user must be hurled into a situation where he wants to buy the container for itself because it is attractive. The ultimate target was to make the container as appealing [as], not to say more so [than], ... the content."[243, p. 201]

The TPCA did not prevent manufacturers from using the package for advertising or for conveying a brand's image. Indeed, with the TPCA in place, manufacturers introduced modified packages for many of the major brands.

Some packages bear advertising slogans. "Traditional Taste • Reduced Irritation" is on Player's Light Smooth. "Made with naturally mellowed, premium tobacco for a smooth, full flavour" is on Export "A" Smooth. These slogans help the tobacco companies get around advertising constraints. With other forms of communication restricted, the package is a critical marketing tool. Kevin Sheridan of Lawson Mardon Packaging, an international firm supplying Canadian tobacco companies, said, "The answer to the question whether pack design can beat restrictions on cigarette advertising must be a very positive 'yes'."[543, p. 99]

The potential impact of plain packaging

Health groups have argued that the alluring aspects of cigarette packages could be eliminated if cigarettes came in plain packaging, sometimes referred to as generic packaging or standard packaging. Perhaps the best descriptor is *dissuasive packaging*, a term coined by Dr Fred Bass of the BC Medical Association.[29]

With plain packaging, the only distinguishing feature would be the brand name, printed in small, standard script in black ink. The main colour of all packages — on the outside and on the inside — would be dull brown or gray or some other specified unattractive colour. In every other respect — size, texture, material, method of opening — packages would be identical. This would eliminate tin containers, glossy finishes, and embossed letters (except possibly for the health warning). The health warning and list of toxic contents would be given more prominence. The packaging requirements would also apply to carton wrappings and any other form of packaging seen by consumers.

Plain packs could significantly decrease the effectiveness of sponsorship promotions and make it much more difficult for consumers to make the association between the sponsorship and the brand. The standard colour required for plain packaging would also reduce the influence of any foreign advertising entering Canada and of any advertising people may have seen in the past.

Plain packaging would remove the imagery from cigarette trademarks. Said Rothmans in its 1994 annual report,

> plain packaging ... would have the impact of confiscating the Company's trademark values, leading to a changed competitive environment in which the Company's most important competitive assets would be diluted or nullified.[516, p. 9]

Indeed, plain packaging would create negative imagery. Instead of being a badge product to be proudly displayed, the ugly pack would be a source of embarrassment.

As Rothmans indicated, trademarks are a tobacco company's most important assets. As far back as 1971, BAT had 38 000 trademark registrations worldwide.[300] Marlboro, the world's top cigarette brand, has a trademark with an estimated global value of US $39 billion.[570] Without trademarks, a company can be reduced to nothing. Without a brand name, a cigarette is nothing special. Here is what Imperial Tobacco's Brown has to say:

> The product itself ... is very interesting, because in the cigarette business there is very little to distinguish, particularly in Canada, because we all use the same kind of tobacco, we do not flavour our tobaccos. So the discrimination in product terms, pure blind product terms, without any packaging or name around it is very limited. You can tell if it's very mild or very strong, and you might get some case characteristics that are different. But it's very difficult for people to discriminate, blind tested. Put it in a package and put a name on it, and then it has a lot of product characteristics.[53]

Tobacco companies use package colour to influence consumers' perceptions of cigarette strength. So-called light and mild cigarettes are typically put in packages with lighter colours or with more white space than stronger cigarettes in the same brand family. White suggests purity and cleanliness. As Hoult says, "the packaging is a most important means of communication and consumers have an expectation that the lighter the pack ... or the total pack get-up, the lighter the cigarette."[253] This packaging technique is commonly used with many consumer products: the Diet Coke can is a lighter colour than a regular Coke can, for example. Plain packaging would prevent this marketing technique.

Plain packaging would help reduce smoking in a number of other ways:

- ✦ It would decrease the impact of shelf displays, which are an extremely important promotional tool.

- ✦ It would improve the effectiveness of health warnings by removing the competing prosmoking messages (trademarks, colours, slogans).

- ✦ It would adversely affect some consumers' perception of the quality and taste of the product inside.

- ✦ It would send a strong educational message to the public that tobacco is different from other products and that unique consideration should be given before a purchase decision is made.

Best of all, the implementation of plain packaging would cost the government next to nothing. The industry would bear the implementation cost, a one-time expense that could be passed on to consumers at less than 1 cent a pack. Once implemented, the industry would save millions of dollars with the reduced expenses for package design, market research, and sponsorship and other promotions connected with brand colours.

A number of research studies provide evidence that plain packaging would be effective. In 1993, with the funding of CCS, the University of Toronto's Centre for Health

Promotion examined the potential impact of plain packaging. The study involved 129 Ontario youths 12–17 years old. The study found that plain packaging made the package — and thus the product — less interesting and that packaging had a greater influence on those who were thinking about starting to smoke than on those who were already smoking regularly. Teens used "wimpy," "boring," and "loser" to describe buyers of plain packages; "smart," "fun," and "popular," to describe buyers of brand packages. More than 86% of the smokers preferred being seen with brand packages. Most important, the study found that 40% of the teens thought that fewer teenagers would smoke if cigarettes were sold only in plain packages; 59% thought that there would be no effect; and 1% thought that more teens would smoke.[96]

A follow-up study, funded by the Robert Woods Johnson Foundation, was conducted in 1994 and 1995. This study involved more than 2 000 youths 12–17 years old youth in Ontario and in Chicago, Illinois. Of the Ontario students, 86% said the plain package was "more boring" and 78% said it was "uglier." Sixty-four percent said "cool kids" would smoke cigarettes from the brand package; only 5% said "cool kids" would smoke cigarettes from the plain package.[506]

Similarly, in Australia, a 1992 study of 66 youths 12–20 years old found that plain packaging "would detract from the image of cigarettes."[95, p. 125] Some of the comments of participants included "it's saying: don't buy me," "people would feel like rejects if they carried these," and "the warning is the first thing that strikes you, not the brand."[95, p. 123] In New Zealand, a study of 568 youths 12–14 years old concluded that "plain-packs would serve as a substantial deterrent to the initiation of smoking behaviour."[34, p. 17] The adolescents found plain packs "dull and boring." A study of 1546 regular Marlboro smokers, reported in *Forbes* magazine in 1987, showed that they, too, found plain packs unappealing:

> The proof is that when we offered them Marlboros at half price — in generic brown boxes — only 21% were interested, even though we assured them that each package was fresh, had been sealed at the factory and was identical (except for the different packaging) to what they normally bought at their local tobacconist or cigarette machine.[594, p. 109]

In Canada, the Loblaws grocery store chain tried marketing unbranded, "no-name" cigarettes. Despite a lower cost for consumers and despite the wild success of many other no-name products, these cigarettes failed in the marketplace.

Health committee studies plain packaging

Despite the potential benefits of plain packaging, the idea is relatively new in the field of tobacco control. No country yet requires the measure. In Canada, the CMA first recommended plain packaging in 1986. In 1988, NSRA and others tried unsuccessfully to get the government to amend Bill C-51 to authorize plain-packaging regulations. In subsequent years, health groups again called for plain packaging, but the measure was not high up on the policy agenda.

Thus, in April 1994, the House of Commons Standing Committee on Health was breaking new ground when it began hearings on plain packaging. The hearings were part of the package of measures promised by Prime Minister Chrétien on 8 February 1994, when he announced the tobacco-tax rollback.

Before the hearings began, eight provincial governments expressed support for plain packaging. As well, a legislative committee in Ontario amended Bill 119, the *Tobacco Control Act*, to enhance the provincial government's authority to require plain packaging. Federal Health Minister Marleau, describing cigarettes as "poison," also came out strongly in support, saying "We feel it would do a lot to discourage young people especially from taking up smoking."[48] She said she was ready to take on the tobacco industry. No other national health minister in the world had taken such a forceful position on plain packaging.

The first day of hearings was 12 April 1994, when officials from Health Canada opened the testimony. The Committee room was packed with media, representatives of both tobacco and health interests, and mysterious individuals who refused to identify themselves. It was then that health groups realized how seriously the industry was going to take the Committee's proceedings. Various industry lawyers, lobbyists, and consultants were present on the first and subsequent days. Some even shielded their faces when candid photographs were taken of those in attendance.

No doubt the Minister's strong public support of the measure mobilized the tobacco companies. The industry knew that the stakes were high and had moved rapidly to organize. If the Committee recommended plain packaging and the measure was adopted, there could be a tremendous effect on tobacco sales. An international precedent could be established, leading to a domino effect on other countries.

CTMC increased its staff. David Small, a key player in Jean Charest's campaign for leadership of the federal Progressive Conservatives, was the most prominent of the new people brought on board. Small was responsible for helping to organize the packaging-industry opposition to plain packaging. Throughout the hearings, CTMC published a daily *Plain Packaging Bulletin*. This bulletin, typically one page and available in both English and French, put the industry's spin on the debate. It was sent by fax to the industry's allies, as well as to Committee members.

Rob Parker, the CTMC President, put forward the theory that if cigarette packaging was controlled, liquor could be next. Alcohol interests, however, declined to join the fray.[489] Nonetheless, tobacco companies had no shortage of allies. Companies that made cigarette packages, companies that made the plates used to print the packages, companies that made the paperboard used in the packages, and even companies that made the ink used in printing all testified before the Committee in support of the industry's position. As usual, the main argument presented was jobs. If one-colour packaging was used, they said, then complex, multicolour printing processes would no longer be necessary. The companies would lose business and would have to lay off workers.

Health groups effectively undercut this argument. They suggested the warning could be in a variety of colours, possibly including a photograph. In this way, the complexity of packaging could be maintained or even enhanced. Jobs would be protected.

The tobacco industry and its allies also argued that plain packaging would mean a return to smuggling. The argument was that a simplified package would become easier to counterfeit and pass off as the real thing. Most Committee members rejected this argument. Existing coloured packages were already being counterfeited, albeit in relatively small quantities. Thus, plain packaging would not create a new risk. As well, it was suggested that a multicoloured warning or other package markings could make counterfeiting as complicated as it currently is.

Others supporting the industry included tobacco farmers, distributors, a tobacco workers union, and retailers. A long list of other companies and groups opposed plain packaging in written submissions to the committee.

To buttress the opposition to plain packaging, manufacturers brought in some American heavyweights. Philip Morris and R.J. Reynolds retained Carla Hills, US Trade Representative (USTR) from 1989 to 1993. She submitted to the Committee a signed legal opinion[413] stating that plain packaging would infringe a trademark provision of the North American Free Trade Agreement (NAFTA), a deal she had negotiated while working for the Bush Administration. As well, she asserted that a different NAFTA provision would require the Canadian government to pay compensation for expropriating tobacco-company trademarks. Further, she stated that a General Agreement on Tariffs and Trade (GATT) agreement on intellectual property would be infringed. Her former government deputy, Julius Katz, appeared before the Committee to present the arguments in person (see Figure 15). Katz got a rough ride. Said Committee Chair Roger Simmons, "The net message that I hear is this: yes, smoking kills, but we've got a right to do it. That argument lacks integrity."[545, p. 9:48] Simmons called Katz a "hired gun."[545, p. 9:47] MP Andy Scott said that industry trademarks were "encumbering our warning"[540, p. 9:51] and that the Committee was faced with two options: saving "Canadian lives or accommodating the principle you spoke of — trademarks."[540, p. 9:52]

Committee members had a right to be upset. The industry's position was outrageous. The industry was saying that even if plain packaging would reduce the number of deaths from tobacco-caused lung cancer, NAFTA prevented Canada from implementing the initiative.

In anticipation of the international-trade arguments Katz would present, health groups retained Jean Castel, respected professor of international law at Osgoode Hall Law School, and lawyer Michael Robinson of the Toronto firm Fasken Campbell Godfrey. Castel and Robinson traveled to Ottawa to be present during Katz's testimony and were able to blunt his effectiveness by releasing to the media legal opinions opposite to that of Hills and Katz.[93,167] The industry may not have anticipated this countermove — it was quite something to see the jaw of one industry lawyer drop when Castel and Robinson entered the room.

Figure 15. Plain packaging hearings before the House of Commons Standing Committee on Health. Seated left to right: David Palmeter, law firm Mudge Rose Guthrie Alexander & Ferdon; Julius Katz, Hills & Company, International Consultants; Richard Dearden, law firm Gowling Strathy and Henderson. All three are representing R.J. Reynolds Tobacco Co. and Philip Morris International Inc. Standing immediately behind those seated is Progressive Conservative Senator William Kelly, Chairman of Rothmans Inc.

Castel told the media that "it's simply preposterous if the Canadian government could not protect the health of its citizens without having to pay millions of dollars."[397] He pointed to health exceptions in both GATT and NAFTA that would justify government action.

Philip Morris threatened to pull jobs out of Canada. In a letter to the Committee, the President of Philip Morris International, William Webb, wrote that "if Canada adopts legislation in total disregard of internationally recognized trademark rights, this would be a significant consideration in any new investment decisions."[626, p. 2] He noted that Philip Morris owned Kraft General Foods Canada Inc. With 4 700 employees and 11 plants, Kraft was the largest packaged-food maker and distributor in Canada. Prominent brands of Kraft General Foods included Tang, Jell-O, Post and Nabisco cereals, and Nabob and Maxwell House coffees. Webb, a former head of Benson and Hedges (Canada) Inc., then a wholly owned Philip Morris subsidiary, was attempting to use economic pressure to influence the Committee's deliberations. A spokesperson for Philip Morris reiterated the threat in an interview with the *Globe and Mail.*[398]

The threat backfired. Health Minister Marleau asserted that "no US multinational tobacco manufacturer or its lobbyists are going to dictate health policy in this country."[597] Canadian nationalists were also outraged. Letters to the editor strongly criticized Philip Morris. The company's tactic was called "arrogant," giving "corporate thuggery a bad name," putting "corporate profits and proprietary interests ahead of Canadian lives," and an invitation to consumers to boycott Kraft General Foods brands.[23,384] Even *Marketing* magazine, an organ of Canada's marketing industry, criticized the "corporate blackmail" and "crass bullying tactics" in an editorial entitled "Get lost, Mr. Webb, get lost."[381] The overall reaction was so strong that Philip Morris later denied that it made a threat in the first place.[3]

The industry's main argument throughout the hearings was a familiar one — there was no proof plain packaging would reduce smoking. Packaging only affected market share, not overall demand, the tobacco lobbyists claimed. The industry rejected the studies health groups put forward showing that plain packaging would work.

The industry tried another traditional tactic, asking for a delay. It urged the Committee to hold off on plain packages until a Health Canada study on the subject was complete, the impact of the new health warnings was measured, and the Supreme Court of Canada ruled on the constitutionality of the TPCA.

Some industry witnesses even argued that plain packages would be counterproductive and might increase smoking among youth. This argument implies that attractive packages decrease consumption, an absurdity.

Throughout the hearings, health groups were united in their support of plain packaging. Organization after organization testified in favour. As well, Ontario Ministry of Health representatives and University of British Columbia marketing professor Richard Pollay expressed support. Nova Scotia's Health Minister, Dr Ron Stewart, presented an eloquent, persuasive endorsement of the measure.[570]

Representatives of some health groups attended all hearings. CCS prepared a detailed response to each argument raised against plain packaging. CCS also obtained signed statements from 23 marketing professors stating that in their opinion it was more likely than not that plain packaging would reduce consumption. The Lung Association brought in Stephen Woodward of Britain's Action on Smoking and Health to demonstrate international support for the proposed measure.

CTMC was the last witness to testify before the Committee. Parker appeared, accompanied by a team of consultants. No company executives appeared with Parker: they were not even in the room and thus not available to answer questions. Parker repeated the same arguments others had previously made. He emphasized the (false) argument that government interventions in the past had not decreased smoking in Canada and thus further regulation was unwarranted. Parker also submitted two further opinions that plain packaging violated international agreements. This last step was curious indeed. Canadian manufacturers were arguing against a proposed law that foreign companies said discriminated **in favour of** Canadian firms.

In the end, the Committee supported plain packaging in a carefully worded recommendation:

> In the interest of the health of Canadians, as suggested by the evidence available to the Committee to date and in the absence of evidence to the contrary, the Committee affirms that plain or generic packaging could be a reasonable step in the overall strategy to reduce tobacco consumption.[268, p. 29]

---

[3]E. Hayes, ABC journalist, personal communication, 1994.

The Committee recommended that the federal government establish a legislative framework to implement plain packaging but that regulations be introduced only if results of an ongoing Health Canada study "support the available evidence that such packaging will reduce consumption."[268, p. 29] The Committee criticized the industry for disparaging the studies supporting plain packaging and not providing any of its own studies.

All of the Liberals on the Committee supported the recommendation, as did Reform MP Margaret Bridgman. Reform MP Dr Keith Martin dissented,[385] to the dismay of many health groups — given that he had been a vocal opponent of reduced tobacco taxes. However, at a news conference, Martin said he would change his view if the Health Canada study provided sufficient evidence. The separatist Bloc Québécois Committee members dissented in a highly political minority report.[143] With a Quebec provincial election then on the horizon, it was not expedient to endorse an initiative proposed by the federal Liberals.

In March 1995, Health Canada released its study on plain packaging, 457 pages in length.[201] This was by far the most comprehensive examination of plain packaging ever conducted in the world. The study concluded as follows:

> Plain and generic packaging of tobacco products (all other things being equal), through its impact on image formation and retention, recall and recognition, knowledge, and consumer attitudes and perceived utilities, would likely depress the incidence of smoking uptake by non-smoking teens, and increase the incidence of smoking cessation by teen and adult smokers. This impact would vary across the population. The extent of change in incidence is impossible to assess except through field experiments conducted over time.[201, p. 15].

The study found that plain packages generated more negative images about smokers and smoking than did regular packages and that plain packages depicting a pair of lungs generated even more negative images. Plain packaging was found to reduce brand-name recall in respondents who had been shown a package earlier. According to teenage respondents, plain packaging would bother them a lot (24%); result in fewer teenagers starting to smoke (49%); result in teenagers smoking less (36%); and result in more teenagers quitting (38%).[201]

The final chapter in the plain-packaging story has yet to be written. If plain packaging is implemented, the biggest beneficiaries will be Canada's young people — and young people are the most strategically important segment of the market for the tobacco industry.

PART IV

Strategies of the Combatants

CHAPTER 13

Masters of Manipulation: Tobacco-industry Tactics

Washington Post Writers Group. By Wiley

The cigarette industry is peddling a deadly weapon. It is dealing in people's lives for financial gain. ... The industry we seek to regulate is powerful and resourceful. Each new effort to regulate will bring new ways to evade. ... Still, we must be equal to the task. For the stakes involved are nothing less than the lives and health of millions all over the world. But this is a battle which can be won ... I know it is a battle which will be won.
    —US Senator Robert Kennedy, [First] World Conference on Smoking and Health, 12 September 1967, New York, NY, USA[331, pp. 6, 13]

Industry survival: the nine D's

Tobacco companies know they are under siege. Thus, the basic strategy is to hold off the inevitable. The industry undoubtedly realizes that in the long term, many decades from now, there will be almost no smoking in Canada, just as there was almost no cigarette smoking in the mid-1800s. Meanwhile, until the inevitable happens, the industry seeks to reap massive profits. And, as will be talked about in a later chapter, tobacco companies are moving aggressively into developing countries to enhance the industry's future.

The industry's survival strategy can be summarized through the nine D's:

1. **Deny** the health consequences of smoking.

2. **Deceive** consumers about the true nature of cigarettes through marketing and PR.

3. **Damage** the credibility of industry opponents.

4. **Direct** advertising to women and youth, in addition to men, to maximize sales volume.

5. **Defeat** attempts to regulate the industry or control smoking.

6. **Delay** legislation if it can't be defeated.

7. **Destroy** legislation once it passes, either by trying to overturn the law in court, by disobeying the law, or by exploiting loopholes.

8. **Defend** lawsuits filed against the industry.

9. **Develop** new markets around the world.

Preceding chapters have described industry actions supporting this strategy, including using voluntary restrictions to prevent regulation, creating and promoting products that lessen the impact of high taxes, and supplying products that become contraband. This chapter looks at other industry tactics that deserve to be exposed in greater detail.

The use of front groups

Tobacco companies know that their credibility is widely dismissed, so others make pro-tobacco arguments. Michel Gadbois, the head of ADA, which organized opposition to high tobacco taxes, said,

> They [the companies] know that few people will listen when they publicly demand a reduction in taxes. But the average citizen has more sympathy for small retailers, who are selling less cigarettes because taxes are too high. And the manufacturers know this too.[441, p. 9]

If one digs deep enough into a pro-tobacco organization, a link to the industry will almost always be found.

The Smokers' Freedom Society (SFS) was a classic example of an industry front group. SFS was created and funded by the tobacco industry. It was not possible to become a member of SFS or to vote for the executive. The organization only had "supporters." Even though a significant proportion of its 8 000 supporters were tobacco farmers or employees of tobacco companies, the organization tried to portray itself as a grass-roots group representing the interests of Canada's 6 million smokers. SFS actively opposed laws restricting smoking and campaigned for a reduction in tobacco taxes. SFS arguments typically echoed industry viewpoints. After taxes were reduced in 1994, the organization and its telephone number ceased to be operational, a step that would not have been taken so quickly if SFS were truly a grass-roots group.

The use of front groups is a typical industry tactic around the world. In Canada, the industry has been the driving force behind the Coalition Against Crime and Contraband Tobacco and the Committee for Fair Tobacco Taxation. In the United Kingdom, the Freedom Organization for the Right to Enjoy Smoking Tobacco (FOREST) has industry links. In the United States, the industry is behind the National Smokers Alliance.

Tobacco manufacturers expand their leverage by joining many associations. In addition to CTMC, tobacco manufacturers have been members of numerous other organizations, including ADA, the Coalition québécoise pour la justice en taxation du tabac (Quebec coalition for fairness in tobacco taxation), the National Association of Tobacco and Confectionery Distributors, the Packaging Association of Canada, the Patent and Trademark Institute, the Canadian Manufacturing Association, the Canadian Advertising Foundation, the Association of Canadian Advertisers, and the Point of Purchase Advertising Institute. All these organizations have raised concerns about, or have opposed, additional regulation or taxation of the industry on one or more occasions. As members, tobacco companies are in a direct position to influence the organizations' decisions. Of these groups, one of the most visibly pro-tobacco is the National Association of Tobacco and Confectionery Distributors. Its Executive Vice-President, Luc Dumulong, is a former vice-president of SFS.

The wall of flesh

The industry's virtually unlimited resources permit it to mount a wall of flesh to fight back opponents. The wall typically consists of large numbers of PR specialists, lawyers, and lobbyists.

One of the PR firms retained by the tobacco industry in Canada and elsewhere has been Burson-Marsteller, the largest PR firm in the world. Although tobacco may be one of the ultimate PR challenges, Burson-Marsteller has had its share of difficult clients in the past. The firm was retained to deal with Union Carbide's 1984 Bhopal disaster, the *Exxon Valdez* oil spill, Dow-Corning breast implants, Argentinian generals, and the Three Mile Island nuclear mishap.[431]

Tobacco companies use teams of lawyers to vigorously defend any lawsuits brought by smokers for smoking-caused disease or death. Only a few cases have been filed against the industry in Canada, but in the United States hundreds of cases have been initiated. In the famous *Cipollone* case, which the industry lost in 1988 (the industry had the decision overturned on appeal), as many as three dozen lawyers were on the case. Estimates of industry spending on the case range up to US $75 million.[339] The industry fights hard to win every case because it knows that if a case is ever lost, a flood of other cases might follow. So far, the industry has never paid damages as a result of losing a case, but in 1996 a US tobacco company, Liggett Group Inc., agreed to an out-of-court settlement for the first time.

In an internal memo, an American lawyer for the industry described the litigation strategy of tobacco companies:

> The aggressive posture we have taken ... continues to make these cases extremely burdensome and expensive for plaintiffs' lawyers. ... To paraphrase General Patton, the way we won these cases was not by spending all of [RJR]'s money, but by making that other son of a bitch spend all of his.[321]

In Canada, an example of using the wall of flesh to lobby was the industry's efforts to oppose implementation of the second round of health warnings in 1993. After draft regulations had been published, the industry sought and obtained a meeting with the government. David Mair, then an assistant to Health Minister Bouchard, recalls that there must have been nearly 40 people in the room, only 4 of whom were from the Department. The other side was represented by industry executives, lawyers, and accountants, CTMC personnel, and packaging-company presidents. The various industry representatives presented all sorts of technical, legal, financial, and employment reasons for not going ahead with an early implementation date or any new warnings at all. In the end, the government went ahead with revised regulations but with a delayed implementation deadline.

Suppression of research

Over the decades, the tobacco industry has done its own health-related research on smoking. Early on, some of that research uncovered previously unknown information about the health consequences of smoking. Not only was that new knowledge concealed from the public, but the industry continued to publicly deny that smoking was harmful.

Although little is known about the research done in the laboratories of Canadian firms, it is known that Canadian tobacco companies have worked closely with their corporate sisters in other countries. For example, Imperial Tobacco participated in annual research conferences with other subsidiaries of BAT.[549]

Some of what was going on inside US tobacco companies has come to light. In 1956, Philip Morris scientists were writing memos saying that nicotine and carbon monoxide were causing "harm to the circulatory system as a result of smoking."[26, p. 186] In 1961, a memo to Philip Morris executives from the Research Director identified 15 compounds in cigarette smoke "as carcinogens" and 2 others as cancer promoters.[405, p. F2] A letter from the Philip Morris vice-president for research to his counterpart at a rival company (Lorillard) indicated that the industry had strict internal guidelines on the kind of research it would support. Excluded were "developing new tests for carcinogenicity" and "conduct[ing] experiments to show addictive effects of smoking."[406]

A key player in tobacco-industry research has been the US-based Council for Tobacco Research (CTR). Set up in 1954, ostensibly to fund independent scientific research on tobacco, CTR has been a PR and lobbying vehicle for the industry. CTR was largely created by the PR firm Hill & Knowlton. Indeed, CTR offices were initially located one floor below those of Hill & Knowlton in New York's Empire State Building. CTR did not try to get to the bottom of smoking and health issues, as it purported to do, but instead created a body of evidence that the industry could use to keep "open" the scientific debate.

In 1964, CTR created the Special Projects division. Directed by lawyers, the division provided funds for particularly touchy projects. The projects were directed by lawyers because legal rules protect the confidentiality of lawyer–client communications. The theory was that any special projects that produced undesirable results could effectively be buried. To date, that theory has been successfully put into practice.

Lawyers had their hands all over CTR work, even research not considered a special project. Lawyers intervened in the drafting of study reports, sometimes attended while work was being conducted in the laboratory, canceled projects that started to show that smoking could cause cancer, and denied future funding to some scientists who would not play ball.[185] Lawyers were involved in deciding which projects would be funded. Scientific merit was not the driving factor in funding decisions. Project results were used to create positive publicity for the industry and to shift attention away from tobacco as a health risk.[37]

Documents from Brown and Williamson (Imperial Tobacco's US-based sister company) further reveal that the company took steps to bring all potentially damaging internal scientific documents under lawyer control, thus making them "privileged" information, unobtainable by those suing the company. Further, the company moved important documents offshore and instructed employees not to make lists or notes of the documents being removed.[220]

In the following excerpt from the *Cipollone* case, Marc Edell, the plaintiff's lawyer, is cross-examining Kinsley vanR. Dey, the President and CEO of Liggett & Myers, a US tobacco company. Note how the witness characterizes the research that had been undertaken.

Q: When you talk about paintings, this was testing with respect to the relationship between cigarette smoking and cancer; is that correct?
A: No.
Q: It wasn't with respect to tar and nicotine on mice?
A: It was smoke condensate put on the backs of mice.
Q: The purpose of that was to see whether or not they would produce cancer; is that correct?
A: Yes.
Q: Tumors?
A: Produce tumors, yes.
Q: And Arthur D. Little did a study for you and they found that when you use this palladium catalyst that it significantly reduced the incidence of tumors and carcinomas in mice, didn't it?
A: Yes.

Q: And that there was some discussion as to using palladium in your cigarettes; isn't that correct?

A: Yes.

Q: Why?

A: Because the mouse painting test done ... with this particular substance reduced the amounts of tumors on the backs of mice.

Q: In fact, the use of palladium was never incorporated in your cigarettes, is that correct?

A: That is correct.

Q: And originally it was going to be done not for test purposes but because it was felt it was going to be safer. Is that correct?

A: No.

Q: Just for test purposes?

A: It was done in answer to the Wynder test who tried to reduce the tumors on the backs of mice.

Q: So the purpose for your company's attempts to use palladium in its cigarettes was to avoid mice developing cancers on their skins when scientists would spread tar and nicotine on them; is that correct?

A: Smoke condensate.

Q: Smoke condensate?

A: Yes.

Q: Is that correct, sir? That was the purpose of this?

A: To try to reduce tumors formed when smoke condenses on the backs of mice, yes.

Q: It had nothing to do with the health and welfare of human beings; is that correct?

A: That's correct.

Q: Do you know how much that study cost, sir?

A: A lot of money through the years.

Q: How much is a lot? A lot of money is different to different people.

A: ... I would say it is well over probably ... $15 million or more.

Q: And this was to save rats, right? Or mice? You spent all this money to save mice the problem of developing tumors; is that correct?

A: I have stated what we did.[108, pp. 3.265–3.266]

One way the industry publicizes research denying the harm of ETS is to hold a symposium. The industry invites sympathetic scientists, many of whom have received industry funding, to present papers at a gathering of many like-minded individuals. Although the papers are not peer reviewed, they end up being cited by the industry as evidence that there is not yet proof that ETS is harmful. One such symposium was held at Montreal's McGill University in 1989. Although the university did nothing more than allow one of its rooms to be booked, industry spokespeople refer to the McGill Symposium as if it had been some significant scientific assembly. The industry even published its symposium "proceedings" in book form[159] and ensured that it was distributed to libraries in Canada and elsewhere.

Suppression of freedom of expression

Tobacco companies portray themselves as great defenders of freedom of expression, but they are quick to deny others the same freedom. For example, Imasco and Rothmans have refused to allow distribution of shareholders' resolutions addressing health issues. Also, when NSRA changed *Player's* to *Slayer's* in a protest against the Player's tennis tournament, Imperial Tobacco threatened to take legal action for trademark infringement. In 1988, when SMART members from the University of Toronto law school charged a Shoppers Drug Mart outlet for selling tobacco to a minor, Imperial Tobacco refused to make a donation to the law school's annual conference. This refusal occurred despite the fact that Imperial had regularly donated in previous years and that the conference organizers had no connection with the students who charged Shoppers. Nonetheless, a spokesperson for Imperial told a conference organizer that the students "were biting the hand that feeds them."

In 1976, *Death in the West — the Marlboro Story*, a film for television, was broadcast in Britain. The film showed six real American cowboys, all of whom had been heavy smokers and were now dying from emphysema or cancer. Their doctors were quoted as attributing the diseases to smoking. The film contrasted the cowboy in Marlboro television commercials with the six dying real cowboys. After *Death in the West* was shown in Britain, the American television program *60 Minutes* was interested in bringing the film to the United States. Philip Morris quickly went to court in Britain to get an injunction to prevent the producer, Thames Television, from selling or rebroadcasting the film. Under the terms of an out-of-court settlement, all copies of the film were destroyed except one that was to be locked in a Thames vault. Mysteriously, a copy of the film resurfaced in 1981 in the United States. Over time, *Death in the West* was widely broadcast.[582]

Public deception

The terrible reputation of the tobacco industry has not come about by accident. Tobacco companies have earned it. To put it kindly, truth has not been a priority for the industry. For virtually every possible regulatory intervention, the industry denies that the regulations would reduce smoking yet carries on with its lobbying to prevent the regulations from being adopted. Deception also comes in the form of misinformation about the health consequences of smoking, advertising that misleads consumers about the true nature of the product, and misinformation to health departments and parliamentary committees developing public-health policies.

One telling example of deception comes from a Brown and Williamson document, "Smoking and Health Proposal," which is undated but appears to be from around 1969.

The document discusses a possible aggressive PR campaign on health issues. One of the explicit objectives was

> to set aside in the minds of millions the false conviction that cigarette smoking causes lung cancer and other diseases; a conviction based on fanatical assumptions, fallacious rumours, unsupported claims and the unscientific statements and conjectures of publicity-seeking opportunists.[52, p. 11]

The jobs argument

The industry regularly uses the threat of job loss in arguing against tobacco-control measures. But should World War II have been prolonged to protect jobs in the munitions factories? Should drinking and driving be permitted just to protect jobs in bars? Should Canadians be encouraged to smoke to prevent the loss of jobs?

The jobs versus lives argument is without merit. The addictiveness of nicotine means that any decrease in tobacco consumption will be gradual. Decreases in employment can be dealt with principally through attrition (quitting and retirement) instead of layoffs. More important, as less money is spent on tobacco, more money will be spent on other items, thereby increasing jobs in other sectors and offsetting any job loss in the tobacco sector. There is evidence that tobacco results in a net economic loss to society,[28] such that a decrease in smoking is economically beneficial. This is particularly so in the eight Canadian provinces that have no manufacturing activity and little or no tobacco farming.

Few major industries are as mechanized as the tobacco industry. In 1992, in the Canadian tobacco-manufacturing sector, production per worker stood at an incredible $725 485, an amount that would be even higher if all tobacco taxes were included.[563] A single machine can produce 14 000 cigarettes per minute. Walking through a factory, one wonders where all of the employees are. RJR–Macdonald President Pierre Brunelle has boasted that from the moment leaf tobacco is cut until the cigarettes are fully made and boxed ready for shipping, no person touches the product.[421] Total industry sales in 1992 were higher than in 1962, but the number of tobacco-industry employees fell from 9 081 to 4 930 over the same period.[149,563] This was the direct result of increased automation (which makes more workers redundant) and industry consolidation (corporate takeovers).

A major report by University of British Columbia professor Robert Allen examined jobs in the tobacco industry. Allen concluded that "the choice between 'lives' and 'jobs' is a false dilemma. Canadians can have a progressive health policy without causing substantial economic dislocation."[13, p. 30] If all full-time jobs in tobacco growing and manufacturing disappeared overnight, the unemployment rate would not even rise by 0.01%. This does not even take into account the new jobs that would be created by reallocated consumer spending or by productivity improvements from a healthier work force. If manufacturers moved production to the United States, the job loss would be even smaller because most jobs in marketing, sales, warehousing, and distribution would remain in

Canada. Allen concluded that threats of production shifts should be ignored because such shifts are inevitable with more efficient American factories and the Free Trade Agreement with the United States. Former Imperial Tobacco President Jean-Louis Mercier has said that with free trade the tobacco industry in North America will become continental in scope and that in time the Canadian market will be too small to support the three manufacturers it currently has.[647]

The perceived economic importance of the tobacco industry was a stronger deterrent to government action in the 1960s and 1970s than it is today. Declines in smoking have not had the major adverse economic impact that was once feared. Nevertheless, the industry continues to advance economic arguments. It is able to do so in part because many of its economic interests are concentrated (in the tobacco-growing belt and in manufacturing centres). Nonsmokers, on the other hand, are geographically diffuse and much harder to organize.

Political connections

Chapter 3 already pointed out some of the industry's political connections, but a few more should be noted. CTMC President Rob Parker is a former Progressive Conservative MP. CTMC lobbyist Mark Resnick is a former policy director for the Liberal Party of Canada. Jodi White, former Chief of Staff to Prime Minister Kim Campbell, became Vice-President, Corporate Affairs for Imasco in 1994. In 1994, CTMC hired Marie-Josée Lapointe as Vice-President. Lapointe had been press secretary to Benoît Bouchard when he was Transport Minister and later worked as press secretary to Prime Minister Mulroney. In 1996, Imperial Tobacco hired Mulroney's former Chief of Staff, Norman Spector, to head the company's lobbying section.

In the United States, the tobacco industry donates heavily to members of Congress and state legislatures. Studies show that members who receive tobacco money are more likely to vote against tobacco-control measures than members who receive none. In Canada, the industry's financial contributions to political parties are substantial and seem to be surpassed only by those from the major banks. In 1993 alone, Imasco gave $194 700, including $120 500 to federal and provincial parties, $9 200 to foundations and fundraising events, and $65 000 to leadership campaigns.[279] During the 1990 federal Liberal leadership race, Imasco contributed to several campaigns, including those of winner Jean Chrétien and runner-up Paul Martin. In its 1993 annual report, Imasco says that it "has never sought, expected, or received any consideration for political donations other than the satisfaction of having contributed to the proper functioning of the democratic political process."[279, p. 16] In 1992, Rothmans gave $3 833 to the federal Progressive Conservatives and $2 455 to the federal Liberals. From RJR–Macdonald in the same year, each of these parties received $30 000.[75] Tobacco companies gave no money to the NDP, which has a policy of refusing donations from corporations other than small businesses.

Charitable contributions to enhance public image

Knowing of their beleaguered image, some tobacco companies and executives make contributions to charity. These contributions are over and above event sponsorships, which are really marketing and not charity.

In 1993, Imasco's Corporate Donations Committee gave more than $3 million to 620 organizations, including hospitals, universities, art galleries, the Girl Guides of Canada, the Boy Scouts of Canada, the Victorian Order of Nurses, the Ontario Pharmacists Association, the Council on Drug Abuse, the Ontario Games for the Physically Disabled, the Pollution Probe Foundation, various YMCAs, and many others. Imasco sponsors the National Imasco Scholarships for Disabled Students through the Association of Universities and Colleges of Canada.[280]

Nicotine manipulation

Despite public assertions by the industry that nicotine is not addictive and that nicotine is only important to smokers in terms of taste, the true, critical role played by nicotine has long been understood inside tobacco companies. The knowledge inside the industry was decades ahead of what was known by the scientific community generally. The industry concealed this knowledge, thus delaying progress in research vital to public health.

As early as 1945, "Role of Nicotine in the Cigarette Habit," a study reporting the results of research supported by the American Tobacco Company, concluded that "with some individuals, nicotine becomes a major factor in the cigarette habit."[377] In 1962, a document written by Sir Charles Ellis, a scientific adviser to BAT, stated that "nicotine is not only a very fine drug, but the technique of administration by smoking has distinct psychological advantages and a built-in control against excessive absorption" and that "smoking is a habit of addiction."[392] A 1963 document written by Addison Yeaman, general counsel to Brown and Williamson, stated, "We are, then, in the business of selling nicotine, an addictive drug effective in the release of stress mechanisms."[649] A 1972 internal industry document obtained in a US court case shows a remarkable appreciation of the role nicotine plays:

> As with eating and copulating, so it is with smoking. The physiological effect serves as the primary incentive; all other incentives are secondary. ... Without nicotine, the argument goes, there would be no smoking. Some strong evidence can be marshaled to support this argument: (1) No one has ever become a cigarette smoker by smoking cigarettes without nicotine. (2) Most of the physiological responses to inhaled smoke have been shown to be nicotine-related.
>
> Why then is there not a market for nicotine per se, to be eaten, sucked, drunk, injected, inserted or inhaled as a pure aerosol? The answer, and I feel quite strongly about this, is that the cigarette is in fact among the most awe-inspiring examples of the ingenuity of man. ...

The cigarette should be conceived not as a product but as a package. The product is nicotine. The cigarette is but one of many package layers. There is the carton, which contains the pack, which contains the cigarette, which contains the smoke. The smoke is the final package. The smoker must strip off all these package layers to get to that which he seeks. ...

Think of the cigarette pack as a storage container for [a] day's supply of nicotine. ... Think of the cigarette as a dispenser for a dose unit of nicotine. ... Think of a puff of smoke as the vehicle of nicotine. ... Smoke is beyond question the most optimized vehicle of nicotine and the cigarette the most optimized dispenser of smoke.[155]

Another document, written in 1972 and entitled "RJR confidential research planning memorandum on the nature of the tobacco business and the crucial role of nicotine therein," stated that

in a sense, the tobacco industry may be thought of as being a specialized, highly ritualized, and stylized segment of the pharmaceutical industry. Tobacco products uniquely contain and deliver nicotine, a potent drug with a variety of physiological effects.[583]

Attempts by the industry to understand nicotine have been far reaching. A 1974 study of the "hyperkinetic child as a prospective smoker" stated that "We wonder whether such children may not eventually become cigarette smokers in their teenage years as they discover the advantage of self-stimulation via nicotine."[538] The study tracked school children, starting with Virginia students in the third grade.

In 1983, Philip Morris researchers completed a study showing that nicotine was addictive in rats. The paper was peer reviewed and accepted for publication, but the company had it withdrawn. The company later closed the researchers' laboratory and eliminated evidence of their work.[151, p. 3] The company did not release findings of the research; it was not until 1994 that the study became public, but without the company's consent.

The critical role played by nicotine in smoking behaviour was well illustrated in 1992, when BAT was considering whether to purchase a manufacturer of nicotine patches. According to confidential documents, corporate researchers from subsidiaries in different countries compared cigarettes and the patch for their relative merits as nicotine-delivery devices. In Canada, Patrick Dunn, Imperial Tobacco's Vice-President of Research and Development, wrote in a confidential memo to CEO Mercier that there would be benefits to owning a nicotine-patch manufacturer:

One could make an argument for the industry supporting development of alternative nicotine delivery systems by considering them in the same philosophical light as brand extensions or, in this case, a business extension. ... An effective quitting aid based on nicotine could have a serious impact on our business and it would be better for us than someone else to profit from it.[154, p. 1]

In the end, BAT rejected the acquisition because of the risk that this would contribute to the US Food and Drug Administration's regulating nicotine as a drug.[539]

A 1992 draft report by a senior Philip Morris employee openly describes cigarettes as a "nicotine delivery system," considers nicotine gum and nicotine patches as competitive rivals to cigarettes, states that the main reason why people smoke is to get nicotine into their bodies, and refers to nicotine as being chemically similar to drugs such as cocaine.[184]

Just as coffee companies can decaffeinate coffee, tobacco companies have the ability to remove nicotine from cigarettes. Despite this, tobacco companies leave nicotine in cigarettes at levels that create and maintain addiction. In the United States, Philip Morris test marketed a brand of cigarettes, Next, from which nicotine had been removed, but the brand failed in the marketplace and was withdrawn.

Companies have the ability to control nicotine levels in their cigarettes and the ability to adjust cigarette design to affect the amount of nicotine absorbed by the smoker. They can do this in a number of ways, such as selecting certain tobacco blends and adding additives. A 1991 handbook on leaf blending and product development from one US company describes how ammonia can be added to tobacco as an "impact booster" to make it easier for smokers to absorb nicotine.[333, pp. 365–366]

In the United States, numerous methods for manipulating nicotine levels have been patented. There are eight patents to increase nicotine content by adding nicotine to the tobacco rod; five patents to increase nicotine content by adding nicotine to parts of the cigarette, such as the filter; eight patents to extract nicotine from tobacco; and nine patents to develop new chemical variants of nicotine.[332]

In the 1980s, Brown and Williamson patented Y1, a specially bred variety of flue-cured tobacco with twice the normal level of nicotine. Y1 was grown in Brazil and imported by Brown and Williamson to the United States for use in some brands. In Canada, the federal Department of Agriculture conducted research, funded by tobacco companies, that successfully bred tobacco plants with much higher nicotine levels than was normally found in Canadian crops.[82] A 1995 study found that the concentration of nicotine in the tobacco in Canadian cigarettes had risen substantially over the period 1968–95.[488]

"Evidence of Nicotine Manipulation by the American Tobacco Company," a 1994 staff report of a US Congressional subcommittee, contained this conclusion:

> The ATC documents submitted to the Subcommittee reflect an intense research and commercial interest in nicotine. From 1940 to 1970, ATC funded over 90 studies on the pharmacological and other effects of nicotine. From 1963 to 1980, ATC researchers experimented with numerous methods to increase nicotine levels in cigarettes. On at least one occasion, in Seattle in 1969, nicotine-enriched cigarettes were test-marketed by ATC to the public.[377, p. 5]

In a tobacco-industry trade journal, an ad placed by one industry supplier, LTR Industries (a subsidiary of Kimberley-Clark), talked of the ability to control nicotine. Under the headline, "More or less nicotine," was the following text:

> Nicotine levels are becoming a growing concern to the designers of modern cigarettes, particularly those with lower 'tar' deliveries. The Kimberley-Clark tobacco

reconstitution process used by LTR Industries permits adjustments of nicotine to your exact requirements. These adjustments will not affect the other important properties of customized reconstituted tobacco produced at LTR Industries: low tar delivery, high filling power, high yield, and the flexibility to convey organoleptic modifications. We can help you control your tobacco.[322, p. 153]

Another supplier, the Contraf Group, described itself in an ad as "The Niche Market Specialists" and listed "Pure Nicotine and other special additives" as available from the company.[151, p. 5]

Despite all their knowledge about the effects of nicotine, the tobacco manufacturers deny that nicotine is addictive or that they manipulate nicotine levels in cigarettes. When the US Surgeon General released his 1988 report on nicotine addiction,[605] the industry vigorously ridiculed the report's conclusions, despite the existence of industry-generated knowledge endorsing the Surgeon General's view.

The "light" cigarette myth

A major response by the industry to health concerns has been the introduction and promotion of so-called light cigarettes. The industry began to lower the tar and nicotine yields in the 1950s, following reports of smoking as a cause of cancer. Tests done for *Reader's Digest* found that between 1957 and 1961, tar yields for many Canadian brands fell:

- ✦ Export "A" filter, from 30.9 mg to 26.2;

- ✦ du Maurier filter, from 22.1 mg to 18.9;

- ✦ Matinée filter, from 27.1 mg to 15.7; and

- ✦ Craven "A" filter, from 29.8 mg to 13.8.

Many "milder" brands still had extremely high yields. In 1961, Player's Mild (no filter) had 30.1 mg of tar, and Player's Medium (no filter) had 27.7 mg.[481]

Lowered yields continued as a trend in the 1960s. In the mid-1970s, there was a shift toward "ultra light" cigarettes. In 1974, only 0.3% of cigarettes sold had tar yields of 5 mg or less. The comparable market shares for different tar ranges for 1977 and 1989 are shown in Table 1.

Table 1. Market shares corresponding to different tar levels, 1977 and 1989.

Tar (mg)	Market share (%)	
	1977	1989
1–5	4.0	7.9
6–9	4.2	13.8
10–14	26.7	50.4
15–18	64.7	27.9

Source: Imperial Tobacco.[290]

There is evidence that switching to low-tar cigarettes may reduce the risk of lung cancer, but it has to be emphasized that the reduced risk is extremely modest compared with quitting altogether. For heart disease, one leading study found that lower yield cigarettes did not reduce the risk of disease.[460] There is no such thing as a safe cigarette. Describing a cigarette as "light" is like describing a poison as "cyanide light" or "arsenic mild."

Tobacco advertising seeks to portray lower yield cigarettes as safer for health, as these excerpts from marketing documents indicate:

Overall Positioning Objective
The objective for Medallion is to associate the brand with **the lowest** recognized level of mildness (Ultra-Mildness) and 'safety', with as little sacrifice or trade-off on image elements. ...

Strategies
Positioning
Reinforce Medallion's **lowest tar**, 'safest', perception [emphasis as in original].
— Imperial Tobacco Ltd, "Medallion," circa 1982–89[301, p. 3]

Player's Extra Light continues to be positioned as a milder, therefore healthier, version of Player's Light. It remains a health oriented alternative for interested Player's smokers. Its role will continue to be as such.
— Imperial Tobacco Ltd, "Player's 1988"[305, p. 4]

Opportunities
a) ... Due to continuing anti-smoking publicity, the public continues to be aware of and concerned with the suggested hazards of cigarette smoking. Matinée is then in an ideal position to take advantage of this situation with its low T & N and 'safer for health' propositions.
— Imperial Tobacco Ltd, "1971 Matinée Marketing Plans"[292, p. 50]

VIII. Advertising Plan
2. Copy Strategy
G. Rationale: As consumers shift from full flavour cigarettes to brands with lower 'tar' and nicotine levels, they will desire as much flavour and satisfaction as possible while easing their concerns about the smoking/health controversy. Because there are many new and established brands competing in this segment, it will be necessary to aggressively communicate that Export 'A' Lights is the **only** brand that has successfully combined full flavour **and** lightness in one cigarette [emphasis as in original].
— RJR–Macdonald Inc., "Canada. R.J. Reynolds Tobacco International. 1978 Annual Business Plan. Marketing Plans: Export 'A' Lights"[492, p. 2126]

As indicated by this last excerpt, tobacco companies seek to alleviate smokers' health concerns by providing a light cigarette that still has the taste (nicotine fix) smokers want. In reality, it is impossible to deliver such a contradictory combination, but advertising has created the perception that such a cigarette is available. For example, in 1965, Player's King Size was launched with the slogan "Come on over to smoothness, with no let down in taste." In 1972, a Matinée package redesign was accompanied by advertising that included the words "New Matinée gives you more of what you don't want: more taste, less strength."

In 1988, an ad for Rothmans Lights had the slogan "The Full-Flavour Lights!" and a package of Rothmans floating among the clouds.

Many smokers believe that low-tar and low-nicotine cigarettes are safe alternatives to quitting. Said Imperial's Donald Brown, "We target at people who are looking for milder brands and we are well aware that the primary reason many of them are looking for milder brands is because they believe a milder brand is better for their health."[55] The industry normally does not explicitly claim that light cigarettes are healthier, but cigarette advertising has clearly given this impression to consumers. When pressed, the industry will deny that low-tar and low-nicotine cigarettes are less dangerous for health.[254] For consistency, the industry has to take this position because it denies that any cigarettes are dangerous for health.

The meaning of *light* varies wildly between brands. Tar yields for light brands range between 4 and 15 mg; for extra light and ultra light brands, between 1 and 12 mg; and for regular brands, between 8 and 21 mg. Thus, there is the highly misleading situation where some extra light brands yield more tar than regular brands.[420] When roll-your-own products are considered, things get even more confusing: the tar yield of Rothmans Extra Light is 18 mg, that of Player's Extra Light is 19.7 mg, and so on.

Many light cigarette brands are not light at all; for example, Player's Light has 13 mg of tar, and Player's Extra Light has 11 mg. These two brands have a tar level almost as high as the 15 mg maximum allowed in the European Union, a maximum that will fall to 12 mg in 1998. How can Imperial get away with describing a yield of 13 mg as light? According to spokesperson Michel Descôteaux, "'light' is relative to each brand. There is no strict logic behind it. Ultimately it's the consumer who decides which cigarette is light for him."[420, p. 64]

What makes things worse is that the tar, nicotine, and carbon monoxide yields reported on a package represent only an average. The actual yield in an individual cigarette may vary greatly. In the case of Export "A" Ultra Light King Size, with an average tar yield of 9 mg, test results reported to the government and obtained under the *Access to Information Act* showed that most yields ranged between 6 and 12 mg.[499] This 6-mg spread is large — normally it's much less.

In quarterly reports submitted by Imperial Tobacco to Health Canada, the tar, nicotine, and carbon monoxide yields for all its products are accompanied by a disclaimer (on every page) stating that "the values for the above periods may not necessarily correspond to the mean values on products currently being produced, or the numbers printed on packages currently available for sale."[291]

Most people are unaware of just how misleading the reported yields of tar and nicotine can be. These yields are based on machine tests that purport to simulate the smoking behaviour of the average person. A small machine actually smokes a cigarette by taking periodic puffs (for example, every 60 seconds), by puffing for a specified duration (for example, 2 seconds), by inhaling a certain amount of smoke per puff, and by continuing to puff until a specified butt length is reached. The problem, of course, is that not all consumers smoke like the machine.

Many consumers believe that if a package says that the tar yield is 6 mg of tar, then each cigarette will deliver this much tar no matter how a cigarette is smoked. After all, they know that a bottle of beer will contain a certain percentage of alcohol no matter how it is drunk, and a container of yogurt will contain a certain number of calories no matter how it is consumed. In the case of cigarettes, though, the amount of toxic constituents inhaled depends directly on how a cigarette is smoked: an intensely smoked cigarette labeled as yielding 6 mg of tar could actually yield four times that much.

One technique to reduce machine-measured yields is to speed up the burn rate of the cigarette. With such cigarettes, the machine takes fewer puffs and inhales less smoke by the time the specified butt length is reached. Smokers, on the other hand, may adjust to the modified burn rate by reducing the interval between puffs, thus still taking their normal number of puffs per cigarette and inhaling their normal amount of tar and nicotine.

The main technique to reduce machine-measured yields to ultra low levels is to ventilate filters through small air holes. As the smoking machine inhales, it draws air through the holes to mix with the smoke. The machine receives more air and less smoke; consequently, tar and nicotine yields are lower. In 1975, only 0.7% of cigarettes sold in Canada were ventilated; by 1983, 42% were.[290] Ventilation has become even more widespread in the 1990s, but exact figures are not available.

Some ventilation holes created by lasers are so small they are undetectable by the naked eye. If the holes are covered by the smoker's lips or fingers, the levels of nicotine and tar inhaled can jump dramatically. Scientists have found that 32%–69% of smokers of low-yield cigarettes block the ventilation holes.[332]

The critical importance of ventilation is illustrated by the yields from roll-your-own tobacco. The government requires this type of tobacco to be tested in a filtered cigarette tube that has no ventilation. As Table 2 illustrates, there is very little difference in the reported yields from brands of roll-your-own tobacco, but there is a sharp difference among cigarette brands. And when a brand of roll-your-own is compared with the same brand of cigarettes, it may be seen that the roll-your-own product has much higher yields of toxic constituents.

As noted, smokers of low-yield cigarettes often change the way they smoke to compensate for the nicotine they are missing. Compared with the standard machine-test method, smokers might take more puffs, take longer puffs, smoke a cigarette closer to the butt, smoke more cigarettes, or even cover the ventilation holes in the filter. Thus, the reported quantities of tar and nicotine may be meaningless. Here is what the tobacco industry told the Isabelle Committee in 1969 while opposing a proposal to list tar and nicotine yields on packages:

> Human smokers differ greatly in the frequency and intensity of their puffing and the amount of each cigarette they smoke. Thus there may be little relation between the figures reported from the machine and the actual exposure of any given smoker with any given cigarette.[4, p. 1652]

Table 2. Comparison of tar, nicotine, and carbon monoxide yields
for selected brands of cigarettes and roll-your-own tobacco.

Brand	Cigarettes			Roll-your-own		
	T	N	CO	T	N	CO
Rothmans	15	1.3	16	19	1.5	18
Rothmans Extra Light	10	1.0	10	19	1.5	17
Matinée	9	0.8	11	21	1.6	18
Matinée Extra Mild	4	0.4	4	19	1.4	17
Player's	15	1.2	16	20	1.7	17
Player's Extra Light	10	0.9	10	20	1.4	17
Export "A"	16	1.3	15	20	1.6	18
Export "A" Ultra Light	7	0.8	6	19	1.5	19

Source: Imperial Tobacco;[291] RJR–Macdonald;[498,499] and Rothmans, Benson & Hedges.[510,511]

Note: T, tar; N, nicotine; CO, carbon monoxide. Reported yields of tar and carbon monoxide for some brands have been rounded. The roll-your-own version of Export "A" is sold with the brand name Export. All cigarettes are regular size except for Rothmans and Rothmans Extra Light, which are only sold in king size.

Some smokers of low-yield cigarettes may inhale more strongly than necessary to compensate for what they are missing. This means that a smoker may actually draw in more toxic constituents with light brands, thereby making light cigarettes more hazardous to health. For some potential smokers, including teenage girls, low-yield cigarettes may make it easier to start smoking.

Internal Imperial Tobacco research in 1975 found that smokers change their smoking techniques to get the nicotine they want: "[a smoker] adjusts his smoking habits when smoking cigarettes with low nicotine and [tar] to duplicate his normal cigarette nicotine intake."[51] Minutes from BAT's 1974 Group Research and Development Conference state that "whatever the characteristics of cigarettes as determined by smoking machines, the smoker adjusts his pattern to deliver his own nicotine requirements."[214] Research has shown that there is little correlation between machine-reported nicotine levels and the total amount of nicotine actually in cigarettes or found in the bloodstream of smokers.[35] Despite this knowledge of smoker compensation, the tobacco industry has never advised smokers that different smoking techniques can result in yields far higher than reported on the package.

Manufacturers can adjust the pH (acidic) level of tobacco so that the amount of nicotine absorbed by the body increases. Thus, two cigarette brands, each with the same nicotine yield according to machine tests and each smoked in identical fashion by the smoker, may actually deliver different quantities of nicotine to the blood.

The most distressing aspect of the emergence of low-yield cigarettes is how this has inhibited smokers from quitting, as indicated by the following excerpts from tobacco-industry marketing documents:

> We have evidence of virtually no quitting among smokers of those brands [of under
> 6 mg of tar], and there are indications that the advent of ultra low tar cigarettes has

actually retained some potential quitters in the cigarette market by offering them a viable alternative.

> — Imperial Tobacco Ltd, "Response of the Market and of Imperial Tobacco to the Smoking and Health Environment," 1978[287, p. 2]

The third objective [of Project Plus/Minus] was to explore brand selection patterns and the perceptions of light brands. The latter was approached in particular as regards the view of light brands as potential substitutes for quitting.

> — Kwechansky Marketing Research Inc., "Project Plus/Minus," prepared for Imperial Tobacco Ltd, 1982[344, p. 2]

Perceptions of Low-Tar Brands

LTNs [low tar and nicotine] allow consumers to smoke under social duress. As a category, the low-tar brands are seen as **a means** to yield to health considerations, social pressures and personal guilt feelings [emphasis as in original].

> — Marketing Systems Inc., "Project Eli Focus Groups Final Report," prepared for Imperial Tobacco Ltd, 1982[382, p. 21]

The desire to quit smoking altogether and the rationalization offered by many consumers that their going down in tar and nicotine brings them closer to the inevitable step of giving up smoking may actually increase the market considerably.

> — Marketing Systems Inc., "Project Eli Focus Groups Final Report," prepared for Imperial Tobacco Ltd, 1982[382, pp. 45–46]

Hence, Quitters may be discouraged from quitting, or at least kept in the market longer, by either of the two product opportunities noted before. A less irritating cigarette is one route. (Indeed, the practice of switching to lower tar cigarettes and sometimes menthol in the quitting process tacitly recognizes this.) The safe cigarette would have wide appeal, limited mainly by the social pressures to quit. ...

Strategically, it would seem that reducing quitting is the most viable approach. But it would also seem that a product solution may not be sufficient on its own. An advocacy thrust may be necessary; disaffected smokers do need some reassurance that they are not social pariahs.

> — The Creative Research Group Ltd, "Project Viking," Volume III: *Product Issues*, prepared for Imperial Tobacco Ltd, 1986[126, p. 8]

The tobacco manufacturers, the masters of manipulation, have a lengthy record of misbehaviour, but the marketing of low-yield cigarettes is one of their most deplorable offensives, exceeded only by the marketing of cigarettes to young people.

Youth: Target Group 12–17

The Toronto Star Syndicate; ©King Features Syndicate, by Jim Borgman

The critical importance of new young smokers

To continue to prosper, the tobacco industry needs new smokers to replace those who quit or die. Very few adults take up smoking, so new smokers must come from the ranks of teenagers and preteens. The industry vigorously denies targeting young people below the age of 18. Health groups and many politicians summarily dismiss industry denials.

Regardless of the intentions of tobacco companies, advertising has a tremendous affect on young people. Seeing tobacco ads everywhere may be the reason young people in many countries consistently overestimate the percentage of the population that smokes. In the United States, Camel cigarettes are widely promoted by a cartoon character, Joe Camel. A study found that Joe Camel was as recognizable to 6 year olds as Mickey Mouse: recognition ranged from 30% for 3 year olds to 91% for 6 year olds.[176]

Tobacco companies have paid to have movie stars smoke certain brands in feature films. In *Superman II*, not only did Lois Lane smoke Marlboros, but Marlboro trucks and advertisements appeared in various scenes. *Superman II* was not a movie aimed at grand-parents. In return for a US $500 000 fee, Sylvester Stallone agreed to use Brown and Williamson tobacco products in no less than five feature films, including *Rambo* and *Rocky IV*.[590]

In Canada, the trial to decide the constitutionality of the TPCA unearthed many details of the industry's marketing practices. Records indicate that Imperial Tobacco regularly conducted large surveys that garnered detailed information from respondents as young as age 15. Marketing documents referred to the "youth" market, sometimes specifically referring to groups younger than 18.

Project 16

In 1977, Kwechansky Marketing Research conducted four focus groups for Imperial Tobacco, two in Peterborough, Ontario, and two in Toronto.[343] The research was known as Project 16. Even though it was illegal in Ontario to sell cigarettes to people under 18 and even though the industry's voluntary code prohibited advertising to those under 18, the participants in the study were exclusively 16 and 17 year old smokers. Two groups were boys, and two groups were girls. Observers from Imperial Tobacco watched the focus-group sessions on closed-circuit camera, as did observers from McKim Advertising and Spitzer Mills and Bates, both firms that did work for Imperial. The purpose of the study, as outlined in the report "Project 16," was quite direct:

> Since how the beginning smoker feels today has implications for the future of the industry, it follows that a study of this area would be of much interest. Project 16 was designed to do exactly that — learn everything there was to learn about how smoking begins, how high school students feel about being smokers, and how they foresee their use of tobacco in the future.[343, p. 1]

As part of the study, there were discussions about the merits and demerits of various brands of cigarettes, the rationale for brand selection, and the teenagers' reactions to various tobacco advertisements. A Player's ad featuring horses

> was perceived most often as the most teen-oriented cigarette ad, and as teen-oriented as any other ad. It depicted honesty, freedom and no one around to 'hassle' them. Besides, riding is something young people do, not parents.[343, p. 89]

The summary of findings included the following:

> There is no doubt that peer group influence is the single most important factor in the decision by an adolescent to smoke. ...
>
> While some enjoy their first cigarette (both taste and self-image), many are rewarded for their daring with nausea. This perceived failure spurs them on to try again, and not fail. ...

Serious efforts to learn to smoke occur between ages 12 and 13 in most case [*sic*]. Playful experimentations, especially by children from smoking homes, can take place as early as 5 years of age, but most often around 7 or 8. ...

Whether schools do or do not officially tolerate smoking, it occurs in any case, but consumption is probably greater in school [*sic*] where smoking is officially allowed.

During school hours, smoking is a social activity and a way to pass time. ...

There is no question that the respondents believed that smoking is a hazard to health. ...

However intriguing smoking was at 11, 12 or 13, by the age of 16 or 17 many regretted their use of cigarettes for health reasons and because they feel unable to stop smoking when they want to.

By the age of 16, any peer pressure to initiate others to smoking is gone. In fact, smokers openly bemoan the sight of 11 or 12 year olds that they see smoking, and in effect, the 16 year olds now act towards their juniors as their own parents act towards them. ...

The health warning clause is perceived as an intrusion by government on individual rights, and a sham since governments make vast sums on tobacco tax, and alcohol, also perceived as dangerous, bears no warning clause.

The 'avoid inhaling' words are singled out for the strongest derision since smoking a cigarette in this way is seen as a waste and, in their word, 'goofy'.[343, pp.i–ii, iv–vii]

Project Plus/Minus

In 1982, Kwechansky Marketing Research conducted Project Plus/Minus for Imperial Tobacco.[344] The project's purpose was to build upon Project 16. Six focus groups were held in Toronto: four groups of smokers (males 16–18 and 19–24; females 16–18 and 19–24) and two groups of ex-smokers (males 19–24; females 19–24).

The project had four objectives: to examine why young people smoke; to learn how smokers feel about their environment, especially about nonsmokers and ex-smokers, but also including their attitudes toward the health issue; to explore youth perceptions of light brands, including as "potential substitutes for quitting";[344, p. 2] and to "probe the area of quitting among both smokers and former smokers.[344, p. 2]" The study highlights included the following:

Starters no longer disbelieve the dangers of smoking, but they almost universally assume these risks will not apply to themselves because they will not become addicted.

Once addiction does take place, it becomes necessary for the smoker to make peace with the accepted hazards. This is done by a wide range of rationalizations. ...

The desire to quit seems to come earlier now than before, even prior to the end of high school. In fact, it often seems to take hold as soon as the recent starter admits to himself that he is hooked on smoking. However, the desire to quit, and actually carrying it out, are two quite different things, as the would-be quitter soon learns.[344, p. i]

The top two motivations for quitting were sports and peer pressure. For those who succeeded in quitting, success came from internal resolve. As for the first brand chosen, the brand of peers "who set the smoking example will most often be the one initially adopted."[344, p. 58]

"Starting"

One research study done for Imperial Tobacco had an extensive section, "Starting," on why people began smoking.[124] The study had 1 022 subjects of all ages, including a group in the 15–19 age category. The subjects were classified into four groups, "non-experimenters" (the 35% who said they had never tried tobacco), "experimenter/rejectors" (the 5% who tried tobacco but never took it up seriously), "never starters" (the 40% that constituted the first two groups), and "starters" (the remaining 60%).

The study was detailed. It looked at 16 personality traits, 15 lifestyle descriptions, various personal activities and interests, assorted attitudes to smoking and health issues, and the relationship of these characteristics to each group. Non-experimenters were asked why they had not started smoking:

> Roughly equal numbers of about one in four point to a simple lack of desire to start, to health concerns, to social concerns (mainly pressure from family) and to physical reactions. In the latter area, problems with other people's smoking are described, but also, as has been noted, some dabbling on their own behalf is evident among a few, who do not consider that 'really experimenting'.[125, p. 10]

For experimenter/rejectors,

> while there was a high incidence of starting smoking among their peers when they decided to reject smoking, there was also a high level of pressure from within the home not to start. Peer pressure was not sufficient to encourage serious smoking. A major part of the reason for this was the physical reaction to the cigarette. Lack of physical tolerance is the major reason given for rejection of cigarettes. The products tried were just too harsh and irritating and caused symptoms Experimenter/Rejectors were not prepared to endure (unlike Starters).[124, p. 11]

Other documents

In "Fiscal '80 Media Plans,"[293] Imperial outlines the target groups for 1980 for each of the company's brands. Target groups were defined on the basis of demographic character-istics such as age, sex, and education. Some brands were targeted to smokers; others were targeted to both smokers and nonsmokers, despite industry claims that advertising is only directed to smokers. Imperial weighted the target groups and used these numbers (with the help of a computer) to select magazines in which to place targeted ads. Ads for certain brands were targeted to "men" and "women" aged 12–17. Sometimes, this age group was weighted more heavily than older age groups. The target groups for each brand are shown in Table 3.

An Imperial Tobacco document for the following year, "Fiscal '81 National Media Plans," contained a comparable target market strategy expressed in a similar format. For some brands, 12–17 year olds continued to be the most important and heavily weighted target group.[295]

Table 3. Target groups for Imperial Tobacco brands, 1980.

Brand	Advertising language	Target group Category	Age(years)	Assigned weight
Player's Filter	E	Men	12–17	1.0
			18–24	1.0
			25–34	0.7
			35+	0.0
	F	Men	12–17	1.0
			18–24	0.9
			25–34	0.7
Player's Light	E	Men	12–24	1.0
			25–34	0.7
			35+	0.0
	E	Women	12–24	1.0
			25–34	0.7
			35+	0.0
	F	Men	12–17	0.8
			18–24	1.0
			25–34	0.6
	F	Women	12–17	0.7
			18–24	0.9
			25–34	0.5
du Maurier	E	Men, women	12–34	
	F	Men, women	12–34	
Matinée	E	Smokers: men, women, some HS+	18–49	
	F	Smokers: men, women	18–49	
Matinée Extra Mild	E	Smokers	18–24	0.7
			25–49	1.0
			50–64	0.3
	F	Smokers	18–24	0.7
			25–49	1.0
			50–64	0.3
Cameo family		Smokers: women	18–49	
Peter Jackson Extra Light	E, F	Smokers: men	18–24	0.8
			24–64	1.0
	E, F	Smokers: women	18–24	0.6
			25–34	0.8
			35–64	0.9
	E, F	No HS		0.0
		Some HS		0.7
		Grad. HS		1.0
Medallion	E, F	Men, women	25–49	1.0
			50–64	0.9
	E, F	Grad. HS.+		1.0

Source: Imperial Tobacco.[293]

Note: Language for advertising: E, English; F, French. Education: Grad. HS, graduated from high school.

The 1981 English Canada target market for Player's Light was described in a different document as "young people under 35 years of age with particular emphasis on the under 20 year old age group, geographically weighted towards areas where Export 'A' is biggest and weakening."[306, p. 41] Creative guidelines for this target market emphasized somewhat the "under-20-year-old group in its imagery reflection of lifestyle (activities) tastes"; at the same time, Imperial was being "cautious in terms of alienating the older end of the total group."[306, p. 42] For Player's Filter, creative guidelines stated that activities depicted in ads

> should not require undue physical exertion. They should not be representative of an elitist's sport nor should they be seen as a physical conditioner. ... The activity shown should be one which is practiced by young people 16 to 20 years old or one that these people can reasonably aspire to in the near future.[296, p. 1]

In 1970, an Imperial Tobacco document said, "Young smokers represent the major opportunity group for the cigarette industry, we should therefore determine their attitude to smoking and health and how this might change over time."[292, p. 11] By 1981, Imperial Tobacco's market share for people under 20 was about 68%, far higher than the company's overall market share of about 45%.[224] In 1988, another company document, "Overall Market Conditions — F88," included these comments:

> If the last ten years have taught us anything, it is that **the industry is dominated by the companies who respond most effectively to the needs of younger smokers**. Our efforts on these brands will remain on **maintaining their relevance to smokers in these younger groups** in spite of the share performance they may develop among older smokers [emphasis as in original].[304, p. 6]

By 1995, Imperial's cigarette market share had risen to 67%. Clearly, the attraction of young people to Imperial Tobacco's brands has been a major contributor to the company's market-share growth.

Other research studied young people. Project Huron examined the appeal of a flavoured cigarette targeted primarily at males aged 15–25.[478] "Youth Target 1987,"[127] a general study with a custom component done for RJR–Macdonald, provided an in-depth examination of smoking among the young. Conducted by The Creative Research Group, the study covered 1 022 subjects aged 15–24. Before the study began, RJR–Macdonald wrote to the research firm to request that the report deal with the 18–24 age group, since "our industry does not market its products to those aged under 18."[620] Nevertheless, the report dealt with the entire 15–24 age group. At around the same time, The Creative Research Group was preparing a report for Imperial Tobacco that analyzed research from respondents as young as 15.

The following excerpts from various documents further demonstrate the significance of the youth market to the industry:

> Advertising Implications
> Export should continue to appeal to younter [*sic*] males who
> ◆ Are sports oriented;

◆ Drink beer;

◆ Enjoy popular music;

◆ Are most comfortable in bluejeans and T-shirts, etc.

However, to maintain our current franchise and attract lapsed users and Players smokers, Export's masculine, rugged image needs to be placed in a more social/socially acceptable context communicating that it's alright to smoke, especially Export.

> — McCann–Erickson Advertising of Canada Ltd, "RJR–Macdonald Inc. Brand Family and Smokers Segmentation Study ('85): Key Findings and Communications Implications," prepared for RJR–Macdonald Inc., 1986[391, p. 695]

◆ It is hypothesized that very young starter smokers choose Export 'A' because it provides them with an instant badge of masculinity, appeals to their rebellious nature and establishes their position amongst their peers. As they mature, they gain more confidence through experience (move from the educational environment into the workforce), acquire other symbols of their masculinity (cars, clothing, etc.) and strive for social and peer group acceptance.

◆ It is at this transition point (ages 18–24) that Export 'A' is declining in its ability to hold the young adult males, as they go through the maturing process, due to its outdated, irrelevant image.

> — RJR–Macdonald Inc., "Export Family Strategy Document," 1982[493, p. 7299]

F88 Overall Marketing Objectives

1. **RE-ESTABLISH clear distinct images** for ITL brands with particular emphasis on relevance to younger smokers. Shift resources substantially in favour of avenues that allow for the expression and reinforcement of these image characteristics [emphasis as in original]

> — Imperial Tobacco Ltd, "Overall Market Conditions – F88," circa 1987[304, p. 11]

In order to move Player's Light up on the masculinity dimension, we will continue throughout F'89 to feature creative which reflects freedom, independence and self-reliance in a relevant fashion for young males.

> — Imperial Tobacco Ltd, "Player's 1988"[305, p. 4]

They [Québécois subjects] are sorry that they ever started smoking because it's harmful but they feel somewhat trapped. They are constantly reminded of their lack of willpower. To defend themselves they tend to put on a jaunty air. They do this to save face because they would really like to quit and not appear to be slaves to their cigarettes. ... Those who have tried to give up smoking have found the experience very painful. It made them realize that, although they thought they could quit easily, they have become slaves to their cigarettes.

> — Kwechansky Marketing Research Inc., "Project Plus/Minus: Young People and Smoking, Behaviours and Attitudes [Quebec]," a study prepared for Imperial Tobacco Ltd, 1982[478, p. 18]

Rationale

1. By younger modern smokers, we mean people ranging from starters of the smoking habit up to and through the seeking and setting of their independent adult lifestyle.

Relevant lifestyle is the key to the brand's positioning, and the youthful emphasis is a psychological not a chronological one.

2. At a younger age, taste requirements and satisfaction in a cigarette are thought to play a secondary role to the social requirements. Therefore, taste, until a certain nicotine dependence has been developed, is somewhat less important than other things.
— Spitzer, Mills & Bates, "The Player's Family: A Working Paper,"
prepared for Imperial Tobacco Ltd, 1977[554, p. 14]

In the West, and particularly B.C., the brand [Player's] has a special role for young people starting the smoking habit.
— Spitzer, Mills & Bates, "The Player's Family: A Working Paper,"
prepared for Imperial Tobacco Ltd, 1977[554, p. 17]

New, Non-traditional Media
We have frequently discussed the problems that our media-restricted, C.T.M.C.-controlled environment cause in terms of effectively communicating with smokers, especially young smokers. This situation will likely get worse in the future. ...

What we are talking about is having our **imagery** reach those difficult to reach, non-reading young people that frequent malls in an impactful, involving first-class way that makes them, us, mall managers, etc. happy [emphasis as in original].
— Imperial Tobacco Ltd, document entitled "Strictly Confidential,"
circa 1984[303, p. 10]

A 1973 R.J. Reynolds document from the United States is also telling. The document, a memorandum written by Claude E. Teague, Jr, then the company's Assistant Director of Research and Development, said that "realistically, if our Company is to survive and prosper, over the long term we must get our share of the youth market," defined as "the approximately twenty-one year old and under group."[584, p. 1] Teague wrote that imagery starts people smoking, and "physical effects" keep them smoking:

For the pre-smoker and 'learner' the physical effects of smoking are largely unknown, unneeded, or actually quite unpleasant or awkward. The expected or derived psychological effects are largely responsible for influencing the pre-smoker to try smoking, and provide sufficient motivation during the 'learning' period to keep the 'learner' going, despite the physical unpleasantness and awkwardness of the period.

In contrast, once the 'learning' period is over, the physical effects become of overriding importance and desirability to the confirmed smoker, and the psychological effects, except the tension relieving effect, largely wane in importance or disappear.[584, p. 2]

The memorandum recommends that in a new cigarette for the youth market the "rate of absorption of nicotine should be kept low by holding pH (acidity) down, probably below 6" and that "the smoke should be as bland as possible" because "the beginning smoker and inhaler has a low tolerance for smoke irritation."[584, p. 4] Teague recommended that the marketing department review current high school history books to find a good brand name and image theme. The memorandum recommended the following imagery characteristics for a product:

> a new brand aimed at the young smoker must somehow become the 'in' brand and its promotion should emphasize togetherness, belonging and group acceptance, while at the same time emphasizing individuality and 'doing ones own thing'.[584, p. 6]

These documents reveal much about tobacco-industry ethics. Even though industry research showed that teens start young and became addicted, the industry continued to direct advertising to teens. This evidence makes the case for a legislated ban on all advertising and promotion all the more compelling. With comprehensive advertising restrictions in place, the industry would no longer be able to continue its documented behaviour.

CHAPTER 15

Women:
"You've Gone the Wrong Way, Baby"

Alan King, The Ottawa Citizen

Women's smoking increases and so does women's lung cancer

A fundamental change in the tobacco market this century has been the increase in tobacco use by women. At the turn of the century, it was socially unacceptable for women to smoke — and they were the ones leading the drive to ban cigarettes — but by the end of World War II that had all changed. Women were smoking in unprecedented numbers. A 1966 government survey found that 32% of the women aged 15+ and 43% of the women 20–24 years old regularly smoked. The comparable figures for men were 54% and 60%.[227]

The rise in smoking among women has led to a rise in smoking-caused disease and death among women. As Figure 1 (Chapter 2) shows, the lung cancer mortality among men has leveled off, but it continues to increase among women. Lung cancer mortality for women rose a startling 405% between 1970 and 1996.[428] As illustrated in Figure 16, deaths from lung cancer among women now exceed deaths from breast cancer, and the situation is expected to get worse.

At one time, it didn't seem that smoking was affecting women's health as seriously as it was affecting men's. For example, the lung cancer rate for men in 1961 was almost seven

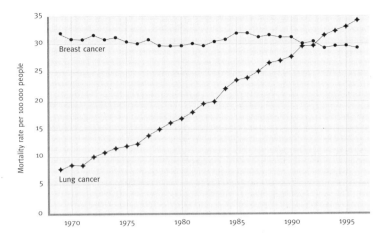

Figure 16. Age-standardized death rates for lung cancer and breast cancer among Canadian women, 1969–96.[428]

times that for women, even though men did not smoke seven times as much as women.[567] Now we know why — the men had a head start. The 1980 US Surgeon General's Report, "The Health Consequences of Smoking for Women," laid to rest any doubt that smoking was an equal-opportunity killer.[603] When women and men have the same smoking patterns (number of years smoked, number of cigarettes per day, etc.), the risks of illness are likely to be similar.[106] As Elinor Wilson of the Heart and Stroke Foundation notes, "When women smoke like men, they die like men."

Some health risks of smoking are unique to women. Smoking is associated with menstrual disorders, early menopause, and osteoporosis (bone thinning) after menopause. A woman who smokes while pregnant is risking the health of her baby (see Chapter 2). Smokers who take birth control pills have an increased risk of stroke.[17]

Why women smoke

Why do women smoke? They smoke for many of the same reasons men do: they're addicted; and both men and women may smoke to enhance social acceptability, to improve self-esteem, or to relieve stress. But many more women than men use smoking as a form of weight control. This is particularly true of teenage girls who may be obsessed with their weight. Many are afraid they will gain weight if they quit smoking.

More women may be smoking because more women are working and can afford to smoke. Another reason is that changing social norms made it socially acceptable for women to smoke. Some women smoke because they grew up in households where the mother smoked. In earlier years, women may have taken up smoking because it was glamorously portrayed in Hollywood movies by stars such as Betty Grable, Marlene Dietrich, and Lauren Bacall.

Marketing targets women

Another reason why women smoke is that the tobacco companies want them to. Industry marketing tactics include advertisements, sponsorship promotions, and special brands deliberately targeted at women. For many girls, there is a gap between actual and desired self-image. The industry portrays cigarettes as something that can fill the gap.

In Canada, the first ad with a woman smoking appeared on the social page of the *Montreal Gazette* on 26 May 1927 (see page 85). The caption read "His favourite brand — and mine!" The brand was Player's. Before this, men and women had appeared together in advertising, but the woman was not smoking. Many other advertisements had featured an attractive woman, no doubt to catch the attention and patronage of men.

Once Player's broke the advertising taboo, many other ads featured women smokers. This development was greeted with tremendous excitement in the tobacco industry. In 1927, an article in the August issue of the *Canadian Cigar and Tobacco Journal* commented that "this advertising will effect a widespread adoption of the cigarette mode" and that "the result will, of course, be seen in greatly increased sales for the tobacconists."[536] Another article in the same issue indicated that

> Retailers hope that such advertising will continue. ... Retailers report the nonchalant manner in which more women than ever come into the tobacco stores to make their own purchases of cigarettes. Where it used to be in perfumed and special brands, it is now the regular 'he-man smoke'.[72]

Another sign of the times was that more jewellery stores started to add a line of cigarette cases.

In the 1930s, Guinea Gold cigarettes came in several versions. One had rouge tips to go with ladies' lipstick, and another had amber tips, providing a more masculine appearance. Advertising for Guinea Gold sometimes featured women modeling the latest fashion designs from New York.

One of the ads for Winchester cigarettes in the 1930s showed women engaged in social and sporty activities. "These ads were oriented towards the women who aspired to the elite class and the ones who already belong to it," according to Imperial Tobacco.[297, p. 1]

In the United States, Lucky Strike's well-known campaign that began in 1928[213, p. 4] encouraged women to "Reach for a Lucky instead of a sweet," deliberately zeroing in on weight concerns. Candy manufacturers protested, so the slogan was changed to "When tempted Reach for a Lucky instead," but the message was still the same. One ad, featuring the shadow of a woman with a double chin, contained the following text:

> Avoid that future shadow by refraining from overindulgence, if you would maintain the modern figure of fashion. We do not represent that smoking Lucky Strike Cigarettes will bring modern figures or cause the reduction of flesh. We do declare that when tempted to do yourself too well, if you will 'Reach for a Lucky' instead, you will avoid overindulgence in things that cause excess weight and, by avoiding overindulgence, maintain a modern, graceful form.[645]

A 1950 item in the *United States Tobacco Journal* included the following:

> A massive potential market still exists among women and young adults, cigarette indus-
> try leaders agreed, acknowledging that recruitment of these millions of prospective
> smokers comprises the major objective for the immediate future and on a long term
> basis as well.[601]

For years, many brands were promoted to both men and women, but the advertisements targeted at the two groups were different. In the late 1960s, Philip Morris launched
Virginia Slims, a cigarette brand specifically targeted at women. The cigarette's name and
width suggested thinness. Advertisements played on the theme of freedom, independence,
and women's emancipation, using the slogan "You've come a long way, baby." A 1994
study published in JAMA reported the following results:

> [In] girls younger than 18 years, smoking initiation increased abruptly around 1967,
> when tobacco advertising aimed at selling specific brands to women was introduced. This
> increase was particularly marked in those females who never attended college.[477, p. 608]

One of the early Virginia Slims models was Cheryl Tiegs, who went on to become a well-
known fashion model. In 1989, an American advertising account executive for a leading
feminine brand said, "We try to tap the emerging independence and self-fulfilment of
women, to make smoking a badge to express that."[619, p. B1] The irony today, however, is
that the women who are the most emancipated in terms of education and career are those
least likely to smoke.

In Canada, brands targeted at women have included Matinée, Cameo, and Contessa.
Slim cigarettes have included Matinée Slims, Contessa Slims, and Craven 'A' Superslims.
Imperial Tobacco's President Donald Brown has described Matinée Special Mild as a brand
having a direction for "modern young women." The brand was positioned "to be more modern, more up-to-date, certainly clearly for women, ... for women who today, in their busy
life, increasingly felt that they would like a moment of relaxation and self-indulgence."[54]
One ad for the brand featured a woman smoking while relaxing in a bathtub.

Other product innovations also make smoking more attractive to women. Luxury-
length cigarettes (100 and 120 millimetres) suggest fashionableness and thinness the same
way slim cigarettes do. Indeed, American Tobacco boasts how well its long, slim brand
Misty is doing in the US "fashion segment."[591, p. 52]

As previously noted, the emergence of light cigarettes may make it easier for teenage
girls to begin smoking. In fact, women are more likely than men to smoke low-yield tar
and nicotine cigarettes. Perfumed cigarettes with attractive fragrances have re-emerged in
some markets, such as happened with the Chelsea brand in the United States.

Imperial Tobacco's internal documents from around 1984 shed light on one adver-
tising campaign aimed at women. The documents discuss ads being prepared for Matinée
Extra Mild cigarettes. The series of ads was to suggest "a typical day in the life of our
[Matinée Extra Mild] woman."[302, p. 1] The following describes the creative rationale:

> Our woman is front and center. She is unquestionably the star. She is happy and healthy.
> She is not a physical fitness fanatic but loves to take part in healthy fun activities. And

while she is good at them, she is not a champion. She is a good week-end skier and cyclist but is equally exhilarated by impromptu volleyball games or tobogganing.

As the strategy dictates, her activities are not too strenuous or aerobic. Smoking a low T & N cigarette would be a logical extension of the lifestyle depicted. ...

The theme **Feeling extra good. Smoking Extra Mild.** is a reflection of the feeling that seems to be indicated by prior research; that is: 'Even though I smoke, I like to be active and look after myself — so I smoke an extra mild cigarette' [emphasis as in original].[302, pp. 1–2]

The target group was described as "females under 49 years of age with greater emphasis on the 25–34 age group, weighted towards good very low T/N markets."[480, p. 2] The advertising objective was to

communicate to the target group that [Matinée Extra Mild] is:
1. A very low T/N product delivering a relatively high degree of satisfaction;
2. projecting a lifestyle image from which low tar smoking is a positive extension; and
3. a brand for women.[476, p. 2]

After the TPCA imposed advertising restrictions, sponsorships of women's fashion-related activities increased, notably through Matinée Ltd.

Smoking: a feminist issue

Tobacco products are the leading cause of premature death among women. Clearly, smoking is a feminist issue. However, prominent women's groups in Canada and other countries have been conspicuously quiet in calling for government action to control tobacco companies. Feminist organizations may not appreciate the significance of tobacco-related harm. More often, organizations feel they do not have the resources to take on another issue, especially when it appears that so many other groups are fighting against tobacco use. The National Action Committee on the Status of Women, however, did support the campaign to pass the TPCA in 1988.

Success at reducing women's smoking

Canada has seen a decline in smoking among women, although the decline has not been as significant as among men. Imperial Tobacco data show that between 1971 and 1993,[4] smoking prevalence declined from 39% to 28% among women and from 55% to 30% among men.[279,290]

Canada's strategy of tax increases and regulation has had a notable impact on reducing women's smoking: the rate of decline accelerated after 1982, when higher tobacco taxes

---

[4] 1993 data are derived by taking the general 1993 prevalence figure of 29% provided by Imperial Tobacco and using a 2% spread in smoking rates for men and women (30% for men; 28% for women), a spread comparable to that found in other surveys.

and new regulations were implemented. Imperial Tobacco data show that smoking among women dropped from 35% in 1981 to 28% by 1993, a decrease of 7% after having seen virtually no net change over the previous two decades.[279,290,508] Among teenage girls, the decline was even more pronounced. Government data show that the prevalence of smoking among women 15–19 years old decreased from 42% in 1981 to 25% in 1991. Those continuing to smoke in 1991 were more likely than before to be occasional smokers than to be daily smokers.[229,445,446,447,564]

This progress is impressive. The 1994 tax decrease, however, may halt or reverse a decade of progress. Unless high taxes return and the ban on tobacco advertising that was overturned by the Supreme Court is reimposed, the prospect for reducing smoking among women becomes bleaker.

CHAPTER 16

Farmers on Tobacco Road

Alan King, *The Ottawa Citizen*

Tobacco farming in Canada

Canada's success in controlling smoking is all the more notable given the large quantity of tobacco leaf grown in Canada. Tobacco is both a significant cash crop and an important agricultural export. Canada is the world's sixth largest producer of flue-cured tobacco.[553] When all types of tobacco are included, Canada is one of the world's top 20 producers.

About 90% of the tobacco grown in Canada is produced in a highly concentrated area in southwestern Ontario, especially near the towns of Delhi and Tillsonburg close to the north shore of Lake Erie. The remainder is grown near Joliette, Quebec (98 farmers), and there is a smattering in New Brunswick (5 farmers), Nova Scotia (9 farmers), and Prince Edward Island (35 farmers).[89]

At one time, most of the tobacco used in Canada was imported from the United States. What was grown in Canada was principally cultivated in Quebec, but some was grown in Essex and Kent counties near Windsor, Ontario. Tobacco growing had been introduced in these counties by United Empire Loyalists, who brought seeds from their tobacco farms in the United States.

A number of events stimulated domestic tobacco farming. The American Civil War (1861–65) raised the price of US tobacco, which prompted companies in Canada to look for other sources of supply. In the early 1880s, the federal government's National Policy stimulated domestic growing by setting taxes on domestic tobacco at lower levels than the tariffs on imported tobacco. Other fiscal changes in 1897 gave further protection to Canadian growers. The amount of tobacco grown increased from 726 000 kg in 1870–71 to 7 938 000 kg in 1910.[289] Part of the growth was attributable to the introduction in 1900 of flue-cured tobacco in the Leamington area of southern Ontario by the Empire Tobacco Co., a forerunner of Imperial. By 1920 the upswing of Canadian-grown tobacco continued, but still two thirds of the tobacco used in Canada was imported. It was in the 1930s that tobacco started to be produced in great quantities in what today is Ontario's tobacco belt, much of which was once a sandy dustbowl. By the 1950s, 99% of the tobacco in Canadian cigarettes was grown in Canada.

Historically, tobacco companies have encouraged and helped farmers to begin growing tobacco. Naturally, a strong domestic supply of tobacco leaf can be nothing but beneficial for the industry because more farmers means a more secure supply and lower prices. More tobacco farmers also means more political clout.

Not surprisingly, tobacco farmers have always been strong opponents of tobacco-control measures: measures that reduce tobacco use may have a direct impact on their income. MPs in regions representing tobacco growers have typically taken strong pro-tobacco positions.

Today, there is no doubt that tobacco continues to make a huge contribution to the local economies of four Ontario counties: the Regional Municipality of Haldimand–Norfolk in particular and Brant, Elgin, and Oxford counties to a lesser extent.

Canadian tobacco farmers are sometimes perceived as innocent victims harmed by decreases in smoking. However, the majority of tobacco farmers probably began farming **after** the government started efforts to reduce smoking, so presumably they knew of the financial risks. In fact, tobacco farmers do very well financially. In 1990, according to Statistics Canada, tobacco farmers earned an average income of $79 062, more than any other type of farmers. The average among farmers in general was far lower, at $47 426.[81] In 1990, the income of the average tobacco farm exceeded the income of about two thirds of Ontario families.[561]

Although the amount of tobacco grown has declined since the early 1980s, farmers have done remarkably well maintaining production in the face of the "health scare." Total 1993 Ontario flue-cured crop sales of 70 761 600 kg is barely below the annual average of 76 204 800 kg for the years 1961–65.[456] The total number of cigarettes sold in Canada in 1994 was still higher than in the early 1960s or any time before that.

During the 1960s and 1970s, Canada's growing population more than offset the modest decreases in per capita tobacco consumption. Total cigarette sales increased, resulting in more demand for tobacco leaf. In the late 1960s and much of the 1970s, average raw leaf production exceeded 90 000 000 kg a year. This growth prompted more farmers to grow tobacco, farmers who would soon have to get out when the massive decline in smoking began in the 1980s.

Tobacco farmers have also been affected by two other situations. First, manufacturers have been paying farmers less for their crop. In 1981, the average price per pound was $1.52. In 9 of the 12 subsequent years, farmers received a lower price. In 1993, the average price was $1.44.[456] This, combined with increased costs due to inflation, has caused the net income per pound to fall. Second, manufacturers are using less tobacco per cigarette, partly to save money and partly to lower the tar and nicotine yields. New manufacturing processes "puff up" tobacco so that less is needed to fill each cigarette. Health Canada researchers reported that the average amount of tobacco in a 1991 cigarette was 0.77 grams, less than half of the amount in a 1952 cigarette (1.67 grams). With lower tobacco prices and less tobacco per cigarette, the cost of tobacco per cigarette fell from two thirds of a cent in 1950 to just over a quarter of a cent in 1990. As a result, the researchers concluded, the tobacco industry saved as much as $229 million between 1982 and 1990, mostly at the expense of farmers.[324]

The number of flue-cured tobacco farmers in Canada decreased from 2 916 in 1981 to 1 326 in 1992.[85,89] The major reason for the decrease was that declining sales and prices had made tobacco farming financially unattractive to many. The decrease is also partly explained by better technology, bigger farms, and improved efficiency and economies of scale. These trends have been found in many agricultural sectors. An additional consideration is that some of the farmers who left in the early 1980s retired.

Canadian tobacco farmers are known as producers of high-quality leaf; at the same time, they are high-cost producers because of the cold climate and the high cost of labour. To address the inherent inefficiencies of growing tobacco in Canada, a supply-management system was established. The Ontario Flue-Cured Tobacco Growers' Marketing Board, created by law, pushes up prices by restricting how much tobacco can be grown. Manufacturers, for their part, help tobacco farmers stay in business by paying them far more than the world prices for tobacco used in Canadian cigarettes. This higher price is passed on to consumers; in effect, Canadian smokers subsidize tobacco farmers. As is the case in some other farming sectors, the government helps farmers by allowing them to import seasonal workers from Jamaica and Latin America to work for minimum wage.

About 40% of the tobacco grown in Canada is exported. Thus, even when Canadian tobacco-consumption decreases, a large portion of farmer sales remains unaffected; as well, more tobacco becomes available for export, albeit at lower prices. Canadian exports have mostly gone to the United Kingdom, the United States, and recently Hong Kong (often on their way to China), but some tobacco has also been exported to Egypt, Ghana, Cameroon, Bangladesh, Trinidad and Tobago, and Indonesia.

Spokespeople for tobacco farmers sometimes assert that fewer pesticides are used in the growing process in Canada because of the colder weather, so Canadian leaf tobacco is "cleaner" and thus safer for health. This very unusual concern for the health of Canadians is commendable, but the representatives offer no studies to support their assertion.

Early manufacturer exploitation of farmers

In his 1968 book *Tobacco in Canada*, tobacco grower Lyal Tait described in detail how leaf buyers, including manufacturers, resisted farmers' efforts to organize and to get higher prices for tobacco crops. During the 1930s, and even earlier, representatives of leaf buyers went to individual farms to negotiate prices. This "barn buying" system was comparable to a "divide and conquer" strategy. Buyers were in a powerful bargaining position; farmers were not. Often there was little competition among buyers; farmers might receive only one offer, or maybe none.[577] Farmers had almost no room to negotiate.

Low prices at the beginning of the buying season in 1932 prompted the *Tillsonburg News* to write in an editorial that "the tactic as reported employed by some of the buyers during the past few days in intimidating the growers, is so degrading and dastardly that one might think we were back in slavery days." [577, p. 127] The situation prompted some dissident growers to organize a selling cooperative. The dissidents sent a petition to the federal government expressing the opinion "that the Imperial Tobacco Co., Canadian Leaf Tobacco Co., Macdonald Tobacco Co., and other manufacturer dealers are combining for the purpose of regulating, controlling the purchase, and fixing the price of tobacco." An investigation was started, but "no combine among buyers to affect prices or limit competition was discovered."[577, p. 128]

In 1936, because of farmer dissatisfaction, the Flue-Cured Tobacco Marketing Association of Ontario was established in Simcoe. Seven of the 23 Board members represented buyers, a clear sign that the organization's role was not to act just in the best interest of farmers. According to Tait, the Association made progress, but there were still "gross inequalities, patronage, graft (and above all, fear) in the marketing of the leaf and in the allotment of basic acreage."[577, p. 146] (Basic acreage referred to how much a farmer could grow.)

In 1951, the Ontario Minister of Agriculture authorized a vote for an all-grower marketing board under the provincial *Farm Products Marketing Act*. This would have benefited the farmers, but the idea was vigorously opposed by the Association. Tobacco companies hired PR experts to help in the No campaign, and the Association paid the bills. Thus, farmer money was being used against farmer interests. After a virulent campaign, the proposal was defeated by a vote of 1 752 to 369. In 1954, buyer influence increased when the Association bylaws were amended to provide equal representation for farmers and buyers.

The Association controlled membership and often prevented new growers from joining. In 1954, there were 304 such excluded independent farmers. Being excluded from the Association meant the independents had no basic acreage rights. They had to wait until Association members' crops were sold before they could sell their own, usually at a much lower price. Thus, buyers had a clear financial incentive for keeping new growers out of the Association — the greater the number of independents, the greater the opportunity for the tobacco companies to pay low prices at the end of the season. In 1956, the federal Restrictive Trade Practices Commission investigated and strongly criticized this closed arrangement.

In 1957, the Ontario government authorized another vote to create an all-grower board. Once again, the Association aggressively opposed the proposal, and once again it hired PR experts to help in the No campaign. The campaign played on farmers' fears about keeping acreage rights and losing bank credit. For example, the special committee campaigning for the Association sent local bankers and lawyers letters suggesting that banks had the right to foreclose on anyone voting in support of the proposal. But in the end, the Yes side won 64% of the votes; 92% of the eligible voters voted.[577] This led to the creation of the Ontario Flue-Cured Tobacco Growers' Marketing Board, a body made up exclusively of tobacco farmers. The Board is still functioning today. Under the marketing-board system, it is illegal for individuals to grow flue-cured tobacco unless they have a quota to do so. All tobacco has to be sold through a Board-organized auction.

After the Board was created, the farmers and the buyers continued to have disputes, but at least the farmers were organized and better able to take a position. Ten years after the Board was established, said Tait, there remained "little trust or cooperation on either side."[577, p. 484] Today, the relationship is better. The Board and the buyers get together to negotiate crop size before the farmers do any planting, thus reducing uncertainty for farmers. There are still disagreements over prices, but according to Board Chairman George Gilvesy, "both sides recognize that each other is one of the few friends they have left."

Attempt to create a national tobacco marketing agency

In January 1985, federal Agriculture Minister John Wise announced plans to create a Canadian Flue-Cured Tobacco Marketing Agency. The national agency had been proposed by Ontario tobacco farmers, and Wise, whose Elgin riding was in the tobacco belt, was supportive. Farmers strongly supported the proposed agency because it would strengthen their hand in negotiations with buyers. The agency would control supply, establish a pricing formula, and limit imports. Tobacco farmers would be subsidized through higher prices charged to manufacturers. Tobacco exports would be subsidized through a levy on manufacturers.

Not surprisingly, tobacco manufacturers strongly opposed the proposed agency. Rothmans, for example, threatened to suspend purchases of Canadian tobacco for 1 year if the agency was created.[552]

To health groups, it made no sense that one hand of government would promote tobacco while the other was discouraging it. One of the agency's functions would be to "undertake and assist in the promotion of the consumption and use of unmanufactured flue-cured tobacco."[455, p. 36] As well, the agency was to look for new markets inside Canada and elsewhere. To the health groups, this seemed intolerable. When the National Farm Products Marketing Council held public hearings on the proposal, the health groups got together and campaigned against the proposal. NSRA took out a two-page ad in *Maclean's* magazine.

After the hearings, the Council submitted recommendations (which were never made public) to the Minister of Agriculture, but tobacco manufacturers went to Federal Court, arguing that the hearings had been improperly conducted. The Court agreed and ordered that hearings be reopened. However, hearings never really resumed because the health lobby had succeeded in making a national marketing agency politically undesirable. The idea of a national agency eventually died away altogether, prompting the national health lobby to claim victory, albeit this time with substantial help from the tobacco companies.

Government support for tobacco farmers

The federal government has a long history of supporting tobacco farming. Around the turn of the century, when most tobacco leaf was imported, the Department of Agriculture worked hard to encourage a domestic growing sector. Officials saw tobacco as bringing tremendous economic benefits and wanted Canada to have a piece of the action. The Department conducted research and experiments on growing tobacco and sought help from knowledgeable US sources. The Department even made arrangements to exhibit Canadian leaf tobacco at the 1900 Paris Exposition.

In 1906, the Department created the Tobacco Branch. Three years later, a tobacco station was established in Harrow, Ontario, to conduct research. This later became the Dominion Experimental Station for all of Southwestern Ontario. In 1933, the Department of Agriculture established the Delhi Research Station. (The station is still functioning, although its mandate is no longer just tobacco research.)

It is through research that government has provided an indirect subsidy worth millions and millions of dollars to farmers. Research has resulted in more pest-resistant, better growing, higher quality strains of tobacco with altered tar and nicotine ratios. Research also led to the development of a Canadian tobacco seed industry, and farmers no longer had to import seeds from the United States. To publicize research developments, the Department of Agriculture put out its own publication, *The Lighter* (1931–90).

A 1964 inquiry into the tobacco-growing industry found that "tobacco research in Ontario has been marked with close and harmonious relations among government departments, firms, and organizations remotely as well as closely connected with the industry."[577, p. 490] Some research projects have been jointly funded by Agriculture Canada, CTMC, and the Ontario Flue-Cured Tobacco Growers' Marketing Board.[289, p. 24]

Provincial governments, especially the Ontario government, have also supported tobacco farmers. The Ontario Ministry of Agriculture and Food sponsors an Extension Service that provides farmers with advice on growing their crops. The Transition Crop Team has helped farmers establish new or alternative crops. Federal and Ontario government representatives sit on the Ontario-based Tobacco Advisory Committee along with members representing the farmers, manufacturers, and other leaf buyers. The Committee is designed to promote cooperation between the various parties.

Today, neither the federal government nor the provincial governments provide direct financial subsidies to tobacco farmers the way governments in the United States and the European Union do. However, tobacco farmers have been able to take advantage of other programs designed to benefit all farmers. These programs have included farmer loans, debt relief, advance payments for crops, and a $500 000 capital-gains tax exemption. The Canadian Rural Transition Program helps farmers move into nonfarming employment. On the export side, farmers, through their marketing board, have been able to benefit from government-sponsored trade missions, the services of Canadian Embassies and High Commissions, and the Program for Export Market Development of the Department of Foreign Affairs and International Trade. In the last case, the use of the program has been small, with no net cost to the government. The Export Development Corporation has supported leaf tobacco sales in nontraditional markets and has provided financial guarantees in established markets.

Federal and Ontario government officials have traveled abroad to help promote Canadian tobacco leaf. In 1988, for example, Agriculture Canada sponsored technical seminars in China to help Ontario tobacco growers sell surplus tobacco.[211] This initiative was successful and led to new sales. Also in 1988, three agronomists from China spent 3 months at the Delhi Research Station to receive training in tobacco research and production technology. A departmental document stated that "these trainees expressed their sincere gratitude prior to their departure from Canada and assured us that they would make suggestions and proposals to increase the imports of Canadian tobaccos into China."[7, p. 2]

A 1989 Agriculture Canada document discussing tobacco exports to China stated that "it is important that all possible efforts be made to expand this market in support of our tobacco industry."[163, p. 1] The document discussed a forthcoming visit of a Chinese delegation to Canada. From the Department's perspective, the objective was "to ensure that the Chinese are aware of the on-going efforts to improve the already high quality of Canadian tobacco through research and biotechnology and to reinforce their confidence in the Canadian capacity to supply tobacco in order to facilitate sales to China."[163, p. 1]

In 1994, representatives of the Ontario Flue-Cured Tobacco Growers' Marketing Board accompanied federal Agriculture Minister Ralph Goodale on a trade mission to China and other Asian countries. Goodale defended the trip: "They (tobacco growers) are a part of agricultural production in the country ... so it's a matter of us discharging our normal commercial responsibilities."[454]

Specific programs to help tobacco farmers exit from tobacco farming have been part of Canada's overall strategy to reduce tobacco, although sometimes these programs have been underrecognized. Few countries have implemented initiatives comparable to Canada's. Between 1987 and 1993, more than $50 million was paid by federal and provincial governments to farmers who stopped growing tobacco. A further $13 million was spent on projects helping to find alternative crops.[627] These initiatives have had three obvious practical and political benefits:

✦ They assisted affected farmers;

✦ They reduced the number of people with a vested economic interest in opposing tobacco-control measures; and

✦ They gave governments a handy response when faced with farmer complaints about efforts to reduce smoking.

Federal aid to help farmers exit from tobacco farming was critical in assisting passage of the TPCA. Easily the most expensive part of the government's comprehensive tobacco-control policy announced in 1987, the aid allowed the Agriculture Minister to remain substantially silent as the Health Minister championed the ban on tobacco advertising and other health measures.

The Tobacco Diversification Plan, announced in 1987, was funded by the federal and provincial governments. The plan had two components: the Tobacco Transition Adjustment Initiative (commonly known as Redux) and the Alternative Enterprise Initiative. Redux provided compensation to farmers who had left tobacco and financial incentives for other farmers to cease tobacco production. Farmers who retired 50% of their quota and sold the remaining 50% on the open market could get up to $65 000 compensation. By all accounts, the program helped with an orderly downsizing of tobacco farming. Remaining farmers were also in a better position because they were able to grow a higher percentage of their quota.

By 1990, Redux had helped about one third of tobacco growers across Canada exit from tobacco production. Of the Ontario farmers who exited, half said they would have exited had there been no program, and a third said the program prompted them to discontinue farming. Many farmers eligible for Redux did not take advantage of the program because they were better off continuing to grow tobacco. Of the Ontario and Quebec farmers who did leave, about 40% were still involved afterward in tobacco growing, typically as employees of other farmers.

The Alternative Enterprise Initiative provided financial support for the development of new crops, or the marketing and processing of existing nontobacco crops unless this disrupted crop production by other farmers. However, the program was not very successful. Some of the funds were not used because farmers were reluctant to leave a high-income crop (tobacco) for a riskier low-income activity. Large amounts of money were given to various ventures that often failed. A peanut cooperative, for example, went bankrupt. The Southern Ontario Tomato Cooperative was given money to run a tomato-processing facility, but this was "a very controversial, problem-ridden project," according to a government evaluation.[8, p. 13] The tomato venture failed. The problem was that farmers did not have the necessary knowledge base or marketing skills to suddenly jump into new big projects.

It is often said that the land on which tobacco is grown cannot support crops other than tobacco. This is wrong. In almost every case, tobacco is grown in rotation with other crops: for example, tobacco and rye are grown in alternate years on the same plot. This is proof that the land can support a different crop. It would be fair to say, however, that no other crops can replace the income that tobacco brings.

Since the early 1980s, many farmers who once grew tobacco have used their land to produce alternative crops, including ginseng, baby carrots, rhubarb, spanish onions, zucchini, coriander, garlic, melons, early and sweet potatoes, buckwheat, and hay.[267] Government programs have contributed to this diversification, but the biggest factor has been the free market. As the demand for tobacco fell in the 1980s, farmers realized they could make more money by growing something else.

According to an Agriculture Canada report, university and government researchers feel that the current tobacco belt will be the horticultural centre of Ontario by the year 2020. The report states that

> the tobacco region is widely regarded as holding the most potential in the province for horticulture, because of its favourable climate and abundance of water, proximity to large markets, and sandy soil that permits early and late field work.[8, p. 15]

Already, urban encroachment is prompting growers from the nearby Niagara Peninsula to move into the tobacco region. These growers bring with them expertise in growing non-tobacco crops.

By the late 1980s, tobacco farming had stabilized, and the number of farmers exiting from tobacco production slowed to a trickle. As a result, the amount of money needed for diversification initiatives also decreased. The Ontario Tobacco Diversification Program, funded by the federal and Ontario governments, had $6 million available for 1994–96. The program subsidizes projects to help the local economy shift away from its dependence on tobacco.

In the short term, tobacco farmers will probably be secure and continue to make good money. The current farmers are getting older, with many approaching retirement. Farmers' children are much less interested in taking over the family farm than would have been the case two decades ago. The "abuse" directed toward tobacco farmers and the uncertain future of tobacco have prompted the pursuit of other careers. It is expected that retiring tobacco farmers will sell their farms to neighbours. Those remaining will be fewer and wealthier, with more acreage under their direction.

The long-term future of tobacco farming may be shaky because of the inefficiency of growing tobacco in Canada compared with other countries, especially low-cost developing countries. If Canadian manufacturers ever change their minds about the current practice of paying farmers prices above world levels and if manufacturers find a suitable raw-leaf substitute for the somewhat unique taste of Canadian tobacco, many Canadian farmers could be in big trouble. Meanwhile, the marketing boards keep the prices of domestic leaf tobacco high. It is ironic that farmers vigorously protest regulation by government, when it is regulation that helps them stay in business and provides them with millions of dollars of extra revenue each year.

CHAPTER 17

Why Canada Has Been Successful

The Toronto Star Syndicate, by Larter

A record of achievement

In 1990, the Seventh World Conference on Tobacco and Health, held in Perth, Australia, endorsed a resolution commending the Canadian Government for "its leadership in improving the health of Canadians and for setting an outstanding example in comprehensive tobacco control policy."[157, p. 966] The *Wall Street Journal* reported in 1991 that "Canada is widely seen as a model for governments trying to reduce smoking through a combination of regulation and taxation."[200, p. B1] Dr Hiroshi Nakajima, the Director General of WHO, said in May 1995 that "Canada's comprehensive approach to tobacco control is an outstanding example of a well thought out public health policy" and that "Canada has taken many groundbreaking initiatives which have been emulated by other countries."[422, p. 1]

At RBH's 1990 annual meeting, President Joe Heffernan said that "the impact of taxation and regulatory interference has been severe," noting the substantial decrease in industry sales and the even greater decrease in RBH sales.[574]

In 1970–72 and again in 1980–82, per capita consumption of cigarettes (including roll-your-own) was higher in Canada than in any other country in the world.[644] By 1990–92, Canada had fallen to 13th place,[644] a clear demonstration of Canada's impressive tobacco-control efforts.

The principal factor behind this large reduction has been the implementation of a comprehensive package of antismoking interventions, mainly by government. Other factors, such as social pressure and a better public understanding of health risks, have also contributed. Canada's leadership is shown by the country's record of achievement:

* ✦ The annual per capita (age 15+) consumption of cigarettes (including roll-your-own) in 1992 was 40% lower than in 1982.

* ✦ The prevalence of smoking among 15–19 year olds fell from 47% in 1979 to 22% in 1991. Over the same period, daily smoking fell from 42% to 16%. Some surveys in 1994, however, found a rise in youth smoking compared to 1991.

* ✦ Canada was the first country to ban smoking on all domestic and international flights of its domestic airlines.

* ✦ Canada was the first country to require health warnings covering 20% of the package front and back; it was also the first country to require black and white health warnings at the top of the package and covering more than 30% of the front and back (25% plus a border).

* ✦ Canada was one of first countries to require health warnings on addiction and on second-hand smoke.

* ✦ Canada is one of few countries to require health warnings on packages sold in duty-free stores.

* ✦ Canada was the second country in the Western Hemisphere (after Cuba) and the second English-speaking country (after Singapore) to ban tobacco advertising, although this ban was struck down as unconstitutional in 1995.

* ✦ New Brunswick, followed by other provinces, was the first jurisdiction to legislatively require stand-alone antismoking publicity at point of sale.

* ✦ Ontario was the first jurisdiction in North America to prohibit pharmacies from selling tobacco.

* ✦ The first smoke-free Olympics were held in Canada (1988 Calgary Winter Games). All Olympic venues were smoke free, and tobacco advertising and sponsorships were not allowed in association with Olympic events.

* ✦ Canada was the first country to require manufacturer reporting to government of ingredients in tobacco products on a brand-by-brand basis [unfortunately, the reports are not publicly available].

* ✦ Canada was the first country to have a parliamentary committee conduct a detailed investigation into the feasibility of plain packaging.

* ✦ Before the federal tobacco-tax rollback in 1994, Newfoundland had one of the highest rates of tobacco taxation (federal and provincial) ever imposed in the world. After the tax decrease, the total tax in Newfoundland is still among the world's highest.

✦ In 1993, Canada implemented perhaps the most advanced tobacco-control policy for any navy in the world at the time, banning smoking on the interior of any ship; restricting smoking in shore facilities; ending ship-board cigarette sales (although this was changed in 1995 to simply ending tax-exempt ship-board sales); and introducing smoking-cessation and education programs.

✦ Canada was one of the first countries to establish a national ban on kiddie packs (packs with fewer than 20 cigarettes).

✦ Canada is one of the few countries with a meaningful program to help farmers exit from tobacco growing.

✦ The federal government was one of the first governments to produce antismoking promotional material mocking the tobacco industry and its denials that it does not market to young people.[226]

✦ Canada proposed a resolution, adopted in 1992 by the International Civil Aviation Organization (a United Nations agency), that called on countries "to take necessary measures as soon as possible to restrict smoking progressively on all international passenger flights with the objective of implementing complete smoking bans by 1 July 1996."[311]

✦ Canada was the spark plug behind the resolutions at the World Health Assembly in 1995 and 1996 calling for the adoption of an international convention on tobacco control.

✦ Canada was a driving force at the 1995 meeting of Commonwealth Health Ministers. Canada's Minister of Health, Diane Marleau, strongly urged tough action on tobacco.

Key success factors

Why has Canada enjoyed the success that it has? Of a long list of factors, the three most important are political will; bureaucratic support and expertise; and effective advocacy outside government. These three are key to the success of tobacco control — had any one of these factors been absent, Canada's progress in tobacco control would have been impeded.

Most tobacco-control measures require government action, so there has to be the political will to introduce, implement, and enforce such measures. Political support starts with the appropriate minister, usually the Minister of Health. If this Minister is not on side, it is extremely unlikely the government as a whole will take action. The Health Minister, once convinced, must then be able to convince Cabinet and caucus colleagues. The Minister must overcome points of resistance. Jake Epp's support for the advertising ban, Benoît Bouchard's push for stronger health warnings, and Ontario Health Minister

Ruth Grier's backing of the provincial *Tobacco Control Act* are all examples of the pivotal role played by a minister.

It happens sometimes that a Health Minister is miles ahead of the Health Department. When Dr Ron Stewart became Nova Scotia's Health Minister, he was a much stronger believer in legislation than his department, which had traditionally focused on education in its antismoking strategy. When legislation was being prepared, he had to tell departmental staff on four occasions that he wanted a complete ban on vending machines. "Are you sure?" staff kept asking him.

The Health Minister is not the only possible political driving force. The Minister of Labour may push for workplace smoking regulations, or the Minister of Finance may push for tobacco taxes. The push may come from caucus. Backbenchers can press Ministers to take action. Lynn McDonald, who introduced Bill C-204 and persistently pressured the government on tobacco issues, showed that even an opposition MP can play a critical role. In Ontario, Progressive Conservative opposition member Norm Sterling played a key role in pressuring the government to introduce the *Smoking in the Workplace Act.*

Usually, Ministers cannot achieve results without the help of others. At the departmental level, bureaucratic support, expertise, and resources are necessary. Officials have to know which types of initiatives are most effective and must be prepared to recommend implementation. Government decision-making must be influenced from the bottom up. Officials need to be familiar with the tobacco industry and the tactics used to thwart attempts at regulation. Accurate information to counter industry misinformation must be readily available to assist Ministers in political fights. When the political climate presents a window of opportunity, officials have must have an action plan ready for approval and implementation.

During the TPCA adoption process, the federal government was fortunate to have on staff Neil Collishaw, now recognized as one of the world's most knowledgeable tobacco-control experts. Had it not been for this expertise, adoption of the TPCA would likely not have happened.

If governments are to act, strong public pressure is needed. That is why advocacy (lobbying) by antismoking and health groups is so important. Advocacy is necessary to ensure that the most effective measures are adopted, and it is here that the Canadian anti-smoking lobby has shown a particular excellence. Lobbying has persuaded politicians that they had to take action. Often the only reason there is political will is because advocacy has created that will. Pressure on governments to do something about tobacco has also led governments to assign more officials to the tobacco file, which in turn enhances the likelihood of good policy.

A tobacco-control campaign has more likelihood of success if the politicians, bureaucrats, and advocates perform their roles effectively and if their roles as members of the public-health team complement each other. These team members should collaborate as much as their respective roles allow. They are on the same side and pursuing the same goal: public health. Part of Canada's success has been due to collaboration between governmental and nongovernmental sectors. Sharing of knowledge and ideas leads to better policy.

However, collaboration has its limits: politicians are required to make cabinet decisions in confidence, bureaucrats are required to provide impartial policy advice in confidence, and nongovernmental organizations (NGOs) are required to answer to their constituencies.

The weight of medical evidence

In the 1960s, as part of industry efforts to block legislation, the tobacco lobby vigorously denied that smoking had any health consequences. Although the industry still maintains this position, it no longer emphasizes this as a tactic in light of the weight of medical evidence to the contrary. Not only has a causal link between tobacco and disease been established, but our current knowledge of the magnitude of the epidemic makes the case for action even stronger.

Increasing knowledge of addiction and the harmful consequences of ETS

The emergence of information on the harm ETS causes to nonsmokers means that smoking is no longer just a matter of personal choice — it is now an issue of concern to smokers, nonsmokers, and society as a whole. Similarly, given the increased understanding of the addictiveness of nicotine, smoking cannot be considered merely an individual decision. Addiction removes choice. The addiction issue is even more relevant because almost all smokers begin as teenagers.

Decreased smoking rates

The decreasing proportion of smokers in the population has made tobacco regulations easier to implement. More nonsmokers means more public support for controls.

Just as smoking has decreased among the general population, it has also decreased among key decision-makers, journalists, and community leaders. Politicians and bureaucrats who smoke have historically been more likely to resist antitobacco legislation than nonsmokers. Smokers may rationalize away concerns and feel that the need for action is not strong. An exception was John Munro, who took a strong stand against tobacco when he was Health Minister, despite the fact that he was a heavy smoker.

Whether a company's CEO is a smoker seems to have an effect on whether smoking is permitted in the company workplace.

Here is an illustration of the potential impact of smoking status on one's perspective: a scientist writing in 1947 in *Science Digest* said, "I must furthermore admit, with some embarrassment, that my transformation from heavy smoker to non-smoker has profoundly influenced my scientific attitude toward tobacco."[628, p. 78]

Comprehensive strategy

Canada has recognized that a comprehensive strategy is necessary to minimize tobacco use. Instead of focusing on just one or two measures, such as education programs, Canada's strategy includes taxation, legislation, and programs.

It has taken a long time for some governments and some health groups to come around to the view that legislation should be used to control tobacco. In the 1950s and early 1960s, most of the emphasis was on medical research on the consequences of smoking. In the late 1960s and 1970s, the emphasis was on education, although there were some who unsuccessfully pushed for legislation. Fortunately, the reluctance of the past has been substantially reduced. Today, the health community recognizes the pivotal role that legislation and taxation play in reducing smoking.

Legislation targets the tobacco industry (the source of the problem) instead of just individual smokers (the victims). There are more than 6 million smokers in Canada, but there are only three main tobacco companies. A focus on curbing the industry is the most effective, and cheapest, component of a comprehensive strategy. Indeed, failing to address the industry is like trying to prevent malaria while ignoring the mosquito.

The benefits of legislation can be seen in other policy areas. Tougher drinking and driving penalties and more active enforcement, for instance, accomplished what public education programs alone could not.

Interdepartmental cooperation

Although the Health Department (federal or provincial) usually takes the lead on tobacco-control initiatives, it benefits from working with other parts of government. Cooperation can prompt action by other departments, or reduce opposition to Health Department initiatives. The Labour Department deals with smoking policies for the private-sector workplace. Treasury Board, in the case of the federal government, is responsible for smoking policy in the government workplace. The Transport Department restricts smoking on airlines and other modes of transportation. The Justice Department drafts laws and represents the government when those laws are challenged in court. The Finance Department can raise taxes and initiate anticontraband measures.

Possible points of resistance must be addressed. The Agriculture Department, responsible for the interests of farmers, might oppose legislation, as might the Industry Department or the Finance Department (which may be concerned with decreased tobacco-tax revenue). Nevertheless, within the federal government and some provincial governments, interdepartmental efforts have strengthened the overall strategy.

Getting health groups involved as active lobbyists

Most of the time before the mid-1980s, health groups did very little lobbying for anti-tobacco legislation. The approach they took was grounded in the "medical model," in which finding cures had priority over preventing disease. By the late 1970s, NSRA was working substantially without active help from the major health organizations. This rankled NSRA Executive Director, Gar Mahood — the contribution of smoking to lung disease, heart disease, and cancer was no secret. In 1978 Mahood even went to court and laid a charge against CCS for failing to post a sign required by the City of Toronto No-Smoking Bylaw. During National Non-Smoking Week in 1983, 1984, and 1985, Mahood publicly attacked health charities for their inactivity. He said that by not targeting the industry, they were failing to focus on preventive medicine.

Some individuals in CCS shared Mahood's frustration. By 1985, Doug Barr had become the Society's CEO. He had experience with advocacy and recognized the potential benefits. In late 1985, CCS organized a National Advocacy Workshop for key Society decision-makers. The American Cancer Society Vice-President of Public Affairs told participants that the American Cancer Society had been involved in lobbying for 10 years. A former Manitoba Cabinet Minister encouraged CCS to get involved politically. A lawyer explained that CCS would not risk losing its charitable status. The workshop led to the creation of the Public Issues Committee.[132]

In the tobacco-control arena, CCS was a "sleeping giant." The largest voluntary charity in Canada, CCS had offices across the country and a budget of tens of millions of dollars. The CCS reputation would give stature to any campaign. No one could dismiss CCS as a fringe or extremist group.

The Society hired Ken Kyle as a full-time advocate in 1986 and opened a Public Issues Office in Ottawa. Later in the year, somewhat fortuitously and somewhat because of CCS lobbying, the federal government announced its decision to prohibit smoking on flights of under 2 hours. The government's decision gave CCS some positive reinforcement and convinced it of the benefits of advocacy. In 1988, when the TPCA campaign resulted in another success, the value of lobbying became more apparent.

There had been a concern that public lobbying activities would hurt CCS fundraising efforts. Those fears never materialized. In fact, it is believed that the frequent exposure in the media has increased the CCS profile and actually helped fundraising efforts. Some volunteers from other charities saw this publicity and wondered why their organization was not doing more active lobbying. CCS helped make it easier for other charities to become more involved in advocacy.

Prominent health organizations carry a lot of weight with the public and with government. Even just saying "cancer," "lung," or "physician" in connection with tobacco sends a strong public-education message itself.

After the TPCA victory, Barr made these comments on lobbying:

If we are willing to learn the political ropes and mobilize our volunteers to exercise their political clout, our organizations can bring about significant legislative change that can reduce disease, that can prevent deaths and, in the long run, do more for the health of Canadians than all the hospitals in this country put together. And in the final analysis, isn't that what we are really all about?[400]

In 1989, the Heart and Stroke Foundation (formerly the Canadian Heart Foundation) decided to become more active. During a strategic planning process, the Foundation concluded that public policy should be one of its three focus areas.

Incremental approach

No major group calls for an outright ban on tobacco, even though surveys show that a significant percentage of the general population supports such a move. Nicotine's addictive qualities would quickly undermine a total ban. The experience with alcohol prohibition suggests that contraband would be widespread. But all measures short of a total ban should be pursued.

Historically, progress in tobacco control has been incremental. Once a measure is in place, lobbying for further restrictions becomes easier. For example, municipal bylaws initially banned smoking in only a few places; more and more places were added over the years. Normally, once a tobacco-control measure is adopted it is there for good, at least until it is replaced by something stronger. The 1994 tobacco-tax reduction and the invalidation of the ban on tobacco advertising were exceptions.

Although early implementation of the strongest antitobacco measures may be desirable, this is not always politically possible. Sometimes a compromise is necessary to get anything through. A case in point is the *Tobacco Sales to Young Persons Act*. When the bill came before Parliament, the House Leader allowed only a few hours for consideration. Health groups were pressing for amendments. When it was clear that the government would not even consider the bill if there were to be amendments, the health groups backed off.

Initiatives from three levels of government

In Canada, antismoking initiatives can be taken by the federal, provincial, and municipal levels of government. The best example is tobacco taxes, whereby increases by either federal or provincial governments can increase the overall price.

One level of government also has the opportunity to pick up the slack when another level has failed to act. Municipalities have enacted smoking bylaws where provincial governments have not. If a province adopts a province-wide smoking restriction and a municipal bylaw already exists, the more restrictive of the two provisions usually applies. After the federal government restricted cigarette-vending machines to bars and taverns, Nova Scotia and Ontario went further and banned such machines altogether.

In the United States, the tobacco lobby has been successful in getting "pre-emption" provisions included in laws. These provisions prevent lower levels of government from taking stronger measures. For example, US federal law prevents states from restricting many types of advertising or requiring their own health warnings on cigarette packages. Some state laws that restrict smoking prevent municipalities from taking further action.

Public opinion

The public has been increasingly supportive of measures to control the tobacco industry and to restrict smoking. Such support adds momentum to the process of introducing legislation. As well, supportive newspaper editorials influence governments to take action.

Voluntary initiatives

Voluntary initiatives have often preceded legislated ones. Many newspapers voluntarily decided to refuse tobacco advertising before the adoption of the nationwide legislated ban. Many pharmacies in Ontario voluntarily stopped selling tobacco before the adoption of the provincial ban. The CBC announced that it would stop accepting tobacco advertising before the Isabelle Committee recommended a total ban on such advertising. Many employers prohibited or restricted smoking in their workplace before legislation was introduced. The move by some restaurants, like McDonald's, to completely prohibit smoking on their premises will stimulate legislation applicable to all restaurants. Although voluntary measures are no substitute for legislation, they can demonstrate the feasibility of a proposed policy.

Availability of Canada-specific research

Research specific to Canada is useful to those who are developing or supporting a Canadian policy. Helpful research data have come from monitoring smoking rates, measuring the health impact of tobacco, calculating the economic costs of smoking, assessing the toxicity of various tobacco products, and so on. Just knowing how many deaths in Canada each year are attributable to tobacco provides a compelling reason to act. Other research includes tracking the adoption of municipal bylaws and assessing the impact of tobacco-control initiatives.

Research from outside Canada, such as that contained in the annual report of the US Surgeon General, has also been beneficial in providing evidence and reasons that justify restrictive measures.

The National Clearinghouse on Tobacco and Health

Tobacco Reporter, an industry trade journal, described the lobbying between pro-tobacco and antitobacco forces as a "War of Information."[150, p. 5] The description is accurate. Once government decision-makers have the correct information, they very often decide to act — the case against tobacco is just that compelling. The problem is getting the information to government decision-makers, especially in light of industry misinformation.

The National Clearinghouse on Tobacco and Health collects and disseminates information, often organizing it into user-friendly form. Jointly funded by federal and provincial governments and health organizations, the Clearinghouse collection of tobacco-related materials is one of the biggest in the world (outside the industry). The library contains an estimated 12 000 items, including published books and journal articles, news clippings, pamphlets, companies' annual reports, government documents, text of laws, transcripts of court proceedings, court exhibits, slides, videos, photographs, product packages, and tobacco-promotion materials. The Clearinghouse enables others on the front lines of tobacco control to do better work. The Clearinghouse also produces various publications, including fact sheets (on youth, the tobacco industry, advertising, smoke-free schools, etc.), an Advocate's Guide, and a handy directory of individuals and groups working on tobacco.

The National Strategy to Reduce Tobacco Use

The Steering Committee of the National Strategy to Reduce Tobacco Use has representatives from the federal, provincial, and territorial governments and eight health organizations. Formed in 1985, the National Strategy pursues three basic goals: smoking prevention, smoking cessation, and protection from ETS. The National Strategy sets target levels for smoking reduction and also sets priorities for action. For example, Cheryl Moyer of CCS notes that after the Steering Committee designated the prevention of tobacco sales to minors as a priority, a proliferation of provincial laws banning such sales arose during the first half of the 1990s.

The Steering Committee was behind the creation of the National Clearinghouse. It also initiated the National Conference on Tobacco or Health in 1993, resurrecting a forum long absent in tobacco control. Organized mostly by CCSH, the 1993 conference exposed attendees to improved information on current tobacco-control issues and strengthened the informal network of contacts.

The Steering Committee provides a forum for intergovernmental and government–NGO collaboration. As well, the Steering Committee gives provincial government officials, especially those new to the tobacco field, an opportunity to obtain information about effective measures being implemented in other provinces. Once one province has taken action, it is a lot easier for others to do likewise. Wisely, the governments and health organizations have excluded tobacco manufacturers from membership on the Steering Committee. An industry presence would merely provide manufacturers with an opportunity to discover and frustrate proposed initiatives.

Use of effective advocacy techniques

Successful lobbying by health groups is without a doubt the main reason Canada has been more successful at controlling the tobacco industry than all but a few other countries in the world. One factor behind the good advocacy is that the health groups offer the government solutions, not just problems. Instead of just saying, "smoking is a problem — do something about it," the groups make the government's job easier by presenting plans detailing proposed measures. Submissions to government provide the content for desired policies, as well as justification for their implementation. Very often, leading health advocates have an experienced and extremely sophisticated understanding of tobacco-policy issues.

Health groups recognize there is strength in numbers and have been most effective when advocating as coalitions. The more groups there are in a coalition, the broader the base of public support. Coalitions decrease duplication of effort and reduce the chance that natural allies will work at cross-purposes. Years of working together have given health groups lots of experience in the difficult craft of coalition management.

CCSH is an umbrella organization with 28 members, including major health organizations and 10 provincial interagency councils. Each of these provincial councils in turn has provincial health organizations as members, although in some provinces the councils are inactive. In Ontario, Quebec, and Nova Scotia, the provincial councils have staff, adding to their effectiveness. At the local level, especially in Ontario, the councils are again replicated and serve as local coalitions. As a result, there is an extensive network of organizations available for lobbying campaigns. At the national level in particular, CCSH plays a coordinating role for the coalition.

In addition to health and antismoking organizations, coalitions have sometimes included consumer, religious, and women's organizations. Drug companies that sell the nicotine patch have occasionally provided financial support. Coalitions are most effective, but the impact of a single individual must not be underestimated. A determined person can really make things happen, especially in a province or municipality with a smaller population. Many of the important early victories were really driven by a small number of people.

A key factor to successful lobbying has been hiring professional full-time staff and placing them in Ottawa to work close to government. Paid staff tend to be around for a longer time than volunteers and are able to develop expertise and lasting contacts. Government officials and media get to know who to call. NSRA has had a full-time Executive Director, Gar Mahood, since 1976 and a full-time lawyer, David Sweanor, since 1985. CCSH increased its effectiveness when it hired a full-time Executive Director in 1987. The same can be said of Physicians for a Smoke-Free Canada, which first had full-time staff in 1993.

As important as professional staff are, volunteers can and do make an important contribution. Some of the volunteers who have made especially effective contributions to tobacco control are lawyers. Lawyers often have experience with the legislative process and are accustomed to advocating a case on behalf of a particular position. Doctors have very significant public credibility, and they too can be effective volunteer spokespersons. Health charities often have large networks of volunteers upon which to draw.

Hiring staff and running campaigns cost money. Adequate financial resources are needed to fight an industry that has seemingly bottomless pockets. In addition to private-sector donations, CCSH and NSRA have received critical financing from government. The government grants have enabled them to better contribute to effective public policy.

In dealing with the tobacco industry, health groups must be able to respond quickly when necessary. Action might be needed within days or even hours. A fast-track decision-making system avoids the cumbersome, slow process that committee approval in a large organization can entail. Most, but not all, the prominent groups in the health lobby have established procedures to make quick decisions.

When lobbying, groups use a wide array of tools, including letter writing and phone calls to MPs, newspaper ads, letters to the editor, written briefs, face-to-face meetings with government officials and elected representatives, commissioned opinion polls, appearances before parliamentary committees, and most of all, the media.

Tobacco-control advocates have wisely placed heavy emphasis on the media. News outlets can broadly disseminate a viewpoint and respond to industry misinformation in a way underfinanced organizations could not otherwise afford. Media coverage forces politicians to respond to issues. Media coverage affects public opinion and prompts letter writing by concerned citizens. Media coverage is also an incredibly cost-effective tool for educating millions of people about the dangers of smoking. Over the years, the advertising value of the media's coverage of smoking and health issues has been worth tens, if not hundreds, of millions of dollars.

Tobacco-control advocates have developed a reputation of being a reliable source of information. Advocates have also caused many stories to break and have framed stories to increase media coverage, such as releasing reports in a hospital setting or on the day a parliamentary session resumes. Some advocates have prompted coverage by attending tobacco company annual meetings and asking questions on health issues and social responsibility.

Another technique has been to use freedom of information laws to obtain internal government documents, as well as industry documents sent to government. This helps the advocates know what is really going on and understand which industry arguments need a reply.

During campaigns, advocates now try to frame the debate in terms of health, particularly health of children. In the 1970s, the discourse was oriented more toward rights, as symbolized by the name of the Non-Smokers' Rights Association. The emphasis today is on addressing the tobacco epidemic, on reducing disease, and on saving lives. If this issue positioning is done successfully, as it often has been, the health lobby has an advantage over the industry, which seeks to frame the debate in terms having nothing to do with health, such as freedom, jobs, or law and order. After the TPCA battle, CTMC's Neville made the following observation:

> Clearly one of the aims — and to give them their due one of the successes — of the anti-tobacco lobby was to make this appear to be a health issue. And when that happens that's a difficult area for the industry.[400]

One of the reasons the industry succeeded in getting tobacco taxes rolled back was that the smuggling issue was in large part positioned and seen as one of law and order.

When necessary, health groups can play tough and criticize the government for inaction. But this criticism is also tempered with praise and thank yous when the government takes commendable initiatives. Health organizations have presented awards to Ministers in recognition of a particular contribution.

Canadian health advocates participate in an extensive worldwide network of tobacco-control colleagues. Knowledge of international developments can be of significant benefit. Precedents established elsewhere and an awareness of previously used industry tactics all help the advocates counter the industry in Canada. Foreign organizations have assisted by writing letters to the Canadian government and occasionally by sending representatives to testify at parliamentary committees.

People to make it happen

Tobacco-industry representatives often wonder what drives tobacco-control crusaders. What is the answer? As suggested in the Preface, very often the more people learn about the industry, the angrier they get. That motivates people to try to stop industry misbehaviour.

One of the critical factors in the success of the antismoking lobby has been the quality, and increasingly the quantity, of people and groups that make things happen. Some of the key players have been around for years and have learned valuable lessons from the successes and failures of past lobbying.

As long ago as 1986, the industry trade journal *Tobacco Reporter* described Canada's "vociferous" antitobacco lobby as "one of the fiercest in the world."[223, p. 44] At the time, the antismoking lobby was dominated by NSRA. Each year, the movement gets stronger as more organizations become more active and more effective. More than 400 people from across the country attended the 1993 National Conference on Tobacco or Health, a number far exceeding expectations. This was symbolic of the increasingly broad-based organized opposition facing the industry.

There are some amazing stories of commitment. Those who fight the industry passionately believe in their cause and work long hours to make things happen.

In 1992, when Dr Mark Taylor was a Major and surgeon in the navy, he leaked a report showing that 53% of junior noncommissioned personnel were smokers, far above the Canadian average. Cigarettes were sold on ships at the incredibly low price of $1.50 a pack. Taylor publicly criticized the navy, calling for remedial steps to end the "smoking epidemic"; he also called for an end to the on-board sale of cigarettes. For this, some in the navy considered court-martialing him, but in the end no charges were brought. The publicity surrounding the report and the efforts of Captain Larry Myette, the Maritime Command surgeon, brought about the navy's advanced antismoking policy.

In the late 1970s, the Toronto Transit Commission voted 5 to 0 to defeat a proposed ban on tobacco ads. When a *Toronto Star* reporter ribbed NSRA's Mahood about "losing that one," the ever-tenacious Mahood offered to bet $100 that the battle was not lost. Eventually, the Commission reversed its position and banned the ads.

Countless other examples of individual efforts exist.

Using the courts

Even though Canadians are less litigious than their American neighbours, Canadians have sometimes used the courts in an effort to advance tobacco-control objectives. In 1987, Physicians for a Smoke-Free Canada used the courts — unsuccessfully — in an attempt to have tobacco added to the *Hazardous Products Act*. In 1990, Les Hagen of Action on Smoking and Health laid a charge against RBH for placing a sticker over the health warning on packages of Black Cat cigarettes. The case never made it to trial, but media coverage exposed industry practices.

The potential for using the courts to make progress in tobacco control is largely untested in Canada. If finances permit, this should be a route used more frequently by the health lobby.

Ontario's *Tobacco Control Act:* a model of success

After the federal TPCA was passed in 1988, health groups in Ontario called for a modern provincial law to prevent the sale of tobacco to minors. Representatives of the health lobby prepared briefs, met with government officials, and held news conferences. There was some interest in government but no action. Hopes were raised in 1990 when the social democratic NDP came to power.

At this time, inside the Ministry of Health, a growing team of officials was gaining expertise in tobacco. These officials started to push upwards for increased action on tobacco. The Deputy Minister of Health, Michael Decter, was a strong supporter of tobacco legislation and pushed the issue at senior government levels. Health groups began campaigning for a comprehensive tobacco-control act, not just one dealing with sales to minors. In the 1991 budget the government announced that legislation would be forthcoming.

After persistent lobbying, the government released a discussion paper in January 1993 that detailed proposed measures. The government indicated that it would introduce legislation several months later in the spring. Public hearings were held, but by late spring there was still no legislation. A meeting between health advocates and key ministers indicated that neither introduction of a bill nor its contents were assured. The health lobby decided to step up the heat.

NSRA, the provincial heart, cancer, and lung organizations, and the Ontario Medical Association collectively put more than $250 000 into a coalition already operating as the Ontario Campaign for *Action* on Tobacco (OCAT). To add to the lobbying effort, Michael Perley was hired as full-time Director of the campaign. Perley had previous experience as Executive Coordinator of the Canadian Coalition on Acid Rain.

OCAT used a number of tactics to increase the pressure on government. The government was strongly criticized in public for failing to live up to its promises to bring in legislation. Lawyers in the health lobby drafted a model bill, thus illustrating the speed with which legislation could be prepared. Grass-roots lobbying was extensive, and OCAT headquarters sent out periodic "Campaign Updates." These went out on a fax modem to more than 350 points around the province and suggested action local groups could take. A draft full-page advocacy ad criticizing the government's inaction was prepared but never published. However, the ad did make its way to senior levels of government, where it made an impression.

In the late summer of 1993, a list of the government's priorities was leaked to the press. The government did not intend to introduce the proposed tobacco legislation at any time before the next provincial election, due in 1995. That news was a major setback. So the health lobby stepped up the campaign a notch and pressured the government House Leader. Inside caucus, Member of Provincial Parliament (MPP) Larry O'Connor led the push to garner support among NDP MPPs. Health Minister Ruth Grier led the fight in Cabinet.

Finally, on 17 November 1993, Bill 119 was introduced. The Bill banned the sale of tobacco from pharmacies and vending machines, set a minimum purchasing age of 19, restricted smoking in certain public places, and gave the government authority to regulate packaging. After second-reading approval in December, health groups participated actively in committee hearings on the Bill. The pharmacy issue was the most controversial, and pharmacy chains led the opposition, although pharmacists were divided. In the end, the pharmacy ban remained. The Bill was strengthened in committee, including giving municipalities more authority to pass smoking bylaws and including a provision clarifying the government's authority to require plain packaging. This last change prompted two opposition MPPs, each having a riding with a packaging firm, to fight the bill. OCAT's ongoing efforts countered this new opposition. The protest delayed passage, but Bill 119 received final approval in June 1994.

The end result was good legislation brought about by the classic blend of political will, expert officials, and effective advocacy. The legislation complemented other aspects of the Ontario government's tobacco strategy, including its award-winning commercials aimed at youth, its funding support for local public health units, and its funding of smoking-related research.

Opportunities for improvement

Canada has had success, but obviously there remains tremendous room for improvement. Some 31% of adults continue to smoke. Canada still needs plain packaging, a reimposed ban on tobacco advertising, elimination of sponsorship promotions, higher tobacco taxes, further smoking restrictions, control of industry profits, and regulation of product design. These items require government action, so the blame for failing to implement the necessary measures lies principally with government. Some measures that were first recommended by national health organizations in the 1960s have still not been adopted. This is unacceptable. The cost of delayed implementation is thousands of preventable deaths. At the same time, government deserves substantial credit for the declines in smoking which have occurred given the critical role played by government internventions.

Governments should be allocating more resources to tobacco control. In 1994–95, Alberta and Manitoba had a tobacco-control budget of less than 1 cent a person. Ontario, at $1.87 a person, was the only province spending more than $1 per capita. One dollar a person is not a lot of money to address the leading preventable cause of disease and premature death in society. Each Ministry of Health should have a suitably staffed Tobacco Control Branch. Some provincial governments do not have a single person working full time on tobacco matters.

Health and antismoking groups should have full-time professional lobbyists in every provincial capital. That is not the case at present. The potential for good legislation in many provinces is not being tapped simply because of the absence of full-time staff lobbying for strong laws.

To facilitate networking, the growing number of activists across the country should be linked in a national system of electronic communication, as exists in the United States. This communication system would include a computer bulletin board from which users could instantaneously obtain information on the latest developments. The US-based Tobacco Merchants Association puts out a series of newsletters, the quality of which puts many newsletters by health groups to shame. These newsletters are for the tobacco industry and provide timely information on all key tobacco issues, from legislation to statistics, to trademarks, to a special bulletin called *China Watch*. This information has been accessible on-line since the mid-1980s. The health side should have an information-dissemination network at least as good.

The health charities have made a big contribution to tobacco control, but they could do far more. They could be allocating more of their dollars to advocacy, the most cost-effective contribution they could make to reducing tobacco use. CCS allocates less than 1% of its $77 million budget to lobbying, even though charities are allowed to spend up to 10%. A 1991 Gallup poll found that Canadians felt, on average, that CCS should spend 9% of its funds on government lobbying; in fact, they thought that CCS was actually spending 12% on government lobbying.[190] Given that the principal component of the CCS mission is to eradicate cancer and given that about 30% of cancer deaths are caused by tobacco, the small advocacy budget represents a costly strategic decision. The cure for tobacco-caused cancer is already known. Yet instead of targeting adequate resources to smoking prevention, hundreds of millions has been spent over the last two decades on bio-medical research.

Of the $36 million CCS gives annually to research, almost nothing goes to tobacco-related research. If even just 10% of this research money were directed to well-designed tobacco-related research, incredible gains could be made. The US National Cancer Institute funded smoking-control and tobacco-control research to the tune of $290 million in 1982–91. There is no reason NCIC cannot make a proportionately similar commitment.

The Lung Association and the Heart and Stroke Foundation have placed even less emphasis on advocacy than CCS. For instance, despite the importance of smoking as a cause of heart disease and stroke and despite annual revenues of $60 million, the Heart and Stroke Foundation has never had more than one full-time person lobbying at the national level. Out of the Foundation's revenues, $30 million goes to research, but almost nothing goes to tobacco-related scientific or behaviourial research. Such a strategy impedes progress on tobacco control and improvements in public health.

CMA is another organization that could be more active in antitobacco lobbying, especially when one considers the credibility and impact doctors can have. CMA led the anti-smoking charge in the 1960s, but this is not the case in the 1990s. CMA's relative inactivity was one reason Physicians for a Smoke-Free Canada emerged.

Nurses (including the Canadian Nurses Association) and respiratory therapists are two professional groups that deal with the harm of tobacco use daily, but they have been conspicuously absent from the public fight against tobacco. Increased activity from these sectors would be good for public health.

The failure over the years of the large, well-funded health organizations to allocate more resources to tobacco control has resulted in higher levels of smoking, disease, and death than would otherwise be the case.

PART V

The War Goes Global

CHAPTER 18

Exporting the Epidemic

Brian Gable, *Globe and Mail*, Toronto

Tobacco is a major threat to sustainable and equitable development. ... In the developing world tobacco poses a major challenge, not just to health, but also to social and economic development and to environmental sustainability.

— Bellagio Statement on Tobacco and Sustainable Development, June 1995[5]

An international health disaster

Canada has only 0.5% of the world's population. The harm caused by tobacco products in Canada, as horrific as it is, is but a drop in the bucket compared with the worldwide epidemic. Indeed, the magnitude of the human disaster is so enormous that it is almost impossible to fully appreciate. And the problem is getting worse every year — far worse.

During the 1980s, per capita consumption declined an average of 1.4% per year in developed countries (DCs) but rose an average of 1.7% annually in less-developed countries (LDCs)[6].[642] In 1970–72, per capita consumption was 3.25 times as high in DCs as in

---

[5]This statement was prepared by 22 individuals and international organizations meeting at the Rockefeller Foundation's Bellagio Study and Conference Center in Italy.

[6]In this chapter, *developed country* will be used instead of *Western* or *industrialized country*. *Less-developed country* will be used instead of *developing* or *Third World country*.

Table 4. Global and regional estimates of cigarette consumption, 1970–72, 1980–82, and 1990–92.

	Cigarettes per adult per year		
	1970–72	1980–82	1990–92
World	1 450	1 650	1 640
Developed countries	2 670	2 770	2 400
Less-developed countries	820	1 160	1 370
WHO regions			
Africa	460	560	540
The Americas	2 600	2 490	1 870
Eastern Mediterranean	730	930	910
Europe	2 280	2 470	2 290
Southeast Asia	640	960	1 150
Western Pacific	1 140	1 600	2 000

Source: World Health Organization.[642]
Note: India is included in the Southeast Asia region. China is included in the Western Pacific region.

LDCs. By 1990–92, the ratio had fallen to 1.75. By 2005 or 2010, it is expected that per capita consumption in LDCs will equal that in DCs.[642] As Table 4 indicates, global per capita cigarette consumption has remained fairly stable at 1 450–1 650 cigarettes since the early 1970s, despite all the efforts to reduce smoking and despite declining rates in DCs.

Annual cigarette consumption varies considerably among countries of the world. However, wealthier countries generally have higher consumption rates.[117,323,644]

Figure 17 shows the dramatically increasing global trend in cigarette production since 1950. Production in 1994 was 5.3 trillion cigarettes. Total weight of all tobacco grown for all tobacco products (in 1993) was 7.7 trillion grams.[553] Six countries account for more than 55% of world cigarette consumption: China (31.4%), United States (9.2%), Japan (6.3%), Russia (4.2%), Germany (2.5%), and Brazil (2.0%).[33]

TTCs are using the vast profits they have made and are continuing to make in DCs to finance international expansion. Worldwide, the tobacco-control movement is winning the occasional battle, usually in a DC, but TTCs are easily winning the global war. To the victors go the spoils — massive profits — while the vanquished are left to deal with colossal casualties. Tobacco-industry optimism was well expressed in the Philip Morris *1992 Annual Report*:

> Our worldwide tobacco business has greater opportunities now than ever before. Our strong bases in the United States and Western Europe, our expansion in Eastern Europe and the former Soviet Union, and our growing businesses in Latin America and the Asia/Pacific region position us well to meet the challenges of increasingly linked and prosperous world markets.[469, p. 18]

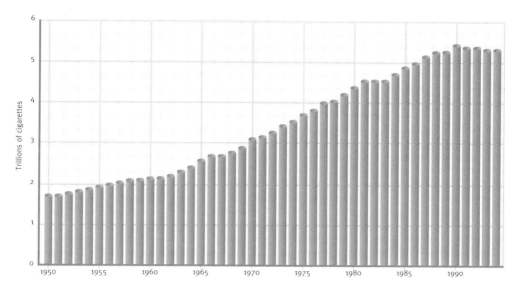

Figure 17. World cigarette production, 1950–94.[499]

In 1995, Geoffrey C. Bible, Chairman and CEO of Philip Morris, enthused that "worldwide, tobacco is going like gangbusters."[471, p. 4]

WHO estimates that worldwide, tobacco kills 3 million people a year: 2 million in DCs, 1 million in LDCs.[466] The 3 million annual deaths translates to one death every 10 seconds, or six deaths every minute. WHO estimates that if current smoking patterns continue, 10 million people will die from tobacco in 2025, 7 million of them in LDCs. That's one death every 3 seconds. Without successful interventions to reduce smoking, the annual death toll after 2025 will exceed 10 million.[466] Of the children and teenagers alive in 1994, it is projected that 250 million will die from tobacco use.[467]

Smoking is already the leading cause of death in DCs. Over the next few decades, it may become the leading cause of death in the world. In some LDCs, like Brazil, tobacco use is already the leading cause of death. According to the World Bank, the deaths from tobacco in 2025 will exceed the deaths from AIDS, tuberculosis, and complications of childbirth combined.[638] What's the explanation for this prediction? Partly it's that the world's population is growing. Partly it's that people are living longer and are more likely to suffer tobacco's effects. But mostly it's that there has been a massive increase in smoking in LDCs over the last several decades. This increase will translate into deaths when the new smokers move into middle age.

Why are smoking rates in LDCs rising? Aggressive marketing by TTCs, the absence of regulations and educational programs, and rising incomes — thus making cigarettes affordable — have all contributed. According to the World Bank, TTC penetration of LDC markets "has been accompanied by very large increases in smoking prevalence, usually among people in their teens and twenties."[637, p. 7]

The future looks great for the conquerors because there are major opportunities for growth. In many LDCs, the average smoker smokes fewer than half the number of cigarettes that the average smoker in DCs does.[644] Many people in LDCs have little knowledge of the health consequences of smoking. Any opposition or antismoking activity is normally unorganized. Some individuals may ignore health advice, believing that longevity is determined by fate or by God. Others may feel somehow that they are physically stronger than smokers in DCs and thus resistant to the dangers of smoking. In some LDCs, smoking rates among youth are now higher than among adults, a telling sign for future trends. In many LDCs, population growth rates are extremely high, meaning that even if per capita consumption were to remain flat, total sales for some regions could still double in 20–30 years. Together, these factors create a tobacco marketer's dream.

As of the early 1990s, the world had an estimated 900 million male smokers (200 million in DCs; 700 million in LDCs) and 200 million female smokers (100 million in DCs; 100 million in LDCs).[642] Although there are significant differences among countries, it has been estimated that about 30% of the world's adults are regular smokers:

- ✦ 48% of the men and 12% of the women in the world;

- ✦ 41% of the men and 21% of the women in DCs; and

- ✦ 50% of the men and 8% of the women in LDCs.[642]

Surveys have found smoking among men to be exceptionally high in some places: it is more than 60% in South Korea, Latvia, Russia, Dominican Republic, Tonga, Turkey, China, and Bangladesh. Prevalence among women is rarely higher than 30% and is lower than 10% in places such as China, Singapore, Albania, Paraguay, and the Philippines. In Muslim countries, smoking prevalence among women is normally less than 10%, even when male prevalence is more than 40%.[644] This means that in certain parts of the world there is a massive female market ripe for exploitation, particularly as social and religious barriers to women's smoking diminish. This evolution in favour of smoking is aided by advertising. As more women obtain employment and income, more women are able to pay for cigarettes. Trends of increasing smoking among women are of particular concern, given that, besides being income earners, women are often role models, primary caregivers, and educators in the home.

In LDCs, tobacco use may result in hardships not found in developed countries. Poor medical systems mean that those who contract cancer or other diseases may not receive suitable, or any, health care. Because high costs may make health care, pain killers, and other drugs unaffordable, suffering may be especially intense. Countries may be too poor to have social-welfare programs to support a family after the premature death of a wage earner. Small, poorly ventilated homes may mean that the health effects of ETS from smoking by a parent or spouse are more severe.

The transnational tobacco industry

The global tobacco industry is dominated by a few giants. In 1993, Philip Morris led the way, with 12% of global market share, followed by BAT at 9.9%, R.J. Reynolds at 5.8%, Japan Tobacco at 5.2%, and Rothmans at 2.9%. The world's biggest company is actually the China National Tobacco Corporation, with roughly 30% of the world market, but because it is a government monopoly it is excluded from this list. The top brands in the world are Marlboro (Philip Morris), Mild Seven (Japan Tobacco), Winston (R.J. Reynolds), and Camel (R.J. Reynolds).[592]

Philip Morris cigarettes, including Marlboro, are sold in about 170 countries. Each Marlboro pack contains the company's coat of arms, featuring the slogan *Veni Vidi Vici* — "I came, I saw, I conquered."

BAT is the world's largest cigarette company outside the United States. It has factories in 50 countries, and its cigarettes are sold in some 180 countries and duty-free markets. In more than 30 of the world's markets, BAT owns the top brand.[31]

Most of Japan Tobacco's sales comes from within its home market. Since 1988, after gaining competitive experience when its domestic market was opened to foreign competitors, Japan Tobacco has expanded internationally. Exports skyrocketed from 1.5 billion units in 1987 to 16.4 billion in 1993. The company concentrates on Korea, China, and Hong Kong, but it has interests in Eastern Europe and is planning further international growth.

The TTCs have become increasingly dependent on overseas sales. In 1983, 40% of the combined cigarette sales of R.J. Reynolds and Philip Morris were to international destinations. By 1993, 65% of their sales were outside the United States.[121] For Philip Morris, international sales in 1993 accounted for 51% of total tobacco profits, up from 17% in 1986.[121]

Penetrating new markets

TTCs have been hugely successful at increasing their global market share and at breaking down trade barriers. In the 1960s, TTCs pushed into many Latin American markets. In the 1980s, TTCs forced their way into Asian countries. In the 1990s, TTCs are moving into the formerly communist countries of Central and Eastern Europe and into communist China and Vietnam. In most cases before the TTCs moved in, the markets were dominated by government-owned monopolies. In the early 1980s, 60% of the world's market was closed to TTCs. Now the opening of more markets (including China) will reduce that to 5%.[18]

How do international tobacco firms penetrate? Dr Judith Mackay, Director of the Asian Consultancy on Tobacco Control, describes a typical four-stage process in which TTCs enter a previously closed market:

1. **The honeymoon.** The initial honeymoon period when the foreign companies enter a country is one of offers of help with technology in farming and manufacturing,

free trips overseas and the co-production of glossy magazines. This is the stage of wooing the country and gaining access.

2. **The marriage.** Next come the joint ventures, a foot in the door. At this stage advertising and promotion often begin to creep in, usually of a sophistication and funding level not used by the national monopoly.

3. **The marriage turns sour.** The relationship then becomes less harmonious, with accusations from the transnational that a monopoly prevents free market access, even with the trade threats ... . Because of the political strength foreign companies can muster, the national monopoly usually must accede to their demands.

4. **The divorce.** Finally the national monopolies weaken or may be disbanded. The foreign tobacco companies come away with what is for them the optimum marriage settlement — domination.[102, p. 46]

To this can be added a few more tactics. Foreign-made contraband may start to appear within a closed market in increasing quantities. This accustoms consumers to a brand's taste and imagery and helps develop a market for the brand. Lost tax revenues from contraband put pressure on the government to allow foreign brands in legally.

At an early stage, a TTC may give the local company a licence to produce a foreign brand, perhaps through a joint venture in the marriage phase of penetration. This seems innocuous enough because domestic jobs are not threatened, but again, it is a way to build market share among the local population. Foreign companies may also visibly engage in charitable activities to create an impression of good corporate citizenship.

The industry has hired big guns to help it expand internationally. Philip Morris hired former British Prime Minister Margaret Thatcher as a consultant on "geopolitical affairs," reportedly paying her US $1 million over 3 years. A 1992 company memo listing issues on which she "may be able to offer guidance and assistance" included "China Entry Strategy," "Vietnam Entry Strategy," and "Singapore Anti-Tobacco Programs."[358] Clayton Yeutter, US Trade Representative from 1985 to 1989, has since joined BAT's Board of Directors. To help break into South Korea, R.J. Reynolds hired Richard Allen, one-time national security adviser to US President Ronald Reagan; Philip Morris hired Michael Deaver, a former White House aide to Reagan. A Philip Morris memo would later boast that Deaver "was given a welcome ordinarily reserved for the highest foreign dignitaries" when he visited South Korea on behalf of the company.[358]

Does it matter whether the supplier of cigarettes in a country is the national government-owned monopoly or a TTC? Absolutely. A government-owned monopoly may acknowledge the health consequences of smoking and may cooperate with government health initiatives. For example, in China all tobacco stores close on World No-Tobacco Day, to the agony of some desperate smokers. A monopoly might not advertise at all, but if it does, its ads will likely be amateurish. Product quality is typically poor, with a harsh, unflavoured taste. Lack of competition means that prices are higher and retail outlets are fewer than would otherwise be the case. Packages may be unalluring. Wholesale distribution may be inefficient.

In contrast, TTCs deny the health consequences of smoking, ruthlessly market cigarettes, vigorously fight against regulatory efforts, and if there is regulation, capitalize on loopholes in the laws. TTCs use attractive packaging, push for an expanded number of retail outlets, and sell flavoured cigarettes that are easier to smoke.

Here's what the industry trade publication *Tobacco Journal International* had to say about the ineffectiveness of monopolies:

> Some monopolies regard their duty as being to do no more than make their tobacco products passively available to smokers who want them; newcomers, domestic or foreign, usually feel the need for more dynamic marketing, aided by thrusting advertisements of a kind that may be new to the target market.[26, p. 132]

From a health perspective, making cigarettes "passively available to smokers" is far more desirable than the approach taken by TTCs.

How have government-owned monopolies fared since the market was opened to competition? Often, not very well. By 1976, TTCs had bought out at least 12 companies in Latin America, the majority of which were former monopolies.[120] By 1988, TTCs controlled 75% of the Latin American market.[119]

There are many examples of TTC tactics to expand profits without regard to the impact on public health. One classic example comes from Sri Lanka. In 1993, BAT's subsidiary, the Ceylon Tobacco Company, organized a news conference to dispute the alleged health effects of smoking. A report of the session in *The Island* newspaper was headlined "Anti-smoking campaign comes under heavy fire" and "Consultants rule out lung cancer, heart." Here are excerpts from the article:

> An international team of consultants hosted by Ceylon Tobacco Company last week insisted that smoking could not be linked to lung cancer and heart disease. They accused the mass media of being biased against smoking. ...
>
> Dr. Sharon Boyse, head of the Smoking Issues Department of the British American Tobacco Corporation in the United Kingdom, said there is `absolutely' no laboratory proof that smoking is directly related to lung cancer or heart disease. ... Lung cancer, she pointed out, could be caused by various other factors also — keeping pet birds and ethnic factors for instance. ...
>
> The issue of passive smoking was dealt with by Philip Witorsch of the George Washington University Medical Center. ... According to him, passive smoking or inhaling what he calls 'Environmental Tobacco Smoke' is not hazardous to one's health as led to believe.[146]

Coverage of the meeting did prompt a backlash from some media, heart specialists, and other concerned citizens.[20]

A similar initiative occurred in South Africa. BAT's local affiliate paid for reporters from South Africa, Malawi, and Mauritius to attend a seminar at a luxury resort. Many of the speakers from the Sri Lanka news conference delivered the same message in South Africa. Other speakers included Jean Boddewyn of Baruch College, New York, who denied that tobacco advertising can affect consumption. The result of the luxury seminar was substantial press coverage favourable to the industry's views.[546] Boddewyn and Philip Witorsch actively work for the industry and have been speakers in many countries. In Canada, both testified in support of the industry before the House of Commons committee considering bills C-51 and C-204.

Another illustration comes from Uganda. In 1988, the Ministry of Health met with BAT to discuss a proposed health warning for cigarette packages. After the meeting, R.M.H. Duncan, the Managing Director of BAT Uganda, wrote to the government seeking to tone down the proposed warning:

> I am afraid that any Health warning clause must be attributable to the Government in some way, e.g. Government Health Warning. ... This is because any unattributable warning might be attributed to B.A.T. and we do not wish this to happen because:
> B.A.T. Uganda 1984 Ltd. does not believe that cigarette smoking is harmful to health.
> B.A.T. Uganda 1984 Ltd. might be held legally liable for any warning which could be attributable to us.[153, p. 1]

The letter also stated that BAT thought "it would be only fair to have a form of words which is not excessively strong" and that the company did not want to put warnings on packages for duty-free or export sales.[153, p. 1]

The industry's pursuit of sales with a apparent lack of concern for the plight of humanity is well illustrated from this excerpt from the 1984 annual report of the BAT subsidiary in Kenya:

> After a promising start, the drought and uncertainty over food supplies created a reluctance among customers, particularly in rural areas, to spend their limited cash resources on items such as cigarettes. Under these conditions volume sales did well to achieve a modest growth of 0.4% and turnover of 7.9% over 1983.[102, p. 18]

The company was noting the fact that some people in a drought-stricken area wanted to spend their money on food instead of cigarettes.

In 1976, both R.J. Reynolds and Philip Morris admitted at hearings before the US federal Securities and Exchange Commission that their international subsidiaries made "questionable" payments totalling $7.4 million to government officials or companies the officials controlled. Philip Morris said that the questionable payment of one of its subsidiaries (US $278 500, mostly cash) was for "what may have been legal political and lobbying expenses," noting that "such payments are customary in the countries involved and apparently condoned by local authorities."[582, p. 264]

In Kenya, 20% of the BAT subsidiary is owned by the national pension fund. This cleverly creates a constituency of those, including retirees, who do not want the government to take action against tobacco because that might hurt their pensions.

The modern opium war

In the early 1800s, British merchants smuggled opium into China and made a fortune; Americans and other Europeans were involved too, but to a lesser extent. Although opium was completely illegal, addictive, and terrible for health, caused all kinds of other social problems, and drained China of vast quantities of silver, the merchants aggressively pushed their product. Apologists for the merchants denied that opium was bad for health. The British argued that if they didn't sell opium, trade would be lost to merchants from other countries. In 1839, after a decade of escalating problems with opium, the Chinese tried to stop the trade by confiscating opium stored by British merchants. This led to the Opium War (1839–42). The British won, and the opium trade continued to flow.

In the 1980s, the American tobacco companies spearheaded a modern-day opium war in the Far East. At the time, Taiwan, Thailand, South Korea, and Japan each had a closed market dominated by a government-owned monopoly. American tobacco companies had no access to these markets. American tobacco companies do not like to be told "No," so they pressured Yeutter, the US Trade Representative, to take action to open the markets. By 1985, the USTR agreed. He warned the four governments that if they didn't open up their markets, the United States would impose severe trade sanctions. Here was the US government, with its health warnings and advertising restrictions to discourage smoking at home, turning around and using threats in order to increase sales abroad. The US government pushed much harder to open the foreign markets for cigarettes than for other American products, no doubt a reflection of the powerful tobacco lobby.

The threat of trade sanctions was a big stick. Taiwan and Japan yielded to the pressure in 1986 and permitted American cigarettes in their markets. South Korea yielded in 1988. During the negotiations with these countries, the US government and the tobacco industry worked closely together. In negotiations with the Taiwanese government officials, when an agreement seemed close at hand, the US government officials would leave the room, speak with American industry representatives, and then return to the negotiating room to say that proposals were not yet acceptable. In Japan, the industry representatives were sometimes waiting just outside the door.[542]

Once the Taiwan market opened up, the American companies flooded the island with tobacco promotions. R.J. Reynolds advertised a concert popular with teens for which the price of admission was five **empty** packs of Winston cigarettes.[120] Attractive young women gave out free cigarettes in bars. Cigarette ads portrayed a desirable Western lifestyle, something to which many local teenagers aspired. The blitz of ads prompted outrage in the country, which in turn prompted the government to consider a law banning tobacco advertising. However, the US government opposed such a ban on the grounds that it would be a protectionist measure to prevent American companies from gaining market share. The Americans even opposed a proposal to ban tobacco ads in magazines read primarily by teenagers on the grounds that "kids these days read everything."[542, p. 86] The Americans also initially opposed a proposal to move health warnings from the side of package to the front. In the end, the warning appeared on the front, but it was smaller than the Taiwan government had originally wanted.[542]

Two years before the American tobacco invasion, a survey of high school students in Taiwan's capital city, Taipei, found that 26% of the boys and 1% of the girls had tried smoking a cigarette. Four years after the invasion, the figures had soared to 48% for boys and 20% for girls.[542]

After the Japanese market opened up in 1986, there was a massive increase in cigarette advertising on television. Some ads even appeared during children's programs. Japan Tobacco, the former monopoly, became one of the big TV advertisers. It had to, to protect its market share from the Americans. Smoking among Tokyo women aged 20–29 increased from 10% in 1986 to 23% in 1991.[116]

In South Korea, tobacco advertisements had previously been banned, but by 1988 cigarettes had become one of the most heavily advertised products in the country.[188]

Of the four countries pressured to open domestic markets, Thailand alone was able to withstand the coercion. The fight is a struggle worth retelling.

In the mid-1980s, large quantities of foreign-made cigarettes were being smuggled into Thailand, in part because of the country's long coastline. Even though Marlboro cigarettes could not be legally sold in the country except in a few duty-free stores, the brand was advertised on billboards and posters and in newspapers and magazines. Foreign cigarette logos also appeared on bumper stickers, kites, children's school notebooks, children's saving banks, chewing gum, women's earrings, T-shirts and other clothing, and shopping bags.[556, p. 565] Tobacco-sponsored boxing, car racing, and soccer were also promoted.

Together, the Marlboro advertising and promotion stimulated demand for contraband and set the groundwork for the anticipated opening of the market. In view of the fact that selling foreign brands was illegal in Thailand, the advertising agency responsible for the Marlboro ads defended the heavy marketing on the grounds that Philip Morris was not **selling** Marlboro cigarettes in Thailand — it was only **advertising** them there.

The Thai Tobacco Monopoly responded with its own advertising on billboards and in print. This continued until 1988, when the government, under pressure from prominent physicians, ordered the Monopoly to stop advertising. The Monopoly did stop, but the TTCs did not, arguing that the Thai Cabinet decision was not a law. It took a new government decree in 1989 to ban all tobacco advertising.

Throughout this period, Thailand refused to open its market, even though it was losing revenue because of smuggling (3%–8% of the market)[430] and it was receiving threats of trade sanctions from the US government. In 1989, the American tobacco manufacturers petitioned the USTR, who began an investigation of Thailand under the US *Trade Act*. This step was necessary before sanctions could be imposed.

Negotiations between the two countries went unresolved because the Thais refused to accept an American demand to repeal the ban on tobacco advertising. The Thai government received support for its position from health groups in Thailand and many other Asian countries. These groups collectively sponsored an ad in the *Washington Times* to express their view. Most important, strong support also came from many quarters in the United States, including the media, members of Congress, and health and antismoking advocates. This US support in turn made headlines in Thailand, boosting the efforts of the Thais to keep the Americans out. Antitobacco activists in the United States and Thailand created an international network and coordinated their campaigns.

Dr Everett Koop, a former US Surgeon General, backed Thailand at hearings in Washington:

> ... the inconsistency between U.S. tobacco trade policy and U.S. health policy increasingly is obvious and denounced in the international health community ... .
>
> At a time when we are pleading with foreign governments to stop the export of cocaine, it is the height of hypocrisy for the U.S. to export tobacco.[430, p. 21]

All of this support helped the Thai government stand firm. The Thai government was under pressure at home from the textiles, furniture, jewelry, and food-processing industries, which would likely suffer if the United States imposed retaliatory trade sanctions. In contrast, the Thai Tobacco Monopoly, conscious that sales were at stake if the market was opened, supported the government. The Monopoly was joined by its unionized workers and by Thai tobacco growers. As luck would have it, a coalition of several parties was in power at the time. If the Thai government backed down, it informed the USTR, there was a risk that one of the parties would back out of the coalition and the government would fall.

In the United States, the US government felt the public heat and referred the issue to GATT, perhaps feeling that if the Thai market were forced open by a neutral body there would be fewer political consequences. American tobacco manufacturers strongly opposed referring the matter to GATT, correctly anticipating that they would have less influence on the outcome than if the issue remained in the American political arena.

The GATT decision, released in 1990, set an important precedent.[192] On the one hand, a GATT panel ruled that Thailand could not have an outright prohibition on foreign cigarettes or a higher tax rate on foreign cigarettes than on domestic cigarettes. On the other hand, the panel ruled that Thailand could implement a whole series of antitobacco measures without violating GATT, provided that domestic and foreign manufacturers were treated equally. Thailand's advertising ban was ruled to be consistent with GATT.

The pending GATT decision and the delay in the Thai–US negotiations gave the Thai government the opportunity to have several tobacco-control measures in place before any foreign companies were in the market.

The invasion efforts of American tobacco manufacturers so galvanized the antitobacco movement in Thailand that this momentum continued long after the opening of the market. As it turned out, the country now has one of the better antitobacco programs in the world. Implemented measures include tax increases, the ban on advertising, a ban on free samples, 10 rotated large health warnings on the front and back of packages, educational efforts, a Quit telephone line for smokers, smoking restrictions in public places, a ban on vending machines, a ban on sales to minors under 18, a ban on tobacco sales from health premises, and a ban on candy cigarettes. The results of this comprehensive program are good: in 1976, 72% of the men had been smokers, but by 1993, the rate was down to 58%;[586] among women, smoking was holding steady at about 5%.[556]

As can be expected, the foreign tobacco industry is trying to find and exploit loopholes in Thailand's law banning advertising. *The Bangkok Post* ran an ad for "Kent Leisure Holidays" showing the cigarette company's logo and promoting "a pleasure trip," but when a doctor called to book a trip, he was refused because the cruise ship was in the Caribbean and would not be coming to Bangkok for 2 years.[158] Advertisements at point of sale have been attempted: a two-storey advertisement was painted on the outside of a store, for example. Clothes bearing cigarette logos are still on sale. International car races feature promotional logos. News of charitable donations appears in the media frequently. Representatives of seven newspapers were given an expense-paid trip to see a tobacco-manufacturing plant in the United States. Enforcement has been a problem for a number of reasons, including, in the words of the Deputy Minister of Health, "an inadequate surveillance system to keep up with the endless tactics and tricks of the tobacco industry."[556, p. 6] In 1995, TTCs were strongly resisting the Thai government's effort to copy a Canadian law requiring the reporting of cigarette additives by brand.[14]

In 1986, Hong Kong was considering a complete ban on smokeless tobacco, regardless of origin. Four US Senators, including Robert Dole, wrote to the Hong Kong Chief Secretary to oppose such a ban, arguing that it would constitute "an unfair and discriminatory restriction on foreign trade — at least that is the way it is likely to be viewed in the United States" and that it could cause "a potential barrier to our people's historic trade relationship."[371, p. 140] Despite these representations and veiled threats of trade sanctions, Hong Kong went ahead with the ban, joining other jurisdictions taking a similar step. Sanctions were not imposed.

In 1993, the pinnacle of hypocrisy was reached when the US Congress passed a law requiring that 75% of the tobacco used in American-made cigarettes be American grown. Foreign growers would be limited to supplying 25% of the needed raw leaf. Whereas a few years earlier the US government had been ruthlessly forcing open free trade in Asian markets, now it was erecting barriers to other countries in its own market. The law would protect American farmers by closing the door on cheaper imports from LDCs. This law was challenged under GATT by numerous parties, including Canada, the European Community, Thailand, and Zimbabwe. In 1994, a GATT panel ruled that the American-content restrictions infringed GATT policies.

China: the ultimate market

China is the largest cigarette market in the world, and TTCs want a piece of the action. Until 1995, this market was pretty well closed and was dominated by the government monopoly. Fewer than 1% of the cigarettes sold were imports. However, that may change as the government prepares to seek admission to the World Trade Organization (WTO), successor to GATT. If China joins WTO, the government will not be able to prevent the entry of foreign-made cigarettes.

China has 300 million smokers, more than the total number of smokers **and** non-smokers in North America. The total number of cigarettes smoked in 1994 in China was 1.67 trillion,[33] up from 943 billion in 1982.[104] The average number of cigarettes a smoker smokes a day has more than doubled since 1972.[557] China's economy is growing rapidly, fueling the prospects for further increases in smoking. Although 61% of Chinese men over the age of 15 smoke, only 7% of women do, leaving a huge untapped market.[644]

The health consequences of smoking are enormous, as one could expect in a country with such a large population. The number of tobacco-caused deaths is projected to increase to 2 million annually by 2025.[466] Surveys apparently show that only 30% of China's people know that smoking is harmful and that 10%–20% even believe that smoking will improve one's health.[50]

Philip Morris, BAT, R.J. Reynolds, and Rothmans, among others, have all firmly entered China with marketing initiatives or joint manufacturing ventures. Some international brand names are being manufactured in the country. At the same time as the TTCs are gaining a foothold, the China National Tobacco Corporation, the government monopoly, is radically improving to prepare for full-scale competition. The monopoly has imported modern manufacturing equipment, has enhanced product quality, and is taking steps to improve distribution.

Smuggling of foreign brands has increased in certain regions of China, thus increasing the pressure on the government to facilitate the marketing of foreign brands. China has a partial ban on tobacco advertising, but this has not stopped Philip Morris from erecting Marlboro billboards that do not show or mention cigarettes. In the company's view, omitting the depiction of cigarettes means that the ad does not fall under the restrictions. The same can be said of television commercials featuring Marlboro cowboys in the rugged outdoors.[102] Although no cigarette is portrayed, consumers know that Marlboro means cigarettes. Tactics like this have made Philip Morris the country's biggest spender on advertising.[328]

Foreign cigarettes are trendy and a major status symbol, despite costing much more than domestically produced brands. Smoking foreign cigarettes "means you're affluent," says Dr Mackay. "It's become almost a mark of business success."[50, p. 1512]

Sponsored events, like the BAT State Express 555 Hong Kong–Beijing motor rally and the Dunhill China Open Badminton tournament prompted the Chinese Minister of Health to make the following comments in 1989:

> It should now be clearly stated that the cigarette companies are very cunning. Since they know they can't have direct advertising, they use deceit to get their commercials placed before the viewing audience. Sport should really be a means of healthy enjoyment and recreation for the public. But propaganda for smoking does precisely the opposite. It's damaging to health, so basically the two things conflict.[102, p. 135]

Free tickets to a rally promoting the Hong Kong–Beijing rally were distributed in the school yards of Beijing elementary schools. Each ticket featured the 555 cigarette logo.[585] As well, product placements for State Express 555 cigarettes were included in the hit television series *A Beijinger in New York*. Ashtrays and other props with "555" on them were shipped to use in filming, even though State Express 555 is not known as a brand in the United States.[585] Other sponsorships include the Marlboro Soccer League and the Marlboro American Music Hour.[158,358]

In 1997, Beijing will host the 10th World Conference on Tobacco or Health, a recognition of the critical role China plays in global tobacco issues.

The TTCs' Canadian subsidiaries have almost always made cigarettes just for the Canadian market. Apart from the contraband situation, very little has been exported other than to supply a small duty-free market in the United States. But that is changing. Imasco's *Annual Report 1993* says that as the Canadian market continues to shrink, "maintaining [Imperial Tobacco] volumes will become increasingly difficult. Consequently, profit growth will become more dependant on productivity improvements and sales to markets outside Canada."[279, p. 8] In 1994 Imperial Tobacco said that it was exploring entry into Asia, especially the China market. An international marketing section was created within the company to pursue this new initiative.[615] Just as the TTCs see the potential for profit in this huge market, so does Imperial Tobacco.

Tobacco economics in LDCs

Around the world, TTCs assert how important tobacco is as a creator of jobs, as a provider of tax revenue, and as a benefit to a nation's economy. Tobacco fetches a higher price than other agricultural crops, it has a growing global demand, it can be preserved for long periods of time without refrigeration, and it can be shipped to markets around the world. Tobacco can be a very lucrative crop.

But that tells only part of the story. Farmers may get a higher price for tobacco than other crops, but the expenses are also higher because of the cost of pesticides, herbicides, fertilizer, seeds, insurance, labour, and capital.

Tobacco companies sometimes point to exports of leaf tobacco from LDCs to show how tobacco benefits the developing world, but this can be misleading because agricultural and manufacturing inputs are sometimes imported from abroad, thus offsetting the trade balance. A cigarette factory may import equipment, filters, cigarette paper, additives, and other supplies. TTCs can take money out of an LDC subsidiary for any of the following: repatriation of profits to the parent company; royalties for using technology, a brand name, or advertisements; directors fees; and salaries to expatriate executives who eventually leave the country. BAT alone made GB £299 million in profits from African operations between 1986 and 1992.[100]

Of 44 African countries, only half exported any tobacco in 1984–85. Some 94% of all tobacco-export earnings on the continent come from just two countries, Malawi and

Zimbabwe, where tobacco makes a huge economic contribution.[100] In Malawi, 73% of the country's entire export earnings come from tobacco; in Zimbabwe the figure is 41%.[600] When one excludes these two countries, though, the remaining countries have a collective negative trade balance in tobacco of US $417 million.[100] Thus, tobacco makes some of the world's poorest countries even poorer.

One of the main beneficiaries of tobacco sales in LDCs and other parts of the world is the United States. R.J. Reynolds boasted to its shareholders that in 1993 exports of American tobacco products helped reduce the US trade deficit by more than US $4 billion.[490]

The World Bank argues that on economic grounds alone, tobacco should be controlled. The Bank's view is all the more significant because the organization is known for its conservative views and its opposition to government regulation in the economy. The Bank recognizes that preventing tobacco use is one of the most cost-effective health interventions available in LDCs. A background paper prepared for the Bank estimates the cost per year of life gained is US $15–$20 for measles immunization, US $20–$40 for anti-smoking prevention, US $100–$500 for cervical cancer screening, US $1 000 for oral cancer treatment, and US $18 000 for lung cancer treatment.[27] A study by one of the Bank's senior economists, Howard Barnum, estimated that when all costs of tobacco around the world are subtracted from all the benefits, the net result is a global economic loss of US $200 billion each year. He estimated that for every additional thousand tonnes of consumption, 650 additional premature deaths will occur and the world economy will suffer a further US $27.2 million economic loss.[28]

In LDCs, tobacco competes with food in two ways. First, the money being spent on cigarettes by consumers is money that is not being spent on food or other necessities for the family. The impact of this should not be underestimated. Many children start out facing so many disadvantages that the last thing they need is to have decreases in nutritional intake. A 1981 Bangladesh study found that the cost of consuming five cigarettes a day by someone in a poor household could lead to a monthly dietary deficit of approximately 8 000 calories for that household.[110]

Second, the growing of tobacco competes with the growing of food. It is true that on some land, few if any other crops could be grown, but most land used for tobacco is suitable for other crops. In Zimbabwe, for example, tobacco is often grown in rotation with maize and other food crops. A 1986 report estimated that tobacco uses land that could otherwise grow food to feed 10–20 million people.[98] A different estimate reported in the *China Daily* in 1994 was that tobacco-growing land in China alone could feed 50 million people.[50]

In LDCs, tobacco may be grown on small plots. When a family with a fixed amount of land decides to increase the amount of tobacco grown, obviously there is less land to grow food. And because farmers tend to invest so much money in their tobacco crops because the production costs are high, food crops may be neglected, thus resulting in an even lower food yield. Furthermore, tobacco consumes soil nutrients faster than other crops. This means that more chemical fertilizers are needed. But if fertilizer is unaffordable, the land's fertility may simply become depleted. Tobacco companies respond in part by saying that water runoff carrying fertilizers used for tobacco results in higher yields for nontobacco crops.

When it comes to paying farmers for tobacco leaf, tobacco companies are as tight-fisted in LDCs as they are in many other countries. In Kenya, BAT opposed the creation of farmers cooperatives to negotiate prices with BAT, on the paternalistic grounds that this was not in the best interests of farmers and would cost the farmers money. One account reports how Kenyan farmers "sometimes had their produce rejected as low quality, but when they dumped it in frustration, BAT employed casuals to pick and grade it, and then bought it at virtually no cost."[345, p. 250] In Uganda, according to one report, "there is a general feeling among farmers that BAT cheats them by paying miserable prices for their crops."[418, p. 255] A farmer's share of the value of the crop sold might amount to just 30%, out of which labour and other costs must be paid.[12] Tobacco companies continue to encourage more farmers to grow more tobacco, knowing that the more tobacco there is on the market, the lower the purchase price will be.

Some steps have been taken toward diversification. In Zimbabwe, about 20% of the country's 68 000 tobacco-growing hectares has been converted to alternative crops such as vegetables, citrus fruits, and roses. The government's goal is 30–35%.[624] Zimbabwean tobacco farmers already produce 20% of the country's maize, produced on land rotated with tobacco growing, as well as 20% of its wheat, and 30% of its prime beef exports.[487] The potential for more diversification remains. One research paper listed 54 agricultural items that could be produced as alternatives to tobacco in Zimbabwe.[625] In Malawi, the government supports diversification, but no progress has yet been reported.

Another point must be mentioned. In many LDCs, child labour is used in the agricultural sector. Tobacco cultivation is no exception, as this excerpt from a Kenya report indicates:

> In the Butonge village of Malakisi, Wycliffe Murunga, a model farmer and teacher, says that it is in seedbed care and picking and the bundling of leaves ready for curing that child labour is primarily used. 'Children between 10 and 15 years appear to be more willing to do such trivial jobs with concentration', says Murunga. Unfortunately, tasks such as harvesting and curing come during the crucial second term of the school year, around June–July, when 'mock examinations' are sat. Children miss school, but teachers, many of whom come from tobacco-growing families, are unable to discipline them or to take parents to task.[345, p. 250]

In Bangladesh, children all across the country roll tobacco into *bidis*, a popular tobacco product consumed by smoking. The children are capable of making 4 000 *bidis* in 8 hours, all the while suffering in poorly ventilated, dust-filled factories for only US $1 a day. Laws prohibiting children under 14 from working in factories are simply ignored,[534] as is the case in many other manufacturing sectors in the Indian subcontinent.

In tobacco growing, as in other agricultural sectors in LDCs, women may be given the most burdensome tasks. This can result in a double-job situation — working on tobacco and working at home — which in turn not only is detrimental to women but also can negatively affect the upbringing of children.[418]

Reducing global smoking rates does not mean that tobacco farmers in LDCs will go out of business. In fact, the large increases in global population will tend to increase the world demand for leaf tobacco, more than offsetting any decrease in smoking rates.

Marketing misbehaviour

In many respects, tobacco companies promote cigarettes in LDCs as they do in DCs — by vigorous marketing. Whether in DCs or LDCs, companies create and propagate brand characteristics associated with various types of imagery. But in LDCs, advertising takes on deeper dimensions. Even though smoking is declining in Western countries and becoming socially unacceptable, advertisements in LDCs portray smoking as an integral part of a desirable, wealthy Western lifestyle. The ads suggest that successful people smoke, that Westerners are successful, and that Westerners smoke. Knowing that most people could never actually afford the lifestyle the images portray, the cigarette companies are marketing smoking as an alternative way for people to fulfill their dreams. Thus, a poverty-stricken African neighbourhood might be overshadowed by a billboard advertising cigarettes and featuring black people in tuxedos and evening gowns in a Paris nightclub. In many LDCs, the industry's advertising budget is greater than the country's entire national health budget.[313]

Tobacco companies know that in time, the number of countries with advertising restrictions will increase. That is why companies are moving early to nurture images for their brands and to recruit loyal smokers. That is also why TTCs are moving to secure indirect forms of promotion such as sponsorships. If advertising is banned but sponsorships are not, then companies still have a way to promote cigarettes.

When it comes to marketing cigarettes, TTCs have a double standard. The TTCs do things in LDCs that they can no longer get away with at home. For example, though Marlboro commercials with the Marlboro man riding on his horse through Marlboro country have not been seen on American television for more than two decades, they are regular fare today in many LDCs. Cigarette packages and advertisements often bear no health warning, or when they do, it is typically weaker than the message required at home. Often the warning is a single, weakly worded message in small print on the side of the package. In the Philippines, cigarettes have had higher tar content than the same brands in the United States.[59]

In Hong Kong in the 1980s, Philip Morris introduced Virginia Slims cigarettes with advertising associating the brand with the usual themes of slimness and women's liberation. At the time, fewer than 1% of Hong Kong women under 40 smoked.[371] The purpose of this campaign was surely to increase smoking among women and not simply to compete for a share of the minuscule market.

TTCs are not the only tobacco firms marketing unethically in LDCs. In some countries, local companies also engage in unethical marketing, but their behaviour is likely to deteriorate even further when a TTC enters the country. After all, TTCs have decades of experience at being unethical, and they can teach the local companies new techniques.

In Africa, tobacco companies have sponsored birthday and wedding parties.[537] In Nepal, the daily summaries of the 1992 Barcelona Olympics on TV were sponsored by Surya Luxury King Size cigarettes, a brand promoted with the slogan "My Nepal, my pride."[113, p. 7] In Guatemala, cigarette billboards often appear on roads as official city-limit signs welcoming travelers.[568] In India, cigarette advertising appears on movie video cassettes. In various countries, cigarette ads are shown in cinemas. In Kenya, shops are painted with cigarette ads. In Ghana, the Miss Ghana beauty contest was sponsored by Embassy cigarettes, and the Minister of Education presented the awards. Also in Ghana it is possible to see a "danger-ahead" street sign and a tobacco ad on the same pole. In Abidjan, Côte d'Ivoire, a Marlboro advertisement occupies the highest point in the city's skyline.[116] In Malaysia, Taiwan, South Korea, and Hong Kong, the Marlboro Adventure Team program is a competition offering lucky entrants a 9-day adventure in the American "Wild West."[21] In the Philippines, where the population is predominantly Roman Catholic, promotional calendars feature cigarette brands under a picture of the Virgin Mary.[358] An article in *Reader's Digest* describes how in Buenos Aires, Argentina, a blonde woman wearing khaki clothing arrives in a Jeep emblazoned with the Camel logo, stops in front of a high school, and gives out free cigarettes to 15 and 16 year old students during recess.[158]

Many ads are culturally imperialistic: they feature caucasian models, use English advertising copy, or suggest that foreign ideals are superior.[99] In francophone Africa, one ad featured a white boy playing tennis and a black boy offering him a cigarette as a sign of friendship.[212]

Tobacco marketing is exemplified by the types of brand names that have been available in LDCs: Long Life (Taiwan), Life (Malawi, Chile), Hollywood (Brazil), Sport (Mexico), Ambassade (Zaire), Diplomat (Ghana), Casino (Latin America), Parisiennes (Argentina), Charms (India), High Society (Nigeria), Full Speed (Ecuador), Sportsman (Kenya), Olympic (Côte d'Ivoire), and Double Happiness (China).[114,120,464,553,585,646] Nelson cigarettes were sold in Senegal and were removed from the market only after the direct personal intervention of South African hero Nelson Mandela.

The behaviour of TTCs in Malaysia is a good example of using loopholes to get around a tobacco-advertising law. Although tobacco ads are prohibited on television, ads for "Salem High Country Holidays" appear on TV. These commercials feature romantic young couples in the pristine, green outdoors, with lively background music. The *Reader's Digest* article reports that when a man tried to book a Salem vacation, he was refused by an office manager who later admitted that the US $2.5 million operation existed only to advertise Salem.[158] These ads sell the lifestyle associated with Salem, which is really known as being a cigarette brand. Indirect ads ostensibly promoting travel have also appeared for

Marlboro and Kent.[102] In Sudan, after a law banning tobacco advertising was adopted, an ad for Marlboro lighters appeared that was almost identical to the previous cigarette ad.[99]

Advertising in LDCs may increase smoking more than advertising in the West does. Because there is often little advertising in LDCs generally, the tobacco advertising stands out. Media have few revenue sources, so tobacco advertisers are more likely to obtain media complicity. As well, sponsorship recipients can become supportive friends.

In opposing restrictions on advertising in LDCs, tobacco companies use the same arguments they use in DCs: advertising is only intended to influence market share and not overall consumption; advertising bans are a restriction on freedom of expression; if tobacco advertising is banned, then restrictions on the advertising of alcohol, sugar, and red meat will be sure to follow; bans will cause jobs to be lost in advertising and media industries; and so on. But there is one difference. In DCs, companies assert that in mature markets, such as for soap or tobacco, it is impossible for advertising to affect anything other than market share. In LDCs, the mature-market argument does not apply because consumption is growing rapidly. Because LDCs are immature markets, the industry's own argument suggests that in LDCs advertising increases overall demand.

Environmental damage

Many people recognize that tobacco is an important health issue in LDCs, but few recognize that tobacco is also an important global environmental issue. The environmental harm in Canada attributable to tobacco use is magnified internationally many, many times. For cigarette paper alone, it is estimated that 350 000 tonnes of paper is used worldwide each year.[101] However, LDCs have a specific concern, sometimes an ecological catastrophe, to deal with. Tobacco leaf needs to be cured (dried) from its natural green to the brownish colour seen in cigarettes. Some types of tobacco, such as burley tobacco, are air cured or sun cured. But other types are fire cured or flue cured, which requires high temperatures for extended periods (say, 1 week). Flue-curing is so called because of the metal pipes, or flues, that permit heated air (instead of direct flame) to circulate through the barn in the curing process. Natural gas or oil is often used in Canada as the energy source for heating, but in LDCs the source is more likely to be wood. Flue-curing using wood fuel is prevalent in Brazil, much of Africa, India, Thailand, and the Philippines.[102]

Estimates of how much wood is needed to cure tobacco vary. One 1986 industry-commissioned report estimated that in the curing barns studied, 7.8 kg of wood, on average, was used to cure 1 kg of tobacco (7.8 kg/kg for short), but this could be as high as 40 kg/kg for individual farms.[182] Other estimates are substantially higher. One report on Uganda states that barns with old, inefficient furnaces use up to 100 kg/kg.[12] In that country, BAT is supporting efforts to introduce more efficient furnaces that use 25 kg/kg.

The result is that tobacco is worsening an already extremely serious world problem of deforestation. In turn, deforestation may contribute to desertification and the greenhouse effect. With trees as a protector gone, fertile land may turn to waste, topsoil may be washed away, and water tables may fall, possibly drying up water sources or tributaries.

Deforestation also means that farmers — or more likely family members — seek wood for curing at increasing distances. Distances by foot of 12 and 17 kilometres from farms have been cited in Kenya and Tanzania.[418,621] If the wood is for cooking fuel, the same distances have to be walked.

Tobacco companies make some efforts at reforestation. They are not shy to publicize this fact, in part to respond to criticism from international environment and development groups. These critics respond that industry efforts are exaggerated and sometimes produce more PR benefits than actual results. BAT gives out millions of seedlings to farmers free of charge, but that does not mean the seedlings are planted, or if planted, survive. There are a number of reasons for this:

✦ The planting season may be short, and a farmer may be too busy planting his own tobacco and other crops to worry about planting trees.

✦ Even if planted, seedlings may die because cattle trample them or because a farmer is still too busy tending his other crops to take care of them.

✦ Farmers may prefer crops with a quicker economic return than possible with the 10 years it takes for a seedling to mature.

✦ A tenant farmer will not be nearly as concerned with the long-term benefits of tree planting as the property owner might be.

✦ A lowered water table may inhibit seedling growth.

In Malawi, the *Special Crops Act 1973* requires tobacco farmers to plant 10% of their land with trees. However, some farmers plant only a handful of trees on their worst 10% of soil, knowing that the seedlings will likely die.[412]

Various pesticides, herbicides, and fertilizers applied in the growing of tobacco are also of concern. Besides the impact the substances may eventually have on a smoker of this tobacco, the substances may contaminate the groundwater and harm the general population in the area. Farm workers who come into direct contact with tobacco leaves also come into contact with harmful chemicals. A 1982 report in *New Scientist* said that BAT Kenya provided farmers with Aldrin, a pesticide banned or severely restricted in many DCs.[375] Warnings on pesticide containers may be of questionable value, as one World Bank report poignantly commented:

> Even if the user can read and understand the warnings, it is not easy to 'avoid contaminating rivers' nor even to 'wash with soap and water after use'. Most users have never seen a physician and certainly are not able to consult one 'immediately' as advised on the label.[636, p. 11]

Apart from the health risks of pesticides and other inputs, those who work with tobacco, including women and children, are susceptible to nicotine poisoning.[600]

Tobacco-control challenges in LDCs

In general, tobacco-control strategies that are appropriate in Canada are also appropriate in countries throughout the world. However, local circumstances present special challenges. For example, high rates of illiteracy in LDCs mean that large segments of the population are unable to read the health warnings on packages or in advertisements, making them ineffective. For this reason, the use of pictures in warnings becomes all the more important.

In countries where few people own televisions, an antismoking advertising campaign using this medium is obviously a poor strategy. Radio may be a better choice; billboards, even better. In a country with many ethnic subgroups, each with its own language, carrying out an effective antismoking publicity campaign can be far more difficult. In parts of Africa and Asia, enforcing laws against selling tobacco to minors is made more difficult because the vendor may be a child selling cigarettes on a street corner. Enforcement of tobacco laws may be arduous if the penalties are inadequate, there is uncertainty over who is responsible for enforcement, there is a lack of public understanding of why a law is necessary, or the tobacco industry simply refuses to obey the law.

In some LDCs, there are high rates of smoking among doctors, in part because doctors can afford to smoke. In China, a survey of medical professionals in five hospitals found a smoking rate of 55% for males.[19] In the Philippines, a study found that 63% of male doctors and 37% of female doctors were smokers. An alarming finding was that 38% smoked regularly in front of their patients. If a large number of doctors smoke (as was once the case in Canada) the credibility of antismoking messages is undermined and it becomes more difficult to convince politicians and the general public of the need for tobacco control. Similarly, high rates of smoking among politicians in many LDCs reduce support for antitobacco legislation.

In many LDCs, the most basic data, such as the prevalence of smoking in the population, are unavailable. LDCs may not have a national registry of diseases or may not record cause of death. Where records are kept, only part of the country may be covered.

Many governments do not have a single official responsible for tobacco control, let alone sufficient expertise to take on the global industry. Given the prevalence of contagious diseases, governments may not see tobacco as a priority. The playing field is tilted in favour of the TTCs.

Most health groups in LDCs are poorly equipped to join the battle against smoking. When representatives in some of the more active African countries were asked what their priorities were, they said "fax machines" and "good-quality typewriters." In 1994, there was only one person in all of Africa working full time on tobacco control.

Cash-strapped governments may not have money to undertake wide-scale programs to educate the public about the dangers of smoking. In such cases, the most effective approach may be to focus the educational component of their antismoking strategy on schools. Schools can deliver the educational messages to children and youth and encourage them to bring the information home to their parents.

Often Ministers of Finance block efforts to control tobacco because they fear a decrease in tax revenue. The percentage of government revenues from tobacco taxes is typically much higher in LDCs than in DCs, exceeding 10% in many countries and reportedly as high as 18% in Sri Lanka and 26% in Zaire.[9] In China, the state tobacco monopoly generates US $6.6 billion a year in taxes, about 12% of all central government revenue.[414] If tobacco-caused health consequences have not yet materialized on a large scale and will not for several decades, convincing Finance Ministers that immediate tobacco control is needed may be a tough sell. That is highly regrettable because the cost of preventing a tobacco epidemic is far less in the early stages than after the epidemic has become entrenched.

Tobacco-tax increases alleviate Finance Ministers' concerns because revenue is increased. A tax on tobacco is normally easy to collect because it is imposed on a handful of manufacturers or importers, instead of millions of citizens. In LDCs, consumers, especially young ones, have very little money. The resulting sensitivity to price increases might reduce overall smoking more than in DCs. This is supported by research from Papua New Guinea.[103] In some countries where borders are poorly patrolled and where neighbours have low tax rates, though, potential smuggling may inhibit a high-tax strategy.

A government could fund a tobacco-control program by dedicating part of the tobacco-tax revenue to it. A surtax on manufacturer profits could also be dedicated. Governments could also impose limits on the proportion of TTC profit leaving the country.

In India, tobacco is available in more than a dozen forms: cigarette, cigar, pipe, cheroot, *bidi*, *chutta*, *dhumti*, *chilum*, and hookah (all consumed by smoking); chewing tobacco, sometimes in the form of betel quid (tobacco mixed with lime and areca nut, rolled in a betel leaf); snuff; *mishri*; and tobacco toothpaste.[102] Some consumers indulge in "reverse-*chutta*" smoking: with this technique it is the lit end of the tobacco that is put in the mouth. Reverse-*chutta* smoking has been associated with higher rates of neck and head cancer. Use of chewing tobacco is high, including among women. In some states, oral cancer is higher for females than for males.[322]

Because there are so many types of tobacco products in India, tobacco control and taxation are complicated — consumers can just substitute one type of tobacco for another. In the case of *bidi*, produced by thousands of small-volume cottage industries around the country, tax laws become extremely costly to enforce.

In the global tobacco-control effort, countries in the same region or countries of comparable economic development would benefit from working together to develop joint strategies. One group might consist of emerging economies, including Brazil, Thailand, Mexico, South Africa, Malaysia, and Singapore. These emerging economies may have higher tobacco-consumption rates than their less-wealthy neighbours, but they also have a more advanced capacity to implement an effective tobacco-control strategy.

Progress toward global tobacco control is painfully slow. One of WHO's goals for 1994 was that 50% of the countries in the world have a national program to reduce tobacco use, let alone an effective or comprehensive program. So far, only 10 countries have comprehensive tobacco-control programs: Australia, New Zealand, France, Portugal, Iceland, Norway, Finland, Sweden, Thailand, and Singapore. Canada was on this list until the TPCA advertising ban was struck down.

Is there any cause for optimism? There are some encouraging signs. In Botswana, 100 people from across the country attended a conference on tobacco, a sign of an organized movement. Botswana's antitobacco program, with its strong advertising restrictions, may be the best in Africa. In Kenya, antismoking activists pressured a car rally to drop its Marlboro sponsorship. Thailand and Singapore have shown that tough laws controlling the industry are possible.

LDCs present a real opportunity. If a strong tobacco-control program is implemented early, before smoking rates take off, there will be incredible long-term health dividends. If at all possible, the time to act is before domestic tobacco companies gain experience at fighting government regulatory efforts and especially before TTCs get a major foothold in the country. Furthermore, when smoking rates have yet to rise to high levels, public opposition to restrictive smoking measures is likely to be less intense than later on when there are more smokers to contend with.

The role of international agencies

A significant contribution to tobacco control is made by some international organizations. One such body is WHO, a United Nations agency based in Geneva. WHO's tobacco initiatives are only modestly visible in Canada, but in LDCs they are much more evident. WHO's parent body, the World Health Assembly, adopted its first resolution on tobacco and health in 1970. Since then more than a dozen resolutions have urged governments to adopt a series of tobacco-control measures, including educational programs, a ban on all advertising, tax increases, health warnings on packages, and protection from ETS. WHO assists governments in implementing a tobacco-control strategy, sponsors World No-Tobacco Day each year, maintains a data centre, awards medals, publishes resource books and a quarterly newsletter, and with other United Nations bodies helps ensure that different agencies are working toward the same objective. WHO's Program on Tobacco or Health does this with only a handful of full-time professional staff. The program's budget of US $2.7 million represents just 0.2% of WHO's total 2-year 1994/95 budget.[335] This amount is unacceptably low, given the magnitude of the tobacco epidemic.

WHO's most valuable contribution is promoting legislation. Given WHO's direct access to Health Ministers in LDCs, this is one area in which WHO can make a huge impact. WHO's testimony before GATT in the Thailand decision clearly had a bearing on the final decision. In what is a sure sign of effectiveness, WHO's antitobacco efforts have been criticized by tobacco interests.

At one time, the World Bank, another agency of the United Nations, gave loans to support tobacco growing and processing. Loans for these purposes totaled more than US $1.5 billion between 1974 and 1988.[102] Such loans are no longer possible. A 1992 policy stipulates that the World Bank will not lend directly for, invest in, or guarantee loans for tobacco production, processing, or marketing, whether for domestic consumption or for export. The Bank will avoid indirect lending to tobacco projects to the extent practicable. Trade-liberalization agreements between countries and the Bank will not cover tobacco, tobacco products, or related items. The Bank will help countries diversify away from tobacco. In its health-sector work, the Bank will include antitobacco activities, such as designing loans with components to reduce tobacco use, examining ways to increase tobacco taxes, and recommending restrictions on tobacco advertising.[637] With a policy like this, the World Bank is an important, highly credible antitobacco advocate.

The Food and Agricultural Organization of the United Nations (FAO) provides governments with assistance for agricultural development and technical advice. Although as a general rule FAO does not encourage the cultivation of tobacco, it may recommend "development of the crop, in such cases where overriding economic considerations so warrant."[179, p. 4] In the past, FAO actively promoted tobacco growing.

The Union internationale contre le cancer (UICC, International Union Against Cancer) established its Programme on Tobacco and Cancer in 1976. Among its initiatives, UICC has organized consultative visits and more than 100 training workshops to help stimulate local tobacco-control initiatives. It also works with its member organizations in more than 80 countries. It sponsors GLOBALink, an international computer network providing instant information on international developments.

Ottawa-based IDRC (the publisher of this book) is coordinating the International Tobacco Initiative. With funds from Health Canada and other partners, the Initiative funds research in LDCs. The LDCs themselves will determine where their research needs lie, and particularly in the fields of health, economics, environment, agriculture, and social science. IDRC has established an international reputation in development, and its decision to become more involved in tobacco is welcome. In 1993, IDRC cosponsored an All-Africa Conference on Tobacco or Health in Harare, Zimbabwe, that attracted 110 delegates from 16 countries.

Other active organizations include the relatively new London-based International Agency on Tobacco and Health, the International Union Against Tuberculosis and Lung Disease, and the International Organization of Consumers Unions. In 1994, 14 NGOs formed a coalition, based in Paris, to work on tobacco control.

Some regions have dedicated organizations, like the Asia Pacific Association for the Control of Tobacco, the Tobacco Control Commission for Africa, and the Latin American Coordinating Committee on Smoking Control. In some countries, religious organizations may be leading advocates of tobacco control.

Every 2–4 years a World Conference on Tobacco and Health is organized by the international tobacco-control community. These forums have proved to be outstanding venues in which to present the latest information on tobacco, to share techniques for fighting the tobacco industry, and to make contacts in other countries. Delegates typically report that attending a world conference is an incredibly motivating experience. The tobacco industry also recognizes the significance of these conferences and quietly sends people to observe the proceedings. Jacques LaRivière, former Vice-President of CTMC, said he was one of about 12 industry representatives attending the 1983 Winnipeg Conference. LaRivière thought that a turning point was reached when tobacco-control activists at this conference made political action, instead of health research, the top priority.[47]

The pro-tobacco side has international organizations at work, too. The International Tobacco Growers' Association was founded in 1984. Its original members — from Argentina, Brazil, Canada, Malawi, the United States, and Zimbabwe — have been joined by other growers since then. The Association emphasizes the economic benefits of tobacco and generally echoes TTC views on smoking issues. The Centre de coopération pour les recherches scientifiques relatives au tabac (Cooperation Centre for Scientific Research Relative to Tobacco), inaugurated in 1956,[111] promotes research cooperation in the tobacco industry. The Tobacco Documentation Centre, formerly known as Infotab, is based in England and helps the industry coordinate its fight against antitobacco measures. Just as health advocates do, tobacco lobbyists learn from their colleagues in other countries how to fight adversaries.

Export promotion of leaf tobacco

Some governments have promoted the international sale of raw leaf tobacco. Following World War II, Canadian tobacco was exported to Europe under the Marshall Plan (1948–52), a plan designed to help reconstruct Europe.[145] In the United States, beginning in 1955, hundreds of millions of dollars worth of American tobacco was given away as part of the Food for Peace donations, although of course no one was going to eat the tobacco. Recipients included South Vietnam, the Philippines, Cambodia, Thailand, Egypt, and Syria.[416] The practice continued for decades, until criticism made it untenable.

Today, both the United States and the European Union subsidize tobacco farmers. This leads to increased production of tobacco leaf for export.

How Canadians can help stop the global epidemic

Despite its small population, Canada makes a tremendous contribution to tobacco control internationally. By taking the lead in implementing tobacco-control measures and setting important precedents, Canada opens the way up for other countries to do likewise. Advocates and politicians elsewhere can (and do) say, "If Canada can do it, why can't we?" Canada is seen around the world as a highly respected, mature, wealthy, and democratic nation. Canada's lowered smoking rates after implementation of its antitobacco measures makes the case for following Canada's strategy all the more persuasive. Canadian laws have been emulated in New Zealand, France, and Thailand, among other places.

Canada is not the world's only role model. Measures implemented in the 1990s by Australia, New Zealand, France, and elsewhere have had their impact. Although the United States is not considered a world leader in tobacco-control regulation, any measures it does implement carry weight simply because of the nation's prominence. US initiatives receive substantial global publicity.

The best thing Canada can do to help the world is to build on its own tobacco-control success. Further, it is important to let the world know about Canada's achievements (and failures).

In 1994, Canada took a further step by making a commitment to provide other countries with direct aid for tobacco control. Health Canada includes an international component in its Tobacco Demand Reduction Strategy and gives financial support to the International Tobacco Initiative coordinated by IDRC. Health Canada has worked with WHO on a project that sees Canadian experts sharing their know-how with foreign countries.

International tobacco ads

The Marlboro Man is seen around the world

Photo: James Lukoski

Gold Coast cigarettes marketed by R.J. Reynolds in San'aa, Yemen.

Ad for L&M cigarettes from Czech Republic. The advertising slogan translates as "This is what America tastes like! New arrival!"

CHAPTER 19

Penetrating Eastern Europe

Brian Gable, *Globe and Mail*, Toronto

Epidemic in progress

In the 1990s, the tobacco situation in the former communist countries of Eastern Europe dramatically changed.[7] Anyone who thinks the war against the tobacco industry is being won should think again. A brief glance at what is going on in these countries will show why.

The tobacco epidemic in Eastern Europe is worse than anywhere else in the world. Consumption in some countries is about twice the world average and still increasing.[115] High smoking rates have been around for decades. WHO estimates that in Eastern Europe there are now 763 000 tobacco-related deaths a year, about one quarter of the world's total.[115] In Eastern Europe, as many as 80% of these tobacco-related deaths occur before the age of 70; the comparable rate in Western countries is estimated at 50% or less.[467] In some parts of Eastern Europe, lung cancer rates in men are the highest ever recorded anywhere in the world.

---

[7] For convenience here, *Eastern Europe* includes the countries of both Central Europe and Eastern Europe.

Poland is the second largest cigarette market in the region (after Russia), and the effects of years of heavy smoking are taking a severe toll on health. Dr Witold Zatonski, head of the Cancer Control Department of Warsaw's Institute of Oncology, says that "middle age male health is worse in Poland today than in many developing countries. One of every two middle aged men will die from tobacco-caused diseases."

There was no commercial advertising under communism, so the fact that smoking rates were high then illustrates that advertising is not the only factor that can contribute to higher smoking rates. However, tobacco advertising now appears on a massive scale and will contribute to yet higher smoking rates, or it will at least delay declines.

Transnationals invade new markets

During the communist era, there was not a lot of contact with foreign cigarette makers, but there was some. In 1974, Philip Morris provided advice to Soviet officials to enable them to improve cigarette quality. In 1975, Philip Morris helped produce a cigarette commemorating the *Apollo–Soyuz* space flight. Between 1978 and 1986, the company exported more than 3 billion cigarettes to the Soviet Union. In Hungary and some other countries, Western brands were manufactured under licence. Before 1989, the legal market share of Western companies was less than 3%.[166] In addition, famous Western cigarette brands could sometimes be found on the black market. In Moscow, a package of Marlboros was as valuable as currency and was a great way to flag a taxi. Beginning in 1989, democratization in the region opened up the countries to the outside world.

In 1990, the Soviet Union faced a drastic shortage of cigarettes. Industry problems in Bulgaria, a traditional supplier to the Soviets, meant that the quantity of imports was less than expected. The shortage caused protests, strikes, riots, and long lines at tobacco kiosks. In August 1990, a Soviet trade representative in Washington contacted the US Department of Commerce to seek export proposals from US manufacturers. Just 3 weeks later, Philip Morris and R.J. Reynolds agreed to sell 34 billion cigarettes to the Russian Republic before the end of 1991. Unexpectedly, the companies had suddenly received a huge boost to their presence in the region.

Since then, TTCs have moved aggressively into the entire East European region, buying up existing government-owned companies and factories. A trickle of investment in 1991 and 1992 turned to a flood in 1993. The potential was so great in 1992 that BAT Chairman Sir Patrick Sheehy exuded, "These are the most exciting times that I have seen in the tobacco industry for the last 40 years."[399] Rothmans International, in a *Globe and Mail* advertisement recruiting sales managers for the region, explained that "Rothmans has clearly identified the markets of Central and Eastern Europe and the [former Soviet Union] as a major growth area for the future."[522]

The takeover of Eastern Europe's tobacco industry by foreign companies moved quickly. By mid-1994, they had bought into more than 30 of the 100 factories, either by 100% takeover or joint venture (foreign companies tend to have a majority stake in joint ventures). Many other factories remained takeover targets and may have been producing foreign cigarettes under licence. The government tobacco monopolies were being quickly dismantled.

Why are companies moving in so fast? The answer is simple: if they don't, competitors will have an advantage. With total sales of 700 billion cigarettes a year, the Eastern European market is roughly 14 times the size of the Canadian market. *Tobacco International's* October 1994 cover story, "The Good War," described the scramble to get market share on what used to be the other side of the Iron Curtain. The fall of barriers to free enterprise was said in the story to provide "some of this century's greatest marketing opportunities."[320, p. 29] Because some governments are desperately seeking hard currency and foreign investment, TTCs have sometimes been able to acquire factories at fire-sale prices.

In 1992, Thomas Marsh, an R.J. Reynolds Vice-President for Eastern Europe, described the intensity with which the industry was going after new markets:

> It's trench warfare, hand-to-hand combat. We talk with each other on certain issues of mutual interest, such as smoking and health issues, advertising restrictions, things like that. We have industry associations where we sit down and act like perfect gentlemen — and then we leave the meeting and go out and battle in the streets again. I don't think there are many other industries that are in as fierce a competition as we are.[219]

Foreign companies are moving in for the long term. In some cases, it will take years for local operations to become profitable. In other cases, the profit is there for the taking now.

In the long run, few domestic East European companies will survive in competition without a foreign partner or owner. Before the influx of foreign firms, existing factories were usually small and inefficient, with outdated equipment. Supply lines were disorganized, and product quality was poor. With insufficient domestic capital, the factories were unable to modernize facilities to compete with the tobacco giants.

Foreign companies bring money, technology, cigarette know-how, and marketing genius with them, so it is not surprising that East Europeans are receptive when foreign suitors come courting. The local companies that still remain appear to be too weak to try to get governments to block the foreign onslaught.

Following the entry of Western firms, many governments weakened or revoked their tobacco-advertising laws. Consequently, cigarette marketing is aggressive and widespread. Once again, ads often portray a successful Western lifestyle. Indeed, West brand is among the top foreign brands in many countries. The fact that the tobacco is "American blend" is often featured prominently on cigarette packages. Much of the advertising has themes of freedom, thus capturing the spirit of new-found democracy in society. English advertising copy can often be seen alongside text in the local language.

Perhaps influenced by advertising, East Europeans perceive smoking as a highly desired, commonplace activity in Western countries. In 1992, a Canadian traveler visiting Moscow and the central Asian republic of Uzbekistan found that men in their twenties were frequently amazed that he, being from the West, did not smoke. "Is it because of sports?" they pressed, only to hear the response that smoking was just bad for health, an answer that seemed to surprise them.

Russian television receives more revenue from cigarette advertising than any other source. During primetime viewing hours, cigarette ads are common. In Moscow, the Camel or Marlboro names and colours are painted on many kiosks. In Romania, Camel advertising has actually been found on the amber light of a set of traffic lights. In Prague, Czech Republic, Camel and Marlboro colours and advertising are painted over the entire exteriors of streetcars. In some Prague tobacco stores, a life-size cardboard Marlboro man greets customers. Some couples in Prague have been married in "Camel" weddings, courtesy of R.J. Reynolds.[358] In Warsaw, one can see Camel-painted taxis.[399] In Latvia's capital city, Riga, the entire side of a six-storey building carries an advertisement for West and the slogan "Test the West."[453] In Hungary, young women dressed in brand colours and stripes distribute free cigarettes in bars and cafés.[358]

In Eastern Europe, smokers are accustomed to cigarettes with a stronger taste than are normally found in the West. Western manufacturers cater to this preference by supplying cigarettes with higher tar yields than in the same brands sold at home. Table 5 shows the results of a 1993 test comparing tar levels in Russian and American versions of the same brands.

In an effort to help prevent adoption of ETS restrictions, the tobacco industry has sent public-health officials from Eastern Europe to conferences in Copenhagen that are sponsored by tobacco-industry related groups, such as Clean Air International. At these conferences, the hazards of ETS are ignored.[121] Tobacco control in Eastern Europe may be a long time coming, for several reasons:

✦ Rates of smoking are very high.

✦ Alcohol may be seen as a more severe problem.

✦ Government personnel have had virtually no experience at regulating companies in a free market.

✦ Governments are faced with many other pressing issues.

Table 5. Comparison of tar levels in Russian and American versions of the same brands, 1993.

Brand	Tar level (mg)	
	Russian	American
Kent	20.2	13.0
Winston	19.0	15.0
Camel	19.2	16.0
Marlboro	21.5	16.0
L & M	16.7	14.0

Source: Kholmogorova and Prokhorov.[334, p. 147]

✦ Governments may be hesitant to restrict freedom so soon after the fall of oppressive governments.

After the market opened up in Russia, alcohol and tobacco advertising in the mass media was prohibited, but this went unenforced. An official in the Russian Press Ministry stated, "We will not take any draconian measures because alcohol and cigarette advertising is a major source of income for many newspapers."[325]

Very often there is little understanding of the magnitude of the problem. When one East European delegate to the Ninth World Conference on Tobacco and Health was telling colleagues at home that 1 500 people would be gathering in Paris, the colleagues found it hard to believe that so many would be concerned about tobacco.

TTCs have the resources and experience to lobby against proposed tobacco-control measures, but the health lobby is usually extremely weak. In Russia, for example, the few people who are working to ensure that the advertising ban is maintained and enforced may not be able to give it much time because they have other full-time jobs.

Interests supporting tobacco advertising are much better organized. The Association of Russian Advertising Agencies was formed in 1993 after the Russian Parliament passed the advertising ban. The same year, the Association gave its support to

> two marketing studies on the effects of the ban, aiming to show that it will have no effect on frequency of use of cigarettes or alcohol but will cause the loss of hundreds of millions of dollars to federal and local budgets.[395, p. I-21]

This is a classic example of results-oriented research by the tobacco industry and its allies.

The beginning of antismoking efforts

Health groups are starting to organize and make modest inroads. A national nonsmoking day is held in November to draw attention to smoking and health issues. This must be having some impact — in Poland, R.J. Reynolds chose that date for a widely publicized draw for Camel smokers and offered a trip to Egypt, a car, and a Harley–Davidson motorcycle as prizes.

In Poland, Dr Zatonski is leading a fight to control smoking. He says that Canada's tobacco experience helps Polish campaigners. "The best example is the taxation and pricing policy," he explains. "The Canadian government was able to achieve two goals: to reduce tobacco consumption and to increase tax revenue. We are using this every day in our advocacy. The second example is the new Canadian health warnings which is helping us a lot."

A 1993 report by Euromonitor, a firm that follows the tobacco industry, dryly predicted that "increasing limits on cigarette advertising are expected to come into force in Poland due to the high death rates caused by the habit."[165, p. 19] Zatonski decries the proliferation of cigarette ads in his country now. "People are probably more sensitive to them because there was no advertising of any kind beforehand," he says, deploring the fact that a package of cigarettes is cheaper than bread. In 1996, final approval was given to a new Polish law banning tobacco advertising on radio and television.

In Lithuania, tobacco advertising was banned following a WHO mission to the country, but since then compliance has been a problem because there are no government officials to enforce the law.

In Czechoslovakia, communism ended in November 1989. By 1991, tobacco ads were starting to appear; by 1992, they were everywhere. Environmentalists led a campaign for a ban, arguing that the ads constituted visual pollution. On 31 December 1992, the last day before Czechoslovakia split into the Czech Republic and Slovakia, the Federal Assembly passed a law to ban tobacco advertising. In 1993, the Czech Republic repealed its ban under pressure from the company Tabak, which by this point had majority ownership from Philip Morris. Tabak, which exported cigarettes to neighbouring Slovakia, repeatedly sent representatives to meet with the Consumer Protection Section of the Slovakian government in an effort to have the ban repealed in Slovakia as well. In 1994, 2 days before World No-Tobacco Day, five foreign tobacco companies held a news conference in Slovakia to give their usual views about why they should have the right to advertise. The more than 40 journalists who attended were offered free cocktails and cigarettes. Nonetheless, the ban remained in place with support from a health coalition. However, there are problems with enforcement and with the definition of advertising.

Slovenia: one country's story

In Slovenia, the northernmost republic of the former Yugoslavia, an estimated 3 500 lives are lost prematurely every year because of tobacco. The tobacco industry has been privatized, and it is one of very few industries in the country doing well after economic liberalization. Germany's Reemstma now has majority control of the country's industry.

Dr Mateja Kožuh-Novak, a physician and for 5 years head of the National Public Health Institute, is now a member of the National Assembly. In 1994, she helped lead a campaign to ban tobacco advertising. A tobacco-control bill before the National Assembly would have required health warnings on packages, restricted smoking in workplaces, prohibited the sale of tobacco to minors, and restricted tobacco advertising. However, the advertising part of the bill was worded in such a way as to make it virtually impossible to get a conviction. Naturally, the tobacco industry liked it this way. Kožuh-Novak introduced an amendment to have a real ban on all direct and indirect tobacco advertising. The amendment passed by almost a two-thirds margin. The next day, newspapers — the recipients of tobacco advertising — came out strongly against the change, saying that it was an attack on smokers and a violation of freedom of expression. "This was despite the fact that an earlier poll found 80% of the population supporting a tobacco ad ban," says Kožuh-Novak. The total ban had the support of the Ministry of Health, but it was opposed by the Ministry of Finance, which was concerned about losing tax revenue. The Ministry of

Economics opposed the ban on the grounds that it was crazy to go after one of the few successful industries in the country.

The tobacco industry claimed that jobs would be lost. That argument made an impact in a country where unemployment had now reached 10% after historically being zero. The industry failed to mention that far more raw leaf tobacco and cigarettes were imported than exported, thus upsetting the balance of payments, and that a ban on tobacco advertising would protect Slovenia brands from further attack by foreign imports. The market share of foreign imports was 20% and rising.

Kožuh-Novak's amendment was repealed, and the weaker provision restricting tobacco advertising was restored. Kožuh-Novak went to the President of the Senate, a lawyer, to urge him to get the Senate to veto the bill. To her surprise, that is exactly what happened. The National Assembly attempted to override the veto but failed to get the needed two-thirds vote. Just 1 week later, a new bill on tobacco advertising was introduced in the Assembly that again had loopholes. "The two people who introduced the bill were not at all interested in health. They were just afraid I would introduce a bill before they did," says Kožuh-Novak. However, health forces mobilized, and eventually many amendments strengthening the bill were adopted. Thousands of letters poured in to parliamentarians, and a demonstration was held outside Parliament on the day of second reading. By early 1996, the bill had yet to receive third and final reading, and its fate was still uncertain.

The attempts to control advertising in Lithuania, Slovenia, and Slovakia may spark some optimism in a region where prospects for tobacco control are bleak. As foreign companies become more dominant, prospects will become even bleaker. As was the case when TTCs entered markets in the developing world, it will be people who will pay the price.

PART VI

Winning the War:
An Agenda for Victory

CHAPTER 20

A Prescription for Health

Brian Gable, *Globe and Mail*, Toronto

The solution to many of today's medical problems will not be found in the research laboratories of our hospitals, but in our Parliaments. For the prospective patient, the answer may not be cure by incision at the operating table, but prevention by decision at the Cabinet table. ... Historically, a nation would look to its doctors for better health. Now they should look to their Members of Parliament.[650, p. 123]

> — Sir George Young, British health minister, in an address to the 1979
> World Conference on Smoking and Health in Stockholm, Sweden

Not all tobacco-control measures have equal impact. But they can all have some impact. Which are likely to be the most effective? As a rule of thumb, the greater the potential effectiveness, the greater the industry opposition will be. Of the items that governments have considered so far, the industry has most strongly opposed high taxes, a total ban on advertising and sponsorship, prominent warnings, plain packaging, and ETS restrictions. Where do we go from here?

Legislative framework

As a start, the Government of Canada should be given complete regulatory authority to control all aspects of the growing of tobacco and the manufacture, importation, advertising, promotion, and sale of tobacco products, other nicotine-delivery devices, and tobacco supplies, such as rolling papers. In this way, the government would have the authority to adopt regulations without the delays that come with introducing legislative amendments in Parliament. An efficient and flexible regulatory process is essential for addressing an epidemic.

A similar framework has long been in place for prescription drugs, hazardous products, pesticides, and radiation-emitting devices. Many provincial governments have had complete regulatory authority over alcoholic products. Tobacco deserves similar treatment, but to date it has been excluded from regulation under the *Food and Drugs Act*, the *Hazardous Products Act*, and narcotics legislation. British Columbia has broad control over tobacco through its *Tobacco Sales Act*, but regrettably the province has passed only a few regulations under the Act. In the 1960s, MP Barry Mather introduced several private-member's bills to place tobacco under the *Food and Drugs Act* or to give the government the same regulatory authority over tobacco as it would have if tobacco were covered by this Act. However, the bills were not voted upon.

Total ban on advertising and promotion

The government should introduce a total ban on all forms of tobacco advertising and promotion, including sponsorships. Also prohibited would be the free distribution of tobacco; the use of tobacco brand names and logos on nontobacco goods like lighters and T-shirts; and the use of games, contests, and other incentives to promote sales. Canada had almost all of these covered under the TPCA; the only exceptions were certain kinds of sponsorship advertising and certain displays of tobacco in retail stores. Measures proposed in the federal government's 1995 blueprint would improve on what had been in the TPCA before the Supreme Court's decision.

Point-of-sale displays are prominent forms of promotion. In 1987, in the period leading up to the enactment of the TPCA, RJR–Macdonald spent $20.3 million (57%) of its $35.3 million advertising and promotion budget on displays and other point-of-sale activity.[497] Imperial Tobacco spent 39% of its marketing budget on retail activities.[288] To address the problem of prominent retail displays, the government should require that tobacco products be stored under the counter.

The need for a total advertising ban is demonstrated by past experience with a partial ban. As previously noted, when the industry voluntarily removed cigarette advertisements from Canadian television and radio in Canada in 1972, tobacco companies simply shifted the expenditures to other types of advertising. When France initially restricted advertising but did not regulate the use of brand names on other goods, the industry promoted Camel lighters and boots with ads identical to those previously used for cigarettes. This loophole was later closed. In the United States, when Congress prohibited television advertising for cigarettes but not for other tobacco products, commercials for smokeless tobacco continued. This contributed to a marked rise in the use of smokeless tobacco. Congress later closed this loophole.

Apart from Canada's experience with the TPCA, total or almost total advertising bans have been adopted by about 20 countries, including New Zealand, Australia, France, Norway, Iceland, Finland, Sweden, Portugal, Singapore, and Thailand. Dozens more have legislated partial restrictions on advertising.

Tax increases and anticontraband measures

High tobacco taxes are a critical component of a comprehensive strategy. All forms of tobacco products should be taxed at a rate equivalent to that for cigarettes to discourage cigarette smokers from switching to cheaper alternatives. For example, tobacco sticks should be taxed at the same rate as cigarettes. The tax on a gram of roll-your-own or raw leaf tobacco should be at least as high as the tax on one cigarette.

With high taxes, measures are needed to prevent the emergence of a sizable contraband market. Packages should be clearly marked to indicate they can be legally sold on the Canadian market. Canada's revised health warnings on packages visibly differentiate licit and illicit products, but a distinct tax marking should also be required. A "tax-paid" marking on individual cigarettes would further help identify licit and illicit products.

Given that cigarette manufacturers fostered the contraband market in the past, measures are needed to control industry behaviour. An effective export tax is needed to prevent exports from reentering Canada. The export tax should be high enough to narrow the gap between the prices of licit and illicit products. An export tax alone is not enough, given that manufacturers might shift some production out of Canada to avoid the tax. If this were to happen, the government would have to respond decisively. For example, if RJR–Macdonald had its American parent company produce Export "A" cigarettes for the Canadian contraband market, then the Canadian government should be in a position to suspend RJR–Macdonald's ability to sell Export "A" in the much bigger legitimate Canadian market. This type of suspension, twice imposed on TTCs by Italy, would give manufacturers a financial incentive to ensure their products only went into legitimate distribution channels and to cooperate with police to identify and shut down illegal operations. Suspension targets the source of the problem. Suspension also sends a message to the industry that the government can play hard ball too.

Contraband may flourish when one jurisdiction has significantly higher tobacco taxes than a neighbouring one. To counter this, the government with the higher taxes should lobby its neighbour to raise taxes. Law-enforcement officials from neighbouring governments should collaborate and share enforcement-related information.

In Canada, tobacco products sold on an Indian reserve are exempt from provincial tobacco taxes. This exemption has sometimes led to abuse. Provincial governments should set limits on the quantity of tax-exempt tobacco entering the reserve and take other steps to ensure that tax-exempt tobacco is not being sold illegally to off-reserve consumers. Better yet, band councils should be able to collect a tobacco tax equal to the provincial tax and then use the revenue for community-development projects.

There should be an end to duty-free sales. Lower duty-free prices encourage consumption and may result in large quantities of tax-exempt tobacco entering the market illegally. As well, governments lose revenue. Ending duty-free sales might best be implemented through reciprocal agreements between neighbouring countries. Alternatively, duty-free status given to tobacco could be phased out over a period such as 5 years.

At the same time, the government should eliminate or reduce the duty-free entitlement for travelers entering Canada. At present, even though most smokers do not exercise their full entitlement, a pack-a-day smoker is nonetheless legally able to bring in almost a 6-week supply tax free (200 cigarettes, 400 cigarette sticks, **and** 400 grams of roll-your-own), not to mention 50 cigars. In addition, it is not unusual for nonsmokers to "give" their allotment to a traveling companion who does smoke.

Tobacco should be taken out of the consumer price index so that increases in tobacco tax do not increase the official rate of inflation.

Smoking bans in all workplaces and public places

Involuntary exposure to ETS should be eliminated from all enclosed workplaces and public places. If smoking is not banned outright, it should be limited to enclosed rooms that are independently ventilated to the outside. The rooms should be used for no purpose other than smoking.

Simply having designated smoking and nonsmoking areas is inadequate. This is like having chlorine and nonchlorine sections in a swimming pool.

Regulation is preferable to letting workers and employers set their own individual policies, the approach advocated by the tobacco industry. The resulting compromise or absence of restrictions might have a particularly negative impact on individuals most vulnerable to the dangers of ETS . Health and safety laws should not be optional. Society does not tolerate voluntary standards for fire protection, automobile safety, or restaurant cleanliness. Besides, employers find that the existence of a law requiring a smoke-free workplace makes implementation easier — management can respond to complaints by citing an external requirement.

Governments should be a model and prohibit smoking in their own workplaces, a step the federal government and most provincial governments have now taken. A complete smoking ban should also apply in all parts of legislative buildings, including offices and rooms for elected members, their staff, and the Press Gallery. When politicians and journalists can work successfully in a smoke-free environment, it makes it a lot easier for them to support a law mandating the same thing for everyone else.

Smoke-free spaces create an environment where nonsmoking is the norm, and this helps prevent teens from smoking. It is important to ban smoking on elementary and secondary school property. Ontario does have such a ban, but many schools across the country still permit students to smoke on secondary school grounds, despite the fact that most, if not all, students are too young to be sold cigarettes. Peer pressure influences teenagers to take up smoking. Teens want to be accepted, especially at school, which is usually the centre of their social lives. Designated smoking areas create an environment where smoking is endorsed, and teens hanging out there may then be seduced into addiction against their better judgment. As well, schools that have a smoking area are undermining the credibility of their own health messages.

Profit controls

Federal and provincial governments should take steps to control the exorbitant profitability (in terms of return on investment) of tobacco manufacturing. The more than $500 million in industry-wide annual aftertax profit in Canada should be reduced by at least 70% to bring profitability into line with that of other industries.

Profit is driving the tobacco epidemic. Reduced profitability would therefore have many benefits:

* The industry would be less able (less money to spend) and less motivated (less profit to defend) to fight tobacco-control efforts.

* Tobacco companies would have less money available for marketing their products.

* The financial incentive for recruiting new smokers would decrease.

* It would eliminate the injustice of manufacturers' earning massive profits at the expense of public health and the taxpayer.

* It would reduce the amount of money that leaves Canada and goes to parent multinationals.

A manufacturer's profit is best controlled by regulating the factory prices it charges. Current factory prices would have to be rolled back to reduce profitability. Government revenue could be increased substantially by increasing tobacco taxes by the same amount that factory prices are rolled back, thus keeping retail prices unchanged. Profitability could also be controlled through new corporate taxes.

Many prices are already regulated in some way, including those for cable television, local telephone service, passenger train travel, local transit, mail, apartments (rent control), patented prescription drugs, taxis, funeral parlours, and medical care. If these products and services beneficial to society can have their prices controlled, there is no reason why the manufactured cigarette, a hazardous product, should be treated differently. Given the health-care costs associated with tobacco use, there is no reason why companies should enjoy profit levels massively surpassing those of all other major industrial sectors. It is ironic that the federal government has put controls on the price of nicotine patches and has rolled back prices but places no controls on prices of cigarettes containing nicotine.

The government should also set a fixed price for the retail sale of tobacco products to prevent retailers from putting tobacco on sale. Such sales pressure competing retailers to lower their own prices, which in turn increases consumption. A fixed price would also prevent stores from selling tobacco at or below cost to draw customers to buy other items, a practice of many gas stations. A fixed retail price would help maintain the benefits of a high-tax strategy.

Health messages

The government should require a series of rotated, prominent, easy-to-understand health messages on tobacco packages — the more space allocated, the better. Warnings should appear on both the front and the back of the package, as well as on the six sides of a carton. Regulations should specify the colours for the messages to prevent companies from choosing colours that blend in with the package design. The specified design and colours should maximize impact.

Messages on packages need not be restricted to health. Other nonhealth messages may be equally or more effective in reducing smoking. Some possible examples are the following:

+ Quit smoking, save money.

+ Men: Smoking increases the risk of impotence and may reduce sexual performance.

+ Cigarettes give you bad breath.

+ Smoking makes your clothes smell.

+ Smoke yellows teeth and fingers.

+ Smoking reduces athletic performance.

+ Life insurance costs less for nonsmokers.

+ Smoking gives you premature wrinkles.

+ Ever tried nicotine gum or the nicotine patch? Details on reverse.

+ Men prefer women who don't smoke.

+ Women prefer men who don't smoke.

+ Out of breath? Don't get left behind. Quit smoking.

Some of these messages may have a much more immediate meaning for teenagers. These messages are harder to dismiss than warnings about heart disease or lung cancer, which teenagers may see as way off in the future and in any event "will not happen to me."

Detailed health information should be provided to consumers, either on a package insert or on the packaging itself. Australia requires a warning on the front, with detailed information explaining the warning on the back. One possibility is to print detailed information on the inside slide portion of the package or on paper laminated to the foil that keeps cigarettes fresh inside packages.

The package should list the product's average and maximum yields of tar, nicotine, and carbon monoxide. The yields of other harmful substances, such as formaldehyde and hydrogen cyanide, should also be listed.

Because a picture sends a thousand words, there could be photographs on packages corresponding to the particular message. Perhaps a photo of a diseased lung, of a cancer patient following chemotherapy, or of a smile with yellow teeth or diseased gums would be à propos. Photographs or graphics help get the message across to those who are illiterate and to those who speak neither official language. Some countries, including Iceland, require some graphic images as part of warnings.

Package warnings can be one of the most effective forms of public education. Messages are targeted directly to smokers and are available for viewing every time the package is opened. Best of all, package warnings cost the government nothing because the industry pays the expense.

Many countries have required warnings for a long time now, but the warnings are often vague, in small print, on the side of the package, and in colour combinations that minimize legibility.

Legislation should also require antitobacco messages on lighters, matchbooks, matchboxes, cigarette carrying cases, and packages containing cigarette tubes, rolling paper, or filters.

Health warnings should also be required for any tobacco advertising or sponsorship advertising permitted during a phase-out period before a total ban. In Canada, some billboard advertising was going to be permitted during the first 2 years of the TPCA, but only if the warning "Smoking causes lung cancer, emphysema and heart disease" occupied the top 20% of the ad. This requirement prompted tobacco companies to voluntarily stop placing billboard advertising in new locations. "We did some mock-up boards and, frankly, find it very unacceptable to put an advertisement for our product out in that manner," said Don Brown, then Imperial Tobacco's Marketing Vice-President. "The first thing you see is a big warning that says 'Smoking causes cancer'. You've got to see it to understand. It's just a feeling."[572]

Point-of-sale signs and pamphlets discouraging the use of tobacco should be required at all retail locations. Point-of-sale messages are read by people waiting in line, including teens who might be thinking about starting to smoke.

The packages should also carry the telephone number of a toll-free Quit Line, as they do in Australia. Smokers could call the hotline to obtain information about smoking and health or to get advice on quitting. Staff answering these lines should be well trained, able to respond to calls in either official language, and on duty at times most convenient to callers. During off hours, a touch-tone–computer-response system could provide some of the more basic information. A toll-free line is an excellent way to reach smokers in rural or remote parts of the country. Manufacturers should be required to pay for the cost of operating the Quit Line.

Packaging controls

All tobacco products and tobacco supplies, such as filters and rolling papers, should be required to come in plain packages. An interesting suggestion is that the standard cigarette package should be too big to fit easily into a pocket.

A cigarette pack might be required to contain no fewer than 20 cigarettes. Canada has had this requirement since 1994 — there are no more kiddie packs (15 cigarettes) or toddler packs (5 cigarettes), which used to make a pack of cigarettes more affordable to low-income consumers, including teens. For a similar reason, it should be illegal to sell single cigarettes, a practice banned in Canada.

A minimum package size of 20 grams could be required for smokeless tobacco, if it is not banned altogether. This would eliminate the 10-gram Skoal Bandits, a product that has come under fire for being aimed at teenage boys.

Product design regulations

Some countries have set maximum limits for tar and nicotine yields, but few have done much to regulate the design of the actual product. Much can be done in this area.

Controls are needed on so-called light and mild cigarettes. For example, *light* should have a consistent meaning across all brands. A preferred approach would be to ban such terms altogether because they are misleading or to require classifications like Player's Poisonous, Player's Highly Poisonous, and Player's Extra Highly Poisonous.

The package could inform consumers that the tar yield depends on how intensely the cigarette is smoked. One desirable option is to require packages of filtered cigarettes to carry a diagram with, say, five circles representing the filter end. Each circle would be a different shade of brown and labeled with a tar level. The darkest circle would represent the highest tar yield. After a smoke, consumers could compare their butts with the diagram and learn how much tar they were exposed to by their style of smoking.

Ventilation holes in filters should be visible to the naked eye. They should be far enough away from the butt end that lips or fingers would not cover the holes.

Slim cigarettes, targeted at and overwhelmingly smoked by women, should be prohibited. Luxury-length cigarettes (100 and 120 millimetre) suggest fashionability and should also be banned.

Perhaps tobacco products could be required to have a more unappealing flavour and odour to diminish the appeal of smoking. Cigarettes with menthol, spearmint, or other flavours should not be permitted. These additives mask the harshness of tobacco smoke that might otherwise make a smoker want to quit. Further, smokers may inhale menthol cigarettes more deeply than the harsher cigarettes, thus increasing the health risks.

Concern over additives in cigarettes is not new. In 1903, MP P. Macdonald told Parliament that the tobacco or paper used for cigarettes was quite possibly laced with narcotics to give the smoker a more pleasurable sensation.[370] Such rumours of adulteration, whether true or not, would remain around for some decades. In 1962, MP Herbert Herridge suggested that cigarette manufacturers should be required to disclose ingredients, but no action was taken.[244–246] Packages should list all the ingredients contained in the cigarettes, including any additives in the filter or cigarette paper. Thousands of food products in grocery stores list their ingredients, and there is no reason why cigarettes should be treated any differently.

Another possibility is to require an unattractive colour for the paper portion of the cigarette. White, the colour almost always used at present, suggests purity (hence manufacturers' use of more white on packaging for light cigarettes). At a minimum, bleached cigarette paper should be prohibited. The colour of the paper covering the filter should also be controlled. The use of colours to suggest a cork should be eliminated. Manufacturers should be required to stop printing brand names and logos on each cigarette. These trademarks reinforce and promote a brand's image.

Some countries have banned smokeless tobacco. Given the small market share of this type of product in Canada, a ban is a feasible and desirable measure.

There could also be a ban on retail sales of roll-your-own and raw leaf tobacco. However, demand for these products could be eliminated if they were taxed at the same rate as cigarettes. These products are usually smoked without a filter, which may increase the health risk. A complementary ban on rolling papers would have a side benefit — they would no longer be available for rolling illegal drugs.

Mandatory fire-safe cigarettes

Cigarettes could be modified to make them less likely to start fires. At present, because of their burn characteristics, cigarettes start fires after smouldering on beds or upholstered furniture. Cigarette paper can be designed to enhance burn or to retard it. Tobacco companies have said that sales would be harmed by fire-safe requirements because cigarettes would be less puffable and would have a bad taste. On the plus side, from a health point of view, such side effects would likely cause some smokers to quit altogether.

Product registration

Manufacturers and importers should be required to register each tobacco product with the government before they place the product on the market. The application form for product registration should require product details, such as the following:

- ✦ Yields of toxic constituents;
- ✦ A list of additives;
- ✦ The pH (acidic) level;

- ✦ The length and circumference;

- ✦ The weight of the tobacco;

- ✦ A description of the blend;

- ✦ A description of ventilation holes and other filter characteristics; and

- ✦ The burn characteristics of cigarette paper.

Manufacturers should be required to file an amended registration **before** they start selling a modification of any product already on the market. The amended registration should describe the intended modification and the impact the change would have.

The registration fees should be high enough to allow the product registry to recover its administrative costs and to allow the government to conduct independent tests of its own on each product.

All the information included on an application for product registration should be available to the public. In addition, the information should be available in a *Nicotine-product Information Book* that the industry would be required to put at each retail outlet where tobacco products are sold. Such a book, which could be in binder format for easy updating, would provide consumers with easily accessible information. The book could also include detailed information on the health consequences of smoking, tips for quitting, and information on the financial costs of being a regular smoker. Information on alternative nicotine products would also be helpful.

Ban on the sale of tobacco to young persons

The vast majority of smokers take up the habit before the age of 18.[225,234] Imperial Tobacco data show that the average age for beginning to smoke regularly is 15.2 years for males and 14.7 years for females. Moreover 20% of male smokers and 22% of female smokers begin regular cigarette use by age 13.[225]

At the very minimum, tobacco should not be sold to anyone under the age of 19. This age is consistent with the minimum drinking age in most provinces and is high enough to help get smoking out of high schools. The minimum age should also apply to rolling papers and other tobacco supplies. Because it is often difficult to judge a person's age, a clerk should refuse to sell tobacco products to customers who appear to be younger than 25 unless they can produce suitable photographic ID. Stores should display a sign to that effect, thus making it easier for a clerk to refuse. The law should not permit a sale even if the minor has a note from a parent. Some jurisdictions set a minimum age for the employees who serve alcohol to customers. If a similar provision were adopted for tobacco, refusing a sale would be made easier because the clerk would be an adult rather than a teenager.

Cigarette-vending machines should be prohibited altogether. At the very least, they should be restricted to bars where minors are refused entry. In jurisdictions that have simply required vending machines to be under adult supervision, minors have had continued success at obtaining cigarettes from the machines.

Counter-top cigarette displays, which might be a temptation to shoplifters of any age, including minors, should be banned. Mail-order sales should also be banned because there is no way to ensure that the recipient is old enough to legally be sold cigarettes.

The federal *Tobacco Sales to Young Persons Act*, passed by Parliament in 1993 with all-party support and proclaimed into force in 1994, sets a minimum age of 18 and restricts vending machines to bars. In the 1990s, several provinces passed their own sales-to-minors laws, some of which replaced antiquated laws passed in the 1890s. The new provincial laws vary, but some have set 19 as the minimum age, banned vending machines altogether, required signs at retail, and provided for a suspension to vendors convicted of selling to minors.

The most effective way to reduce illegal sales to minors would be to hold manufacturers responsible for youth smoking. The government should conduct an annual survey of youth smoking rates and estimate each company's share of the youth market. The government should charge each company a fee based on the estimated retail value of the company's share. The tobacco industry would then have a financial reason to **reduce** youth smoking and reverse the present situation. Manufacturers would quickly take steps to make sure retailers were not selling to minors. At present, manufacturers do nothing meaningful to prevent retailers from making illegal sales.

Public-education and smoking-prevention campaigns

Public education is an important part of a comprehensive strategy, but it is only one part. The existence of a modest public-education effort should not be an excuse for failing to adopt other tobacco-control measures, as has sometimes been the case.

Governments should undertake an extensive antismoking campaign using the mass media. Just as large scale tobacco advertising campaigns can increase consumption, large scale antitobacco advertising campaigns can decrease consumption. Media advertising can effectively communicate an antismoking message, whether through TV, radio, movie theatres, billboards, print, or otherwise. The government should have a professional advertising firm create maximum-impact advertisements. Market research should be undertaken to determine what ad content would be most effective. Campaigns should be intensive to best reach target groups. California has a major antismoking advertising campaign, and there is evidence that this has contributed to a decline in smoking.[271,476] Perhaps the tobacco industry agrees, given how hard it sought to block the campaign.

Between 1967 and 1970 in the United States, the Federal Trade Commission required antismoking messages on television and radio to balance cigarette commercials. At the peak, about 1 minute of antismoking airtime appeared for every 3 minutes of cigarette commercials. Per capita consumption fell during each year of the campaign and rose again when the mandated messages stopped.[607] The American antismoking commercials spilled over into Canadian homes and may have contributed to a Canadian decline in per capita consumption during much of this period.

The media can have a tremendous educational impact. News coverage about the health consequences of smoking has a broad reach and costs antitobacco activists almost nothing. Even reports surrounding the debate over proposed laws can heighten the public's awareness of the dangers of tobacco. For example, the release of the 1964 Report of the Advisory Committee to the US Surgeon General generated a great deal of spontaneous publicity and led to reduced smoking.

Given the influence that doctors and nurses have as role models, professional organizations should have a campaign to encourage their members to be nonsmokers and certainly to abstain from smoking while at work.

It should be mandatory for elementary and secondary schools to teach about the hazards of tobacco. Programs should be suitably designed for different ages and should be conscious of gender differences.

National Non-Smoking Week, held in Canada in January every year, started out as an educational activity in 1977 and now has a life of its own. On Weedless Wednesday during that week, smokers are invited to give up smoking for 1 day. The week is often used to organize activities in schools or to host media events. Ministers of Health occasionally announce new initiatives that week. The concept of a week or day with a nonsmoking theme is not a new idea. Starting in about 1960, British Columbia designated May 31 as a nonsmoking day, an event that continued for decades. Coincidentally, WHO now uses May 31 each year to mark World No-Tobacco Day, an event of some significance in many countries. In the United States, the American Cancer Society sponsors the 1-day Great American Smokeout in November every year.

Physician counseling

Doctors should counsel patients on the importance of not smoking. At present, even during regular checkups, many general practitioners neither ask patients about their smoking behaviour nor provide counseling, despite the critical role smoking can play in a person's health.

The 1994 *Canadian Guide to Clinical Preventive Health Care* strongly recommends that physicians provide smoking-cessation counseling and offer nicotine-replacement therapy.[83] A 1996 American clinical practice guideline recommends that doctors "use officewide systems to identify smokers, treat every smoker with a cessation or motivational intervention, offer nicotine replacement except in special circumstances, and schedule follow-up contact to occur after cessation."[550, p. 1270] There is evidence that physician counseling leads to higher cessation rates.[340,550]

Other primary-care clinicians, such as dentists, nurses, physician assistants, and respiratory therapists, also have a role to play in patient counseling.

Limited distribution

In an ideal world, only government-owned or government-controlled stores would be allowed to sell tobacco, as is currently the case for alcohol in many provinces. Some countries, including France, have implemented this measure for tobacco. In any case, tobacco should not be sold in hospitals, pharmacies, or other health-care centres. Neither should it be sold from vending machines, on the premises of educational institutions or athletic facilities, from outlets in government buildings, or from establishments in which alcoholic beverages are served.

Reducing the number of distribution outlets would make it less convenient to purchase cigarettes, would decrease point-of-sale promotions, and would decrease the acceptability of tobacco. In the absence of price controls, limited distribution would reduce the likelihood of price competition, thus pushing up the price. Limited distribution would also make it easier to enforce tobacco laws, such as those banning sales to minors.

A store should be required to obtain a licence to sell tobacco. This would make it easier to identify retailers to target for education about legal obligations. If a retailer were to sell tobacco to minors, sell contraband, or infringe other tobacco laws, the licence (and selling privileges) would be suspended. This would provide a meaningful economic incentive to obey the law. A licencing fee provides revenue for enforcement.

In most countries outside North America, pharmacies that sell tobacco are unheard of. But in the United States and Canada, with the exception of Ontario, pharmacists have become major tobacco vendors despite being licenced health professionals with a monopoly over the sale of prescription drugs. From an ethical point of view, pharmacists should not be permitted to sell both remedial drugs and the leading cause of preventable death. Tobacco sales mean that pharmacists profit when customers smoke and profit again when prescriptions are filled to treat an illness. Those pharmacists who voluntarily refuse to sell tobacco should not be placed at a competitive disadvantage because they are acting ethically. Banning tobacco sales in pharmacies would eliminate a conflicting message, especially to children, about the health risks of smoking.

The same conflicting message is given by hospitals and other health-care institutions that allow the sale of tobacco products on their premises. The tobacco industry knows this. Imperial Tobacco's 1971 marketing plans positioned Matinée as a low-tar brand that was "safer for health." As part of the campaign, Imperial Tobacco proposed to place Matinée ads on vending machines in hospitals and health-care centres.[292]

Some pharmacies, especially chains like Shoppers Drug Mart, do more than just sell tobacco. They actively promote tobacco through prominent shelf and counter-top displays and through advertising. Shoppers has often put tobacco on sale, thereby putting pressure on other retailers in the community to also lower their prices. The economic impact of selling tobacco may warp a pharmacist's sense of professional duty. One Ottawa pharmacist from a major chain (then selling tobacco) said, "We can't appear to do anything against tobacco."[130, p. 467]

Industry reporting

Tobacco manufacturers, importers, and wholesalers should be required to report sales volumes by brand and package size to the government. The government could use this information to monitor both market developments and progress on tobacco-control initiatives. All of this information should be publicly disclosed. Disclosure facilitates the work of researchers and assists the efforts of health groups.

Each company should annually report how much it spent on each type of marketing activity (for example, sponsorships, print advertising, retail display space) in the event that some marketing activity continues to be permitted. A copy of all advertisements and packaging should be filed with the government. This would help governments and health organizations monitor industry strategies.

Funding for cessation programs

Smoking cessation benefits public health, reduces health-care costs, and increases worker productivity. However, smokers participating in smoking-cessation programs have to absorb the cost themselves. This should change — government should fund cessation programs. Participants could be reimbursed through provincial health insurance plans or federal income-tax credits. Ideally, tobacco manufacturers would be responsible for reimbursing the cost of participation in cessation programs.

Permitting advertising for nicotine substitutes

In Canada, it is illegal to advertise prescription drugs in the consumer market. An exception should be made for nicotine substitutes, such as the patch, nicotine gum, nicotine inhalers, and nicotine nasal sprays. Advertising nicotine substitutes would increase their market share of the nicotine market, especially in the absence of tobacco advertising. It is already legal to advertise Nicorette, though, because gum with 2 mg of nicotine or less no longer requires a prescription. In the United States, advertisements for the patch are legal, although there are some constraints.

Insurance discounts for nonsmokers

Despite decades of evidence that smokers die at a younger age than nonsmokers, it was not until the 1980s that life insurance discounts for nonsmokers were widely available in Canada.[439] Later, it became common for insurance companies to offer lower nonsmoker premiums for fire and car insurance as well. Higher premiums for smokers provide an additional economic incentive to quit, and they provide an unimpeachable message about the reduced life expectancy for smokers. In Canada, the competitive marketplace has ensured that lower nonsmoker premiums are obtainable, so government intervention now seems unnecessary.

Agricultural measures

Federal and Ontario governments should continue their programs, especially cash incentives, to encourage farmers to exit from tobacco farming.

Subsidies for tobacco growing should not be allowed, although in Canada there are no direct subsidies. However, research and technical assistance programs provided by the federal and Ontario governments amount to an indirect subsidy and should be discontinued in their present form. Neither taxpayers nor a government committed to a tobacco-free society should be assisting in the development of a lethal product. The cost should be borne by those who are benefiting, namely, the tobacco growers and manufacturers.

Marketing boards artificially inflate the revenues of inefficient farmers. These boards should be disbanded so that leaf tobacco is sold at world prices and farmers are not rewarded with excessively high income for growing a deadly crop.

Tobacco growers participate in government-sponsored international trade missions, use the services of Canadian embassies abroad, and take advantage of other programs of the Department of Foreign Affairs and International Trade. By permitting this, the government is supporting the export of raw leaf tobacco to less developed countries. The government should withdraw this support.

Enforcement

Adopting legislation is not good enough if the legislation is not enforced. Past experience shows that in the absence of strict enforcement, the tobacco companies take bolder and bolder steps to avoid compliance with laws.

In drafting legislation, it is important that legislators provide adequate deterrents to illegal activity: fines must be sufficiently high; and the courts must have the option of jail terms for corporate executives. Further, the legislation should give the government the ability to impose the type of cease and desist orders found in some consumer-protection laws. That is, if a company is breaking the law, the government should have the ability to order immediate compliance, instead of having to wait for the delays and pay the costs inherent in the legal process. A company could appeal the order, but meanwhile it has to obey the direction.

In the case of enforcing chronically disobeyed sales-to-minors laws, the best strategy is to impose a fee on manufacturers based on their market share of the youth market, as previously discussed. The next most effective strategy is to use unannounced purchasing tests. In such a test, a health official sends an underage teenager into the store to try to buy cigarettes. If the teen is successful, the official issues a ticket to the store and suspends the store's licence to sell tobacco for a short period (such as 1 day or 1 week) if this is the first offence, for longer periods if it is not. This gives the retailer a strong financial incentive to obey the law.

The municipality of Woodridge, Illinois, a suburb of Chicago, used this test-purchase strategy and achieved 100% compliance by retailers. In Woodridge, some of the retailers who were suspended after failing the test smartened up when they saw customers go to competitors to buy cigarettes. The bottom line for Woodridge was that the proportion of local junior high school students reporting they were regular smokers fell from 16% to 5%.[315] An increasing number of municipal and state governments in the United States and some provincial governments in Canada are adopting test-purchase enforcement strategies.

Are test purchases entrapment, thereby giving a defence to an accused store? No. Test purchases can be organized in such a way as to avoid legal difficulties. Test purchases have been so successful in some parts of the United States that the American tobacco industry and its allies have taken steps to undermine the use and effectiveness of this strategy. Pro-tobacco forces have lobbied for laws that prohibit journalists, interested citizens, researchers, or stores themselves from conducting test purchases; that contain loopholes making convictions almost impossible; that repeal stronger municipal laws; that prohibit health officials from enforcing the law; and that limit enforcement to a state's least-capable agency.[588] The industry has even opposed studies that measure compliance rates, even if test purchases do not lead to charges.

Product liability

Provincial laws should make it easy for tobacco victims to sue tobacco manufacturers. Provincial laws should provide that manufacturers and importers are strictly liable for the damages caused by tobacco products. Thus, plaintiffs would not face many of the delays or legal costs that have characterized much American litigation. With proper wording, plaintiffs would only have to prove that it was more likely than not that smoking caused their emphysema, throat cancer, etc., for a court to award damages. For certain diseases, this will often be relatively easy to prove. Where a person has smoked cigarettes made by different companies, liability could be divided up proportionately among those companies.

Because tobacco-industry defendants have deep pockets, creating an economic imbalance between the plaintiff and the defendant in tobacco lawsuits, the government could go a step further and provide financial support for a test case or a class-action lawsuit.

Until the end of 1994, only one liability lawsuit had been filed against a tobacco company in Canada. That was the case started in Vancouver in 1988 by Roger Perron for damages attributable to smoking-caused Buerger's disease (see Chapter 1). By early 1996, the case was still working its way through preliminary procedures.[465] In January 1995, a major development occurred when four smokers filed a lawsuit in Ontario against Canada's three major companies and sought to have their case certified as a class action.[91] If the case, *Caputo et al.* v. *Imperial Tobacco Ltd. et al.*, is certified by the court, millions of smokers could potentially be part of the lawsuit. Potential damages could be in the billions of dollars. Although the legal process will take years, a successful case — by no means certain — could devastate the industry.

The statement of claim filed by lawyer Richard Sommers of the Toronto law firm Sommers and Roth on behalf of the plaintiffs presents a lengthy list of allegations against the industry. The allegations, which have not been proved in court, include that the defendant tobacco companies

+ Concealed their own research about the addictiveness of nicotine and misinformed the public about that research;

+ Conspired to target advertising at women and children;

+ Controlled the amount of nicotine contained in cigarettes;

+ "Intentionally attempted to create, heighten and maintain addiction to nicotine so as to promote and ensure continued purchase of their products and thereby replace with new, young and healthy recruits who died or became diseased";[91, p. 11] and

+ Engaged in a conspiracy that "constitutes a wanton and outrageous disregard for the health and wellbeing of the plaintiffs."[91, p. 30]

Previous American lawsuits against the industry were unsuccessful for two main reasons: juries blamed the smoker, not the tobacco company; and industry wealth was able to wear down plaintiff lawyers. Class actions undermine these factors, especially if many lawyers act for the plaintiffs. In the United States, 60 major personal-injury law firms are working together in a series of class-action lawsuits. Not including lawyers' time, the law firms have each been contributing US $100 000 a year toward the cost of taking on the industry. This gathering of resources pitted against the industry is unprecedented and enhances the chances for success.

Other new American developments with huge potential are the lawsuits filed by several state governments to recover smoking-related Medicare costs from tobacco companies. State governments have large financial resources and legal departments. It is difficult for juries to blame the health consequences of smoking on plaintiff governments. Provincial governments in Canada could file similar lawsuits, but they have not yet done so.

Criminal liability

The Criminal Code says, "Every one is criminally negligent who (a) in doing anything, or (b) in omitting to do anything that it is his duty to do, shows wanton or reckless disregard for the lives or safety of other persons." The offence of "causing bodily harm by criminal negligence" has a maximum penalty of 10 years imprisonment. The offence of "causing death by criminal negligence" has a maximum penalty of life imprisonment.

When he was a lawyer at the firm of McCarthy and McCarthy, David Doherty (now a justice of the Ontario Court of Appeal) wrote a legal opinion for NSRA concluding that under certain circumstances tobacco companies could be guilty of criminal negligence. Given the duty of companies to design safe products, and given the duty of companies to not make negligent statements about their products, and given the duty of tobacco companies to warn consumers of the health risks of tobacco, and given the failure of tobacco companies to fulfill these duties, a case may someday be made that companies have violated criminal law.

Provincial Attorneys General are responsible for enforcing the Criminal Code. They should instruct that an investigation of manufacturer practices be launched and subsequently, if appropriate, that charges be laid and prosecuted against tobacco companies and executives. Possible charges to investigate are criminal negligence, conspiracy, and fraud.

Government annual report

Federal and provincial legislation should require an annual government report on tobacco. Responsibility for the report should be assigned to a designated official, such as a province's Chief Medical Officer of Health or the federal Director of the Office of Tobacco Control. The report should monitor smoking rates, evaluate the effectiveness of legislation and government initiatives, and recommend improvements. In the United States, the annual reports of the Surgeon General provide authoritative statements on the state of tobacco-related knowledge and have helped galvanize public and political support for legislation.

Ban on candy cigarettes

Candy cigarettes and other products designed to resemble a tobacco product should be banned. Thailand and at least one Australian state have such a ban. So does Nova Scotia, although the provision has not been proclaimed into force.

An American study found that repeated candy cigarette purchases were significantly correlated with experimental tobacco use.[336] Candy cigarettes legitimize the social acceptability of smoking to very young kids. Similarly, products like Big League Chew bubble gum legitimize the social acceptability of chewing tobacco. A child too young to smoke may see candy cigarettes or bubble gum wads as a playful way to imitate an adult behaviour seen as desirable.

In the United States, tobacco manufacturers have been slow to take major action against companies for selling candy cigarettes in packages with trademarks imitating those of cigarette brands. This suggests that tobacco companies have historically had no real objection to these products.

Boycotts of tobacco stocks

Investment managers for pension funds and mutual funds have an obligation to act in the best interests of their clients by maximizing return on investment. Even though it may be ethically desirable to avoid purchasing tobacco-company securities, investment managers may feel hindered in making this decision on ethical grounds alone. Managers should be able to refuse tobacco securities, just as some jurisdictions supporting an end to apartheid gave managers discretion to boycott companies with South African investments. Investment legislation should be amended accordingly.

A successful boycott of tobacco stocks would further isolate tobacco companies and increase public support for regulation. Already, some organizations and institutions have decided not to invest in tobacco stocks. The institutions include Harvard University, Johns Hopkins University, and the City University of New York.

CHAPTER 21

A Research Plan

Ron Tandberg, *Sydney Morning Herald*

The need for research

Much is already known about what has to be done to reduce tobacco use. Nonetheless, more research is needed, both in Canada and around the world. Research can help make political decision-makers aware of the need for action within their own country and can help policymakers design more effective tobacco-control policies and programs. However, research should never be used simply as an excuse to delay real action.

The type of research a particular country needs may depend on how advanced the country's tobacco-control strategy is. An LDC intending to implement a strategy might need research on the prevalence of smoking or on the rates of lung cancer — the type of research that was conducted in Canada in the 1960s. Canada, on the other hand, can pioneer in research that would help the country expand its antitobacco strategy.

Health research

Every year, research on tobacco use uncovers more "bad news." Ever-growing knowledge about the health consequences of smoking, ETS, and nicotine addiction further makes the case for strong action by policymakers.

Compared with DCs, where countless health studies already exist, the LDCs have a greater need for health research because the tobacco epidemic in those countries is not yet as severe. The tobacco industry has frequently argued that a lack of local health evidence in LDCs means that there is no proof that smoking is harmful to local residents.[622] As false and as racist as such industry claims may be, good research helps to counter the industry's position.

In many LDCs, basic epidemiological research is needed to determine the risks of smoking for a particular population, especially where risks of certain diseases may be higher than they are in DCs. For example, in parts of China the residents have a heavy salt diet, so they already have an elevated risk of heart disease. Tobacco consumption might also worsen existing endemic conditions, such as low birth weight due to poor maternal nutrition, bladder cancer due to schistosomiasis, or cancer due to unregulated exposure to environmental carcinogens.[474]

Economic research

Given that the industry is quick to emphasize the economic benefits said to arise from tobacco, research into the economic costs from tobacco can provide valuable information for decision-makers. So can information that a domestic company is exporting earnings through dividends to an expatriate parent company. Knowledge of the industry's high profitability can help make the case that profit has to be reduced. Similarly, research demonstrating that tobacco imports are adversely affecting the balance of trade can be powerful information for a country with a significant import market but scarce foreign exchange. Such economic considerations might be enough to persuade the government in question to take strong action against tobacco. Knowledge of how much is spent annually on tobacco by consumers, in LDCs especially, can illustrate how money is not being spent on the necessities of life. This gives a further reason why tobacco should be controlled.

Environmental and agricultural research

Much more research needs to be done to better understand how the growing and curing of tobacco lead to environmental damage. More needs to be learned about the extent of deforestation and soil depletion. Existing research has concentrated on Africa, but little is known about Asia, including China. In the short term, designing fuel-efficient curing barns might reduce environmental damage.

Research into alternative crops can help farmers exit from tobacco growing. Research into the occupational health problems of tobacco growers, especially in LDCs, might provide further reasons for discouraging the growing of tobacco.

Market research

Regular, ideally annual, surveys of the prevalence of smoking are needed. The surveys should be broken down by demographic group (age, sex, region, socioeconomic status, urbanization, ethnic subgroup, and so on). These breakdowns are important for monitoring trends among different groups. Surveys help analysts evaluate the effectiveness of existing prosmoking and antismoking interventions. Surveys also help policymakers design better tobacco-control strategies.

Also needed is continuous updated behavioural research. Why do people start smoking? Why do they continue to smoke? Why do they attempt to quit? Why do they succeed in quitting? There needs to be an understanding of the products being consumed (cigarettes versus roll-your-own, the preference for various tar and nicotine yields, the preference for menthol cigarettes, and so on). Growth in certain market segments may reveal industry strategies and highlight the need for new remedial interventions. The market is continuously changing, and those working in the tobacco field must keep on top of things. Imperial Tobacco knows this and boasts that one of the company's most important strengths is "a deep understanding of consumers gained through extensive market research."[281, p. 11]

Survey methodology must be culturally sensitive. Thus, in countries where smoking is socially unacceptable for women, interviewers should be women who receive special training. In LDCs, a survey might find a high smoking prevalence among health-care professionals, thus indicating a need for a targeted educational program. Monitoring market changes following entry by TTCs can show other countries why they should — and how they can — keep TTCs out of their own markets.

Policy research

Policy research is needed to help countries design and implement effective tobacco-control policies. Research could take many forms. One initiative might be to assemble a collection of the laws enacted by other governments. A complementary initiative would be to prepare model laws that municipalities, provinces or states, or countries could adopt, as appropriate. Opinion polls could determine how much public support there is for various tobacco-control measures. Politicians place great value on public opinion. A list of tobacco industry arguments, together with counterarguments, would provide a useful reference for advocates campaigning for new tobacco-control measures.

It is important to monitor tobacco-control developments in other places. News reports are helpful for this: in a "war of information," it is essential to keep on top of current events. In addition, case studies detailing successful and unsuccessful campaigns describe lessons learned so that the same mistakes do not have to be repeated elsewhere.

In each policy area, research can help determine the need for a proposed measure or the best way to implement one. There are hundreds, if not thousands, of possible research questions worth investigating. A few, given below, illustrate what can be pursued.

In the realm of taxes, helpful initiatives would be to track prices in different provinces; to measure the impact of higher taxes on consumption; to determine whether higher taxes on cigarettes cause consumers to switch to other tobacco products; and to measure whether taxes are keeping up with inflation and increases in disposable income. Any rise in smuggling should be documented, as should any direct or indirect industry contributions to the problem. Documenting problems make it easier to design remedial actions.

In the realm of advertising, numerous research questions might provide further evidence related to advertising restrictions. One might investigate the impact of advertising on consumer perception of brand imagery; the ability of children to recall advertising; the influence of advertising on consumer perceptions of the safety of light cigarettes; or the influence of advertisers on the news content of magazines and newspapers. It would be helpful to document industry violations of voluntary restrictions on advertising and to investigate how the industry exploits loopholes in existing laws. More research on the promotional value of packaging could provide evidence that would be useful in the inevitable legal challenges to the implementation of plain packaging. Documenting sponsorships, charitable donations, and political contributions is a way to monitor the tobacco industry's PR and promotional activity.

In the realm of smoking restrictions, many questions still need research. What percentage of workers have a smoke-free workplace? How quickly are employers moving to restrict smoking in workplaces? Do 100% smoke-free policies for workplaces influence smokers to quit smoking or reduce their daily consumption? How many restaurants have voluntarily banned smoking? How many health-care institutions are smoke free? Are the consequences of ETS more severe in homes with poor ventilation and open fires? What steps can be taken to make it easier to implement smoke-free policies? How does a city bylaw banning smoking in all restaurants affect restaurant sales?

In the realm of laws prohibiting tobacco sales to minors, researchers could measure the effect of retailer educational programs on compliance. Surveys could measure the compliance rate in a community and identify retailers not complying with the law. Generally, all laws should be monitored for the extent to which they are obeyed. Identifying how laws are being disobeyed is the first step to ensuring compliance.

In the realm of product design, researchers could measure the levels of toxic substances in tobacco products; analyze the content of new or modified products; estimate the impact of banning the use of menthol or other flavouring; investigate ways to control deceptive filter ventilation; or determine ways to make the taste of cigarettes deliberately less palatable.

In the realm of health warnings, researchers could examine which messages are the most effective; determine which photographs or graphics accompanying a warning would have the greatest impact; measure the impact of existing messages; track changes over time in consumer knowledge of health consequences; or determine which nonhealth messages would be most effective on packages.

In the realm of alternative nicotine products, research on nicotine gum and nicotine patches, for example, might result in products better able to substitute for cigarettes. Such research might be conducted by the drug companies already manufacturing nicotine alternatives.

In determining research priorities, researchers should work together with policy-makers and policy advocates. A coordinated approach helps avoid a situation in which insufficient research is being conducted on the most important issues or the research conducted is redundant or of little value.

Program research

Research for designing effective programs should be carried out. What types of school-based educational messages work best for boys and for girls in various age groups? How can physicians achieve the best results when counseling patients about smoking? What types of antismoking advertisements have the greatest impact? How effective are various educational and smoking-cessation programs? What initiatives implemented elsewhere could be copied locally?

Tobacco-industry activity

It is essential that the activities of the tobacco industry and its allies be monitored. With-out knowledge of what the tobacco industry is up to, it is not possible to plan counterac-tions. When the industry releases studies of its own, a thorough analysis may expose faults in assumptions, methodology, conclusions, and so on. Publicly released industry research is frequently flawed. A good rebuttal can effectively undermine the advocacy outcome the industry intended. Some of the best information on industry activity has been found in corporate documents. Such documents, to the extent available, should be collected and made accessible for easy reference.

Paying for research

The least-expensive way to pursue research is to require tobacco manufacturers to publicly disclose internal industry research. Another inexpensive research initiative is to collect what has already been done. Existing studies may provide enough answers on a particular ques-tion to make further research unnecessary.

To pay for research, one option is to earmark revenue raised through taxes on tobacco products or industry profits. Much research in California and Massachusetts has been funded this way. Persuading NCIC and the Heart and Stroke Foundation, and to a lesser extent similar organizations, to allocate funds to tobacco policy research would be highly desirable. The major health charities already spend large sums on research, but virtually nothing is spent on studies relevant to tobacco control.

Disseminating research

Once research has been conducted, it is important to disseminate the findings and make them accessible to others working in the tobacco-control field. The Ontario Tobacco Research Unit, headed by Dr Roberta Ferrence of the Addiction Research Foundation, assists in this respect by linking a network of researchers, hosting an annual conference, publishing a series of working papers, and publishing a monthly report called *Current Abstracts on Tobacco*. A documentation centre, similar to Canada's National Clearinghouse on Tobacco and Health, could be set up to collect relevant literature in one place. Key documents, or at least their abstracts, should be translated into other languages to make them useful in other parts of the world. The availability of new studies could be posted on the Internet.

Finally, new research should be brought to the attention of the media. As previously noted, media publicity can in itself be an important educational tool.

PART VII

Final Thoughts

CHAPTER 22

Into the Lion's Den

In 1994, I attended the Tabexpo 94 exhibition in Vienna, Austria. This exhibition, Toward 2000 — Challenges of Changing Markets, was the tobacco industry's international equivalent of the World Conference on Tobacco and Health. Organizers promoted Tabexpo 94 as "by far the largest tobacco exhibition and congress ever held!" This was a chance to view the industry from the inside.

At least 6 000 people came to see what 366 companies from around the world had to offer. The whole exhibition, with 205 display booths, occupied more than 19 000 square metres.[390] Large indeed! I meandered about as unobtrusively as possible, feeling like a lamb in the lion's den. The exhibition hall was packed with booths set up by the tobacco manufacturers. Also well represented were the suppliers of related products: raw leaf tobacco, rolling papers, filters, glue, flavouring, packaging, cellophane tear tapes, testing equipment, tobacco publications, matches and lighters, reconstituted tobacco, and more. The whole tobacco "family" was there. In fact, there were so many exhibitors that conference organizers needed a second hall. Some equipment manufacturers had monstrous machines actually producing cigarettes on site.

The congress itself attracted 867 delegates. It began on Tuesday morning, 25 October, with a keynote address by James W. Johnston, the Chairman and CEO of R.J. Reynolds

Worldwide. When the tall American was being introduced, he was commended for his "outstanding" performance before a US Congressional subcommittee earlier in the year. At this hearing, Johnston and other CEOs had faced an onslaught of hostile questions from Congressmen.

It was soon clear from the attentiveness of the audience that Johnston was widely respected by these delegates. His basic message was a call to action. It was time for all sectors of the industry to fight the antitobacco movement, to "stand up and make our voices heard," he said, perhaps amazingly, given that the industry had been making itself heard for a long time now.

He described the "antis" as formidable adversaries who were smart, sophisticated, well organized, and well funded, and who learned from their counterparts in other countries. "All of us need to take their efforts very seriously." He also noted with concern that the attacks against the industry were spreading into new countries.

Johnston told the story of a US warship traveling to one of the world's hotspots. A blip appeared on the radar. The ship was heading straight for the blip, so the control room radioed ahead telling the other ship to change its course 15 degrees. The reply was immediate: "Change **your** course by fifteen degrees." The control room radioed back "This is a US aircraft carrier. Change your course 15 degrees." Again, the reply came "Change **your** course 15 degrees." The Admiral, hearing this exchange, grabbed the radio and barked "I am an Admiral in the United States Navy, and I order you to change your course immediately." There was a pause. And then came the reply. "I am a lighthouse. I suggest that you change your course."

The point of this story was that the industry was facing a lot of lighthouses these days, and it was the industry that would have to change its course. At one time, the industry could count on having a relatively easy time getting its own way, but no more.

Johnston lamented the industry's lack of commitment to addressing emerging issues. "If we do nothing, we can watch our revenues dwindle," he warned. "They will succeed unless we fight back, and fight back hard." He said that in the United States, the industry has begun to fight back and has become far more aggressive. He suggested that the tobacco industry "leverage" the tobacco-tax rollback in Canada to prevent tax increases worldwide. Canada's experience with contraband could be used to deter other countries from adopting a high-tax strategy. Johnson said that in the past couple of years, his company had spent "millions of dollars on programs designed to fight antismoking efforts. It's going to take a similar commitment from every company in this room for our industry to be effective on a worldwide basis."

On the evening of the first day, there was a glittering gala dinner at the opulent and historic Hofburg Palace for a cost of US $125 for those who chose to go. Dinner was preceded by a cocktail reception sponsored by R.J. Reynolds.

At Tabexpo, one point that continually came through was how much people in the industry had rationalized away any notion of the harm they were causing. There was no apparent comprehension of the impact on public health. Throughout the entire 3 days, I heard "cancer" only once, and that was when someone derided the claim that ETS caused lung cancer. One person who worked for a supplier to the industry said that the "industry is horrible, but the money is great and the people are nice."

Companies went to Tabexpo to do business and to make deals. At the back of each exhibitor's display booth, there was usually a separate, enclosed work area where a private meeting could be held. Many booths offered free alcoholic beverages as a way to entice attendees in for a chat to hear more about the host company. Some booths offered food. Cigarette companies routinely had free cigarettes available. Some firms, like Rothmans, had "cigarette girls" offering samples to passers-by.

The Ontario Flue-Cured Tobacco Growers' Marketing Board had a booth at the exhibition. An official from the Ontario Ministry of Agriculture and Food was one of the booth personnel promoting tobacco sales.

The Aluminum Company of Canada, better known as Alcan, had a booth at which its European subsidiaries promoted sales of foil inner wrap. A sign in the booth boasted that Alcan was a "Partner to the Tobacco Industry." Lawson Mardon Packaging, which started in London, Ontario, but is now based in England, gave out promotional souvenirs featuring a cute, fuzzy critter holding up a banner that proclaimed, "Supporting the tobacco industry worldwide."

At the R.J. Reynolds booth, several televisions repeatedly played commercials for cigarettes. Some featured the Camel man in daring jungle and adventure situations, relaxing afterward with a Camel cigarette. Others featured sponsorship of rock concerts or Salem vacations in Malaysia. Philip Morris sponsored the Central and Eastern European Lounge, where refreshments were served.

The various session topics covered China, Eastern Europe, technology, the emerging importance of flavourings, and voluntary advertising codes as an alternative to regulation. At a session on leaf tobacco, optimism was bubbling all around the room because of growing world demand and solid future prospects.

A session entitled "Cowboys and Camels: Cigarette Branding Today and Tomorrow" was led by Spencer Plavoukos, President of Lintas Worldwide, a major advertising agency that does work for R.J. Reynolds. Plavoukos gave an insightful presentation, noting that the tobacco industry had been responsible for most of the innovations in the field of marketing. He described a European campaign his firm was doing for Winston to attract smokers 18–24 years old. This "Myths and Symbols" campaign built on Winston's existing American image. The slogan "The Genuine Taste of America" was used with such recognizable American icons as the Lone Ranger, Fifth Avenue, and Alcatraz. The ads were said to position Winston "as a brand at ease with itself in today's world where values of freedom, confidence, informality, and fun are pre-eminent."

Another campaign, dubbed the "Success" campaign, was doing well in Poland, Russia, and the Middle East. It involved a series of TV commercials in soap-opera style: the man — the "Winston hero" — meets the woman and they fall in love. The commercials produced astonishing recall levels and were described as entertaining, convincing, and relevant to 18–35 year olds.

Plavoukos told how in various countries sales volume increased by 25% during a promotion offering a chance to win trips to the United States to see World Cup Soccer, Disney World, and car racing. In Lebanon alone, 400 000 entries were received. Plavoukos compared cigarette marketing with hockey star Wayne Gretzky. Gretzky knows that scoring a lot of goals means knowing not only where the puck **is**, but where the puck **will be**. Noting that increasing advertising restrictions were expected to come about, Plavoukos said that "it makes sense to maximize investment in brand building today, using all appropriate tools, while they are still available, while we develop new brand-building tools for tomorrow."

One of the most insightful sessions, held on the last day of the congress, was a panel discussion, "Tolerance and Common Sense — How to Tackle the Information Battle." The panel featured leading tobacco lobbyists from the United States, United Kingdom, Germany, Sweden, and Austria. The panel discussed how to counter the "antismoking industry." All agreed that tobacco manufacturers had never before been under so much pressure.

Bo Aulin, Vice-President Legal and Public Affairs of the Swedish Tobacco Company, said that

> the anti-tobacco forces are by now so well coordinated, trained and goal-oriented and in such a strong position that I don't think they can be stopped by merely political activities, PR-activities, and with facts and arguments regardless of the strength in them. ... This coordination, this global strategy, the international network, the professionalism and the fundings are factors that I think justify the term: the anti-tobacco industry. ... It is an industry that is effecting the biggest and most powerful lobbying campaigns that the world has ever seen.

Several speakers referred to the lack of credibility that tobacco manufacturers had because of their position denying the health consequences of smoking, a position taken to defend against product-liability lawsuits in the United States. Germany's Harald Konig, Secretary-General of Verband der Cigarettenindustrie, commented that it would not be much of a victory if "we win the last litigation case and the last smoker has just quit smoking."

Clive Turner, Executive Director of Industry Affairs for Britain's Tobacco Manufacturers Association, emphasized how important it was that companies get together and have a common position on each issue and to stand behind it. "It can take a lot of time and effort, but it is worth it." He said that in the United Kingdom, 31 such issues have been identified, the most important of which is ETS.

According to Turner, the industry should never run away from an issue, and spokespersons should "never, never, never get angry." He recounted how recently he had participated in a radio phone-in show. One caller said, "You are a slug. You should be stepped on. You are in a disgraceful business. You are a ... murderer, and you are a scumbag."

Turner's suggested response in such circumstances is to say "Just a minute. I hear what you say but that is an opinion. Now here are the facts 1, 2, 3." Turner noted how Britain's Tobacco Manufacturers Association had a policy of responding immediately to every adverse media story.

Turner derided antismoking lobbyists:

> I call them the shower adjusters. I think if they could get into your bathroom they would adjust the temperature of the water because they know what is good for you. The antis are quite extraordinary people. They have a sort of missionary glint in the eye. ... They think that they have a monopoly on wisdom. They are self-righteous. I think they are seized with a need to tell everybody else how to run their affairs and how to run their lives.

Turner added that "anytime the words 'passive smoking' are said, I think they have an orgasm. I really do. They get all hot and flush and quite excited by it all." He said the industry has to respond with facts to the misinformation presented by the other side. "Many people believe the doctors. Many people believe the antitobacco careerists."

Aulin had a more moderate view. "There are fanatics," he said, "but they are not all fanatics. There are a lot of credible, caring, good people. There is valid, solid support for action against tobacco — we must respect that."

Turner replied that "not everyone is a fanatic, but the problem is that the single-issue fanatics get more media attention."

Added Walker Merryman, Vice-President of the Tobacco Institute, "In the United States, if there are reasonable people, I have not met them. The leaders of the antis are fanatics."

Turner deplored the complacency in the industry and urged listeners to respond to Johnston's call to action:

> The antis in some places of the world that I have been to are just over the hill. They have assembled all their troops there, all their armament. Everything is ready. Some-times, in some parts of the world, at the bottom of the hill, there we are. We have no foot soldiers ready, no armament, no ammunition, and we are complacent.

To illustrate this, Turner mentioned talking with someone from a tobacco company in Indonesia who said that nothing would happen there for 25 years. But within a few months the issue of constituent labeling came up, and the Indonesian tobacco industry was screaming for help.

Konig said that "we must keep up smoking as socially acceptable" but that so far in Germany this was not as big an issue as in the United States. "We have to follow developments in the United States, Canada, Australia, New Zealand because we get spillover and it has an impact on us."

Merryman commented that the political will for a tax increase in the United States was not there,

> in large part because of activities undertaken by the tobacco industry. Other factors were involved, to be sure, but we put up an extraordinary, vigorous, cohesive campaign.

Without our opposition, there certainly would have been an extraordinary increase in the tax [in 1994].

In this session and others, the industry seemed most concerned about taxation, ETS, and advertising bans, a sure sign that health advocates working on these issues have been on the right track.

CHAPTER 23

Where the Future Lies

Tribune Media Services, by Mike Peters

The tobacco epidemic cannot be prevented. It is already here. All we can hope to do is slow it down. Canada has made tremendous progress in reducing smoking, but the high rates of disease and death caused by smoking will persist for years to come.

Smoking will be around for decades. The rate of smoking will decline in the future, but the speed of that decline will directly depend on how soon and how effectively governments implement tobacco-control measures. Even with a very successful tobacco-control strategy, though, the smoking rate will decline slowly. A tremendous but unlikely accomplishment would see Canada's smoking rate fall from 31% to 20% by the year 2005, a decline of about 1% per year. If smoking drops to 10% of the Canadian population by the year 2015, that will be an incredible and even more unlikely victory for public health.

Over the past 45 years, Canada's tobacco war has increased in intensity. In the 1950s there were just skirmishes, but by the late 1980s and 1990s confrontations had escalated to full-scale battles. Now the industry is under attack on many fronts.

The war will continue. Forthcoming battles include the fight to again ban tobacco advertising and to defend the ban in court, to implement plain packaging, to eliminate sponsorship promotions, and to ensure that tobacco taxes are as high as they can reasonably go.

By 2005, if not earlier, it is probable that smoking will be prohibited in almost all workplaces and public places in Canada, including bars and restaurants. This will be brought about by a combination of voluntary action, legislation, and legal proceedings.

Over time, many of the measures recommended in this book will be implemented. Governments in Canada will begin to start controlling design of the cigarette itself. If the industry continues to earn wildly exorbitant profits — and without intervention, it will — governments will have no choice but to regulate profits by controlling manufacturer prices.

By 2025, comprehensive tobacco-control legislation not only will be in place in Canada but also will enjoy tremendous public approval. Measures that today are so widely contested by the industry will have such widespread acceptance in Canada that people will wonder what took previous generations so long to get the measures adopted.

Worldwide, the factors that have already led to higher global smoking rates will push rates up further. Tragically, predictions of a dramatically increased death toll from smoking will be realized. On the bright side, the current trend of increasing regulation around the world will also continue. As more countries ban advertising, restrict smoking, and legislate other measures, other countries will be motivated to do likewise. The pace at which governments take action will directly affect global smoking rates. In time, there will be an international treaty on the control of tobacco.

In Canada and other DCs, the tobacco industry will continue to do whatever it can to maintain sales. Sales mean profits, and the industry has no desire to give up its profits. The tobacco industry has repeatedly shown that it has the ability to overcome obstacles, and it will continue to use its traditional tactics to delay, weaken, defeat, or overturn legislation. Without a doubt, the industry has the resources necessary to fight in the tobacco war.

The best thing the industry has going for it is the addictiveness of tobacco. Nicotine is the single biggest factor preventing a rapid demise of the tobacco industry. The development of a highly effective, nontobacco nicotine-delivery device or a satisfactory nonaddictive substitute for nicotine would speed the downfall of the tobacco industry.

If manufacturers start losing product-liability lawsuits, this would speed up the downfall even more. Although the companies have successfully defended all cases to date (except for one out-of-court settlement in 1996), the winning streak will not last forever. The breakthrough will probably come in the United States because of the number of cases already before the courts there. A flood of successful cases, or even one or two major class-action successes, would financially cripple or even bankrupt the companies. From such a weakened position, the industry would not be able to oppose the unprecedented level of regulatory control that would be sure to follow.

Act now

Millions have suffered needlessly or died prematurely because of the actions of tobacco companies. The tragedy has been monumental. As a society we have been lamentably slow to respond, surely a sign of the industry's power. What else would explain the credence given to the cigarette, a toxic, carcinogenic product that can be lethal when used exactly as intended but that has little or no socially redeeming value?

The tobacco industry has perpetrated the largest consumer deception the world has ever seen. Death upon death has been the result, but the industry has never apologized to or compensated the family of any victim. Instead, the industry has denied responsibility and advertised its products in a way that attracts teenage recruits to replace dead customers.

Enough is enough. The global harm caused by tobacco use is the leading health issue of our day. The case for tobacco control is overwhelming. The excuses used to justify inaction or delay are simply unacceptable. Decisive and comprehensive measures are needed now. The future health of a generation of youngsters hangs in the balance.

Postscript

Brian Gable, [Regina] Leader Post

The campaign for new federal legislation

By the end of August 1996, the federal government had still not announced the content of new tobacco legislation. The long delay was causing much anxiety among health groups. Nevertheless, the government was getting closer to completing its legislation, with a bill expected to be introduced in the fall parliamentary sitting.

The most contentious issue will be that of sponsorships, as was the case in 1987–88 during the Bill C-51 campaign. "There must be a total ban on sponsorship advertising," says Nancy Roberts of the Lung Association. Adds NSRA lawyer Eric LeGresley "the Supreme Court endorsed a ban on lifestyle advertising, and sponsorship promotions are lifestyle advertising: 100% imagery." Recipients of arts and sports sponsorship money, however, will be vocal in resisting any sponsorship restrictions.

The battle over new tobacco legislation will be a vigorous dogfight, with the tobacco industry in a position to spearhead opposition. On the health side, it may be that the three key success factors leading to effective tobacco control measures are present: Minister Dingwall is personally very committed to strong antitobacco legislation; there is tobacco control expertise and support at the bureaucratic level inside Health Canada; and the health lobby is larger and far better organized than in 1987–88 during the Bill C-51 campaign.

Tobacco advertising resumed in February, 1996 with RBH advertising its Canadian Classics brand using the slogan "Pure Canadian Classics" and depicting such scenes as hockey gloves on the ice, the shadow of a moose, and a toque on snow. Almost immediately afterwards, RJR-Macdonald advertised Export "A" Smooth cigarettes in an ad depicting an electric guitar and an acoustic guitar, together with the slogan "Either you like it or you don't." This prompted criticism that the ad was attractive to young people. "Electric guitars are not exactly targeted at senior citizens," said NSRA's Heather Selin. Health Minister David Dingwall rebuked the industry. "I'm pissed off at the manufacturers in terms of what they've done," he said. "It seems to me they're focusing on young people when they've indicated previously they weren't going to do that." One ad was located directly across the street from a high school in Hull, Quebec, in violation of the voluntary code. This received media attention and was quickly taken down.

On 25 April, the Canadian Cancer Society filed a lengthy list of complaints with the Tobacco Advertising Supervisory Committee, set up by the industry to enforce the voluntary code. On 4 June, the Committee confirmed that most of the complaints were indeed violations, including 31 examples of placing ads inside stores located within 200 metres of schools. The tobacco industry responded to this by promptly weakening its code to allow such ads to continue. This industry move was comparable to an environmental polluter being convicted, having no fine to pay, and then being allowed to rewrite the law to continue polluting all it wants. The Committee also ruled that point of sale ads had been erected without the required health warnings.

On 9 July, the Heart and Stroke Foundation of Canada, the Canadian Cancer Society, and the Lung Association released an Environics poll showing strong public support for tobacco control measures. Fully 71% supported a ban on advertising, 68% supported plain packaging, 61% agreed that tobacco products should not be visible until a purchase is made, and 93% supported mandatory listing on the package of all product ingredients. But only 44% supported a ban on tobacco sponsorships.

The federal government received a major boost on 23 August when US President Bill Clinton announced new regulations adopted by the Food and Drug Administration. Nicotine is now regulated in the United States as an addictive drug, and cigarettes and smokeless tobacco are now treated as drug-delivery devices. The regulations ban all forms of sponsorship promotions, impose significant restrictions on advertising, prohibit the use of tobacco trademarks on nontobacco goods, and create national measures to curb youth access, such as a minimum age of 18 and banning vending machines except in locations where teenagers are denied entry.

Dr Michael Goodyear of the Hamilton Regional Cancer Centre said that seeing what the United States has done gives momentum to the Canadian campaign. Adds Melodie Tilson of the Heart and Stroke Foundation, "If the Americans can ban sponsorship promotions, a bold step, so can we."

Clinton emphasized that his objective was to prevent smoking among young people. Health Minister David Dingwall can be expected to convey a similar message when trying to garner support for Canadian legislation.

Optimism in Quebec

Persistently high smoking rates in Quebec have long frustrated members of the health community. Not only are smoking rates higher than anywhere else in Canada but also, according to at least one survey, the prevalence of smoking among adult women (38%) is higher than any country in the world. Smoking retains substantial cultural acceptance in Quebec. And the province is home to three of four of the country's main cigarette factories. But now there are some encouraging signs.

The province's Health Minister, Dr Jean Rochon, who previously worked for the World Health Organization, has spoken out strongly against tobacco. He said that he intends to introduce strong provincial antitobacco legislation in the fall of 1996. Support for a tough antitobacco effort is also growing within the public service and within regional health units. "The opportunity for progress in Quebec has never been so good," says Maurice Gingues of the Canadian Cancer Society.

On the ground, the antismoking forces have been bolstered by a new coalition and by the addition of full-time staff. Louis Gauvin (previously with the public health system) and Heidi Rathjen (formerly of the Coalition for Gun Control) head the Quebec Coalition for Tobacco Control. Launched on 6 June 1996, the coalition is made up of 40 member organizations. François Damphousse now heads the Quebec Office of the Non-Smokers' Rights Association, which opened in 1995.

Local Bylaw Campaigns Heat Up

In 1995, Guelph, Ontario became the first municipality in Canada to ban smoking in restaurants, but the ban was being phased in and would not be fully in place until the year 2000. Still, the development was significant in that Guelph is home to an Imperial Tobacco cigarette factory.

1996 has seen vigorous local campaigns seeking to ban smoking in restaurants and bars. Campaigns are particularly visible in British Columbia and Ontario. The city of Vaughan, Ontario, located just north of Metropolitan Toronto, became the first municipality with a bylaw in force banning smoking in all restaurants. In Vancouver, City Council banned smoking in all restaurants. Several other municipalities in the Greater Vancouver Regional District have followed, or are planning to follow, with their own bylaws banning smoking in all restaurants. In BC's Capital Regional District, which includes Victoria, a new bylaw banned smoking in all restaurants and bars effective in 1998. Toronto adopted a widely publicized bylaw banning smoking in all restaurants and bars. The Toronto bylaw has been the subject of so much controversy that it might be reconsidered before the scheduled implementation date of 1 January 1997.

Litigation activity increases

In the United States, the tobacco industry suffered a significant lawsuit defeat on 9 August 1996 when a jury in Jacksonville, Florida, ordered Brown and Williamson to pay US $750 000 to Grady Carter and his wife Millie Carter. Mr Carter had smoked for 44 years before contracting lung cancer. Some jury members explained that a key factor in their decision was the fact that the company publicly denied that cigarettes were addictive while internal company documents explicitly said the opposite. The verdict, which the industry is appealing, sent US tobacco industry shares sharply downward.

Andreas Seibert of Sommers and Roth, the law firm that filed the proposed class action in Ontario, commented that "We have always known that the industry can be beaten. The *Carter* verdict just spreads that message a little wider."

A more significant US development is the growing number of state governments filing lawsuits against the industry to recover health-care expenditures attributable to smoking. By the end of August, the total had risen to 14: Arizona, Connecticut, Florida, Kansas, Louisiana, Maryland, Massachusetts, Michigan, Minnesota, Mississippi, Oklahoma, Texas, West Virginia, and Washington. Los Angeles County and San Francisco have also filed suit, and more states and municipalities are expected to do likewise. The total amount of money being sought is in the tens of billions of dollars. While tobacco companies are fully capable of putting up a vigorous defence, the industry has never before faced such a large legal assault. More lawsuits from individual plaintiffs are scheduled to go to trial in the fall of 1996, with the first trial in a state lawsuit slated for 1997.

Canadian Cigarette Brand Family Ownership by Company

Imperial Tobacco	Rothmans, Benson & Hedges	RJR–Macdonald
Avanti	Accord	Camel*
Buckingham	Belmont	Contessa
Cameo	Belvedere	Export
du Maurier	Benson & Hedges	Export "A"
John Player	Black Cat	Macdonald
Kool	Canadian Classics	More*
Matinée	Craven	Salem*
Medallion	Craven "A"	Smooth
Pall Mall	Dunhill	Vantage
Peter Jackson	Holiday	Winston*
Player's	Mark Ten	
Sweet Caporal	Number 7	
	Oxford	
	Peter Stuyvesant	
	Rothmans	
	Sportsman	
	Viscount	

* Imported from the United States from parent company, R.J. Reynolds.

APPENDIX 2

Chronology

1st century BC .. The Mayas of Central America smoke tobacco in religious ceremonies.

1492 . . . . Columbus "discovers" tobacco upon arrival in America.

1535 . . . . Jacques Cartier encounters tobacco on his second voyage to Canada.

1560 . . . . France's ambassador to Portugal, Jean Nicot, ships tobacco seeds to the Queen Mother of France, believing that tobacco would cure many diseases.

1604 . . . . King James I writes *A Counterblaste to Tobacco*, condemning smoking.

1670 . . . . New France's Sovereign Council imposes duties on tobacco.

1676 . . . . Residents of New France are prohibited from smoking or carrying tobacco on the streets.

1739 . . . . Canada exports tobacco to France for first time.

1761 . . . . In England, first known clinical report links tobacco with cancer.

1854–56 . . . . . Soldiers return home to England and France from Crimean War with hand-rolled cigarettes obtained from the Turks, increasing the popularity of cigarettes.

1858 . . . . Macdonald Tobacco is established in Montreal.

1878 . . . . House of Commons defeats resolution to abolish tobacco taxes.

1881 . . . . Cigarette-making machine is patented. (Machine becomes operational in 1884.)

1890s . . . . Safe, portable match is developed.

1891 . . . . British Columbia prohibits the sale of tobacco to minors. (Other jurisdictions soon follow: Ontario and Nova Scotia in 1892; New Brunswick in 1893; and Northwest Territories in 1896.)

1895 . . . . American Tobacco Company moves into Canada.

Canadian Cigar and Tobacco Journal is established and would continue to be published until the late 1950s.

1903 . . . . House of Commons passes resolution supporting a ban on cigarettes, but no law is passed.

Minister of Justice Charles Fitzpatrick introduces *Criminal Code* amendment bill that includes a provision banning the sale of tobacco to persons under 18. The tobacco provision is dropped from the bill at the committee stage.

Royal Commission reports on the American Tobacco Company's anti-competitive practices in Canada.

1904 . . . . House of Commons again approves resolution to ban cigarettes.

Bill to ban cigarettes receives second reading and committee approval in House of Commons, but does not receive final passage.

1906 . . . . Benson & Hedges moves into Canada.

Federal Department of Agriculture establishes the Tobacco Branch.

1908 . . . . Parliament passes the *Tobacco Restraint Act* prohibiting the sale of tobacco to persons under 16, and prohibiting such persons from purchasing or possessing tobacco.

Imperial Tobacco is established through a formal merger of the American Tobacco Company and the Empire Tobacco Company.

1911 . . . . US Supreme Court, in an antitrust case, orders the breakup of the American Tobacco Company's controlling position of the US tobacco industry.

1912 . . . . The present Imperial Tobacco is incorporated as a successor to the Imperial Tobacco formed in 1908.

1914 . . . . House of Commons Select Committee on Cigarette Evils conducts public hearings but makes no policy recommendations.

1914–18 . . . . . . Cigarettes are sent over to soldiers during World War I, thus providing a tremendous endorsement for cigarettes when soldiers returned home.

1921 . . . . Canadian Pacific Railway announces that it will add railway sleepers with smoking rooms for female passengers.

Imperial Tobacco acquires the General Cigar Company.

1927 . . . . *Montreal Gazette* publishes the first Canadian advertisement with a woman smoking.

1930s . . . . Ontario tobacco belt begins to develop.

1930 . . . . Imperial Tobacco acquires the Tuckett Tobacco Company.

1931 . . . . Agriculture Department first publishes *The Lighter*, a publication specializing in tobacco research. The publication would continue until 1990.

1938 . . . . A Commission concludes that tobacco companies are price fixing. Charges are laid, resulting in convictions; on appeal, all convictions but one are overturned on a technicality.

Raymond Pearl finds that smokers have a lower life expectancy than nonsmokers.

1939 . . . . F.H. Müller finds a statistical link between lung cancer and smoking in a small-scale but seminal study.

1943 . . . . Judicial Committee of the Privy Council (then Canada's highest court) rejects challenge to provincial ability to impose tobacco taxes.

1947 . . . . Canadian Dr Norman Delarue finds a statistical association between lung cancer and smoking, but the study has a small sample size and is not published.

1949 . . . . Imperial Tobacco acquires Imperial Tobacco (Newfoundland) Ltd, just as Newfoundland was entering Confederation.

1950 . . . . First large-scale epidemiological studies showing a statistical association between lung cancer and smoking are published.

1950s . . . . Big shift towards filter cigarettes occurs.

Tobacco advertising and media reports contribute to increased sales for brands with lower tar yields.

1951 . . . . National Cancer Institute of Canada draws attention in newsletter to possible link between lung cancer and smoking.

House of Commons, with the support of Health Minister Paul Martin, Sr, votes down proposal to establish a special committee to examine the "entire cigarette problem."

A vote in Ontario for an all-grower marketing board is defeated.

1952 . . . . Federal government reduces tobacco taxes after a rise in smuggling.

1953 . . . . Federal government further reduces tobacco taxes.

Ernest Wynder and Evarts Graham find that the painting of cigarette smoke condensate ("tar") on the backs of mice produces cancer.

1954 . . . . Preliminary results from an American prospective study led by Cuyler Hammond and Daniel Horn, and from a British prospective study led by Richard Doll and Bradford Hill, find that smoking is associated with increased lung cancer.

In Canada, the tobacco industry gives its first grant to the National Cancer Institute of Canada to study lung cancer.

Canadian Medical Association issues first public warning on the hazards of smoking.

Federal Department of Health and Welfare initiates major study of the health effects of smoking, with Canadian war veterans as the participants.

US-based Tobacco Industry Research Committee is established (later renamed Council for Tobacco Research).

In the United States, the industry faces its first product liability lawsuit in *Pritchard* v. *Liggett & Myers* (dropped by plaintiff 12 years later).

Benson & Hedges (Canada) becomes a Philip Morris subsidiary.

1957 . . . . Rothmans of Pall Mall enters the Canadian market.

Ontario Flue-Cured Tobacco Growers' Marketing Board is established.

1958 . . . . National Cancer Institute of Canada concludes that cigarette smokers have a greater risk of dying of lung cancer than nonsmokers and that risk increases with amount smoked.

1960s . . . . Transnational tobacco industry actively enters markets in Latin America.

1960 . . . . First results of veterans study show that the group of cigarette smokers had 60% more deaths than the group of nonsmokers and that cigarette smoking was associated with an increase in lung cancer and heart disease.

1961 . . . . Canadian Medical Association concludes that cigarette smoking causes lung cancer.

1962 . . . . Royal College of Physicians of London in the United Kingdom issues historic report on the health consequences of smoking and recommending remedial action.

National Cancer Institute of Canada declares that smoking is a cause of lung cancer.

Benson & Hedges (Canada) acquires Tabacofina of Canada.

1963 . . . . Federal Health Minister Judy LaMarsh declares that smoking is a contributory cause of lung cancer and may also be associated with chronic bronchitis and coronary heart disease.

MP Barry Mather introduces Bill C-75, a private member's bill that would regulate tobacco. The bill is not passed. Several dozen private member's bills would be introduced over the next 10 years.

Canadian Medical Association President urges doctors to stop cigarette smoking, at least during professional duties.

National Conference on Smoking and Health is held.

Canadian Tobacco Manufacturers' Council is established.

1964 . . . . Advisory Committee to US Surgeon General concludes that cigarette smoking is a cause of lung and laryngeal cancer in men, a probable cause of lung cancer in women, and the most important cause of chronic bronchitis.

Canadian smoking and health program starts.

Canadian tobacco industry adopts its first voluntary code on marketing practices.

Imperial Tobacco begins to diversify.

House of Commons Agriculture and Colonization Committee holds hearings on tobacco.

1965 . . . . The Department of National Health and Welfare commissions a national survey on smoking and, to the surprise of many, a bare majority of adults are nonsmokers.

US Congress requires a warning on cigarette packages (warning first appears in 1966).

United Kingdom bans broadcast advertising of cigarettes.

1966 . . . . Canadian per capita consumption peaks. (It begins to fall slowly in subsequent years.)

1967 . . . . Federal Cabinet approves a recommendation of Health Minister Allan MacEachen to prepare legislation to require tar and nicotine levels on packages and in advertising and to prohibit misleading cigarette advertisements, but legislation is not introduced.

First World Conference on Smoking and Health is held in New York.

An antismoking film, *The Drag*, is produced by the National Film Board. The film goes on to be nominated for an Academy Award in the animated cartoon category.

In the United States, starting 1 July, the "Fairness Doctrine" results in widespread antismoking commercials in the broadcast media, some of which spill over into Canadian homes.

US Surgeon General concludes that smoking is the principal cause of lung cancer.

1968 . . . . House of Commons Standing Committee on Health, Welfare and Social Affairs begins extensive investigation into tobacco issues. In testimony before Committee, Health Minister John Munro condemns tobacco advertising.

Health and Welfare Canada releases results of its testing of tar and nicotine yields for major cigarette brands, a practice that would be repeated yearly for some time.

1969 . . . . CBC voluntarily stops accepting tobacco advertising.

House of Commons Committee on Health, Welfare and Social Affairs recommends that tobacco advertising be banned and that many other tobacco-control measures be adopted.

1970 . . . . Incentive promotions peak at 63% of the Canadian cigarette market. Tobacco companies announce voluntary end to such promotions.

First World Health Assembly resolution to prevent the harms caused by tobacco is passed.

Imasco Ltd is created as a holding company for Imperial Tobacco and other subsidiaries.

1971 . . . . US ban on cigarette advertising and radio comes into effect on 2 January.

Health Minister John Munro introduces Bill C-248 to ban cigarette advertising and require a warning on packages, but the bill is neither debated nor passed.

Tobacco companies announce that effective 1972 they will voluntarily place a warning on cigarette packages and will not advertise cigarettes on radio or television.

British Columbia bans tobacco advertising.

Air Canada introduces no-smoking sections on planes.

US Surgeon General finds that maternal smoking during pregnancy exerts a retarding influence on fetal growth.

1972 . . . . US Surgeon General concludes that smoke-filled rooms have carbon monoxide levels equal to or exceeding the legal limits for ambient air quality.

BC Supreme Court rejects tobacco industry constitutional challenge to provincial advertising ban, ruling that the ban is within provincial jurisdiction. Nevertheless, BC government replaces total advertising ban with partial restrictions.

1973 . . . . Canadian National Railway sets aside nonsmoking sections on some trains between Montreal and Toronto.

1974 . . . . Canadian Council on Smoking and Health is founded.

Non-Smokers' Rights Association is founded.

R.J. Reynolds buys Macdonald Tobacco, renaming the new subsidiary RJR–Macdonald Inc.

Canadian Motor Coach Association makes voluntary recommendation that the first five rows of buses be non-smoking.

MP Ken Robinson introduces Bill C-242, a private member's bill requiring nonsmoking sections in planes, trains, and intercity buses. Although the bill received second reading in 1975 and was the subject of committee hearings, the bill did not receive final approval.

Minnesota adopts landmark comprehensive state law restricting smoking in public places.

Mid-1970s . . . . . Trend to ultra light cigarettes of 5 mg of tar or less begins.

1975 . . . . Tobacco industry's voluntary code is amended so that sponsorship promotions will not appear on television; the health warning will be included in print, transit, and some point-of-sale advertising; tar and nicotine yields will appear on packages and print advertisements; and the total industry spending limit on advertising can be increased with inflation.

1976 . . . . City of Ottawa passes first municipal bylaw in Canada restricting smoking in public places. (Bylaw comes into effect in 1977.)

1977 . . . . National Non-Smoking Week begins as an annual event in Canada.

Swedish law comes into force requiring a series of rotated warnings on cigarette packages.

1978 . . . . Imasco acquires Shoppers Drug Mart.

1979 . . . . Toronto Transit Commission votes to stop accepting tobacco advertising effective in 1980.

Nicotine gum appears in Canadian market on a prescription basis.

Early 1980s . . . . Much stronger evidence accumulates that ETS harms nonsmokers.

1981 . . . . US Surgeon General concludes that there is no safe cigarette and that any risk reduction associated with lower yield cigarettes would be small compared with quitting smoking.

1982 . . . . Total annual market size in Canada peaks at about 73 billion cigarettes, including fine-cut equivalents.

Tobacco taxes start to increase at a rate faster than inflation.

1983 . . . . Dramatic decline in per capita consumption begins, although there had been a small decline in 1982.

Fifth World Conference on Smoking and Health is held in Winnipeg, Manitoba.

1984 . . . . *Kingston Whig-Standard* stops accepting tobacco advertising.

Top skiers Steve Podborski and Ken Read refuse to accept trophies they had earned in the Export "A" Cup, the national ski championships.

US Congress adopts law requiring four rotational health warnings on cigarette packages and advertisements.

1985 . . . . Federal tobacco taxes are increased by $2.00 a carton.

National Strategy to Reduce Tobacco Use is established.

Federal government announces it will stop funding any amateur sport organization that accepts a new tobacco sponsorship.

Federal Agriculture Minister John Wise proposes to create a Canadian Flue-Cured Tobacco Marketing Agency; hearings are eventually held, but the agency is never established.

Treasury Board announces voluntary guidelines on workplace smoking for federal public servants.

Physicians for a Smoke-Free Canada is established.

Federal public servant Peter Wilson wins right to a smoke-free workplace in an adjudication before the Public Service Staff Relations Board. The ruling is appealed and later overturned on technical grounds.

Aspen, Colorado becomes the first municipality in North America to ban smoking in all restaurants.

1986 . . . . *Globe and Mail* [Toronto] stops accepting tobacco advertising.

Vancouver passes bylaw restricting smoking in the workplace.

Quebec adopts law restricting smoking in some workplaces and public places. (Law comes into effect in 1987.)

Rothmans of Pall Mall Canada and Benson & Hedges (Canada) merge to form Rothmans, Benson & Hedges Inc.

Air Canada becomes first North American carrier to introduce flights that are entirely smoke free.

US Surgeon General concludes that involuntary smoking is a cause of disease, including lung cancer, in otherwise healthy nonsmokers.

Advisory Committee to the Surgeon General concludes that smokeless tobacco can cause cancer and can lead to nicotine addiction.

MP Lynn McDonald introduces Bill C-204, the *Non-smokers' Health Act*, in Parliament.

Taiwan and Japan yield to US pressure and open their markets to American cigarettes.

1987 . . . . Smoking is banned on domestic flights of 2 hours or less.

Northwest Territories bans smoking in all government workplaces. In subsequent years, many provincial governments would do likewise.

Federal and provincial governments announce Tobacco Diversification Plan to help farmers exit from tobacco growing.

House of Commons Agriculture Committee releases report recommending measures to assist tobacco growers.

Health Minister Jake Epp introduces Bill C-51, the *Tobacco Products Control Act*, in Parliament.

1988 . . . . Parliament passes *Tobacco Products Control Act* banning tobacco advertising and *Non-smokers' Health Act* restricting smoking in federally regulated workplaces and public places. (Both come into force in 1989.)

Three major tobacco companies each file a constitutional challenge to the *Tobacco Products Control Act*. The trial would begin in 1989.

Calgary Winter Olympics become first smoke-free Olympics.

In New Jersey, a jury awards US $400 000 to Rose Cipollone, the first time a tobacco company loses a verdict in court. The award would be overturned on appeal.

First Canadian lawsuit by a smoker against a manufacturer is filed against RJR–Macdonald.

US Surgeon General concludes that the pharmacologic and behavioural processes that determine tobacco addiction are similar to those that determine heroin and cocaine addiction.

World Health Organization initiates World No-Tobacco Day, held annually on May 31.

South Korea yields to US pressure and opens its market to American cigarettes.

National Clearinghouse on Tobacco and Health is established.

1989 . . . . Four legislated health warnings appear in rotation on front and back of cigarette packages.

Smoking ban in federal public service comes into effect.

Smoking is banned on all domestic air flights.

Smoking is prohibited on interprovincial bus travel.

Ontario law restricts smoking in workplaces.

Federal tobacco taxes are increased by $4.00 a carton.

1990s . . . . Transnational tobacco companies begin to penetrate markets of Central and Eastern Europe.

1990 . . . . Manitoba law sets 18 as the minimum age and restricts smoking in public places.

GATT decision dismisses American argument that Thailand's ban on tobacco advertising violates GATT provisions.

Seventh World Conference on Tobacco and Health endorses resolution commending Canadian government for "its leadership in improving the health of Canadians and for setting an outstanding example in comprehensive tobacco control policy."

A further resolution "recognises and congratulates the Cancer Societies in Canada, New Zealand and Australia for their leadership in stimulating and sustaining tobacco control initiatives in their respective countries and encourages all other non-government health organisations to learn from, and be encouraged to follow these examples."

1991 . . . . Quebec Superior Court declares federal ban on tobacco advertising unconstitutional.

Federal tobacco taxes are increased by $6.00 a carton.

1992. . . . . Federal government imposes export tax to curb cigarette smuggling, but this is repealed within 2 months.

US Environmental Protection Agency classifies environmental tobacco smoke as a group A (known human) carcinogen and completes major report on the health effects of ETS.

International Civil Aviation Organization adopts resolution urging nations "to take necessary measures as soon as possible to restrict smoking progressively on all international flights with the objective of implementing complete bans by 1 July 1996."

Nicotine patch appears in the Canadian market on a prescription basis.

Nicotine gum of a dosage of 2 mg or less is allowed to be sold over the counter without a prescription.

1993 . . . . Lung cancer surpasses breast cancer as the leading cause of cancer deaths among Canadian women.

Parliament passes *Tobacco Sales to Young Persons Act* setting 18 as the minimum age and prohibiting cigarette-vending machines except in bars. (Act comes into force in 1994, at which point the repeal of the *Tobacco Restraint Act* comes into effect.)

Quebec Court of Appeal reverses lower court and upholds constitutionality of tobacco-advertising ban.

National Conference on Tobacco or Health takes place in Ottawa, with more than 400 in attendance.

Smuggling into Canada, which had been rising for several years, reaches its peak year at about 25–31% of the market. Exports to United States also peak in this year.

Navy introduces comprehensive antismoking initiative.

Ontario Tobacco Research Unit is established.

1994 . . . . Federal government and five provincial governments set major reductions in tobacco taxes to curb smuggling.

Federal Government announces it will spend $185 million over 3 years in an antismoking program funded by increased corporate taxes on tobacco companies.

House of Commons Health Committee recommends adoption of plain packaging provided that results of a Health Canada study provide further evidence that plain packaging will be effective at reducing smoking.

Parliament bans kiddie packs, which contain fewer than 20 cigarettes.

Eight revised health warnings appear in rotation in black and white at the top of the front and back of the packages.

New Brunswick requires retailers to post detailed health warnings at point of sale.

British Columbia, Ontario, New Brunswick, Nova Scotia, and Newfoundland laws prohibiting the sale of tobacco to persons under 19 come into force. Ontario and Nova Scotia ban cigarette-vending machines outright.

Ontario bans sale of tobacco in pharmacies and restricts smoking in certain public places.

Newfoundland law restricts smoking in workplaces and public places.

British Columbia repeals provincial advertising restrictions.

Smoking is banned on all international flights of Canadian air carriers.

McDonald's announces that all of its company-owned restaurants in North America will be smoke free.

Imperial Tobacco announces that it is exploring entry into Asia, especially China.

Several US states file lawsuits against tobacco manufacturers to recover Medicare costs attributable to smoking. (Other states filed their own lawsuits in subsequent years.)

Large set of internal documents from US tobacco company Brown and Williamson become public.

1995 . . . . Supreme Court of Canada, in a 5 to 4 decision, declares advertising restrictions and unattributed health warnings under the *Tobacco Products Control Act* unconstitutional infringements of freedom of expression.

Health Minister Diane Marleau releases a blueprint recommending a comprehensive tobacco-control policy, including a new legislative framework and a renewed complete ban on tobacco advertising. A week later, the tobacco industry adopts a new voluntary advertising code.

Four Ontario smokers file a proposed class-action lawsuit against the three large Canadian manufacturers.

Federal and Quebec governments impose small increases in tobacco taxes.

Federal government cuts funding for 3-year $185 million antitobacco program by more than 40%.

US Food and Drug Administration proposes to regulate cigarettes and smokeless tobacco as drug-delivery devices. Strong restrictions on advertising are proposed.

Imasco sells United Cigar Stores to Hachette Distribution Services of France.

1996. . . . . Tobacco companies resume advertising.

Tobacco industry weakens voluntary code to permit advertising inside stores near schools after a ruling finds that such advertising is a violation of the code.

City of Vaughan, Ontario, becomes first municipality with a bylaw banning smoking in restaurants. Vancouver bans smoking in restaurants. Toronto bans smoking in restaurants and bars (effective 1 January 1997), although the bylaw was being reconsidered. Other municipalities adopt bylaws restricting smoking in restaurants and/or bars.

Liggett Group Inc., the smallest of the five major American tobacco companies, agrees to settle *Castano* class-action lawsuit and some lawsuits filed by state governments.

A Florida jury awards US $750 000 to Grady Carter and his wife Millie Carter in a product liability case against Brown and Williamson. The industry appeals.

US President Bill Clinton announces final regulations of the Food and Drug Administration. The regulations require a minimum national age of 18, restrict vending machines to adult only premises, prohibit sponsorship promotions, prohibit the use of trademarks on nontobacco goods, and restrict advertising.

By late August, 14 US states had filed lawsuits against tobacco companies to recover health costs attributable to smoking. More states were expected to file suit.

Federal Health Ministers Since 1944

Minister	Period	Party
Brooke Claxton	1944–46	Liberal
Paul Martin, Sr	1946–57	Liberal
Waldo Monteith	1957–63	Progressive Conservative
Judy LaMarsh	1963–65	Liberal
Allan MacEachen	1965–68	Liberal
John Munro	1968–72	Liberal
Marc Lalonde	1972–77	Liberal
Monique Bégin	1977–79	Liberal
David Crombie	1979–80	Progressive Conservative
Monique Bégin	1980–84	Liberal
Jake Epp	1984–89	Progressive Conservative
Perrin Beatty	1989–91	Progressive Conservative
Benoît Bouchard	1991–93	Progressive Conservative
Mary Collins	1993	Progressive Conservative
Diane Marleau	1993–96	Liberal
David Dingwall	1996–	Liberal

World Conferences on Tobacco and Health

1967	World Conference on Smoking and Health, New York, NY, USA
1971	2nd World Conference on Smoking and Health, London, UK
1975	3rd World Conference on Smoking and Health, New York, NY, USA
1979	4th World Conference on Smoking and Health, Stockholm, Sweden
1983	5th World Conference on Smoking and Health, Winnipeg, MB, Canada
1987	6th World Conference on Smoking and Health, Tokyo, Japan
1990	7th World Conference on Tobacco and Health, Perth, WA, Australia
1992	,8th World Conference on Tobacco or Health, Buenos Aires, Argentina
1994	9th World Conference on Tobacco and Health, Paris, France
1997	10th World Conference on Tobacco or Health, Beijing, China

Resolutions from the Ninth World Conference on Tobacco and Health

This appendix reprints resolutions adopted at the Ninth World Conference on Tobacco and Health, held on 10–14 October 1994 in Paris, France.

This conference resolves that

1. All nations implement the International Strategy for Tobacco Control. [outlined below]

2. The Prime Ministers of Germany, the United Kingdom and the Netherlands be informed by formal letter from the President of this conference and individual letters from conference participants that their governments' action in blocking the implementation of the Directive on Tobacco Advertising in the European Union is an international scandal and is detrimental to the health of all citizens of the European Union, and by example of the citizens in all developing regions of the world who look to the European Union for leadership in Public Health Policy.

3. The International Strategy for Tobacco Control (resolution 1) should be implemented by all the governments of Central and Eastern Europe. Moreover, the Western governments which have the headquarters of the transnational tobacco companies (which now control a majority of the tobacco production capacity in the Central and Eastern European region) should share the responsibility for ending the tobacco epidemic and assist governments in the region to implement the strategy.

4. This conference further resolves that:

   a) Duty free sales of tobacco products be prohibited.

   b) National Governments, Ministers of Health, and the World Health Organisation should immediately initiate action to prepare and achieve an International Convention on Tobacco Control to be adopted by the United Nations as an aid to enforcement of the International Strategy for Tobacco Control (resolution 1) adopted by the Ninth World Conference on Tobacco and Health.

   c) Leaders of all religious communities be urged to adopt an official position and take action to protect humanity from the dangers to health from tobacco.

   d) An Islamic Council for Tobacco Control be established.

   e) National governments should be encouraged to take measures leading to the adoption of generic packaging as a means of reducing inducements to tobacco consumption.

f) In view of the vital importance of information and data exchange, the European Commission is strongly urged to maintain its support for BASP [Bureau for Action on Smoking Prevention] to enable this organisation to continue its major contribution to tobacco control in the European Union.

An International Strategy for Tobacco Control

Since measures to deal with the tobacco problem must be comprehensive and long term, the following individual actions should form the basis of such a strategy.

1. Legislation to ban all direct and indirect advertising and promotion of tobacco products.

2. Legislation to protect young people from tobacco promotion and sales.

3. Policies to discourage the onset and maintenance of tobacco use, including:

   a) intensive health education and information to young people and adults;

   b) wide availability of support for tobacco users who wish to stop.

4. Economic policies to discourage production and use of all tobacco products, including:

   a) progressive significant increases in taxation above inflation (and the growth of disposable income), and the allocation of a specific proportion of such taxes for tobacco control purposes;

   b) action to discourage tobacco production and marketing by the abolition of all subsidies and protection for tobacco growers and the development of alternative economic, agricultural and international trade policies;

   c) removal of tobacco from national cost of living indexes;

   d) measures to control smuggling of tobacco products.

5. Effective health warnings and regulation of tobacco product packaging and on such promotional material still permitted.

6. A policy for the regulation of tar and nicotine content of tobacco products.

7. "Smoke-free" public policies — to protect the health and rights of people in all common environments.

8. Policies to block future marketing initiatives of the transnational tobacco industry.

9. Effective national monitoring of the tobacco pandemic and the enforcement of these control measures.

Key Contacts

Canadian nongovernmental organizations

Action on Smoking and Health
Aberhart Centre
3rd Floor
11402 University Avenue
PO Box 4500
Edmonton, AB, Canada T6E 6K2
Tel: (403) 492-5454
Fax: (403) 492-0362

Canadian Cancer Society
Suite 200
10 Alcorn Avenue
Toronto, ON Canada M4V 3B1
Tel: (416) 961-7223
Fax: (416) 961-4189

Canadian Council on Smoking and Health
Suite 1000
170 Laurier Avenue W
Ottawa, ON, Canada K1P 5V5
Tel: (613) 567-3050
Fax: (613) 567-2730
http://www.ccsh.ca/index.html

Canadian Medical Association
1867 Alta Vista Drive
Ottawa, ON, Canada K1G 3Y6
Tel: (613) 731-9331
Fax: (613) 731-1779
http://www.cma.ca/idx.htm

Heart and Stroke Foundation of Canada
Suite 200
160 George Street
Ottawa, ON, Canada K1N 9M2
Tel: (613) 241-4361
Fax: (613) 241-3278

The Lung Association
Suite 508
1900 City Park Drive
Blair Business Park
Gloucester, ON, Canada K1J 1A3
http://www.lung.ca/index.html

National Clearinghouse on Tobacco and Health
Suite 1000
170 Laurier Avenue W
Ottawa, ON, Canada K1P 5V5
Tel: (613) 567-3050
Fax: (613) 567-2730
http://www.ccsh.ca/ncth/

Non-Smokers' Rights Association
Suite 221
720 Spadina Avenue
Toronto, ON, Canada M5S 2T9
Tel: (416) 928-2900
Fax: (416) 928-1860

Ontario Tobacco Research Unit
33 Russell Street
Toronto, ON, Canada M5S 2S1
Tel: (416) 595-6888
Fax: (416) 595-6068
http://www.arf.org/otru/
e-mail: otru@arf.org

Physicians for a Smoke-Free Canada
PO Box 4849, Station E
Ottawa, ON, Canada K1S 5J1
Tel: (613) 233-4878
Fax: (613) 567-2730

Note: The Canadian Cancer Society, the Heart and Stroke Foundation, and The Lung Association have units at the provincial and local levels.

Federal, provincial, and territorial governments

Canada

Office of Tobacco Control
Health Canada
Room 513, Tower A
11 Holland Avenue
Ottawa, ON, Canada K1A 1B4
Tel: (613) 941-3723
Fax: (613) 941-1551

Alberta

Paula Finlayson, Consultant
Health Planning Branch
Alberta Health
24th Floor, 10025 Jasper Avenue
Edmonton, AB, Canada T5J 2N3
Tel: (403) 427-2653
Fax: (403) 427-2511

British Columbia

Linda Brigden, Senior Adviser
Tobacco Reduction Strategy
Office of Health Promotion
Population Health Resource Branch
British Columbia Ministry of Health
Main Floor, 1520 Blanshard Street
Victoria, BC, Canada V8W 3C8
Tel: (604) 952-1701
Fax: (604) 952-1713

Manitoba

Barbara Hague, Manager
Community Health and Mental Health Services
  Division
Public Health Branch
Manitoba Health
Suite 301, 800 Portage Avenue
Winnipeg, MB, Canada R3G 0N4
Tel: (204) 945-1062
Fax: (204) 948-2040

New Brunswick

Bill Howard, Consultant
Health Promotion and Disease Prevention
Branch
Department of Health and Community Services
PO Box 5100, Carleton Place
2nd Floor, 520 King Street
Fredericton, NB, Canada E3B 5G8
Tel: (506) 457-4983
Fax: (506) 453-2726

Newfoundland

Eleanor Swanson, Director of Health Promotion
Health Promotion Division
Community Health Branch
Department of Health
1st Floor, Confederation Building, West Block
PO Box 8700
St. John's, NF, Canada A1B 4J6
Tel: (709) 729-3940
Fax: (709) 729-5824

Northwest Territories

Rick Tremblay, Youth Addiction Consultant
Department of Health and Social Services
6 Precambrian Building
PO Box 1320
Yellowknife, NT, Canada X1A 2L9
Tel: (403) 920-3299
Fax: (403) 873-7706

Nova Scotia

Merv Ungurain, Director
Tobacco Control Unit
Nova Scotia Department of Health
10th Floor, 1690 Hollis Street
PO Box 488
Halifax, NS, Canada B3J 2R8
Tel: (902) 424-6259
Fax: (902) 424-0663

Ontario

Lorne Widmer, Acting Manager
Tobacco Control Strategy Unit
Health Promotion Branch
Ontario Ministry of Health
5th Floor, 5700 Yonge Street
North York, ON, Canada M2M 4K5
Tel: (416) 314-5476
Fax: (416) 314-5497

Prince Edward Island

Emily Bryant, Health Education Coordinator
Prince Edward Island Health and Community
  Services Agency
4 Sydney Street
PO Box 2000
Charlottetown, PE, Canada C1A 7N8
Tel: (902) 368-6509
Fax: (902) 368-6136

Quebec

Yves Archambault
Agent de recherche et de planification
  socio-économique
Direction de la santé publique
Ministère de la Santé et des Services sociaux
3ième étage, 1075, chemin Sainte-Foy
Québec (PQ), Canada G1S 2M1
Tel: (418) 643-6084
Fax: (418) 646-1680

Saskatchewan

April Barry, Director
Health Promotion Unit
Population Health Branch
Saskatchewan Health
3475 Albert Street
Regina, SK, Canada S4S 6X6
Tel: (306) 787-4086
Fax: (306) 787-3823

Yukon Territory

Jean Kapala, Program Coordinator
Public Health and Safety
Yukon College
8–5110 5th Avenue
Whitehorse, YT, Canada Y1A 1L4
Tel: (403) 668-5201
Fax: (403) 668-5210

Note: Individual government contacts are
subject to change.

International organizations

International Agency for Research on Cancer
150, cours Albert Thomas
Cedex 08
Lyon, France 69372
Tel: 33 (72) 73 84 85
Fax: 33 (72) 73 85 75
http://www.iarc.fr/

International Agency on Tobacco and Health
c/o Action on Smoking and Health
109 Gloucester Place
London, UK, W1H 3PH
Tel: 44 (171) 935-3519
Fax: 44 (171) 935-3463

International Non-Governmental Coalition
  Against Tobacco
c/o Service de pneumologie
Hôpital Saint-Louis
Coquelicot 5
1, avenue Claude-Vellefaux
Cedex 10
Paris, France 75475
Tel: 33 (1) 4249-9307
Fax: 33 (1) 4249-9395

International Tobacco Initiative
c/o International Development Research Centre
250 Albert Street
PO Box 8500
Ottawa, ON, Canada K1G 3H9
Tel: (613) 236-6163
Fax: (613) 567-7748

International Union Against Cancer
3, rue du Conseil-Général
1205 Geneva, Switzerland
Tel: 41 (22) 809-1820
Fax: 41 (22) 809-1810
http://www.uicc.who.ch/

International Union Against Tuberculosis and
Lung Disease
68, boulevard Saint-Michel
Paris, France 75006

Tobacco Control: An International Journal
c/o BMA House
Tavistock Square
London, UK, WC1H 9JR

Tobacco Products Liability Project
Cushing Hall
102 The Fenway
Boston, MA 02115, USA
Tel: (617) 373-2026
Fax: (617) 373-3672

World Health Organization
20, avenue Appia
1211 Geneva 27, Switzerland
Tel: 41 (22) 791-3423
Fax: 41 (22) 791-4851
http://www.who.ch/programmes/psa/toh.htm
e-mail: collishaw@who.ch

Abbreviations and Acronyms

ABC	American Broadcasting Corporation
ADA	Association des détaillants en alimentation du Québec [Quebec association of food retailers]
AIDS	acquired immune deficiency syndrome
BAT	B.A.T Industries plc
BC	before Christ (when used as part of a date)
BC	British Columbia
CBC	Canadian Broadcasting Corporation
CCS	Canadian Cancer Society
CCSH	Canadian Council on Smoking and Health
CEO	Chief Executive Officer
CMA	Canadian Medical Association
CTMC	Canadian Tobacco Manufacturers' Council
CTR	Council for Tobacco Research
CTV	Canadian Television Network
DC	developed country
EPA	Environmental Protection Agency [US]
ETS	environmental tobacco smoke
FOREST	Freedom Organization for the Right to Enjoy Smoking Tobacco
FAO	Food and Agriculture Organization of the United Nations
GASP	Group Against Smokers' Pollution
GATT	General Agreement on Tariffs and Trade
IDRC	International Development Research Centre
JAMA	*Journal of the American Medical Association*
kg	kilogram(s)

LDC	less-developed country
MATRAC	Mouvement pour l'abolition des taxes sur le tabac [movement to abolish tobacco taxes]
mg	milligram(s)
MP	Member of Parliament
MPP	Member of Provincial Parliament
NAFTA	North American Free Trade Agreement
NCIC	National Cancer Institute of Canada
NDP	New Democratic Party
NGO	nongovernmental organization
NSRA	Non-Smokers' Rights Association
OCAT	Ontario Campaign for Action on Tobacco
PGA	Professional Golfers' Association
PR	public relations
RBH	Rothmans, Benson & Hedges Inc.
RCMP	Royal Canadian Mounted Police
SFS	Smokers' Freedom Society
SMART	Student Movement Aimed at Restricting Tobacco
STOP	Society to Overcome Pollution
TPCA	*Tobacco Products Control Act*
TTC	transnational tobacco company
UICC	Union internationale contre le cancer [International Union Against Cancer]
US	United States
USTR	United States Trade Representative
WCTU	Women's Christian Temperance Union
WHO	World Health Organization
WTO	World Trade Organization
YMCA	Young Men's Christian Association

Bibliography

1.   Abbott, D. 1952. House of Commons debates. 8 Apr, p. 1258.

2.   Abbott, D. 1953. House of Commons debates. 19 Feb, pp. 2132–2133.

3.   Ad Hoc Committee of the Canadian Tobacco Industry. 1963. Some scientific perspectives for consideration of smoking and health questions. A presentation to the Conference on Smoking and Health of the Department of National Health and Welfare, 25-26 Nov, Ottawa, ON, Canada.

4.   Ad Hoc Committee of the Canadian Tobacco Industry. 1969. A Canadian Tobacco Industry Presentation on Smoking and Health. A presentation to the House of Commons Standing Committee on Health, Welfare and Social Affairs. *In* House of Commons Standing Committee on Health, Welfare and Social Affairs, minutes of proceedings and evidence. 5 Jun, pp. 1579–1689.

5.   Adler, I. 1912. Primary malignant growths of the lungs and bronchi. Longmans, Green and Co., New York, NY, USA. *Cited in* Wynder, E.L.; Graham, E.A. 1950. Tobacco smoking as a possible etiologic factor in bronchiogenic carcinoma. A study of six-hundred and eighty-four proved cases. Journal of the American Medical Association, 143(4), 329–337.

6.   Advocacy Institute, Smoking Control Advocacy Resource Center. 1995. Action alert. Issue: Support needed to save OSHA's smokefree workplace proposal. 12 Dec.

7.   Agriculture Canada. 1989. Summary. [Document obtained from Agriculture Canada under the *Access to Information Act.*]

8.   Agriculture Canada. 1990. Evaluation of the Tobacco Diversification Plan: (Tobacco Transition Adjustment Initiative; Alternative Enterprise Initiative) executive report. Audit and Evaluation Branch, Program Evaluation Division, Agriculture Canada, Ottawa, ON, Canada. 6 Dec.

9.   Agro-Economic Services Ltd; Tabacosmos Ltd. 1987. The employment, tax revenue and wealth that the tobacco industry creates. Table A3.6. *Cited in* Chapman, S.; Leng, W.W. 1990. Tobacco control in the Third World: a resource atlas. International Organization of Consumers Unions, Penang, Malaysia. p. 53.

10. Air Canada. 1994. History of non-smoking flights at Air Canada. Fact Sheet.

11. Airspace Non-smokers' Rights Society. 1994. Breathers' dining guide. Pamphlet.

12. Aliro, O.K. 1993. Uganda: paying the price of growing tobacco. The Panos Institute, London, UK.

13. Allen, R.C. 1993. The false dilemma: the impact of tobacco control policies on employment in Canada. Feb.

14. Anan, N.W. 1995. Cigarette firms in Thai market fume over plan. Wall Street Journal, 8 Sep, p. A5A.

15. Angus Reid Group, Inc. 1995. No smoking bylaw survey. Submitted to Metropolitan Board of Health of Greater Vancouver, BC Lung Association, Canadian Cancer Society, and Heart and Stroke Foundation of BC and Yukon. May.

16. Anti-Tobacco Association of Saint John, New Brunswick, ed. 1889. Prize essays on tobacco. Daily Telegraph Book and Job Press, Saint John, NB, Canada.

17. Ashley, M.J. 1995. The health effects of tobacco use. Prepared for the National Clearinghouse on Tobacco and Health by the Ontario Tobacco Research Unit. Mar.

18. Asia Pacific Tobacco News. 1993. Across region. Asia Pacific Tobacco News, Bulletin No. 3, Nov, p. 1. *Citing* [Hong Kong] Sunday Morning Post, 31 Oct 1993, p. 8.

19. Asia Pacific Tobacco News. 1994. China. Asia Pacific Tobacco News, Bulletin No. 5, Jan, p. 9. *Citing* WHO Collaborating Centre for Tobacco or Health Anti-Tobacco Newsletter, 15 Dec 1993.

20. Asia Pacific Tobacco News. 1994. Sri Lanka. Asia Pacific Tobacco News, Bulletin No. 6, Feb, p. 7. *Citing* Sri Lanka Link, 13 Jan 1994, p. 1.

21. Asia Pacific Tobacco News. 1994. Hong Kong. Asia Pacific Tobacco News, Bulletin No. 12, Aug, p. 4. *Citing* [Hong Kong] South China Morning Post, 13 Jul 1994, p. 8.

22. Association des conseils des médecins, dentistes et pharmaciens du Québec; Canadian Cancer Society; Canadian Council on Smoking and Health; Canadian Teachers' Federation; National Action Committee on the Status of Women; Non-Smokers' Rights Association; Physicians for a Smoke-Free Canada. 1988. How many thousands of Canadians will die from tobacco industry products may largely be in the hands of these two men. Globe and Mail, 25 Jan, p. A3. Advertisement.

23. Austin, D.R.; McBurney, M.; Kieran, M.; Lindsay, D.; Greenaway, T. 1994. A new low in corporate thuggery. Globe and Mail, 18 May, p. A21. Letters.

24. Authier, P. 1987. Citizen to drop tobacco ads, ban smoking. The Ottawa Citizen, 2 Oct, p. C1.

25. Barford, M.F. 1991. Tobacco Journal International, Feb. *Cited in* Connolly, G.N. 1994. Freedom from aggression: a guide to resisting transnational tobacco companies' entry into developing countries. *In* Building a tobacco-free world. 8th World Conference on Tobacco or Health, 30 Mar – 3 Apr 1992, Buenos Aires, Argentina. American Cancer Society. pp. 125–158.

26. Barnet, R.J.; Cavanagh, J. 1994. Global dreams: imperial corporations and the new world order. Simon & Schuster, New York, NY, USA.

27. Barnum, H. 1994. The economic burden of the global trade in tobacco. Paper presented at the 9th World Conference on Tobacco and Health, 10–14 Oct 1994, Paris, France.

28. Barnum, H. 1994. The economic burden of the global trade in tobacco. Tobacco Control, 3(4), 358–361.

29. Bass, F. 1994. House of Commons Standing Committee on Health, minutes of proceedings and evidence. 3 May.

30. BAT Industries plc. 1994. Clearing the air. The Leaflet, Nov/Dec, pp.2, 6.

31. BAT Industries plc. 1994. Factfile. BAT Industries. Tobacco.

32. BAT Industries plc. 1995. Annual review and summary financial statement 1994.

33. BAT Industries plc. 1995. Factfile. BAT Industries. Tobacco.

34. Beede, P.; Lawson, R.; Shepherd, M. 1991. The promotional impact of cigarette packaging: a study of adolescent responses to cigarette plain-packs. Department of Marketing, University of Otago, Dunedin, New Zealand.

35. Benowitz, N.L.; Hall, S.M.; Herning, R.I.; Jacob, P., III; Jones, R.T.; Osman, A.-L. 1983. Smokers of low-yield nicotine do not consume less nicotine. New England Journal of Medicine, 309(3), 139–142.

36. Benson & Hedges Tobacco Co.; Imperial Tobacco Products Ltd; Macdonald Tobacco Inc.; Rothmans of Pall Mall Canada Ltd. 1972. Cigarette advertising code of the Canadian Tobacco Manufacturers Council. Revised May.

37.   Bero, L.; Barnes, D.E.; Hanauer, P.; Slade, J.; Glantz, S.A. 1995. Lawyer control of the tobacco industry's external research program: the Brown and Williamson documents. Journal of the American Medical Association, 274(3), 241–247.

38.   Best, E.W.R.; Josie, G.H.; Walker, C.B. 1961. A Canadian study of mortality in relation to smoking habits: a preliminary report. Canadian Journal of Public Health, 52(3), 99–106.

39.   Best, E.W.R.; Walker, C.B. 1964. A Canadian study of smoking and health — second report. Canadian Journal of Public Health, 55(1), 1–11.

40.   Bickerdike, R. 1903. House of Commons debates. 1 Apr, p. 820.

41.   Bickerdike, R. 1903. House of Commons debates. 1 Apr, p. 822.

42.   Bickerdike, R. 1903. House of Commons debates. 1 Apr, p. 823.

43.   Bigney, L. 1889. Tobacco. *In* Anti-Tobacco Association of Saint John, New Brunswick, ed., Prize essays on tobacco. Daily Telegraph Book and Job Press, Saint John, NB, Canada. pp. 55–74.

44.   Blain, R. 1907. House of Commons debates. 4 Mar, p. 4058.

45.   Blain, R. 1907. House of Commons debates. 4 Mar, p. 4059.

46.   Blanchard, S. 1988. Les Grands perdants : les petits événements sportifs et culturels. Le Devoir, 8 Jun, p. 17.

47.   Bloom, J. 1993. Fear and irony on Tobacco Road: notes from the Fourth Tobacco International Exhibition and Conference. Tobacco Control, 2(1), 46–49.

48.   Brennan, R. 1994. Minister promises plain-pack smokes. The Ottawa Citizen, 8 Apr, p. A3.

49.   Brigham, J.; Gross, J.; Stitzer, M.L.; Felch, L.J. 1994. Effects of a restricted work-site smoking policy on employees who smoke. American Journal of Public Health, 84(5), 773–778.

50.   Brooks, J. 1995. American cigarettes have become a status symbol in smoke-saturated China. Canadian Medical Association Journal, 152(9), 1512–1513.

51.   Brown and Williamson document. 1988. Chronology of Brown and Williamson smoking and health research. p. 27. *Cited in* Slade, J.; Bero, L.A.; Hanauer, P.; Barnes, D.E.; Glantz, S.A. 1995. Nicotine and addiction: the Brown and Williamson documents. Journal of the American Medical Association, 274(3), 225–233.

·52. Brown and Williamson document. Circa 1969. Smoking and health proposal. Page numbering unclear.

53.   Brown, D. 1989. Transcript, *RJR–Macdonald Inc.* v. *Canada (Attorney General).* 28 Sep, p. 661.

54.   Brown, D. 1989. Transcript, *RJR–Macdonald Inc.* v. *Canada (Attorney General).* 2 Oct, p. 711.

55.   Brown, D. 1989. Transcript, *RJR–Macdonald Inc.* v. *Canada (Attorney General).* 3 Oct, p. 909.

56.   Brown, D. 1989. Transcript, *RJR–Macdonald Inc.* v. *Canada (Attorney General).* 4 Oct, p. 1050.

57.   Brown, K.S.; Taylor, T.E.; Madill, C.L.; Cameron, R. 1996. The relationship between the tobacco tax decrease and smoking among youth: results of a survey in southwestern Ontario. Ontario Tobacco Research Unit, Toronto, ON, Canada. Working Paper Series, No. 14.

58.   Bruner, M. 1991. The history of smoke. Doctor's Review, Sep, 87–92.

59.   Brunneman, K.D.; Hoffman, D. 1988. Determination of tar, nicotine and carbon monoxide in Philippine cigarettes. American Health Foundation. 12 Apr. *Cited in* Mackay, J. 1990. Political and promotional thrusts in Asia by the transnational tobacco companies. *In* Durston, B.; Jamrozik, K., ed., The global war. Proceedings of the 7th World Conference on Tobacco and Health. Organis-

ing Committee of the 7th World Conference on Tobacco and Health, Perth, WA, Australia. pp. 139–141.

60. Burns Fry Limited. 1994. Canada's tobacco industry — continued profit growth likely despite concerns. 29 Jun.

61. Canadian Cancer Society. 1993. What's your poison? Poster.

62. Canadian Cancer Society. 1994. Protecting health and revenue: an action plan to control contraband and tax-exempt tobacco. Jan.

63. Canadian Cancer Society. 1995. In support of public health. A submission to the United States Food and Drug Administration respecting proposed tobacco regulations under the *Food, Drug and Cosmetic Act*. Dec.

64. Canadian Cancer Society; Canadian Council on Smoking and Health; Canadian Medical Association; Heart and Stroke Foundation of Canada; Non-Smokers' Rights Association; Physicians for a Smoke-Free Canada. 1990. Sustaining a successful policy: the treatment of tobacco taxation in the 1991 Federal Budget. A Submission to the Minister of Finance, The Honourable Michael Wilson. Dec.

65. Canadian Cancer Society; National Cancer Institute of Canada. 1969. Brief to the Standing Committee on Health, Welfare and Social Affairs of the House of Commons together with a supplementary statement by the National Cancer Institute of Canada. *In* House of Commons Standing Committee on Health, Welfare and Social Affairs, minutes of proceedings and evidence. 19 Jun, pp. 2014–2051.

66. Canadian Cigar and Tobacco Journal. 1899. Tobacco and pulmonary diseases. Canadian Cigar and Tobacco Journal, Feb, 71.

67. Canadian Cigar and Tobacco Journal. 1902. The year's trade. Canadian Cigar and Tobacco Journal, Sep, 477.

68. Canadian Cigar and Tobacco Journal. 1903. Smoking on street cars. Canadian Cigar and Tobacco Journal, Nov, 11.

69. Canadian Cigar and Tobacco Journal. 1906. Growth of smoking habit. Canadian Cigar and Tobacco Journal, Apr, 47.

70. Canadian Cigar and Tobacco Journal. 1915. Soldiers and cigarettes. Canadian Cigar and Tobacco Journal, Jul, 13.

71. Canadian Cigar and Tobacco Journal. 1921. The W.C.T.U. objects. Canadian Cigar and Tobacco Journal, Jul, 39.

72. Canadian Cigar and Tobacco Journal. 1927. Cigarette advertising for women. Canadian Cigar and Tobacco Journal, Aug, 21.

73. Canadian Cigar and Tobacco Journal. 1933. Smoking in theatres. Canadian Cigar and Tobacco Journal, Aug, 28.

74. Canadian Cigar and Tobacco Journal. 1942. Eminent American physician blasts Tunney for his tirade on tobacco. Canadian Cigar and Tobacco Journal, Jun, 6.

75. Canadian Council on Smoking and Health. 1993. Contributions to major political parties by major tobacco companies for the fiscal period ending December 31, 1992.

76. Canadian Medical Association. 1969. The Canadian Medical Association brief Re: Smoking and Health to the House of Commons Standing Committee on Health, Welfare and Social Affairs. *In* House of Commons Standing Committee on Health, Welfare and Social Affairs, minutes of proceedings and evidence. 27 Feb, pp. 689–698.

77. Canadian Medical Association. 1987. Physicians asked to vote against any MP who opposes Bill C-51. 25 Sep. News Release.

78. Canadian Medical Association. 1987. All CMA members asked to call their MPs on Bill C-51. 19 Oct. News Release.

79. Canadian Press. 1983. Bégin's aides try to clear air on cigaret pricing proposal. Globe and Mail, 13 Jul, p. 8.

80. Canadian Press. 1989. Warnings don't stand out. The Ottawa Citizen, 31 May, p. A11.

81. Canadian Press. 1993. Tobacco farmers top list. Globe and Mail, 28 Apr, p. B4.

82. Canadian Press. 1994. Tobacco bred for high nicotine. Globe and Mail, 26 Apr, p. A1.

83. Canadian Task Force on the Periodic Health Examination. 1994. The Canadian guide to clinical preventive health care. Minister of Supply and Services, Ottawa, ON, Canada.

84. Canadian Tobacco Grower. 1993. Tobacco industry and anti-smoking groups agree and disagree. Canadian Tobacco Grower, Jul, pp. 25, 31.

85. Canadian Tobacco Manufacturers' Council. 1982. Tobacco in Canada 1981. 15 Mar.

86. Canadian Tobacco Manufacturers' Council. 1987. A brief to the Legislative Committee of the House of Commons on Bill C-51. 11 Dec.

87. Canadian Tobacco Manufacturers' Council. 1988. Comments by the Canadian Tobacco Manufacturers' Council on principles for the development of tobacco regulations under the *Tobacco Products Control Act* (C-51, 1988). 31 Aug.

88. Canadian Tobacco Manufacturers' Council. 1992. Tobacco company sponsorship of cultural and sports events: a brief from the Canadian Tobacco Manufacturers' Council. Mar.

89. Canadian Tobacco Manufacturers' Council. 1993. Tobacco in Canada 1992. 1 Jun.

90. Canadian Tobacco Manufacturers' Council. 1993. Untitled. [Summary of Canadian and American tobacco sales, including sales of Canadian contraband.]

91. *Caputo, et al.* v. *Imperial Tobacco Ltd., Rothmans, Benson & Hedges Inc. and RJR–Macdonald Inc.* 1995. Statement of claim. Ontario Court, General Division. File No. 95-CU-82186.

92. Carroll, W. 1977. Tobacco sponsors pulling out. Financial Times of Canada, 6 Jun, pp. 1, 14.

93. Castel, J.-G. (Distinguished Research Professor and Professor of International Business Law, Osgoode Hall Law School, York University). 1994. Letter to J. Michael Robinson (Fasken Campbell Godfrey). Would plain packaging for cigarettes violate Canada's international trade obligations? 11 May.

94. Cédilot, A.; Trottier, E. 1993. La Contrebande dans les réserves amérindiennes : la GRC bafouille. La Presse, 16 Jul, p. A3.

95. Centre for Behavioural Research in Cancer. 1992. Paper 13: Adolescents' reactions to cigarette packs modified to increase extent and impact of health warnings. *In* Health warnings and contents labelling on tobacco products. Report prepared for the Ministerial Council on Drug Strategy Tobacco Task Force, Anti-Cancer Council of Victoria, Melbourne, Australia. pp. 121–125.

96. Centre for Health Promotion, University of Toronto. 1993. Effects of plain packaging among youth. 30 Nov.

97. Centrepoint, Sunday Morning. 1994. CBC Radio, 10 Apr.

98. Chandler, W.U. 1986. Banishing tobacco. Worldwatch Institute, Washington, DC, USA. Worldwatch Paper No. 68. *Cited in* Barry, M. 1991. The influence of the U.S. tobacco industry on the

health, economy, and environment of developing countries. New England Journal of Medicine, 324(13), 917–920.

99. Chapman, S. 1986. Great expectorations: advertising and the tobacco industry. Comedia Publishing Group, London, UK.

100. Chapman, S. 1993. Tobacco trade in Africa: a bright picture, indeed? *In* Yach, D.; Harrison, S., ed., Proceedings of the All Africa Conference on Tobacco or Health. 14–17 Nov 1993, Harare, Zimbabwe. pp. 28–33.

101. Chapman, S. 1994. Tobacco and deforestation in the developing world. Tobacco Control, 3(3), 191–193.

102. Chapman, S.; Leng, W.W. 1990. Tobacco control in the Third World: a resource atlas. International Organization of Consumers Unions, Penang, Malaysia.

103. Chapman, S.; Richardson, J. 1990. Tobacco excise and declining tobacco consumption: the case of Papua New Guinea. American Journal of Public Health, 80(5), 537–540.

104. Charlton, A.; Mackay, J.; Moyer, C.; Shiru, N.; Hing, L.T. 1993. Smoking and youth in China 1992: review and recommendations. International Union Against Cancer; Cancer Research Campaign, Geneva, Switzerland; London, UK.

105. Chicanot, E.L. 1948. You may puff peacefully while doctors disagree. Saturday Night, 28 Aug, p. 32.

106. Chollat-Traquet, C. 1992. Women and tobacco. World Health Organization, Geneva, Switzerland.

107. Chrétien, J. 1994. House of Commons debates. 8 Feb, p. 1031.

108. *Cipollone* v. *Liggett Group, Inc., et al.* 1988. Transcript of proceedings [excerpt]. Tobacco Products Litigation Reporter, 3(3), 3.251–3.268.

109. Cloutier, L. 1995. Les Festivals et tournois pourraient pâtir de cette victoire du tabac. La Presse, 23 Sep, p. A7.

110. Cohen, N. 1981. Smoking, health and survival: prospects in Bangladesh. The Lancet, 1(8229), 1090–1093.

111. Cole, J.S. 1994. The role of tobacco research. World Tobacco for Russia and Eastern Europe, Vol. II. pp. 49–53, 55.

112. Collishaw, N.E. 1987. Legislative control of tobacco in Canada. Paper presented at the 6th World Conference on Smoking and Health, 9–12 Nov 1987, Tokyo, Japan.

113. Collishaw, N.E. 1992. A plan for tobacco control in Nepal. 7 Aug.

114. Collishaw, N.E. 1993. Tabac ou santé en Côte d'Ivoire : rapport de mission et recommandations. Apr.

115. Collishaw, N.E. 1993. What Canadians can do to end the tobacco pandemic. Paper presented at Tobacco-Free Canada: 1st National Conference on Tobacco or Health, 20–22 Oct 1993, Ottawa, ON, Canada.

116. Collishaw, N.E. 1994. Is the tobacco epidemic being brought under control, or just moved around? An international perspective. Paper presented at the 5th International Conference on the Reduction of Drug-Related Harm, 6–10 Mar 1994, Toronto, ON, Canada.

117. Collishaw, N.E.; Mulligan, L. 1984. Recent trends in tobacco consumption in Canada and other countries. Chronic Diseases in Canada, 4(4), 52–54.

118. Comtois, J.-R. 1973. House of Commons debates. 19 Jun, p. 4927.

119. Connolly, G.N. 1990. Political and promotional thrusts worldwide by the transnational tobacco companies. *In* Durston, B.; Jamrozik, K., ed., The global war. Proceedings of the 7th World Conference on Tobacco and Health. Organising Committee of the 7th World Conference on Tobacco and Health, Perth, WA, Australia. pp. 142–147.

120. Connolly, G.N. 1994. Freedom from aggression: a guide to resisting transnational tobacco companies' entry into developing countries. *In* Building a tobacco-free world. 8th World Conference on Tobacco or Health, 30 Mar – 3 Apr 1992, Buenos Aires, Argentina. American Cancer Society. pp. 125–158.

121. Connolly, G.N. 1994. Tobacco, trade and Eastern Europe. Paper presented at the 9th World Conference on Tobacco and Health, 10–14 Oct 1994, Paris, France.

122. Corti, E.C. 1931. A history of smoking. George G. Harrap & Co. Ltd, London, UK.

123. Crawford, T. 1975. Sailor docked $300. Toronto Star, 22 Mar, p. A8.

124. The Creative Research Group Limited. 1986. Project Viking. Vol. I: A behaviourial model of smoking. Prepared for Imperial Tobacco Ltd. Feb–Mar. Exhibit AG-21A, *RJR–Macdonald Inc.* v. *Canada (Attorney General)*.

125. The Creative Research Group Limited. 1986. Project Viking. Vol. II: An attitudinal model of smoking. Prepared for Imperial Tobacco Ltd. Feb–Mar. Exhibit AG-21B, *RJR–Macdonald Inc.* v. *Canada (Attorney General)*.

126. The Creative Research Group Limited. 1986. Project Viking. Vol. III: Product issues. Prepared for Imperial Tobacco Ltd. Feb–Mar. Exhibit AG-21C, *RJR–Macdonald Inc.* v. *Canada (Attorney General)*.

127. The Creative Research Group Limited. 1987. Youth Target 1987. Prepared for RJR–Macdonald Inc. Exhibit RJR-6, *RJR–Macdonald Inc.* v. *Canada (Attorney General)*.

128. Cross Country Checkup. 1994. CBC Radio, 30 Jan.

129. CTV National News. 1994. Transcript excerpt. 1 Sep.

130. Cunningham, R. 1991. Why banning tobacco sales in pharmacies should reduce tobacco use. Canadian Pharmaceutical Journal, 124(10), 466–468, 476.

131. Cunningham, R. 1995. Enforcing the *Tobacco Products Control Act* and the *Tobacco Products Control Regulations*. A report prepared for the Non-Smokers' Rights Association. 18 Apr.

132. Cunningham, R.; Kyle, K. 1988. Fighting the good fight: a look at the battle that gave Canada the world's toughest anti-tobacco legislation. 1 Sep.

133. Dateline Ontario. 1987. TVOntario. Transcript. 12 Jul.

134. Delarue, N.C. 1990. Smoking or health: an early historical perspective. Annals of the Royal College of Physicians and Surgeons of Canada, 23(6), 431–435.

135. Demers, L.P. 1904. House of Commons debates. 20 Jun, p. 5137.

136. Demers, L.P. 1904. House of Commons debates. 20 Jun, p. 5138.

137. Department of Finance, Government of Canada. 1989. Budget papers. Tabled in the House of Commons by the Minister of Finance, The Honourable Michael H. Wilson.

138. Department of Finance, Government of Canada. 1993. Tobacco taxes and consumption. Jun.

139. Department of National Health and Welfare. 1964. Smoking and health reference book (Canada). Information Services. Queen's Printer, Ottawa, ON, Canada.

140. Department of National Health and Welfare. 1965. Canadian Youth Conference on Smoking and Health, 12–14 May 1965, Ottawa, ON, Canada. Summary Report.

141. Department of National Health and Welfare. 1970. A case history. The Canadian Smoking and Health Program, Department of National Health and Welfare, Ottawa, ON, Canada.

142. Department of Pensions and National Health. 1940. Smoking. Publicity and Health Education Division. King's Printer, Ottawa, ON, Canada. National Health Series, No. 106.

143. de Savoye, P.; Picard, P. 1994. Concerns over plain packaging of cigarettes and issues of a true public health policy. Minority report of the members of the Bloc Québécois. 21 Jun. *In* House of Commons Standing Committee on Health. 1994. Towards zero consumption. Generic packaging of tobacco products. Report of the Standing Committee on Health, Appendix C. pp. 46–60.

144. Devine, J. 1987. Anti-tobacco lobby targets Stewart. The [Barrie, ON] Banner Advance, 25 Nov, p. 1.

145. Diefenbaker, J. 1948. House of Commons debates. 22 Mar, p. 2501.

146. Dissanaike, T. 1993. Consultants rule out lung cancer, heart. Anti-smoking campaign comes under heavy fire. The Island, no page numbers.

147. Doll, R.; Hill, A.B. 1950. Smoking and carcinoma of the lung: preliminary report. British Medical Journal, 2, 739–748.

148. Doll, R.; Peto, R.; Wheatley, K.; Gray, R.; Sutherland, I. 1994. Mortality in relation to smoking: 40 years' observations on male British doctors. British Medical Journal, 309, 901–911.

149. Dominion Bureau of Statistics. 1971. Tobacco products industries 1969. Catalogue 32-225.

150. Doolittle, D.E. 1994. Under siege. Tobacco Reporter, May, pp. 4–5.

151. Douglas, C.E. 1994. The tobacco industry's use of nicotine as a drug. What do the recent revelations mean for tobacco control? American Council on Science and Health, New York, NY, USA. Special Report.

152. Dow Jones; Canadian Press; Globe and Mail. 1990. CAI predicts $40 million revenue dip from smoking ban. Globe and Mail, 17 May, p. B9.

153. Duncan, R.M.H. (Managing Director, BAT Uganda 1984 Ltd). 1988. Letter to the Director of Medical Services, Ministry of Health. 21 Jun.

154. Dunn, P. 1992. Response to BAT Industries' note on transdermal nicotine (28.02.92). Memorandum to Jean-Louis Mercier. 27 Mar.

155. Dunn, W.L. Jr (senior scientist, Philip Morris Tobacco Company). 1972. internal report, title not cited. Exhibit P-5171, *Cipollone* v. *Liggett Group, Inc., et al. Cited in* Douglas, C.E. 1994. The tobacco industry's use of nicotine as a drug: what do the recent revelations mean for tobacco control? American Council on Science and Health, New York, NY, USA. p. 3.

156. Durbin, D.; Meehan, M. 1994. More smoke from the tobacco industry. Statement on Congressional letterhead. 23 Sep.

157. Durston, B.; Jamrozik, K., ed. 1990. The global war. Proceedings of the 7th World Conference on Tobacco and Health. Organising Committee of the 7th World Conference on Tobacco and Health, Perth, WA, Australia.

158. Ecenbarger, W. 1993. America's new merchants of death. Reader's Digest, Apr, pp. 85–92.

159. Ecobichon, D.J.; Wu, J.M., ed. 1990. Environmental tobacco smoke. Proceedings, International Symposium, 3–4 Nov 1989, McGill University, Montreal, PQ, Canada. Lexington Books, Lexington, MA, USA.

160. Edwards, P. 1994. Illegal cigarettes make millionaires out of smugglers. Toronto Star, 5 Feb, pp. A1, A12.

161. Ellison, L.F.; Mao, Y.; Gibbons, L. 1995. Projected smoking-attributable mortality in Canada, 1991–2000. Chronic Diseases in Canada, 16(2), 84–89.

162. Emmerson, H. 1904. House of Commons debates. 20 Jun, p. 5132.

163. Endemann, K. 1989. EEF proposal China/tobacco. 2 May.

164. Epp, J. (Minister of National Health and Welfare). 1985. Letter to Wilmat Tennyson (President, Imperial Tobacco Ltd). 24 Sep.

165. Euromonitor plc. 1993. Tobacco markets in Eastern Europe. Euromonitor plc, London, UK.

166. European Bureau for Action on Smoking Prevention. 1991. Test the East. The Tobacco Industry and Eastern Europe. Feb.

167. Fasken Campbell Godfrey (Robinson, J.M.). 1994. Letter to Garfield Mahood (Executive Director, Non-Smokers' Rights Association). Subject: Proposed Canadian legislation requiring "plain packaging" for cigarettes and tobacco products. 11 May.

168. Fayne, T. 1988. In a word, Knudson doing fine. Globe and Mail, 5 Apr, p. A20.

169. Federal Trade Commission. 1995. Cigarette advertising and promotion in the United States, 1993: a report of the Federal Trade Commission. Tobacco Control, 4(3), 310–313.

170. Feldt, R.H. 1943. This is the truth about tobacco. Maclean's, 1 Nov, pp. 10, 38–40.

171. Fennell, P.J. 1987. House of Commons Legislative Committee on Bill C-204, minutes of proceedings and evidence. 24 Nov.

172. Fennell, P.J. (President and CEO, Rothmans, Benson & Hedges Inc.); Mercier, J.-L. (Chairman and CEO, Imperial Tobacco Ltd); Fitzgerald, C.W., Jr (President and CEO, RJR–Macdonald Inc.). 1989. Letter to G.E. Morehouse (Morehouse G E Limited). 14 Mar.

173. The Financial Post Company. 1993. Imasco Limited. CUSIP No. 452451. 6 May.

174. Finch, E.P. 1968. Letter to Richard P. Dobson (British-American Tobacco Co., Ltd. 11 Dec.

175. Fischer, D. 1994. Du Maurier takes heat for blocking anti-cigarette ad. The Ottawa Citizen, 15 Aug, p. A2.

176. Fischer, P.M.; Schwartz, M.P.; Richards, J.W., Jr; Goldstein, A.O.; Rojas, T.H. 1991. Brand logo recognition by children aged 3 to 6 years: Mickey Mouse and Old Joe the camel. Journal of the American Medical Association, 266(22), 3145–3148.

177. Fisher, I. 1924. Does tobacco injure the human body? Reader's Digest, Nov, pp. 435–436. *Cited in* Ritchie, R; Pollay, R.W. 1995. Reader's Digest's Indigestion of Tobacco: 1924–1994. The History of Advertising Archives, Faculty of Commerce, University of British Columbia, Vancouver, BC, Canada. Jan. p.1.

178. Fitzpatrick, C. 1903. House of Commons debates. 8 Sep, p. 10757.

179. Food and Agricultural Organization. 1979. FAO position paper on tobacco cultivation.

180. Ford, H. 1916. The case against the little white slaver. Privately published.

181. Fortin, P. 1869. House of Commons debates. 7 Jun, p. 637.

182. Fraser, A.I. 1986. The use of wood by the tobacco industry and the ecological implications. International Forest Science Consultancy, Edinburgh, UK. Dec.

183. Fraser, G. 1988. Bills aimed at smoking step away from law. Globe and Mail, 29 Jun, p. A1.

184. Freedman, A.M. 1995. Philip Morris memo likens nicotine to drugs. Wall Street Journal, 8 Dec, pp. B1, B4.

185. Freedman, A.M.; Cohen, L.P. 1993. Smoke and mirrors: how cigarette makers keep health question 'open' year after year. Wall Street Journal, 11 Feb, pp. A1, A10.

186. Freeman, A. 1991. Smokers urged to fight tax with cigarette-pack mail. Globe and Mail, 22 May, p. A8.

187. Freeman, A. 1993. Tobacco rivals strike a match. Globe and Mail, 6 May, pp. B1, B6.

188. Gadacz, O. 1988. US firing up Korean cig ads. Advertising Age, 1 Aug, p. 36.

189. Gallup Canada Inc. 1987. Gallup national omnibus: attitudes toward smoking restrictions. Conducted for Canadian Cancer Society. Oct.

190. Gallup Canada Inc. 1991. National omnibus — Canadian Cancer Society. 19 Dec.

191. Galt, V. 1990. Bid to postpone smoking ban leaves flight attendants burning. Globe and Mail, 30 May, p. A8.

192. General Agreement on Tariffs and Trade. 1990. Thailand: restrictions on importation of and internal taxes on cigarettes. Report of the Panel adopted on 7 Nov 1990. GATT Document DS10/R, 46th sess., 37th suppl., Basic Instruments and Selected Documents (1991) 200.

193. Gervais, H. 1904. House of Commons debates. 20 Jun, p. 5165.

194. Glantz, S.A.; Parmley, W.W. 1991. Passive smoking and heart disease; epidemiology, physiology, and biochemistry. Circulation, 83(1), 1–12.

195. Glantz, S.A.; Smith, L.R.A. 1994. The effect of ordinances requiring smoke-free restaurants on restaurant sales. American Journal of Public Health, 84(7), 1081–1085.

196. Globe and Mail. 1971. Tar, nicotine limits crippling, tobacco industry leader says. Globe and Mail, 11 Jun, pp. 1–2.

197. Globe and Mail. 1977. City to curb smoking Oct. 1 in stores, hospitals, banks. Globe and Mail, 21 Jun, pp. 1–2.

198. Globe and Mail. 1992. Imperial Tobacco completes pact. Globe and Mail, 30 Sep, p. B7.

199. Globe and Mail. 1994. A nation of cheaters. Globe and Mail, 11 Feb, p. A18.

200. Goad, G.P. 1991. Canada's tobacco-ad ban is overturned by judge. Wall Street Journal, 29 Jul, pp. B1, B3.

201. Goldberg, G.E.; Liefeld, J.; Kindra, G.; Madill-Marshall, J.; Lefebvre, J.; Martohardjono, N.; Vredenburg, H. 1995. When packages can't speak: possible impacts of plain and generic packaging of tobacco products. Expert panel report prepared at the request of Health Canada. Mar.

202. Gooderham, M. 1989. Ottawa orders ban on smoking on airlines' international flights. Globe and Mail, 19 Dec, p. A12.

203. Goodyear, M. 1994. Canadian tobacco taxation 1867–1994. Hamilton Regional Cancer Centre, Hamilton, ON, Canada. 7 Sep.

204. Government of Canada. 1967. Cabinet minutes 41-67. 11 May, pp. 7–8.

205. Government of Canada. 1970. Memorandum to the Cabinet [arising from the 9 Jun 1970 meeting of the Cabinet Committee on Social Policy]. Cabinet Document 727/70. 15 Jun.

206. Government of Canada. 1970. Cabinet minutes 37-70. 18 Jun, pp. 6–8.

207. Government of Canada. 1971. Cabinet minutes 6-71. 18 Feb, pp. 5–7.

208. Government of Canada. 1971. Cabinet minutes 18-71. 6 May, pp. 5–6.

209. Government of Canada. 1971. Cabinet minutes 28-71. 7 Jun, p. 9.

210. Government of Canada. 1992. Government announces further measures to counteract tobacco smuggling. 8 Apr. News Release.

211. Gratias, A. 1988. Memorandum to the Deputy Minister. Canada–China Joint Agriculture Committee (JAC) Project 22.9: Technical Tobacco Seminars, 11–17 Apr, 17 May.

212. Gray, N. 1990. Global overview of the tobacco problem. *In* Durston, B.; Jamrozik, K., ed., The global war. Proceedings of the 7th World Conference on Tobacco and Health. Organising Committee of the 7th World Conference on Tobacco and Health, Perth, WA, Australia. pp. 19–25.

213. Greaves, L. 1989. Taking control: an action handbook on women and tobacco. Canadian Council on Smoking and Health, Ottawa, ON, Canada.

214. Green, S. 1974. Notes on the Group Research and Development Conference, 12–18 Jan 1974, Duck Key, FL, USA. Notes for 12 Jan 1974, p. 2. *Cited in* Glantz, S.A.; Barnes, D.E.; Bero, L.; Hanauer, P.; Slade, J. 1995. Looking through a keyhole at the tobacco industry: the Brown and Williamson documents. Journal of the American Medical Association, 274(3), 219–224.

215. Greene, J.J. 1966. House of Commons debates. 2 Mar, p. 2040.

216. Greene, J.J. 1966. House of Commons debates. 2 Mar, p. 2041.

217. Greenspon, E. 1994. Issues of '63 Liberals sound familiar. Globe and Mail, 23 Mar, p. A6.

218. Grimm, R.H. 1988. House of Commons Legislative Committee on Bill C-204 and Bill C-51, minutes of proceedings and evidence. 19 Jan.

219. Hall, M.M. 1992. Tobacco. The 700-billion cigarette habit. Globe and Mail, 19 Dec, p. D5.

220. Hanauer, P.; Slade, J.; Barnes, D.E.; Bero, L.; Glantz, S.A. 1995. Lawyer control of internal scientific research to protect against products liability lawsuits: the Brown and Williamson documents. Journal of the American Medical Association, 274(3), 234–240.

221. Hansell, E.G. 1951. House of Commons debates. 19 Feb, p. 458.

222. Hansell, E.G. 1951. House of Commons debates. 19 Feb, p. 459.

223. Harman, A. 1986. Update Canada: tobacco industry in turmoil. Tobacco Reporter, Aug, pp. 44–47.

224. Harris, J.E. 1989. Cigarette advertising and promotion in Canada: effects on cigarette smoking and public health. Exhibit AG-196, *RJR–Macdonald Inc. v. Canada (Attorney General)*. Aug. Expert Report.

225. Harris, J.E. 1990. Supplementary report. Exhibit AG-197, *RJR–Macdonald Inc. v. Canada (Attorney General)*. 11 Mar. Expert Report.

226. Health and Welfare Canada. 1991. Diary of a teenage smoker. Minister of Supply and Services, Ottawa, ON, Canada. Video.

227. Health and Welfare Canada (Millar, W.J.). 1988. The smoking behaviour of Canadians — 1986. Minister of Supply and Services, Ottawa, ON, Canada.

228. Health and Welfare Canada (Morin, M.; Gallant, J.). 1992. Smoking by-laws in Canada, 1991. Minister of Supply and Services, Ottawa, ON, Canada.

229. Health and Welfare Canada (Stephens, T.). 1991. Canadians and smoking: an update. Minister of Supply and Services, Ottawa, ON, Canada. Jan.

230. Health and Welfare Canada; Department of Finance. 1977. Smoking, health and tax policy. Non-Medical Use of Drugs Directorate, Health and Welfare Canada; Tax Analysis Section, Department of Finance. 12 Aug.

231. Health Canada. 1994. Constituents of tobacco smoke. Fact Sheet.

232. Health Canada. 1994. Passive smoking: nowhere to hide. Fact Sheet.

233. Health Canada. 1994. Quarterly surveillance update: AIDS in Canada. Division of HIV/AIDS Epidemiology, Bureau of Communicable Disease Epidemiology, Laboratory Centre for Disease Control. Apr.

234. Health Canada. 1994. Survey on smoking in Canada, cycle 1. Aug.

235. Health Canada. 1994. Survey on smoking in Canada, cycle 2. Nov.

236. Health Canada. 1994. The benefits of quitting: good news for ex-smokers. Fact Sheet.

237. Health Canada. 1995. Internal report (work in progress). *Cited in* Health Canada. 1995. Tobacco control: a blueprint to protect the health of Canadians. Minister of Supply and Services, Ottawa, ON, Canada. p. 17.

238. Health Canada. 1995. Survey on smoking in Canada, cycle 3. Feb.

239. Health Canada. 1995. Tobacco control: a blueprint to protect the health of Canadians. Minister of Supply and Services, Ottawa, ON, Canada.

240. Health Canada. 1996. 1994 youth smoking survey.

241. Health Canada (Stephens, T.). 1994. Smoking among Aboriginal people in Canada, 1991. Minister of Supply and Services, Ottawa, ON, Canada.

242. Heinrich, J. 1994. Imasco posts record 1st-quarter profit of $75 million. Montreal Gazette, 29 Apr, pp. D1–D2.

243. Hemain, C. 1994. Stripping intolerance. *In* King, T.; Owen, B.; Oldman, M., ed., The tobacco industry 1994. Millenium Press, London, UK. pp. 201–203.

244. Herridge, H.W. 1962. House of Commons debates. 30 Jan, p. 348.

245. Herridge, H.W. 1962. House of Commons debates. 5 Feb, p. 523.

246. Herridge, H.W. 1962. House of Commons debates. 6 Feb, p. 578.

247. Herter, U. 1993. Untitled paper presented at the World Tobacco Symposium, 22–24 Sep 1993, Moscow, Russia. p. 3. *Citing* Report and accounts of Souza Cruz, Brazil, n.d.

248. Himbury, S.; West, R. 1985. Smoking habits after laryngectomy. British Medical Journal, 291, 514–515.

249. Hollobon, J. 1983. Bégin lobbying for tax increase to curb smoking. Globe and Mail, 12 Jul, pp. 1–2.

250. Holmes, R. 1903. House of Commons debates. 1 Apr, p. 826.

251. Hoult, P.J. 1989. Transcript, *RJR–Macdonald Inc.* v. *Canada (Attorney General)*. 27 Sep, p. 401.

252. Hoult, P.J. 1989. Transcript, *RJR–Macdonald Inc.* v. *Canada (Attorney General)*. 27 Sep, p. 397.

253. Hoult, P.J. 1989. Transcript, *RJR–Macdonald Inc.* v. *Canada (Attorney General)*. 27 Sep, p. 399.

254. Hoult, P.J. 1989. Transcript, *RJR–Macdonald Inc.* v. *Canada (Attorney General)*. 27 Sep, pp. 503–507.

255. Hoult, P.J. (President and Chief Executive Officer, RJR–Macdonald Inc.). 1987. Letter to Bill Vankoughnet (Member of Parliament). 10 Mar.

256. House of Commons debates. 1878. 23 Apr, pp. 2122–2140.

257. House of Commons debates. 1904. 23 Mar, pp. 336–364.

258. House of Commons debates. 1904. 30 May, p. 3772.

259. House of Commons debates. 1904. 1 Jun, p. 3978.

260. House of Commons debates. 1904. 2 Jun, pp. 4052–4053.

261. House of Commons debates. 1904. 14 Jun, pp. 4724–4725.

262. House of Commons debates. 1904. 20 Jun, pp. 5129–5166.

263. House of Commons debates. 1907. 4 Mar, pp. 4053–4091.

264. House of Commons debates. 1908. 16 Mar, pp. 5087–5134.

265. House of Commons debates. 1908. 18 Mar, pp. 5251–5255.

266. House of Commons Select Committee on Cigarette Evils. 1914. Second report. 2 Jun. *In* House of Commons Journals, 49, Appendix 3, 6.

267. House of Commons Standing Committee on Agriculture. 1987. The Canadian tobacco-growing industry in crisis. Report of the Standing Committee on Agriculture. Jun.

268. House of Commons Standing Committee on Health. 1994. Towards zero consumption. Generic packaging of tobacco products. Report of the Standing Committee on Health. Jun.

269. House of Commons Standing Committee on Health, Welfare and Social Affairs. 1969. Report of the Standing Committee on Health, Welfare and Social Affairs on tobacco and cigarette smoking. *In* House of Commons Standing Committee on Health, Welfare and Social Affairs, minutes of proceedings and evidence. 9 Dec, pp. 2:1–2:165.

270. Howard, R. 1992. Threats derailed tobacco tax. Companies warning led Ottawa to ease 'war on smugglers'. Globe and Mail, 22 May, pp. A1, A6.

271. Hu, T.; Keeler, T.E.; Sung, H.; Barnett, P.G. 1995. The impact of California anti-smoking legislation on cigarette sales, consumption, and prices. Tobacco Control, 4 (suppl. 1), S34–S38.

272. Hunter, I. 1989. Industry helped dilute smoking rules. The Ottawa Citizen, 26 Jun, p. A5.

273. Ialomiteanu, A.; Bondy, S. 1995. Prevalence of smoking and attitudes toward tobacco control policies: findings of the 1995 Ontario alcohol and other drug opinion survey (OADOS). Ontario Tobacco Research Unit, Toronto, ON, Canada. Working Paper Series, No. 6.

274. Imasco Ltd. 1984. Annual report 1984.

275. Imasco Ltd. 1986. Annual report 1986.

276. Imasco Ltd. 1987–96. Annual reports, 1987–95.

277. Imasco Ltd. 1992. Annual report 1991.

278. Imasco Ltd. 1993. Annual report 1992.

279. Imasco Ltd. 1994. Annual report 1993.

280. Imasco Ltd. 1994. Involvement in the community 1993.

281. Imasco Ltd. 1995. Annual report 1994.

282. Imasco Ltd. 1995. Investor update 1, January to March 1995.

283. Imasco Ltd. 1995. Management proxy circular. 1 Mar.

284. Imasco Ltd. 1996. Annual report 1995.

285. Imasco Ltd; Imperial Tobacco Ltd. 1965–95. Annual reports, 1964–94.

286. Imperial Tobacco Company of Canada Ltd; Macdonald Tobacco Inc.; Rothmans of Pall Mall Canada Ltd; Benson & Hedges (Canada) Ltd. 1964. Cigarette advertising code of Canadian tobacco manufacturers. 16 Jun.

287. Imperial Tobacco Ltd. 1978. Response of the market and of Imperial Tobacco to the smoking and health environment. Exhibit AG-41, *RJR–Macdonald Inc.* v. *Canada (Attorney General)*.

288. Imperial Tobacco Ltd. 1988. Domestic advertising expense summary. Exhibit AG-30A, *RJR–Macdonald Inc.* v. *Canada (Attorney General)*.

289. Imperial Tobacco Ltd. 1988. Imperial Tobacco.

290. Imperial Tobacco Ltd. 1989. The Canadian tobacco market at a glance. Exhibit AG-31, *RJR–Macdonald Inc.* v. *Canada (Attorney General)*.

291. Imperial Tobacco Ltd. 1993. Quarterly report to Health and Welfare Canada "Toxic substances in smoke". 19 Jul.

292. Imperial Tobacco Ltd. Circa 1970. 1971 Matinée marketing plans. Exhibit AG-204, *RJR–Macdonald Inc.* v. *Canada (Attorney General)*.

293. Imperial Tobacco Ltd. Circa 1979. Fiscal '80 media plans. Exhibit ITL-13, *RJR–Macdonald Inc.* v. *Canada (Attorney General)*.

294. Imperial Tobacco Ltd. Circa 1979. Creative guidelines [apparent title]. Exhibit AG-29, *RJR–Macdonald Inc.* v. *Canada (Attorney General)*.

295. Imperial Tobacco Ltd. Circa 1980. Fiscal '81 national media plans. Exhibit AG-223, *RJR–Macdonald Inc.* v. *Canada (Attorney General)*.

296. Imperial Tobacco Ltd. Circa 1980. Player's filter '81 creative guidelines. *In* Various internal Imperial Tobacco documents. Exhibit AG-35, *RJR–Macdonald Inc.* v. *Canada (Attorney General)*.

297. Imperial Tobacco Ltd. Circa 1980s. Entitled 1930–1939.

298. Imperial Tobacco Ltd. Circa 1980s. Entitled 1940–1949.

299. Imperial Tobacco Ltd. Circa 1980s. Entitled 1960–1969.

300. Imperial Tobacco Ltd. Circa 1980s. Entitled 1970–1979.

301. Imperial Tobacco Ltd. Circa 1982–89. Medallion. Exhibit AG-24, *RJR–Macdonald Inc.* v. *Canada (Attorney General)*.

302. Imperial Tobacco Ltd. Circa 1984. Matinée extra mild creative phase 2 rationale. Exhibit AG-212, *RJR–Macdonald Inc.* v. *Canada (Attorney General)*.

303. Imperial Tobacco Ltd. Circa 1984. Strictly confidential. Exhibit AG-36, *RJR–Macdonald Inc.* v. *Canada (Attorney General)*.

304. Imperial Tobacco Ltd. Circa 1987. Overall market conditions — F88. Exhibit AG-214, *RJR–Macdonald Inc.* v. *Canada (Attorney General)*.

305. Imperial Tobacco Ltd. Circa 1987. Player's 1988. Exhibit AG-210, *RJR–Macdonald Inc.* v. *Canada (Attorney General)*.

306. Imperial Tobacco Ltd (Chacra, A.). 1980. Player's trademark F'81 advertising. 5 May. *In* Various internal Imperial Tobacco documents. Exhibit AG-35, *RJR–Macdonald Inc.* v. *Canada (Attorney General)*.

307. Imperial Tobacco Ltd (Woods, J.). 1980. du Maurier trademark F'81 advertising. 5 May. *In* Various internal Imperial Tobacco documents. Exhibit AG-35, *RJR–Macdonald Inc.* v. *Canada (Attorney General)*.

308. *Imperial Tobacco Ltd.* v. *Canada (Attorney General)* (1988), 55 Dominion Law Reports (4th) 555.

309. Informetrica Limited (Jacobson, P.M.; Rodway, P.N.). 1990. Tobacco demand elasticity study. Prepared for Canadian Tobacco Manufacturers' Council. 17 Jan.

310. Insight Canada Research. 1992. Smoking in Canada: warnings. Report of the findings of a nationwide survey conducted on behalf of the Canadian Cancer Society, the Heart and Stroke Foundation of Canada, and the Canadian Council on Smoking and Health. Nov.

311. International Civil Aviation Organization. 1992. Smoking restrictions on international passenger flights. Resolution 7/4. 8 Oct.

312. International Network of Women Against Tobacco. 1994. Continuing a family tradition. World Smoking and Health, 19(2), 4–5.

313. International Tobacco Initiative. 1995. Facts on tobacco — economics of production and consumption. Fact Sheet.

314. James, I. 1604. A counterblaste to tobacco. Reprinted 1954, Rodale Books, London, UK.

315. Jason, L.A.; Ji, P.Y.; Anes, M.D.; Birkhead, S.H. 1991. Active enforcement of cigarette control laws in the prevention of cigarette sales to minors. Journal of the American Medical Association, 266(22), 3159–3161.

316. Jeffery, R.W.; Kelder, S.H.; Forster, J.L.; French, S.A.; Lando, H.A.; Baxter, J.E. 1994. Restrictive smoking policies in the workplace: effects on smoking prevalence and cigarette consumption. Preventive Medicine, 23(1), 78–82.

317. Jelinek, O. (Minister of National Revenue). 1992. Letter to Kell Antoft. 14 Oct.

318. Jenish, D. 1990. Warning smokers. Maclean's, 5 Feb, p. 51.

319. Jerome, J. 1970. House of Commons debates. 5 Oct, pp. 8727–8728.

320. John, G.A. 1994. Scenes from the "good" war. Tobacco International, Oct, pp. 28–30, 32, 36, 38, 40.

321. Jordan, M.J. 1988. Memorandum to unspecified smoking and health attorneys. 29 Apr. *Cited in Haines* v. *Liggett Group, Inc.* 814 Federal Supplement 414 (D.N.J. 1993), p.241.

322. Kabwe, A. 1993. Women and tobacco: trends and prospects in developing countries. *In* Yach, D.; Harrison, S., ed., Proceedings of the All Africa Conference on Tobacco or Health. 14–17 Nov 1993, Harare, Zimbabwe. pp. 46–52.

323. Kaiserman, M.J.; Ducharme-Danielson, C. 1991. Global per capita consumption of manufactured cigarettes, 1989. Chronic Diseases in Canada, 12(4), 56–60.

324. Kaiserman, M.J.; Leahy, K. 1992. Changes in the weight of the Canadian cigarette, 1930–1991. Chronic Diseases in Canada, 13(4), 61–63.

325. Kaplan, F. 1993. Russia cigarette law goes up in smoke. Boston Globe, 29 Aug, p. 2.

326. Katz, S. 1974. Non-smokers fight back — they start to organize. Toronto Star, 8 Oct, p. B3.

327. Katz, S. 1977. The sweet, smoke-free smell of success. Toronto Star, 18 Jun, p. B1.

328. Kelly, F. 1994. China considers banning cigarette advertising. Marketing, 14 Nov, p. 6.

329. Kelso, J.J. 1914. House of Commons Select Committee on Cigarette Evils. Proceedings and evidence of the Select Committee Appointed to Inquire and Report as to the Expediency of Making Any Amendment to the Existing Laws for the Purpose of Remedying or Preventing Any Evils Arising From the Use of Cigarettes. House of Commons Journals, 49, Appendix 3, 51–57.

330. Kennedy, C.; King, C. 1952. Bootleg tobacco. Weekend Picture Magazine, 8 Mar, pp. 2–4.

331. Kennedy, R.F. 1967. Untitled address. *In* Goodman, H.A., ed. 1968. World Conference on Smoking and Health: a summary of proceedings. pp. 4–13.

332. Kessler, D.A. 1994. Statement on nicotine-containing cigarettes. Tobacco Control, 3(2), 148–158.

333. Kessler, D.A. 1994. The control and manipulation of nicotine in cigarettes. Tobacco Control, 3(4), 362–369.

334. Kholmogorova, G.T.; Prokhorov, A.V. 1994. West goes East: the new tobacco situation in Russia. Tobacco Control, 3(2), 145–147.

335. King, T. 1994. Destruction Inc. inside the anti-smoking movement. Tobacco International, Dec, pp. 21–25.

336. Klein, J.D.; Forehand, B.; Oliveri, J.; Patterson, C.J.; Kupersmidt, J.B.; Strecher, V. 1992. Candy cigarettes: do they encourage children's smoking? Pediatrics, 89(1), 27–31.

337. Knight, R.R. 1950. House of Commons debates. 24 May, p. 2822.

338. Knudson, G. 1980. George Knudson. Today Magazine, 21 Jun, p. 3.

339. Koepp, S. 1988. Tobacco's first loss. Time, 27 Jun, pp. 48–50.

340. Kottke, T.E.; Battista, R.N.; DeFriese, G.H.; Brekke, M.L. 1988. Attributes of successful smoking cessation interventions in medical practice: a meta-analysis of 39 controlled trials. Journal of the American Medical Association, 259(19), 2882–2889.

341. KPMG Peat Marwick Thorne. 1990. The smuggling of U.S. manufactured and Canadian duty-free cigarettes into Canada and inter-provincial smuggling. 5 Mar.

342. KPMG Peat Marwick Thorne. 1991. The smuggling of U.S. manufactured and Canadian duty-free cigarettes into Canada and inter-provincial smuggling: an update. 20 Mar.

343. Kwechansky Marketing Research Inc. 1977. Project 16. Report for Imperial Tobacco Ltd. 18 Oct. Exhibit AG-216, *RJR–Macdonald Inc.* v. *Canada (Attorney General)*.

344. Kwechansky Marketing Research Inc. 1982. Project Plus/Minus. Prepared for Imperial Tobacco Ltd. 7 May. Exhibit AG-217, *RJR–Macdonald Inc.* v. *Canada (Attorney General)*.

345. Kweyuh, P.H.M. 1994. Tobacco expansion in Kenya — the socio-ecological losses. Tobacco Control, 3(3), 248–251.

346. Kyle, K.; Du Melle, F. 1994. International smoke-free flights: buckle up for take-off. Tobacco Control, 3(1), 3–4.

347. Laflamme, T.-A.-R. 1878. House of Commons debates. 23 Apr, p. 2131.

348. Lalonde, M. 1974. A new perspective on the health of Canadians: a working document. Department of National Health and Welfare, Ottawa, ON, Canada.

349. Lalonde, M. 1975. House of Commons debates. 28 Nov, p. 9567.

350. LaMarsh, J. 1963. House of Commons debates. 17 Jun, pp. 1213–1214.

351. LaMarsh, J. 1977. Smoking law's dumb — let's repeal it now. Toronto Star, 16 Oct, p. A18.

352. Laurier, W. 1878. House of Commons debates. 23 Apr, pp. 2123–2124.

353. Laurier, W. 1903. House of Commons debates. 1 Apr, p. 846.

354. Laurier, W. 1907. House of Commons debates. 4 Mar, p. 4067.

355. Lauzon, L.-P. 1994. Analyse socio-économique : l'industrie du tabac (1987 à 1993). Université du Québec à Montreal, Montreal, PQ, Canada. May.

356. Laverne, A. 1904. House of Commons debates. 23 Mar, p. 352.

357. Lemieux, L.J. 1914. House of Commons Select Committee on Cigarette Evils. Proceedings and evidence of the Select Committee Appointed to Inquire and Report as to the Expediency of Making Any Amendment to the Existing Laws for the Purpose of Remedying or Preventing Any Evils Arising from the Use of Cigarettes. House of Commons Journals, 49, Appendix 3, 78–87.

358. Levin, M. 1994. Targeting foreign smokers. Los Angeles Times, 17 Nov, pp. A1, A15.

359. Levin, M.L.; Goldstein, H.; Gerhardt, P.R. 1950. Cancer and tobacco smoking: a preliminary report. Journal of the American Medical Association, 143(4), 336–338.

360. Lewit, E.M.; Coate, D. 1982. The potential for using excise taxes to reduce smoking. Journal of Health Economics, 1(2), 121–145.

361. Lewit, E.; Coate, D.; Grossman, M. 1981. The effects of government regulation on teenage smoking. Journal of Law and Economics, 24, 545-569.

362. Lindquist Avey Macdonald Baskerville Inc. 1992. Contraband tobacco estimate. 30 Jun.

363. Lindquist Avey Macdonald Baskerville Inc. 1993. 1992 contraband tobacco estimate. 31 Mar.

364. Lindquist Avey Macdonald Baskerville Inc. 1993. 1992 contraband estimate — an update. 27 Sep.

365. Lindquist Avey Macdonald Baskerville Inc. 1994. The impact of reducing tobacco taxes on the contraband market. 27 Jun.

366. Lindquist Avey Macdonald Baskerville Inc. 1994. Cigarette smuggling in the United States. 15 Aug.

367. Liston, A.J. (Assistant Deputy Minister, Health Protection Branch, Health and Welfare Canada). 1988. Memorandum to manufacturers and importers of tobacco products. 29 Jul.

368. Liston, A.J. (Assistant Deputy Minister, Health Protection Branch, Health and Welfare Canada). 1988. Information letter to manufacturers and importers of tobacco products, retail trade associations and other interested parties. Subject: Proposed tobacco products control regulations. 7 Nov. Information Letter No. 754.

369. Lopez, A.D.; Collishaw, N.E.; Piha, T. 1994. A descriptive model of the cigarette epidemic in developed countries. Tobacco Control, 3(3), 242–247.

370. Macdonald, P. 1903. House of Commons debates, 1 Apr, pp. 843–844.

371. Mackay, J. 1990. Political and promotional thrusts in Asia by the transnational tobacco companies. In Durston, B.; Jamrozik, K., ed., The global war. Proceedings of the 7th World Conference on Tobacco and Health. Organising Committee of the 7th World Conference on Tobacco and Health, Perth, WA, Australia. pp. 139–141.

372. Mackie, R. 1994. Retailers group links protesters, tobacco firms. Globe and Mail, 28 Jan, p. A4.

373. Maclean's. 1989. Openly Canadian. Maclean's, 10 Apr, p. 62.

374. MacQueen, K. 1995. Anti-smoking message on T-shirt burns tobacco sponsor of raft race. The Ottawa Citizen, 15 Aug, p. A12.

375. Madeley, J. 1982. Kenyan farmers risk their lives for smokers. New Scientist, 8 Apr, p. 67.

376. Mahood, G. 1976. Non-smokers may be winning the battle against 'the weed'. Toronto Star, 13 Jan, p. B4.

377. Majority Staff, Subcommittee on Health and the Environment, US House of Representatives. 1994. Evidence of nicotine manipulation by the American Tobacco Company. Staff Report. 20 Dec.

378. Malone, A. 1988. Untitled statement. 31 May.

379. Manitoba Educational Research Council. 1966. A study of cigarette advertising. Report submitted to the Department of National Health and Welfare.

380. Mao, Y.; Morrison, H.; Nichol, R.D.; Pipe, A.; Wigle, D. 1988. The health consequences of smoking among smokers in Canada. Canadian Journal of Public Health, 79(5), 390–391.

381. Marketing. 1994. Get lost, Mr. Webb, get lost. Marketing, 23 May, p. 23.

382. Marketing Systems Inc. 1982. Project Eli focus groups final report. Prepared for Imperial Tobacco. Jul. Exhibit AG-40, *RJR–Macdonald Inc.* v. *Canada (Attorney General).*

383. Marks, J. 1987. Knudson's back in business after fight with lung cancer. Toronto Star, 2 Oct, p. H2.

384. Marlin, R.; Barclay, J. 1994. Putting profit ahead of Canadians' health. Globe and Mail, 21 May, p. D7. Letters.

385. Martin, K. 1994. Dissenting opinion. *In* House of Commons Standing Committee on Health, ed., Towards zero consumption. Generic packaging of tobacco products. Report of the Standing Committee on Health, Appendix D. Jun, pp. 61–63.

386. Masironi, R.; Rothwell, R. 1988. Tendances et effets du tabagisme dans le monde. World Health Statistics Quarterly, 41(3–4), 228–241.

387. Mather, B. 1963. House of Commons debates. 17 Jun, p. 1214.

388. Mather, B. 1964. House of Commons debates. 29 May, p. 3764.

389. Mather, B. 1971. House of Commons debates. 16 Mar, p. 4332.

390. Matlick, D. 1994. Tabexpo 94 a record-breaking success. Tobacco Reporter, Dec, p. 4.

391. McCann–Erickson Advertising of Canada Ltd. 1986. RJR–Macdonald Inc. brand family and smokers segmentation study ('85). Key findings and communications implications. Nov. Exhibit RJR-175, *RJR–Macdonald Inc.* v. *Canada (Attorney General).*

392. McCormick, A. 1962. Smoking and health: policy on research. Minutes. pp. 4, 15–16. *Cited in* Slade, J.; Bero, L.A.; Hanauer, P.; Barnes, D.E.; Glantz, S.A. Nicotine and addiction: the Brown and Williamson documents. Journal of the American Medical Association, 274(3), 225–233.

393. McDonald, N.J. (President, Canadian Tobacco Manufacturers' Council). 1986. Letter to Jake Epp (Minister of National Health and Welfare). 19 Feb.

394. McIvor, D. 1951. House of Commons debates. 19 Feb, p. 454.

395. McKay, B. 1993. Russian agencies unite to fight ban. Advertising Age, 20 Sep, pp. I–3, I–21.

396. McKee, K. 1989. Knudson battled for perfection. Toronto Star, 25 Jan, p. F3.

397. McKenna, B. 1994. Ottawa comes under fire from U.S. tobacco lobby. Globe and Mail, 11 May, pp. A1–A2.

398. McKenna, B. 1994. Jobs in peril, U.S. tobacco firm warns. Globe and Mail, 14 May, pp. A1–A2.

399. McKinsey, K. 1994. Clearing the smoke in Poland. The Ottawa Citizen, 16 Nov, p. A2.

400. MediCinema Ltd. 1989. Lobbying for lives — lessons from the front. MediCinema Ltd, Toronto, ON, Canada. Video.

401. Mercier, J.-L. 1987. House of Commons Legislative Committee on Bill C-204, minutes of proceedings and evidence. 24 Nov.

402. Mickleburgh, R.; McInnes, C. 1994. Provinces join in opposing tax cut. Globe and Mail, 5 Feb, p. A4.

403. Millar, W.J. 1988. Evaluation of the impact of smoking restrictions in a government work setting. Canadian Journal of Public Health, 79(5), 379–382.

404. Miller, H.H. 1908. House of Commons debates. 16 Mar, p. 5106.

405. Mintz, M. 1988. Expert: tobacco firms knew risk, didn't tell public. Washington Post, 5 Feb, pp. F1–F2.

406. Mintz, M. 1991. The pro-corporate tilt. Nieman Reports, Fall, p. 28. *Cited in* Barnet, R.J.; Cavanagh, J. 1994. Global dreams: imperial corporations and the new world order. Simon & Schuster, New York, NY, USA. p. 187.

407. Monteith, J.W. 1962. House of Commons debates. 11 Oct, p. 381.

408. Montgomery, C. 1985. Amateurs to spurn some aid. Globe and Mail, 26 Jan, p. S3.

409. Montreal Gazette. 1987. Gazette won't accept ads for tobacco after Jan. 1. Montreal Gazette, 31 Oct, p. A1.

410. Morrow, R.A.H. 1889. Tobacco and its history. *In* Anti-Tobacco Association of Saint John, New Brunswick, ed., Prize essays on tobacco. Daily Telegraph Book and Job Press, Saint John, NB, Canada. pp. 5–34.

411. Moser, K. 1979. Tobacco firm pulls ads. The Ottawa Citizen, 27 Jun, p. 12.

412. Mponda, F.; Ham, M. 1994. Forests in need of an alternative cure. Panoscope, Oct, pp. 16–17.

413. Mudge Rose Guthrie Alexander & Ferdon (Hills, C.). 1994. Letter to R.J. Reynolds Tobacco Company and Philip Morris International Inc. Subject: Legal opinion with regard to plain packaging of tobacco products requirement under international agreements. 3 May.

414. Mufson, S. 1995. Fight over China's smoking market heating up. The Ottawa Citizen, 3 Jul, p. C9.

415. Müller, F.H. 1939. Tabakmissbrauch und Lungencarzinom. Zeitschrift fuer Krebsforschung, 49, 57–85. *Cited in* Wynder, E.L.; Graham, E.A. 1950. Tobacco smoking as a possible etiologic factor in bronchiogenic carcinoma. A study of six-hundred and eighty-four proved cases. Journal of the American Medical Association, 143(4), 329–337.

416. Muller, M. 1978. Tobacco and the Third World: tomorrow's epidemic? War on Want, London, UK.

417. Munro, J. 1968. House of Commons Standing Committee on Health, Welfare and Social Affairs, minutes of proceedings and evidence. 19 Dec.

418. Muwanga-Bayego, H. 1994. Tobacco growing in Uganda: the environment and women pay the price. Tobacco Control, 3(3), 255–256.

419. Myers, J. 1991. The Fitzhenry and Whiteside book of Canadian facts and dates. Revised and updated by Hoffman, L.; Sutherland, F. Fitzhenry and Whiteside, Richmond Hill, ON, Canada.

420. Nadeau, J.-B. 1995. The filtered truth. Reader's Digest, Jan, pp. 63–65.

421. Nadeau, J.-B. 1995. Imperial Tobacco écrase ses concurrents. Commerce, Feb, pp. 46–48, 50, 52–53.

422. Nakajima, H. 1995. WHO 1995 World No-Tobacco Day. Address, Vancouver, BC, Canada. 31 May.

423. National Campaign for Action on Tobacco. 1994. Tobacco smuggling: who is responsible?

424. National Campaign to Pass the *Tobacco Products Control Act*. 1987. Give kids a chance. Pamphlet.

425. National Cancer Institute of Canada. 1958. Lung cancer and smoking. Canadian Medical Association Journal, 79(7), 566–568.

426. National Cancer Institute of Canada. 1962. Lung cancer and smoking: a second report by the National Cancer Institute of Canada. Canadian Medical Association Journal, 87(16), 879.

427. National Cancer Institute of Canada. 1995. Canadian cancer statistics 1995. National Cancer Institute of Canada, Toronto, ON, Canada.

428. National Cancer Institute of Canada. 1996. Canadian cancer statistics 1996. National Cancer Institute of Canada, Toronto, ON, Canada.

429. National Clearinghouse on Tobacco and Health. 1995. Current Smoking in Canada (%), By Age and Sex, 1965-1995. Jul.

430. National Committee for Control of Tobacco Use, Ministry of Public Health, Royal Thai Government. 1990. Tobacco colonialism threatening Thailand. Moh-Chao Ban Publishing House, Bangkok, Thailand.

431. Nelson, J. 1994. The Zapatistas versus the spin-doctors. Canadian Forum, Mar, pp. 18–25.

432. Neville, W.H. (President, Canadian Tobacco Manufacturers' Council). 1988. Letter to G.E. Mac-Donald (Chief, Legislative and Regulatory Processes, Environmental Health Directorate, Health Protection Branch, Health and Welfare Canada). 17 Aug.

433. Neville, W.H. (President, Canadian Tobacco Manufacturers' Council). 1988. Letter to G.E. Mac-Donald (Chief, Legislative and Regulatory Processes, Environmental Health Directorate, Health Protection Branch, Health and Welfare Canada). 31 Aug.

434. Neville, W.H. (Président, Conseil canadien des fabricants des produits du tabac). 1990. Mémoire adressé à l'honorable Michael Wilson, ministre des Finances, Gouvernement du Canada. Objet : taxation des produits du tabac. 8 Jan.

435. Neville, W.H. (President, Canadian Tobacco Manufacturers' Council). 1990. Letter to the Chief, Legislative and Regulatory Processes, Environmental Health Directorate, Health and Welfare Canada. 6 Apr.

436. Neville, W.H. (President, Canadian Tobacco Manufacturers' Council). 1991. Letter to the Minister of Finance, The Honourable Michael Wilson. 13 Mar.

437. Neville, W.H. (President, Canadian Tobacco Manufacturers' Council). 1991. House of Commons Legislative Committee F on Bill C-10, minutes of proceedings and evidence. 26 Sep.

438. Newton, J. 1992. Where there's smoke. Canadian Business, Oct, pp. 86–95.

439. Nicholson, A. 1979. House of Commons debates. 22 Mar, p. 4441.

440. Noël, A. 1994. Les Épiciers ont crée de toutes pièces le mouvement des « dépanneurs généreux ». La Presse, 27 Jan, pp. A1–A2.

441. Noël, A. 1994. La Route du tabac : quand les médias se font complices. Le 30, Apr, pp. 7–10.

442. Non-Smokers' Rights Association. 1986. A catalogue of deception: the use and abuse of voluntary regulation of tobacco advertising in Canada. A report for submission to The Honourable Jake Epp, Minister of Health, Health and Welfare Canada. Jan.

443. Non-Smokers' Rights Association. 1987. An attempt to outmuscle Parliament: the attack by cigarette manufacturers on bills C-51 and C-204. For submission to Members of Parliament. Dec.

444. Non-Smokers' Rights Association. 1987. Will tobacco industry deception outmuscle Parliament? The Ottawa Citizen, 1 Dec, p. A11. Advertisement.

445. Non-Smokers' Rights Association. 1993. Current smokers 15–19, Canada 1977–1991.

446. Non-Smokers' Rights Association. 1993. Occasional smokers 15–19, Canada 1977–1991.

447. Non-Smokers' Rights Association. 1993. Regular smokers 15–19, Canada 1977–1991.

448. Non-Smokers' Rights Association. 1994. Disposable income and tobacco price index, Canada 1949–1993.

449. Non-Smokers' Rights Association. 1995. World cigarette production 1950–1994. *Citing* data from the US Department of Agriculture.

450. Non-Smokers' Rights Association. 1996. What the tobacco manufacturers do not want you to know about tobacco sponsorship of the arts. ... Corporate philanthropy? Or selling addiction? Flyer.

451. Non-Smokers' Rights Association; Smoking and Health Action Foundation. 1994. The smuggling of tobacco products: lessons from Canada. Jul.

452. Norr, R. 1952. Cancer by the carton. Reader's Digest, Dec, pp. 35–36.

453. O'Connor, M. 1993. Tobacco advertising in Central and Eastern Europe. Tobacco Control, 2(2), 101–102.

454. O'Neil, P. 1995. Goodale sees no problem pitching tobacco to China. The Ottawa Citizen, 25 Apr, p. A4.

455. Ontario Flue-Cured Tobacco Growers' Marketing Board. 1984. Proposal by Ontario Flue-Cured Tobacco Growers' Marketing Board for the establishment of the Canadian Flue-Cured Tobacco Marketing Agency. 15 Oct.

456. Ontario Flue-Cured Tobacco Growers' Marketing Board. 1994. 1994 annual report.

457. Ontario Tobacco Research Unit. 1995. Monitoring Ontario's tobacco strategy: progress toward our goals. Oct.

458. Osler, E.B. 1904. House of Commons debates. 23 Mar, p. 354.

459. Ottawa Sun. 1989. Feds admit law is flawed. Ottawa Sun, 22 Dec, p. 20.

460. Palmer, J.R.; Rosenberg, L.; Shapiro, S. 1989. "Low yield" cigarettes and the risk of nonfatal myocardial infarction in women. New England Journal of Medicine, 320(24), 1569–1573.

461. Paré, P. 1969. House of Commons Standing Committee on Health, Welfare and Social Affairs, minutes of proceedings and evidence. 5 Jun, pp. 1537–1557, 1559–1564, 1566–1578.

462. Pearl, R. 1938. Tobacco smoking and longevity. Science, 87, 216–217.

463. Pepin, J.-L. 1972. House of Commons debates. 2 Jun, p. 2802.

464. Perl, R. 1994. Scenes from Chile. Tobacco Control, 3(2), 161–162.

465. *Perron* v. *RJR–Macdonald Inc.* 1988. No. C883254, Vancouver Registry, British Columbia Supreme Court.

466. Peto, R.; Lopez, A. 1990. Worldwide mortality from current smoking patterns: WHO consultative group on statistical aspects of tobacco-related mortality. *In* Durston, B.; Jamrozik, K., ed., The global war. Proceedings of the 7th World Conference on Tobacco and Health. Organising Committee of the 7th World Conference on Tobacco and Health, Perth, WA, Australia. pp. 66–68.

467. Peto, R.; Lopez, A.D.; Boreham, J.; Thun, M.; Heath, C., Jr. 1994. Mortality from smoking in developed countries 1950–2000: indirect estimates from national vital statistics. Oxford University Press, Oxford, UK.

468. Philip Morris & Co. Ltd. 1929. They're on the air — everywhere. Canadian Cigar and Tobacco Journal, Dec, 26–27. Advertisement.

469. Philip Morris Companies Inc. 1993. 1992 annual report.

470. Philip Morris Companies Inc. 1995. 1994 annual report.

471. Philip Morris Companies Inc. 1995. 1995 mid year update.

472. Philips, A.J. 1954. Mortality from cancer of the lung in Canada 1931–1952. Canadian Medical Association Journal, 71(3), 242–244.

473. Philips, A.J. 1961. A study of deaths in Canada ascribed to lung cancer. Canadian Medical Association Journal, 84(14), 795.

474. Phillips, A.; de Savigny, D.; Law, M.M. 1995. As Canadians butt out, the developing world lights up. Canadian Medical Association Journal, 153(8), 1111–1114.

475. Physicians for a Smoke-Free Canada. 1994. Breaking the link: the case for plain packaging of tobacco industry products. A submission to the House of Commons Standing Committee on Health Regarding the Study of Plain Packaging of Tobacco Products. 5 May.

476. Pierce, J.P.; Evans, N.; Farkas, A.J.; et al. 1994. Tobacco use in California: an evaluation of the Tobacco Control Program, 1989–1993. University of California, San Diego, La Jolla, CA, USA.

477. Pierce, J.P.; Lee, L.; Gilpin, E.A. 1994. Smoking initiation by adolescent girls, 1944 through 1988: an association with targeted advertising. Journal of the American Medical Association, 271(8), 608–611.

478. Pollay, R.W. 1989. The functions and management of cigarette advertising. 27 Jul. Exhibit AG-224, *RJR–Macdonald Inc.* v. *Canada (Attorney General)*. Expert Report.

479. Porter, M.E. 1980. Competitive strategy: techniques for analyzing industries and competitors. Free Press, New York, NY, USA.

480. Publicité BCP ltée. 1984. Matinée Extra-Mild. Shoot book for Imperial Tobacco Ltd. 8 Feb. Exhibit AG-213, *RJR–Macdonald Inc.* v. *Canada (Attorney General)*.

481. Reader's Digest. 1961. Canadian cigarettes: 1961. Reader's Digest, Jul, pp. 32–33.

482. Reaume, B. 1995. An important victory for free speech. Marketing, 6 Nov, p. 31. Letter.

483. *Regina* v. *Imperial Tobacco Products Ltd.* (1971), 22 Dominion Law Reports (3d) 51, (Alberta Supreme Court, Appellate Division), affirming 16 Dominion Law Reports (3d) 470 (Alberta Supreme Court).

484. Reid, J.M. 1973. House of Commons debates. 21 Feb, p. 1493.

485. Report on Business Magazine. 1994. Ranking by profits. Report on Business Magazine, Jul, pp. 70–75, 78–105.

486. Report on Business Magazine. 1995. Ranking by profits. Report on Business Magazine, Jul, pp. 94–99, 102–129.

487. Richards, P. 1993. The tobacco crop in Zimbabwe. *In* Yach, D.; Harrison, S., ed., Proceedings of the All Africa Conference on Tobacco or Health. 14–17 Nov 1993, Harare, Zimbabwe. pp. 138–142.

488. Rickert, W.S. 1995. A historical study of nicotine yields of Canadian cigarettes in relation to the composition and nicotine content of cigarette tobacco (1968–1995): final report. A Health Canada sponsored project. 31 Mar.

489. Riddell, K. 1994. Smoke firms rally opposition to plain packaging. Marketing, 18 Apr, p. 2.

490. RJR Nabisco Holdings Corp. 1994. Second quarter shareholders report. 30 Jun.

491. RJR Nabisco Holdings Corp. 1995. Annual report 1994.

492. RJR–Macdonald Inc. 1977. Canada. R.J. Reynolds Tobacco International. 1978 annual business plan. Marketing plans: Export 'A' Lights. *In* RJR–Macdonald Inc. 1978 business plan of

RJR–Macdonald. Exhibit AG-14, *RJR–Macdonald Inc. v. Canada (Attorney General)*. pp. 2102–2148.

493. RJR–Macdonald Inc. 1982. Export family strategy document. 22 Mar. Exhibit AG-222, *RJR–Macdonald Inc.* v. *Canada (Attorney General)*.

494. RJR–Macdonald Inc. 1984. RJR–Macdonald Inc. Area II — Canada 1985–1987 strategic plan. Exhibit RJR-14, Tab 1, *RJR–Macdonald Inc.* v. *Canada (Attorney General)*.

495. RJR–Macdonald Inc. 1986. Tempo qualitative post-launch evaluation, MRD#85-056/NS. Jan. Exhibit AG-17, *RJR–Macdonald Inc.* v. *Canada (Attorney General)*.

496. RJR–Macdonald Inc. 1986. Export family draft brand positioning statement. 16 Oct. Exhibit AG-8, *RJR–Macdonald Inc.* v. *Canada (Attorney General)*.

497. RJR–Macdonald Inc. 1988 or 1989. Advertising and promotion spending. Exhibit RJR-3, *RJR–Macdonald Inc.* v. *Canada (Attorney General)*.

498. RJR–Macdonald Inc. 1993. Rapport du gouvernement fédéral pour la loi C-51. Résultats de fumage des coupes fines de RJR–Macdonald Inc. pour le 3ième trimestre du 5 juillet 1993 au 24 septembre 1993.

499. RJR–Macdonald Inc. 1993. Résultats de fumage des marques de RJR–Macdonald Inc. pour le 3ième trimestre du 5 juillet au 24 septembre 1993.

500. *RJR–Macdonald Inc.* v. *Canada (Attorney General)* (1991), 82 Dominion Law Reports (4th) 449, 37 Canadian Patent Reporter (3d) 193 (Que. S.C.), (*Sub nom. Imperial Tobacco Ltd.* c. *Canada (P.G.)* (1991), [1991] Recueils de jurisprudence du Québec 2260).

501. *RJR–Macdonald Inc.* v. *Canada (Attorney General)*, [1993] Recueils de jurisprudence du Québec 375, 53 Quebec Appeal Cases 79, 102 Dominion Law Reports (4th) 289, 48 Canadian Patent Reporter (3d) 417.

502. *RJR–Macdonald Inc.* v. *Canada (Attorney General)*, [1994] 1 Supreme Court Reports 311.

503. *RJR–Macdonald Inc.* v. *Canada (Attorney General)*, [1995] 3 Supreme Court Reports 199.

504. Rock City Tobacco Company (1936), Ltd. 1951. World famous fine quality plus nation-wide advertising. Canadian Cigar and Tobacco Journal, Jan, back cover. Advertisement.

505. Ronson, J.; Cunningham, R. 1992. Fighting for health: the Canadian tobacco advertising case. World Smoking and Health, 17(2), 24–25.

506. Rootman, I.; Flay, B.R.; Northup, D.; Foster, M.K.; Burton, D.; Ferrence, R.; Raphael, D.; Single, E.; Donovan, R.; d'Avernas, J. 1995. A study on youth smoking: plain packaging, health warnings, event marketing and price reductions. Key findings. University of Toronto; University of Illinois at Chicago; York University; Ontario Tobacco Research Unit; Addiction Research Foundation, Toronto, ON, Canada.

507. The Roper Organization Inc. 1978. A study of public attitudes toward cigarette smoking and the tobacco industry in 1978. Vol. I. Prepared for the Tobacco Institute. May.

508. Rose, W.H. 1981. The Canadian cigarette industry: the next 20 years. Research paper submitted in partial fulfillment of the requirements for the degree of Master of Business Administration at Concordia University, Montreal, PQ, Canada. Mar.

509. Rosenblatt, R. 1994. How do tobacco executives live with themselves? New York Times Magazine, 20 Mar, pp. 34–41, 55, 73–74, 76.

510. Rothmans, Benson & Hedges Inc. 1993. Cigarette smoking data for quarter ending — 9309.

511. Rothmans, Benson & Hedges Inc. 1993. Cigarette tobacco smoking data for quarter ending — 9309.

512. Rothmans Inc. 1987–95. Annual reports 1987–95.

513. Rothmans Inc. 1988. Annual report 1988.

514. Rothmans Inc. 1991. Annual report 1991.

515. Rothmans Inc. 1993. Annual report 1993.

516. Rothmans Inc. 1994. Annual report 1994.

517. Rothmans Inc. 1995. Management proxy circular. 31 May.

518. Rothmans International plc. 1993. Annual report and accounts 1993.

519. Rothmans International plc. 1994. Annual report and accounts 1994.

520. Rothmans International Research Division. 1958. An announcement of major importance: the Canadian Medical Association and cigarette smoking. Globe and Mail, 23 Jun, p. 27. Advertisement.

521. Rothmans International Research Division. 1958. The International Cancer Congress and cigarette smoking. Toronto Daily Star, 13 Aug, p. 5. Advertisement.

522. Rothmans International Tobacco (UK) Limited. 1992. Opportunities in Central and Eastern Europe and the CIS. Globe and Mail, 9 Dec, p. B24. Advertisement.

523. Rothmans of Pall Mall Canada Limited. 1964. Annual report 1964.

524. Rothmans of Pall Mall Canada Limited. 1970. Annual report 1970.

525. Rothmans of Pall Mall Canada Limited. 1982. Rothmans of Pall Mall Canada Limited 1957–1982.

526. Roxburgh, J. 1964. House of Commons debates. 6 May, p. 2997.

527. Roxburgh, J. 1964. House of Commons debates. 29 May, p. 3767.

528. Royal College of Physicians of London, Committee on Smoking and Atmospheric Pollution. 1962. A report of the Royal College of Physicians of London on smoking in relation to cancer of the lung and other diseases. McClelland and Stewart, Toronto, ON, Canada.

529. Royal Commission on the Exclusive Contract System Adopted by the American Tobacco Company of Canada and the Empire Tobacco Company Thus Creating a Monopoly (McTavish, D.B.). 1903. Report of the Commissioner. *In* House of Commons sessional papers, Volume 13, 3rd session, 9th Parliament. Sessional Paper No. 62. 6 Apr.

530. Royal Society of Canada. 1989. Tobacco, nicotine, and addiction. A committee report prepared at the request of the Royal Society of Canada for the Health Protection Branch, Health and Welfare Canada. 31 Aug.

531. Rubenstein, L. 1987. Knudson's spirits high as fight against cancer begins. Globe and Mail, 1 Jul, pp. D1, D4.

532. Rubenstein, L. 1988. Knudson's sweet swing returns to the tour. Globe and Mail, 27 Apr, p. A18.

533. Rubenstein, L. 1989. Knudson's quest: mastery of swing. Globe and Mail, 25 Jan, p. A15.

534. Samad, S. 1994. Poverty's poisonous brands. Panoscope, Oct, p. 23.

535. Samuels, B.; Glantz, S.A. 1991. The politics of local tobacco control. Journal of the American Medical Association, 266(15), 2110–2117.

536. Sanders, C.F. 1927. Well planned ads are offering cigarettes to women smokers. Canadian Cigar and Tobacco Journal, Aug, 16.

537. Sanwougo, L. 1993. Tobacco and health: the situation in the African region. *In* Yach, D.; Harrison, S., ed., Proceedings of the All Africa Conference on Tobacco or Health. 14–17 Nov 1993, Harare, Zimbabwe. pp. 36–45.

538. Schwartz, J. 1995. Tobacco firm's nicotine studies assailed on Hill. Washington Post, 25 Jul, p. A8.

539. Schwartz, J. 1995. Tobacco firm's inside debate revealed. Washington Post, 9 Oct, pp. A8–A9.

540. Scott, A. 1994. House of Commons Standing Committee on Health, minutes of proceedings and evidence. 10 May.

541. Selikoff, I.J.; Hammond, E.C. 1979. Asbestos and smoking. Journal of the American Medical Association, 242(5), 458–459.

542. Sesser, S. 1993. Opium war redux. The New Yorker, 13 Sep, pp. 78–82, 84–89.

543. Sheridan, C. 1994. Pack leaders to beat the ban. *In* King, T.; Owen, B.; Oldman, M., ed. The tobacco industry 1994. Millenium Press, London, UK. pp. 99, 101.

544. Siegel, M. 1993. Involuntary smoking in the restaurant workplace: a review of employee exposure and health effects. Journal of the American Medical Association, 270(4), 490–493.

545. Simmons, R. 1994. House of Commons Standing Committee on Health, minutes of proceedings and evidence. 10 May.

546. Simpson, D. 1994. Propaganda hit squad at large. Tobacco Control, 3(1), 76–77.

547. Sims, A. 1878. The sin of tobacco smoking and chewing together with an effective cure for these habits. W. Lightfoot & Son, Toronto, ON, Canada.

548. Sims, A. 1894. The common use of tobacco condemned by physicians, experience, common sense and the Bible. A. Sims, Uxbridge, ON, Canada.

549. Slade, J.; Bero, L.A.; Hanauer, P.; Barnes, D.E.; Glantz, S.A. 1995. Nicotine and addiction: the Brown and Williamson documents. Journal of the American Medical Association, 274(3), 225–233.

550. Smoking Cessation Clinical Practice Guideline Panel and Staff. 1996. The Agency for Health Care Policy and Research *Smoking cessation clinical practice guideline*. Journal of the American Medical Association, 275(16), 1270–1280.

551. Sonnenberg, M. 1987. Free trade could stop Bill C-51, Wise tells Tillsonburg audience. Delhi News-Record, 21 Jun, pp. 1–2.

552. Spears, J. 1985. New Rothmans chief takes new tack. Toronto Star, 27 Sep, pp. B1–B2.

553. SpecComm International, Inc. 1994. 1993 Maxwell tobacco fact book. SpecComm International, Inc., Raleigh, NC, USA.

554. Spitzer, Mills & Bates. 1977. The Player's family: a working paper prepared for Imperial Tobacco. 25 Mar. Exhibit AG-33, *RJR–Macdonald Inc.* v. *Canada (Attorney General)*.

555. Sproule, T.S. 1903. House of Commons debates. 1 Apr, p. 843.

556. Srisangnam, U. 1994. Tobacco advertising legislation: Thailand's experiences. Paper presented at the 9th World Conference on Tobacco and Health, 10–14 Oct, Paris, France.

557. Stackhouse, J. 1994. Third World lung-cancer epidemic feared. Globe and Mail, 2 Nov, pp. A1–A7.

558. Stafford, H.E. 1969. House of Commons debates. 12 May, p. 8613.

559. Statistics Canada. 1981–95. Exports by commodity. Catalogue 65-004. Dec issues, 1980-1994 (monthly).

560. Statistics Canada. 1989, 1996. Imports by commodity. Catalogue 65-007. Dec issues, 1988, 1995 (monthly).

561. Statistics Canada. 1990. Family incomes: census families. Catalogue 13-208. p. 23. *Cited in* Allen, R.C. 1993. The false dilemma: the impact of tobacco control policies on employment in Canada. Feb, p. 16.

562. Statistics Canada. 1992. Exports by commodity. Catalogue 65-004. Jan–Jun, 1992 (monthly).

563. Statistics Canada. 1994. Beverage and tobacco products industries, 1992. Catalogue 32-251.

564. Statistics Canada. 1994. Health status of Canadians: report of the 1991 general social survey. Catalogue 11-612E, No. 8.

565. Statistics Canada. 1994. Inter-corporate ownership. Catalogue 61-517. Jul.

566. Statistics Canada. 1995–96. Production and disposition of tobacco products. Catalogue 32-022. Dec issues, 1994–95 (monthly).

567. Statistics Canada. 1996. Age-standardized death rates, Canada and the provinces, cancer of the lung, trachea and bronchus. Health Statistics Division. Unpublished data.

568. Stebbins, K.R. 1994. Making a killing south of the border: transnational cigarette companies in Mexico and Guatemala. Social Science Medicine, 38(1), 105–115.

569. Stephens, T. 1995. Trends in the prevalence of smoking, 1991–1994. Chronic Diseases in Canada, 16(1), 27–32.

570. Stewart, R. 1994. House of Commons Standing Committee on Health, minutes of proceedings and evidence. 12 May.

571. St Laurent, L. 1946. House of Commons debates. 2 Jul, pp. 3078–3079.

572. Strauss, M. 1989. Two tobacco companies to end ads. Globe and Mail, 29 Mar, pp. B1–B2.

573. Strauss, M. 1989. Rothmans chief thinks tobacco will need only two players. Globe and Mail, 26 Jul, p. B9.

574. Strauss, M. 1990. Physician fails to query Rothmans. Globe and Mail, 20 Jul, p. B5.

575. Strauss, M. 1995. IBM gets brand new lease on life. Globe and Mail, 13 Jul, p. B4.

576. Sweanor, D. 1993. Memorandum to CTMC contraband file: over-estimate of smuggling. 22 Apr.

577. Tait, L. 1968. Tobacco in Canada. Ontario Flue-Cured Tobacco Growers' Marketing Board, Tillsonburg, ON, Canada.

578. *Talbot and the Corporation of the City of Peterborough, In re,* (1906), 12 Ontario Law Reports 358 (C.P.).

579. Tandemar Research Inc. 1992. Tobacco health warning messages, inserts and toxic constituent information study final report. Prepared for Tobacco Products Section, Health and Welfare Canada. May.

580. Task Force on Smoking. 1982. Smoking and health in Ontario: a need for balance. Report submitted to the Ontario Council of Health. May.

581. Tate, C. 1989. In the 1800s, antismoking was a burning issue. Smithsonian, 20(4), pp. 107–108, 110–112, 114–117.

582. Taylor, P. 1984. Smoke ring: the politics of tobacco. The Bodley Head, London, UK.

583. Teague, C., Jr. 1972. RJR Confidential research planning memorandum on the nature of the tobacco business and the crucial role of nicotine therein. *Cited in* Hilts, P.J. 1995. US convenes grand jury to look at tobacco industry. New York Times, 26 Jul, pp. A1, A15.

584. Teague, C.E., Jr. 1973. Research planning memorandum on some thoughts about new brands of cigarettes for the youth market. 2 Feb.

585. Tempest, R. 1994. Tobacco industry lights up at mention of China market. Los Angeles Times, 18 Nov, pp. A1, A8–A9.

586. Thailand National Bureau of Statistics. National smoking prevalence survey, 1976–1993. *Cited in* Vateesatokit, P. 1995. Letter to Rob Cunningham. 27 Apr.

587. Thompson, A. 1989. Rothmans sees tobacco firms forced to merge. Toronto Star, 26 Jul, pp. E1–E2.

588. Tobacco Access Law News. 1994. The Empire Strikes Back. Tobacco Access Law News, No. 25, Jul.

589. Tobacco Association of Canada. 1876. Serious loss of revenue to the country.

590. Tobacco-Free Youth Reporter. 1994. What do they have in common? Tobacco-Free Youth Reporter, Summer, p. 3.

591. Tobacco Journal International; Tobacco Reporter. 1994. Catalogue. Tabexpo 94 Exhibition and Congress.

592. Tobacco Reporter. 1994. Maxwell report: world brand leaders. Tobacco Reporter, Jun, p. 6.

593. Toronto Star. 1989. He never knew the word 'can't'. Toronto Star, 25 Jan, p. F3.

594. Trachtenberg, J.A. 1987. Here's one tough cowboy. Forbes, 9 Feb, pp. 108–110.

595. Transport Canada. 1994. 1993 Canadian motor vehicle traffic collision statistics. Oct.

596. Trottier, E.; Cédilot, A. 1993. Un 'Ordre' empêche la GRC d'intervenir dans les réserves. La Presse, 15 Jul, pp. A1–A2.

597. Trueheart, C. 1994. Fuming over cigarette packs: US tobacco industry warns Canada against plain packaging law. Washington Post, 17 May, p. A7.

598. Tunney, G. 1941. Nicotine knockout, or the slow count. Reader's Digest, Dec, pp. 21–24.

599. United Nations. 1995. Statistical yearbook. 40th issue. United Nations, New York, NY, USA.

600. United Nations Conference on Trade and Development. 1995. Economic role of tobacco production and exports in countries depending on tobacco as a major source of income. Study by the UNCTAD Secretariat. 8 May.

601. United States Tobacco Journal. 1950. Cigarette executives expect added volume. United States Tobacco Journal, 154(26), 3. *Cited in* US Department of Health and Human Services. 1994. Preventing tobacco use among young people: a report of the Surgeon General. US Department of Health and Human Services, Public Health Service, Centers for Disease Control and Prevention, National Center for Chronic Disease Prevention and Health Promotion, Office on Smoking and Health, Atlanta, Georgia, USA. p. 166.

602. US Centers for Disease Control. 1991. Smoking-attributable mortality and years of potential life lost — United States, 1988. Morbidity and Mortality Weekly Report, 40(4), 62–63, 69–71.

603. US Department of Health and Human Services. 1980. The health consequences of smoking for women: a report of the Surgeon General. US Department of Health and Human Services, Public Health Service, Office of the Assistant Secretary for Health, Office on Smoking and Health, Rockville, MD, USA.

604. US Department of Health and Human Services. 1986. The health consequences of involuntary smoking: a report of the Surgeon General. US Department of Health and Human Services, Public

Health Service, Centers for Disease Control, Center for Health Promotion and Education, Office on Smoking and Health, Rockville, MD, USA. DHHS Publication No. (CDC) 87-8398.

605. US Department of Health and Human Services. 1988. The health consequences of smoking: nicotine addiction: a report of the Surgeon General. US Department of Health and Human Services, Public Health Service, Centers for Disease Control, Center for Health Promotion and Education, Office on Smoking and Health, Rockville, MD, USA. DHHS Publication No. (CDC) 88-8406.

606. US Department of Health and Human Services. 1989. Reducing the health consequences of smoking: 25 years of progress. A report of the Surgeon General. US Department of Health and Human Services, Public Health Service, Centers for Disease Control, Center for Chronic Disease Prevention and Health Promotion, Office on Smoking and Health, Rockville, MD, USA. DHHS Publication No. (CDC) 89-8411.

607. US Department of Health and Human Services. 1991. Strategies to control tobacco use in the United States: a blueprint for public health action in the 1990's. US Department of Health and Human Services, Public Health Service, National Institutes of Health, National Cancer Institute. NIH Publication No. 92-3316, Smoking and Tobacco Control Monograph No. 1. Dec.

608. US Department of Health and Human Services. 1992. Smoking and health in the Americas. US Department of Health and Human Services, Public Health Service, Centers for Disease Control, National Center for Chronic Disease Prevention and Health Promotion, Office on Smoking and Health, Atlanta, GA, USA. DHHS Publication No. (CDC) 92-8419.

609. US Department of Health and Human Services. 1994. Preventing Tobacco Use Among Young People. A Report of the Surgeon General. US Department of Health and Human Services, Public Health Service, Centers for Disease Control and Prevention, National Center for Chronic Disease Prevention and Health Promotion, Office on Smoking and Health.

610. US Environmental Protection Agency. 1992. Respiratory health effects of passive smoking: lung cancer and other disorders. US Environmental Protection Agency, Washington, DC, USA. Publication No. EPA/600/6-90/006F.

611. US Food and Drug Administration. 1995. Regulations restricting the sale and distribution of cigarettes and smokeless tobacco products to protect children and adolescents. Federal Register, 60(155), 11 Aug, pp. 41314–41375.

612. US Public Health Service. 1964. Smoking and health. Report of the Advisory Committee to the Surgeon General of the Public Health Service. US Department of Health, Education, and Welfare, Public Health Service, Center for Disease Control. PHS Publication No. 1103.

613. US Public Health Service. 1972. The health consequences of smoking: a report of the Surgeon General. US Department of Health, Education, and Welfare. DHEW Publication No. (HSM) 72-6516.

614. US Public Health Service. 1975. The health consequences of smoking: 1975. US Department of Health, Education, and Welfare, Public Health Service, Center for Disease Control, Atlanta, Georgia, USA. Health Services and Mental Health Administration. DHEW Publication No. (CDC) 76-8704.

615. Vallières, M. 1994. Imperial Tobacco sonde le marché chinois. Les Affaires, 15 Oct, p. 16.

616. Vateesatokit, P. 1990. Tobacco and trade sanctions: the next victim after Thailand. In Durston, B.; Jamrozik, K., ed., The global war. Proceedings of the 7th World Conference on Tobacco and Health. Organising Committee of the 7th World Conference on Tobacco and Health, Perth, WA, Australia. pp. 164–166.

617. Vidal, J.-P. 1994. A critique of Léo-Paul Lauzon's socioeconomic balance sheet. Translation by Berman, J. Jul.

618. Voges, E. 1984. Tobacco encyclopedia. Tobacco Journal International, Mainz, Germany.

619. Waldman, P. 1989. Tobacco firms try soft, feminine sell. Wall Street Journal, 19 Dec, pp. B1, B10.

620. Walker, I.A. (Director, Market Research, RJR–Macdonald Inc.) 1987. Letter to Elisabeth Jay (The Creative Research Group Ltd). 30 Jan. Exhibit RJR-5, *RJR–Macdonald Inc.* v. *Canada (Attorney General)*.

621. Waluye, J. 1994. Environmental impact of tobacco growing in Tabora/Urambo, Tanzania. Tobacco Control, 3(3), 252–254.

622. Wangai, P. 1990. Intricacies of Third World tobacco control. *In* Durston, B.; Jamrozik, K., ed., The global war. Proceedings of the 7th World Conference on Tobacco and Health. Organising Committee of the 7th World Conference on Tobacco and Health, Perth, WA, Australia. pp. 818–819.

623. Warner, K.E.; Goldenhar, L.M.; McLaughlin, C.G. 1992. Cigarette advertising and magazine coverage of the hazards of smoking: a statistical analysis. New England Journal of Medicine, 326(5), 305–309.

624. Watts, R. 1994. What went up in smoke is now coming up in blooming roses. Panoscope, Oct, pp. 17–18.

625. Watts, R.; Watts, T. 1993. National dependence on tobacco: a case study. *In* Yach, D.; Harrison, S., ed., Proceedings of the All Africa Conference on Tobacco or Health. 14–17 Nov 1993, Harare, Zimbabwe. pp. 110–127.

626. Webb, W.H. (President and Chief Executive Officer, Philip Morris International Inc.). 1994. Letter to House of Commons Standing Committee on Health. 5 May.

627. Weybrecht, E.W. (External Affairs and International Trade Canada). 1993. Memorandum to Christine Simonowski (External Affairs and International Trade Canada). 26 Oct.

628. Whelan, E.M. 1984. A smoking gun: how the tobacco industry gets away with murder. George F. Stickley Co., Philadelphia, PA, USA.

629. White, L.C. 1988. Merchants of death. The American tobacco industry. Beech Tree Books William Morrow, New York, NY, USA.

630. Wigle, D.T.; Collishaw, N.E.; Kirkbride, J.; Mao, Y.; et al. 1987. Deaths in Canada from lung cancer due to involuntary smoking. Canadian Medical Association Journal 136(9), 945–951.

631. Wilson, C. 1975. No-smoking cabbie on carpet. Toronto Sun, 28 Aug, p. 8.

632. Wilson, M. 1991. The budget speech. 26 Feb.

633. Wilson, R. 1889. The tobacco nuisance, in a letter to John Smith, Esq. *In* Anti-Tobacco Association of Saint John, New Brunswick, ed., Prize essays on tobacco. Daily Telegraph Book and Job Press, Saint John, NB, Canada. pp. 35–54.

634. Woods, R. 1993. Tobacco sponsorship advertising in the Ottawa/Hull region. Prepared for the Canadian Council on Smoking and Health. Dec.

635. Woolfson, A. 1994. Canada's ad ban puts cigarettes out of sight. The [Louisville, KY] Courier-Journal, 4 Aug, pp. 1, 4.

636. World Bank. 1984. World Bank tobacco financing: the environmental/health case. Background for policy formulation. Office of Environmental and Scientific Affairs, World Bank, Washington, DC, USA. *Cited in* Chapman, S.; Leng, W.W. 1990. Tobacco control in the Third World: a resource atlas. International Organization of Consumers Unions, Penang, Malaysia. p. 32.

637. World Bank. 1992. World Bank policy on tobacco. World Bank, Washington, DC.

638. World Bank. 1993. World development report 1993. Investing in health: world development indicators. Oxford University Press, New York, NY, USA.

639. World Health Assembly. 1990. Resolution WHA43.16. May.

640. World Health Organization. 1992. WHO on smoking and travel. Tobacco Control, 1(4), 310–311.

641. World Health Organization. 1992. Tobacco-free workplaces: safer and healthier. Kit for World No-Tobacco Day, 31 May.

642. World Health Organization. 1994. Tobacco or health. Report by the Director-General. World Health Organization, Geneva, Switzerland. Document EB95/27. 24 Oct.

643. World Health Organization. 1995. Tobacco costs more than you think. World No-Tobacco Day advisory kit. Tobacco Alert, Special Issue.

644. World Health Organization. 1996. The tobacco epidemic: a global public health emergency. Tobacco Alert, Special Issue.

645. World Smoking and Health. 1991. World Smoking and Health, 16(2), cover.

646. World Tobacco. 1991. How the brands ranked. World Tobacco, Sep, pp. 60–62.

647. World Tobacco. 1992. Some light at end of Canadian tunnel. World Tobacco, Sep, pp. 13, 16, 18, 20, 89.

648. Wynder, E.L.; Graham, E.A. 1950. Tobacco smoking as a possible etiologic factor in bronchiogenic carcinoma. A study of six-hundred and eighty-four proved cases. Journal of the American Medical Association, 143(4), 329–336.

649. Yeaman, A. 1963. Implications of Battelle Hippo I & II and the Griffith filter. p. 4. *Cited in* Slade, J.; Bero, L.A.; Hanauer, P.; Barnes, D.E.; Glantz, S.A. 1995. Nicotine and addiction: the Brown and Williamson documents. Journal of the American Medical Association, 274(3), 225–233.

650. Young, G. 1979. The politics of smoking. *In* Ramstrom, L.M., ed., The smoking epidemic, a matter of worldwide concern. Almqvist and Wiksell International, Stockholm, Sweden. pp. 123–127.

Index

About the Author

A lawyer by profession, Rob Cunningham has degrees in political science (BA, University of Western Ontario), law (LLB, University of Toronto), and business (MBA, University of Western Ontario). He first became active in tobacco issues in 1988 and has since become a recognized expert in the field of tobacco control. He has worked as a consultant for provincial, national, and international health organizations. As one of the core group of Canadian advocates fighting for tobacco control, Rob has testified before parliamentary committees, given hundreds of media interviews in Canada and the United States, published numerous tobacco-related articles, and initiated private prosecutions for violations of tobacco-control laws. He has presented papers at several conferences, including the Ninth World Conference on Tobacco and Health, held in Paris in 1994. He now works in Ottawa as a senior policy analyst for the Canadian Cancer Society.

About the Organization

The International Development Research Centre (IDRC) is committed to building a sustainable and equitable world. IDRC funds developing-world researchers, thus enabling the people of the South to find their own solutions to their own problems. IDRC also maintains information networks and forges linkages that allow Canadians and their developing-world partners to benefit equally from a global sharing of knowledge. Through its actions, IDRC is helping others to help themselves.

About the Publisher

IDRC Books publishes research results and scholarly studies on global and regional issues related to sustainable and equitable development. As a specialist in development literature, IDRC Books contributes to the body of knowledge on these issues to further the cause of global understanding and equity. IDRC publications are sold through its head office in Ottawa, Canada, as well as by IDRC's agents and distributors around the world.